SOLDIERS AND SCHOLARS
Military Education and National Policy

SOLDIERS
AND
SCHOLARS

Military Education
and
National Policy

BY
JOHN W. MASLAND
AND
LAURENCE I. RADWAY

PRINCETON, NEW JERSEY
PRINCETON UNIVERSITY PRESS
1957

JOHN W. MASLAND and LAURENCE I. RADWAY are members of the Department of Government at Dartmouth College. Mr. Masland has served in the Department of State, the faculty of the Civil Affairs Training School at Stanford University, the headquarters of the Supreme Commander for the Allied Powers in Japan, and the faculty of the National War College. Mr. Radway has served in the Bureau of the Budget, the United States Army, and the Office of Defense Mobilization.

Printed in the United States of America
by the Vail-Ballou Press, Inc., Binghamton, N.Y.

TO
MARY AND PAT

PREFACE

THE traditional distinction between military and civilian affairs in American life has become less significant. Under present conditions at home and abroad, it is obviously not enough for the armed forces to provide good soldiers, sailors, and airmen, and the leaders necessary to command them in battle. Today many of these leaders are called upon to work closely with foreign affairs experts, industrial managers, scientists, labor leaders, and educators. They participate in the drafting and promotion of legislation, in the preparation of a national budget, and in the determination of the American position on a wide variety of foreign policy issues. They are required to understand, to communicate with, and to evaluate the judgment of political leaders, officials of other executive agencies, and countless specialists; they must make sound judgments themselves on matters which affect a wide variety of civilian concerns. They are called upon to evaluate the motivations and capabilities of foreign nations and to estimate the effects of American action or inaction upon these nations. And above all, the new role of military leaders requires of them a heightened awareness of the principles of our democratic society.

The project which follows stems from our interest in this role of the military in government affairs. Military affairs, civil-military relations, and defense policy have been receiving the increasing attention of scholars and informed observers. As we have reflected on this interest, we have noted that one important aspect has been largely neglected, namely the problem of higher education in the armed forces, *much of which is designed to prepare senior officers for precisely those roles in which their decisions are of greatest interest to civilian authorities.* It also has become apparent that few students of public personnel administration have examined military education programs in their search for ideas of general applicability to the preparation of public service personnel.

This volume, then, is a study of military education, with emphasis upon the preparation of career officers for positions involving participation in the formulation of national policy. By way of introduction, it examines first the developments of recent decades that have brought these officers into intimate association with a wide variety of nonmilitary activities and considerations. It then speculates about the qualifications that seem to be called for among officers assigned to these positions. In this connection it takes note of the distinctive context of decision making in military organizations. The principal portions of the book deal with education programs, as they relate to the cultivation of these qualifications.

The armed forces have given much thought to the educational systems by which they seek to develop men capable of coping with the great issues of national security. The policies and practices that distinguish these systems have been, and continue to be, debated within the relatively limited circle of professional military officers. They deserve the attention of a wider audience. Civilians can learn much from the positive accomplishments of military education. They ought also to be aware of its still unsolved problems. To contribute to these ends, and in the hope of uncovering some ways in which military officers may be better prepared to discharge the new burdens thrust upon them, the present study has been undertaken.

To prevent misunderstandings about the assumptions, purpose, and scope of our study we wish to make clear what we are *not* trying to do.

We have not attempted to examine the relationships of the military to all the fields outside of conventional military affairs with which career officers have had to concern themselves. For our purposes we have concluded that consideration of certain selected fields would be adequate. Specifically, we have emphasized the development of national policies in international affairs, strategic planning, and resources planning. We have given some attention to budgetary matters and to scientific research and development.

We do not assume that the armed forces should educate a closed staff corps whose members will devote themselves solely and permanently to policy positions. We are concerned with the education of military generalists, not specialists. Nor do we contend that the armed forces can now minimize the importance of developing leaders with courage, pride, vigor, and other traditional virtues of the fighting man.

We do not deny the need for better preparation of civilians—both at the political level and at the administrative level—for *their* responsibilities. But examination of this urgent problem is beyond the scope of our study.

We do not suggest that military officers ought to play a larger role in the civil functions of government, or that their present role should be taken for granted. Some civilians fear that any effort to give professional officers a more sophisticated knowledge of political and economic affairs can only undermine the leadership of responsible civilian authorities. Many officers are also wary of such efforts for other reasons. As one of the most thoughtful put it to us: "If we make our professional officers part time statesmen, they can no longer perform their primary role of protecting the country, and so automatically lose the stature they might have in the secondary role of the performance of 'civilian' duties."

We would meet the last two points in the following way. Military responsibilities have expanded greatly in the past few generations largely because of changes in science, technology, and political and economic affairs. This process can be curbed, or even reversed somewhat, by policy decisions to rely more heavily on civilian personnel. But we do not think this can eliminate the need for officers more broadly trained than those of 1900. Let us be specific. Civilians may displace military men from certain supervisory activities relating to foreign aid or scientific research. But such activities will remain so vital to military planning that professional officers will continue to have to participate in them and to know something about them. What does this imply for a study of military education? A study concerned with *details* of the curricula of military schools would have to make specific assumptions about the degree of military participation in the civil functions of government; for the extent of this participation would determine the particular detailed information that the schools should try to impart. But no such specific assumption is needed where, as in the present case, the study is concerned with general skills and attitudes, and with such broad knowledge as will be useful to the modern military executive even if he is confined exclusively to strategic planning and to the direction of large operating and supporting forces. Indeed, an important standard of judgment in the latter kind of study will be whether the schools devote too much time to imparting specific data that an officer may never be in a position to use.

It may even be that the government could close the War Colleges and yet succeed in producing more effective national security administrators than these colleges can ever hope to graduate. It could take steps to attract and retain better-qualified professional officers. It could make better use of the natural skills and the practical experience of officers without special schooling. Study of these alternatives is not only appropriate but highly necessary. But we do not think it would weaken the case for the present inquiry. As a practical matter we simply do not believe that any combination of these alternatives can be exploited to the point where it becomes sensible to abandon reliance on formal military education as an additional means of raising the level of performance in the kinds of positions with which we are concerned. As long as this is true such education remains an important subject of study.

We have not attempted to analyze *all* factors that may influence the performance of officers. Little regard, for example, has been given to the extremely important influence of experience on the job. Nor, with a few exceptions, have we considered the social origins of professional officers or the effect on their behavior of the social organization of military life. Specialists in such matters are already studying them. *We wish to make it clear at the outset that we believe these to be at least of equal and perhaps of even greater significance than formal education.* Certainly education alone cannot solve the services' need for highly qualified officers. The best education in the world will not make an "ideal" general out of an officer who has a rigid, inflexible personality.

The study extends to officers of the Army, Navy, Marine Corps, and Air Force. It deals with *career* rather than temporary personnel, since the latter are rarely concerned with the sort of responsibility under review here, except in wartime. Few of them attend the schools with which this book is concerned. Generally speaking, attention is focused on officers in grades ranging from lieutenant colonel to major general, and comparable grades in the Navy. These are the officers who are about to attend, who are attending, or who have recently graduated from advanced schools. Currently, they are performing much of the staff work on which major policy decisions are based. In the next decade they will occupy the top leadership positions in the armed forces.

The schools that are examined in the most detail are the National War College, the Industrial College of the Armed Forces, the Army, Naval, and Air War Colleges, and the three service academies. Some attention is devoted to the Armed Forces Staff College and to the Command and Staff schools. We have not investigated the military schools that are devoted to professional military matters, such as the Infantry School at Fort Benning, or the large number of training programs designed to impart specific skills. The use of civilian institutions by military personnel for advanced education is given some consideration. The Marine Corps schools fall into the category of professional military training, and we have not examined them here. Marine Corps officers, it should be noted, attend the advanced schools of the other services that we have studied, and in that sense are included in the general study.

No book of this sort could fail to reflect the experience, attitudes, and predilections of its authors, and in fairness to the reader ours should be identified. Both of us are products of undergraduate liberal arts colleges. We received our graduate education in universities that are firmly rooted in the liberal arts tradition and our teaching experience likewise has been in such institutions. Personally we are committed to a philosophy of professional education in which the liberal arts occupy a central position.

No military officer need be sensitive to any of the criticism found in this book. Many of the features of the military schools with which we have taken exception prevail in civilian institutions as well. They are weaknesses of American education generally. For the others, we emphasize that our criticism and evaluation are offered in a constructive spirit.

Countless individuals have helped us in this study; without their cooperation and assistance it could not have been conducted and completed. We owe a special debt to Lieutenant General Harold R. Bull USA (Ret.) and to Colonel George A. Lincoln, USA, who inspired us to undertake this study and helped us along the way with wise and friendly counsel. From the start the president of Dartmouth College, John Sloan Dickey, and the provost of the college, Donald Harvard Morrison, have given us every encouragement. They not only have arranged to release us from many of our regular duties so that we might devote time and energy to this project, but have advised us at various stages of our work. Our colleagues in the Department of Government at Dartmouth have accommodated themselves cheerfully to our comings and goings. Professor Harold Sprout of Princeton University arranged for one of us to spend a semester in residence at that university during the initial phase of our study. To him and others at Princeton who are actively engaged in the investigation of military problems we owe special thanks in helping us to define our task and initiate our investigations. Similar thanks are due to Professor William T. R. Fox of Columbia University, chairman, and to the other members of the Committee on National Security Policy Research of the Social Science Research Council, to Professor Harold Stein, director of the Study of Civil-Military Relations of the Twentieth Century Fund, to Professor W. Barton Leach, director of the Defense Studies Program of Harvard University, and to Professor Morris Janowitz of the University of Michigan. Dr. James Shelburne, educational advisor at Air University, has guided us in many ways and has made available his own materials on military education. The officers of the Brookings Institution generously provided a headquarters from which to conduct our field work in Washington. To Mrs. Edna Birkel of Brookings we are particularly grateful for her many courtesies.
A list of officers in the three armed services and others in official positions who have facilitated our work would fill several pages. To them all we owe an apology for the interruptions we have caused and a measureless debt of gratitude for their inter-

est, courtesies, and guidance. At every school we were warmly welcomed, were given opportunity to observe the programs in action and to talk with students and faculty, and were able to secure the information that we sought. We doubt that we could have learned as much about a comparable number of civilian colleges and universities in the same amount of time. Likewise we received the courteous and fruitful help of countless officers in the Office of the Secretary of Defense, the Joint Staff, and in the headquarters of the three services. We would like to acknowledge our debt to many individuals who made this study possible by their frank and candid observations, but we honor their requests for anonymity. We also are deeply indebted to the large number of individuals who have read portions of the manuscript. We have submitted each section to the appropriate military schools and offices for comments and suggestions. As a result of careful consideration by many officers we have eliminated numerous errors of fact and interpretation. Many other friends, military and civilian, who are not presently associated with military education, also have given us the benefit of their criticism of selected chapters. We owe a special debt to Professors Fox and Sprout, who read a draft of almost the entire manuscript.

Dr. Andrew F. Henry, Vanderbilt University, has been associated with us throughout much of this undertaking. He participated in the preparation, administration, and analysis of the questionnaire project, and gave us considerable help in the overall design and conduct of this study. Dr. MacAlister Brown, now of Williams College, has helped with the analysis of some of our data. Numerous Dartmouth colleagues have advised on matters related to their special interests. Miss Virginia Close of the Dartmouth College Library and George J. Stansfield of the National War College Library greatly facilitated the search for materials. Miss Elizabeth J. Likert served throughout much of the project as research assistant and secretary. We are particularly grateful to Mrs. Anne C. Tonseth for her meticulous preparation of the final manuscript and to John Ervin, Jr. of Princeton University Press for his highly valued editorial guidance. A few passages from articles by one or both of us are reproduced from the *Public Administration Review* with permission.

The Carnegie Corporation of New York has made this undertaking possible by a grant to Dartmouth College. We are especially grateful to James A. Perkins, its vice president, for his interest and encouragement. The Carnegie Corporation and Dartmouth College, as well as all others mentioned in this preface, assume no responsibility for what we have written. That responsibility is ours alone.

JWM
LIR

Hanover, New Hampshire
November 1, 1956

A NOTE ON METHOD AND SOURCES

No single method of inquiry has been relied upon in the preparation of this book. In large measure it is based upon interviews and direct observation over a period of three years. In order to gain insight into the nature of the problems facing the armed services, we began our investigations with a series of interviews with officers then or in the recent past engaged in positions involving the formulation of national policy. We corresponded with still others in such positions, including some overseas. At the same time we interviewed many civilians who had been or were currently in positions in the Department of Defense, the Department of State, other executive agencies, and the Congress which brought them into intimate association with military personnel. This group of informants included several individuals at the Cabinet level. After a year of such "open-ended" interviewing of more than 300 individuals, we administered a detailed questionnaire to more than 550 officers on duty in the Pentagon, to gain further information and insight into their duties and the relevance of educational experience to these positions.

We have visited all of the institutions that are described and evaluated, most of them at least twice, and several of them more frequently. One of the authors served on the civilian faculty of the National War College in 1950 and again in 1951 for four and a half months in each instance. He also has participated in conferences and seminars at the three service War Colleges, has served as a consultant to two of them, and has lectured at one, in addition to his visits in connection with this study. It has been our privilege to become personally acquainted with many of the officers stationed as administrators, faculty, and students at these institutions during recent years. We estimate that we have interviewed or met informally in groups with an additional 150 or more students or graduates. We also have discussed military education and the separate military schools with officers in the personnel agencies and other appropriate units in the headquarters of the three services, the Joint Staff, and the Office of the Secretary of Defense.

We have collected and examined a large quantity of documentary materials. These have included service regulations relating to military education and relevant personnel practices, and a number of surveys or reports prepared by staff agencies or special groups. They also have included documents prepared by the various schools for their own use but usually not available for wider distribution, such as descriptive catalogs, curriculum outlines, separate course directives, texts, staff studies, annual reports, and special advisory reports. The hearings and reports of the Congressional armed services and appropriations committees also have been significant sources of information. The official journals *Air University Quarterly Review* and *Military Review*, the semi-official *United States Naval Institute Proceedings*, and the unofficial *Army, Army Navy Air Force Journal, Army Times, Navy Times,* and *Air Force Times* also have been of considerable value.

A number of unpublished theses and other manuscripts have been of very substantial help to us in the preparation of this book. These are: T. J. Barrett, *Mobilization for Education,* M.A. thesis, Ohio State University, 1949; Richard C. Brown, *Social Attitudes of American Generals, 1898–1940,* Ph.D. thesis, University of Wisconsin, 1951; B. F. Fuller, Jr., *Professional Education for United States Air Force Officers,* Ph.D. thesis, Yale University, 1951; Robert K. Johnson, *Air Universities Library Study of Libraries in Selected Military Educational Institutions in the United States,* Air University, 1956; James C. Shelburne, *Factors Leading to the Establishment of the Air University,* Ph.D. thesis, University of Chicago, 1953; William Y. Smith, *The Air Academy: The Growth of an Idea,* seminar paper, Harvard University, 1953; William W. Whitson, *Naval War College Education for Foreign Policy Formulation,* course paper, Fletcher School of Law and Diplomacy, 1954; and C. Henry Wood, *The General Education Movement and the West Point Curriculum,* D.Ed. thesis, Columbia University, 1951.

There is a paucity of published material on military education. There are numerous popular and a few serious histories of the service academies, but accounts of the other schools are limited almost exclusively to magazine and journal articles. We have found that the latter usually are little more than descriptive accounts and soon are outdated. Brief descriptions of military schools are included in *The Officer's Guide, The Naval Officer's Guide,* and *The Air Officer's Guide,* published at frequent intervals by the Military Service Publishing Company, Harrisburg. *Education for the Professions,* published by the United States Office of Education, Washington, in 1955, also contains chapters on the Army, Navy, and Air Force education programs for officers.

A considerable volume of published material is available to the reader who is interested in pursuing a study of the widening scope of military responsibilities. Many of these sources are listed in *Civil-Military Relations, An Annotated Bibliography 1940–1952,* prepared under the direction of the Committee on Civil-Military Relations Research of the Social Science Research Council (New York, 1954), and in an earlier work of similar nature, *Civil-Military Relations: Bibliographical Notes of Administrative Problems of Civilian Mobilization,* prepared under the editorial direction of Pendleton Herring (Chicago, 1940). Paul Van Riper's "A Survey of Materials for the Study of Military Management" (*American Political Science Review,* September 1955, pp. 828–850) is an indispensable bibliographical guide.

CONTENTS

CONTENTS

PART ONE

MILITARY RESPONSIBILITIES

IN THE MODERN AGE

CHAPTER ONE

THE VARIETY OF MILITARY

EXPERIENCE

THE distinctive task of military organization is to plan and conduct military operations. The irreducible minimum function of an officer corps is to train and direct combat forces. In addition, officers are often responsible for securing the equipment and supplies necessary to support operating forces. Within the last generation these traditional functions have expanded enormously. To generalize, they have been modified in two fundamental ways. First, officers have become increasingly concerned with international affairs, that is to say, with the premises of military policy, with the purposes for which and the terms on which military forces will be deployed. They have moved upstream toward the fountain springs of national policy. Second, their support functions—supply, finance, research and development, public relations, manpower management, and the like—have grown more numerous, difficult, and important. They have moved downstream to a point where the river widens into a bay far broader than any they have ever traveled before. Both developments have complicated the task of military education. This book is concerned with the response of the three services to new requirements. In the two introductory chapters it deals first with the dimensions of these developments and some of their implications for career officers.

The Old Order

Prior to world war II, most officers spent most of their careers in assignments traditional to their profession. Interservice, interagency, and intergovernmental contacts were uncommon; and only

3

rarely did they involve issues of overriding importance. Military personnel led a far more cloistered and routine existence than they do today. The change may be a trifle less in the case of Naval officers, who continue to go off to sea in their formative years. But even for them the pattern of fleet and shore assignments was less complex than it is at the present time. In the case of the Army officer, the secluded garrison of the past was not much different from a solitary, self-contained ship. Colonel Ernest Dupuy has drawn a vivid picture of these establishments as they appeared in 1904 —monasteries in which the soldier's father superior was a two-fisted sergeant and his abbott a company commander.[1] Ritual and rectitude were the order of the day, and the immaculate technique was the prized partner of the immaculate uniform. All was on a miniature scale. The total force consisted of a mere 50,000 men and 5,000 officers spread among two score posts, camps, and stations. As late as 1935 the Army had only 125,000 men.

Much of the isolation and austerity that characterized the military forces was pressed upon them by an indifferent or suspicious people. The fear of standing armies had been written into the Constitution. The devotion of the states to the militia system and the egalitarian's hostility to hierarchy and discipline combined to produce an ideal of the citizen-soldier who would spring to arms at the blast of a trumpet, secure the nation as common sense dictated, and return immediately to his farm or trade. After the civil war a nation heavily preoccupied with industrial development and happily remote from the quarrels of Europe gave its soldiers neither attention nor social status nor money.

The political atmosphere also limited severely the demands on strategic planners. War planning before 1917 was a highly suspect activity, and such plans as managed to escape Congressional censure were largely defensive in nature. With this assumption it was unnecessary to provide for overseas bases, overseas transport, or antisubmarine warfare. After world war I, Naval planning was concerned largely with protection of the Philippines, Hawaii, and the Panama Canal. The concern of the Army was simply coastal defense. Military operations were to be undertaken only as a last resort; they were to be undertaken alone; and they did not appear

[1] Colonel R. Ernest Dupuy, "Pass in Review," *Army Combat Forces Journal,* October 1954, p. 25.

to require a total national effort. As the editors of the *Army Combat Forces Journal* have put it: "Such problems as military and industrial mobilization and higher logistics were beyond the interest of the great majority of officers. . . . The problem of allies, of creating an effective coalition force, was beyond [their] terms of reference. . . . In short, there was really no reason for the soldier of the line to be concerned with logistics, allies, military missions, or atomic warfare." [2]

Such was the nature of military service when West Point and Annapolis developed their programs and traditions, and when the Naval and Army War Colleges first struggled to promote the higher military learning in America. It was a service that placed a great value on loyalty, precedent, specific technical skill, and a gentlemanly code of conduct. Officers' duties were limited by the aloofness of civilian society, by a less complicated and more static weaponry, and by the smallness and autonomy of military organizations. Inevitably, all this was reflected in the schools—in their missions, curricula, and methods.

The picture has been overdrawn, of course. Before 1815, Naval officers had conducted negotiations with France, Morocco, and Algiers; later they concluded treaties with Hawaii, Samoa, Japan, and Korea. Army officers went abroad on a variety of missions. At home the Corps of Engineers worked with civil authority to discover and to build a nation. The war with Spain was a definite turning point. It provided a broad range of job experiences and led Secretary of War Elihu Root to urge an Army reorganization that later opened up new high level positions. The variety of duties was also increased by the acquisition of overseas territories, by the emergence of the United States as a great naval power, and by Theodore Roosevelt's readiness to use that power in support of national policy. By the first decade of the twentieth century a limited number of Naval planners had worked on issues in which the interests of the sailor and the diplomat tended to converge.

During and immediately after world war I, military officers were again involved, though only temporarily, in what Root called "almost every branch of civil government." Their relationships with industry and with allied military forces were more extensive than

[2] "The Journal's First Half Century," *Army Combat Forces Journal,* October 1954, p. 19.

ever before. Their participation in the occupation of Germany added the Rhineland to a list that already contained the names of Pekin, Nicaragua, Manila, Havana, Murmansk, and Panama. Throughout most of the 1920's the dominant theme was resumption of garrison and shipboard routine. But here, too, there were exceptions. To preserve the lessons of industrial mobilization, military personnel were assigned to the newly created Office of the Assistant Secretary of War, Army Industrial College, and Army and Navy Munitions Board. A very small number of officers, like Admirals William H. Standley and William V. Pratt, were privileged to attend international disarmament conferences. A somewhat greater number were assigned to the War Department General Staff's Plans Division. The Army officers of this division, which was created in 1921, participated in the tentative joint war planning of the 1920's and represented the Army in its relations with other agencies of the government.

An additional trend of some significance was the assignment of officers to civilian agencies of the government. This practice dates from the early history of the republic. It became common during the New Deal era when experienced administrators were at a premium. Thus by the early 1930's there were numerous precedents, however sporadic, for the utilization of officers in functions not closely related to combat operations.

The Warming-Up Period (1937–1941)

Also at this time a gradual rise took place in the number of officers working in the twilight zone between strategic planning and foreign affairs. Behind this development was the rise of hostile forces in the Far East and Europe. Beginning in 1931 a series of aggressive actions took place in Manchuria, Ethiopia, the Rhineland, Spain, China, Austria, and Czechoslovakia. The anti-Comintern powers appeared to be cooperating in a global plan and America faced the ominous risk of strategic encirclement. The age-old ocean barriers somehow seemed less secure in the light of modern science and in view of the exposed position of the traditional guardian of the seas, Great Britain. The President spoke boldly of "quarantining" the aggressors.

Within the armed services the lead in strategic planning was at first taken by the Navy. The Navy had long been the "ready" service, "America's first line of defense." Since 1920 Naval officers had assumed that the Pacific was the primary danger zone. In 1937, moreover, Japan not only unleashed an attack against China, but refused to limit naval armaments by international agreement. The Navy therefore began to plan a 20 percent increase in strength, and prompted the Joint Board to revise War Plan Orange (Japan). The Joint Board, a kind of forerunner of the present Joint Chiefs of Staff, was composed of the principal operations and plans officers of the Army and Navy. Incidental to these developments, Captain Royal E. Ingersoll, director of naval plans, was sent to London in December 1937 to confer with British Naval authorities. His visit marked a turning point of utmost significance. Although forces of isolationism were still dominant, America was breaking a century-old tradition of unilateral military planning.

By February 1938, when the Joint Board had approved a revised Plan Orange, two major policies were beginning to emerge: first, cooperation with the British; and second, preparedness in the Atlantic as well as the Pacific. The second was a more or less inevitable consequence of the first; for the British obviously had to concern themselves with the dangers closest at hand. After the Munich Pact of September 1938, emphasis on the Atlantic increased. Early in 1939, the Joint Board set its Planning Committee to work on five Rainbow Plans designed to provide varying degrees of hemispheric defense, varying degrees of emphasis on the Pacific, and in one case (Rainbow 5) active participation in a European war.[3] Thus, for the first time in American history, the armed forces were approaching a conflict with a joint war plan developed through peacetime staff work. The role of the Joint Board in this process was underlined in 1939, when it was ordered to report directly to the President.

Another significant development of the period was the addition of Army Air Corps officers to high level strategic planning

[3] Rainbow 5, completed in the spring of 1941, assumed that it might be necessary to send expeditionary forces to Africa or Europe. On prewar planning generally, see Mark S. Watson, *Chief of Staff, Prewar Plans and Preparations,* Office of the Chief of Military History, Department of the Army, Washington, 1950.

councils. In November 1939, President Roosevelt invited not only the chief of staff but General H. H. Arnold of the Air Corps to a momentous White House conference at which he announced an expanded aircraft program—a decision that to some extent delayed the development of the ground force program. In the next three years the position of American air officers was consolidated by two developments abroad. One was the impressive performance of the Luftwaffe in Poland, the Low Countries, and France. The second was the British practice of including senior air personnel in their joint planning councils and, consequently, in the discussions between the United States and Britain that were starting to take place. This led inevitably to the participation of American air officers in combined talks. Also in July 1941 the chief air officer was finally added to the Joint Army and Navy Board.

Step by step there emerged the pattern of joint and combined strategic planning that was to continue throughout the war. Strategic decisions were paralleled by supply discussions in Washington with members of the British purchasing commission. The destroyer-bases exchange was arranged. In September 1940 the Army War Plans Division suggested that a new national policy might be required to facilitate release of munitions to Britain. In November the chief of naval operations proposed more systematic Anglo-American staff talks. As a result, in early 1941, the first lengthy conferences with the British were held in Washington. Nine American officers, supported by many more assistants working anonymously in the war plans divisions of the two services, took part in these so-called ABC-1 conferences. In March 1941, before the talks had been concluded, the lend-lease act was passed. The program of military aid was now on a new basis and by the end of the year it was extended to the Soviet Union and China. In August senior officers accompanied Roosevelt to the Atlantic conference with Churchill, the first of the many meetings between heads of governments. Once again planning staffs were asked to prepare papers and brief their principals. In September 1941 the long months of military planning culminated in a remarkable Joint Board document outlining the national objectives of the United States as a basis for strategic and production planning. This document, signed by Admiral Stark and General Marshall on September 11, 1941, stated much of the political and strategic policy that was to govern American forces in world war II.[4]

Significantly, these prewar planning activities seldom brought military officers into close association with State Department officials. There was one major exception. In 1938 the State Department became concerned over the danger of Nazi infiltration into the Western Hemisphere. This led to the creation of a standing liaison committee composed of the under secretary of state, the chief of naval operations, and the chief of staff. On the other hand military officers became highly active in economic mobilization. In the winter of 1939–1940 they began to work with the Treasury's interdepartmental committee to coordinate foreign and domestic military purchases. After May 1940 they dealt constantly with production and procurement officials of the National Defense Advisory Commission and its successor, the Office of Production Management. On a less extensive basis—because the problems were still less urgent—they dealt with manpower, transportation, price stabilization, consumer protection, and agricultural officials. The Army-Navy Munitions Board began to coordinate a simplified priorities system. In the autumn of 1941 industrial mobilization planning culminated in the preparation of the so-called Victory Program setting forth in gross terms the supply as well as force level requirements for triumph over the Axis powers.

In this same period an increasing number of officers began to participate in major research and development enterprises. They had long participated in the work of the National Advisory Committee for Aeronautics and in such service agencies as the Naval Research Laboratory. Preliminary work on radar and many other devices had begun. But a strange new world of massive involvement with civilian scientists and engineers was presaged in March 1939 when Professor Enrico Fermi of Columbia pointed out to the Navy Department the possibility of exploiting the fission of uranium.

Thus, by December 7, 1941, major aspects of national security policy—joint and combined strategy, international affairs, economic mobilization, foreign aid, scientific research and development—were beginning to come within the orbit of a senior officer's military career.

[4] Robert E. Sherwood, *Roosevelt and Hopkins,* New York, 1948, pp. 410 ff.

World War II

The outbreak of war accelerated this trend. As military victory became the dominant purpose of American life, half of the nation's income and a formidable proportion of its human and physical assets were diverted to military use. It became much harder to locate a dividing line between military and civilian activity or military and civilian personnel. Hastily commissioned officers and millions of draftees did jobs that had been the exclusive function of the regular establishments. Conversely, career officers began to take on the roles of diplomat, economist, scientist, and general manager. They played these roles in every quarter of the globe—in the Persian Gulf, Iceland, Natal, Brisbane, Antwerp, Assam, Tunis, Basra, Moscow, Santa Maria, Calcutta, and Washington.

Day after day high-ranking officers addressed themselves to such questions as these: Should Allied forces deal with representatives of Vichy France? Will projected operations be hampered or rendered impossible by production "slippages" or by inadequate shipping or port facilities? Should the Air Forces bomb industrial centers in Flanders? Should Soviet or Allied armed units liberate Prague? What should be the missions and jurisdictions of Admiral Chester Nimitz and General Douglas MacArthur in the Pacific? Should a limited supply of machine tools be used to produce heavy cruisers for the Navy, planes for the British, or munitions for the Army? How much effort should be made to develop incendiary bombs, proximity fuses, or high muzzle velocity antitank guns? Even officers with the broadest prior experience became involved in novel situations. Thus General Somervell, Army supply chief, found himself in New Delhi worrying with Lord Mountbatten about how General Stilwell might be restored to the good graces of Chiang Kai-shek.[5]

Many of these problems had to be solved in conjunction with civilian officials or with representatives of other services and nations. To improve the machinery for dealing with them many organizational changes were made in the first three months of the war. The Navy established a separate headquarters in Washington for the commander in chief of the United States Fleet, and then

[5] John D. Millett, *The Organization and Role of the Army Service Forces*, Washington, 1954, pp. 76–77.

in effect merged it with the Office of the Chief of Naval Operations by placing Admiral Ernest King in charge of both. The Navy also revised its logistical organization by creating an Office of Procurement and Material. Both changes opened up new high level staff positions to Naval officers. The same effect flowed from the great Army reorganization of February-March 1942, which brought the technical services under the wing of an Army Service Forces organization and gave virtual autonomy, including coordinate representation on the principal joint and combined committees, to the Army Air Forces.

The modest Joint Board organization of 1941 evolved into a highly complex Joint Chiefs of Staff structure, with a host of committees and subcommittees to deal with current war plans, future war policy, logistics, intelligence, munitions assignment, transport, and communications. Although the rise of the Air Forces would undoubtedly have forced such joint action in the long run, the immediate impetus came from the British, who wished international cooperation to extend to many functional areas and who thus precipitated interservice cooperation in the United States. The Combined Chiefs of Staff (U.S.-U.K.) held their first meeting on January 20, 1942, and the first meeting of the Joint Chiefs of Staff followed soon thereafter. The combined committees for strategic planning, intelligence, munitions assignment, and military transportation were paralleled by JCS committees. Overseas all this was reflected in the creation of joint and combined commands.

At home such fields as ocean shipping, land transport, civilian defense, industrial relations, public relations, strategic intelligence, and psychological warfare were either expanded or opened up to military officers. In budgeting and finance, virtual disappearance of normal peacetime Congressional controls was succeeded by appearance of controls over the flow of physical resources and the price of commodities. Allocation and scheduling problems beset the Army Service Forces, the Air Matériel Command, and the technical bureaus of the Navy. The initials WPB and OPA became as familiar to some officers as OPD and CNO. They came to learn that victory would require more equipment than they had first supposed, that America's capacity to produce was greater than they had first imagined, that there were limits beyond which the economy could not be pushed without endangering their own supply needs, not to speak of evoking political objections, and that "bottlenecks" had a nasty habit of moving about from machine tools to materials to plant facilities to component parts to manpower.

The importance of supply became clear to forces overseas. Great naval armadas, thousands of miles from port, had to be made self-sustaining for long periods. Thus when Fleet Admiral King attempted to characterize the great conflict he said "Whatever else it is, so far as the United States is concerned, it is a war of logistics." [6] For this reason such names as Aurand, Burns, Carter, Clay, Echols, Lutes, Robinson, and Somervell must take their place beside those of the great field and sea commanders.

The demand for officers with scientific training also increased tremendously. Many were assigned to such agencies as the Army's New Developments Division, the Air Forces' center at Wright Field, or the JCS Committee on New Weapons and Equipment. The Corps of Engineers created the Manhattan District as a framework under which scientists and military men carried forward the work of developing an atomic bomb. All three services created operations research units to study the performance of their equipment and the effectiveness of their methods in the field.

Interaction with the State Department at the staff level was limited during much of the war. In May 1943 the military asked State to designate an official to advise JCS committees that had to prepare papers in which political considerations could not be divorced from strategic ones. But the State Department preferred to confine itself largely to the exchange of memoranda plus occasional conversations at the secretarial level. After the Moscow conference of foreign ministers in October 1943 it appeared that the terms of the peace might become more important than military operations. A European advisory commission was established in London. Ambassador John Winant headed the American delegation, but both the War and Navy Departments were also represented on it. In December 1943 the State Department created an informal "working security committee" to clear communications between American agencies and the European Advisory Commission. This also included military members. By the end of the year,

---

[6] Ernest J. King, *U.S. Navy at War, 1941–1945: Official Reports to the Secretary of the Navy,* Washington, 1946, p. 34.

moreover, the State Department had begun to furnish the Joint Chiefs of Staff with some political guidance. Finally, in December 1944, a three member State-War-Navy Coordinating Committee (SWNCC) was created. Officers did not sit on the committee but they did sit on the subcommittees that were soon formed. The War Department immediately assigned to the Operations Division of the General Staff responsibility for handling SWNCC papers. In order to represent Naval interests more effectively, and especially to keep abreast of the position of Secretary Forrestal, the chief of naval operations assigned similar responsibility to a newly created politico-military affairs unit.

If collaboration between State and military officers did not emerge until late in the war, this certainly does not mean that officers were inactive in the field of foreign affairs. Military personnel took an active part in many of the great international conferences of the war. The Army alone sent 37 officers to the second Quebec conference and another 20 to Yalta. Military and economic aid programs were administered with the aid of officers from the very moment that the lend-lease act of 1941 was passed. Military participation increased as Congress came to appropriate funds for military aid *directly* to the War and Navy Departments. General Somervell, chief of the Army Service Forces, sat on the President's Soviet Protocol Committee and his staff worked with the British Supply Council in North America. It reviewed British requirements for ground force lend-lease; and it did so with an eye to preventing the British from using lend-lease supplies for postwar economic recovery or for nonessential civilian purposes. Toward the end of the war it supervised the purchase and distribution of civilian supplies in occupied areas.

As Allied power began to press upon the Continent, officers were increasingly drawn into the realm of civil affairs, where diplomatic and military issues were closely interwoven. The Combined Chiefs of Staff established a Civil Affairs Committee. The War Department, which had previously left such matters to the provost marshal general, raised them to a higher echelon by creating a Civil Affairs Division under Major General John Hilldring. But the main impact came overseas. From North African experience, officers realized that the supreme headquarters of any Allied expeditionary force would be the point at which strategy and international policy would merge. General Sir Frederick Morgan, head of the Normandy invasion planning staff, said: "There could hardly be any such thing here as a purely military consideration. Any and every decision by the Supreme Commander must and could only be taken after consideration of the possible and probable political repercussions thereof." [7]

By the autumn of 1943 Morgan had established a small Political Advisers Section, and had secured the services of a diplomatic representative, A. E. Drexel Biddle, Jr. Throughout 1944, according to the official SHAEF historian, General Eisenhower and his staff—including a new general staff division for civil affairs (G-5)—were particularly busy in the political sphere ". . . representing Great Britain and the United States in relations with representatives of France, preparing for civil affairs administration after the liberation of occupied countries, and planning for military government for conquered Germany. Somewhat allied to these activities were those relating to press relations, censorship, and psychological warfare." [8]

The historian of the Operations Division of the War Department General Staff (OPD) likewise traces the growing involvement of military officers in foreign affairs: "As Army forces began going overseas, it became increasingly difficult for military planners to avoid taking foreign affairs into their military calculations. . . . The public clamor over the negotiations which General Eisenhower conducted with Admiral Jean Darlan . . . dramatically illustrated the fact that the Army, even in executing military plans as ordered, and in making decisions on grounds of military necessity, could not avoid becoming involved in the most controversial questions of foreign policy." [9]

Within the Army General Staff, primary responsibility for synthesizing military and foreign policy was exercised by OPD, especially by its Strategy and Policy Group. OPD papers were not merely referred to the chief of staff for consideration at the JCS level. They were also submitted to Secretary Stimson, Under Secretary Patterson, and Assistant Secretary McCloy, the War De-

[7] Lieutenant General Sir Frederick E. Morgan, *Overture to Overlord*, New York, 1950, pp. 219–220.

[8] Forrest C. Pogue, *The Supreme Command*, Washington, 1954, pp. 67–68.

[9] Ray S. Cline, *Washington Command Post: The Operations Division*, Washington, 1951, p. 313.

14

partment's representative on SWNCC. For as the war progressed and strategic designs were in the process of being executed, emphasis inevitably shifted from military to politico-military planning. In the words of the historian of OPD: "Day after day the staff dealt with issues that were not conventionally considered part of the main military task of devising strategy and coordinating operations." [10]

In preparation for the Yalta conference, OPD prepared a memorandum raising 17 questions about the possible consequences of a Soviet declaration of war against Japan. These included questions about whether Soviet participation in the war in Asia might not lead to the absorption of North China.[11] In 1944 OPD officers were still somewhat diffident about discussing such issues. But this too changed shortly. By the time of the Potsdam conference, papers were being prepared on such frankly political topics as Soviet intentions with respect to expansion, American policy toward Indo-China, and the terms of a Japanese surrender. Thus as the war drew to a close the duties of career officers were becoming increasingly complex. From the point of view of this study probably the most significant development of the period was the growth of planning staffs and their intrusion into the field of foreign affairs.

For understandable reasons this intrusion was somewhat greater in the case of Army planners than in the case of Naval or Air Forces planners. Both the latter also had to deal with foreign affairs problems. In the Navy these were greatest in the Pacific, though they arose in other areas as well. In the Air Forces they derived from the rapid growth of air bases on foreign soil and from the need to make delicate decisions about what targets to bomb and how to bomb them. But in the nature of things the Army had a more direct massive contact with the terrain and populations of other nations, especially with the relatively advanced nations of Europe. As a result its officers were more heavily involved in international problems.

Army officers also played a somewhat larger part than Naval or Air Forces officers in many of the other quasi-military fields that have been mentioned. Here, too, the reasons are plain. At the

---

[10] *ibid.*, p. 188.
[11] *ibid.*, p. 331. Of the 86 papers that OPD prepared for Potsdam, Cline estimates that less than half were concerned primarily with military operations.

start of the war the mobilization, supply, and general management problems of the Army *included* those of the Air Forces and throughout the war the Army continued to perform many essential services for the Air Forces. Army officers were more heavily involved in such matters than Naval officers because they started from a lower level of preparedness and they had to build to a higher level—higher in terms of the number of men and the amount of equipment and supplies.[12] Moreover, the build-up process in the Army was largely under the centralized control of professional military officers reporting to the chief of staff. In the Navy, on the other hand, civilian executives with their direct ties to the technical bureaus played a relatively greater part in the "business affairs" of the department.

We shall see that these differences were to some degree reflected in the distinctive educational policies and practices of the services.

1945–1955: The World Scene

The advent of peace did not permit officers to withdraw from their diversified policy-level positions. A principal reason for this was the reluctance of some civilian agencies to assume functions that the military were performing. A case in point was the State Department's long reluctance to assume responsibility for conquered Germany. Another reason was the inability of the government to attract sufficient numbers of capable civilian executives. But the experience of Great Britain and other major powers suggests that even if civilian officials had been able to carry a larger part of the load, they could not have carried it all. Many highly important quasi-military duties would still have devolved upon officers of the armed forces. This was inevitable, given the continued size, urgency, and complexity of the national security function in the decade that followed world war II.

Overseas the first great task was the interim administration of foreign countries, notably Germany and Japan, but also including Austria, Korea, Trieste, and many Pacific islands. The main burden here was assumed by the Army. Between 1945 and 1952 Gen-

---

[12] A notable exception was the field of research and development. Here, again for understandable reasons, Naval and Air Forces officers had at least as great a role as their Army colleagues.

eral MacArthur's headquarters labored to restore Japan to the family of nations. Military officers helped to revise the constitution and laws. They participated in determining the level and structure of industry; in reforming the monetary and financial system; in guiding the trade union movement and political parties; and in supervising the press and the educational system. Finally, they played an important role in the writing of the peace treaty.

In Germany between 1945 and 1949 General Clay and his staff faced similar problems, with the added complication of quadripartite control.[13] Thousands of American officers worked to restore essential services, end inflation, revive trade, and purge the civil administration of individuals who had been leaders in the Nazi ranks. They faced such questions as whether Hamburg and Bremen would receive more shipping than the Low Country ports; what part the Ruhr should play in a German state; and whether the German economy should be organized into four separate compartments or efforts should be made to unify it in whole or in part. Starting in the spring of 1948 they also had to cope with the potentially explosive Berlin blockade and to improvise an airlift to overcome it.

The foreign responsibilities were increased, moreover, by the gradual development of foreign aid programs. In the late winter of 1946–1947 the British requested the United States to assume responsibility for sustaining Greece and Turkey. This gave rise to the announcement of the Truman Doctrine in March 1947. Even as that policy was being promulgated, military officers were working with State Department officials on measures to meet the European dollar shortage. This led to the development of the European Recovery Program in the autumn of 1947. Again, in the spring of 1948, when this program was getting under way, Anglo-American military discussions had begun on the question of transforming the new Brussels Pact association into an Atlantic association to which the United States would belong and to whose members it would supply weapons and equipment. These talks were the first steps along a road that in 1949 led to the creation of the North Atlantic Treaty Organization and inauguration of

---

[13] It is significant that Clay neither sought nor received advice from the State Department before he started out on his tasks. See his own account in *Decision in Germany*, New York, 1950, p. 6.

the Mutual Defense Assistance Program. NATO soon generated a military committee of chiefs of staff, a permanent subcommittee or standing group composed of American, British, and French officers, and a set of allied commands and subcommands served by international staffs, including a supreme headquarters (SHAPE) near Paris. In the Far East there were partly analogous developments in the creation of a United Nations command to conduct the war in Korea and in efforts to build a Southeast Asia Treaty Organization.

To administer billions of dollars of military aid, American officers had to maintain close relations with the State Department, with the Mutual Security Administration and its successor agencies, and with other federal departments. Overseas, officers of all services were assigned to Military Assistance Advisory Groups (MAAG) in the recipient countries. They helped foreign governments compute supply requirements and forwarded deficit lists to higher headquarters. After other officers in Washington had supervised the procurement and shipping of the equipment, the MAAG's supervised its distribution and instructed local personnel in its operation. Two closely related supply functions were also undertaken. One was a program to award contracts in Europe for the equipment needed by Allied nations and paid for with American dollars—the offshore procurement plan. Another was a program to construct lines of communication and support facilities in France for NATO countries—the so-called "infrastructure" plan. In addition, officers of all services were assigned to military missions to supervise or arrange for the conduct of training programs for soldiers of friendly nations. By 1954, about 50,-000 foreign officers and men had received formal training under such programs.

By 1955, American military forces were spread throughout the greater part of the free world. In Europe they wrestled with the problem of German rearmament and participation in NATO. In East Asia, General Maxwell Taylor summarized the unfinished business of his command as: how to resolve the armistice situation in Korea and terminate the disadvantageous conditions imposed on our forces there; how to get Japan into its proper military, political, and economic role in stabilizing the Far East; how to organize and dispose of available resources to attain our agreed objectives in the Far East.[14] Army officers, usually in the company of Naval or Air Force officers, participated in MAAG's or military missions in 35 foreign countries. Other interservice missions were established to carry out American obligations to the United Nations. A United States delegation served the UN military staff committee. Military observers were sent with UN commissions in Pakistan, Indonesia, the Balkans, and Palestine. Air Force officers operated bases in North Africa, the Middle East, the Near East, and the Far East. They collaborated with Canada and other countries in devising early-warning systems of air defense, commanded joint forces in Alaska, and supervised NATO air forces.

Naval officers also became more involved in international affairs than ever before. After 1945 they supervised the repatriation of 4,000,000 Japanese and 1,000,000 Chinese, Koreans, and other Asians to their homelands. They played a major role in determining the status of the mandated islands of the central Pacific. They administered more than 20 active overseas bases and governed natives on such islands as Saipan and Tinian. With the dispatch of the *Missouri* to Istanbul by Secretary Forrestal in 1946, the Navy began to acquire a major interest in waters that had previously been a British domain. Admiral Sherman conducted conversations that led to the creation of American bases in Spain. Admirals Carney and Fechteler commanded Allied forces in southern Europe. The Sixth Fleet was maintained in the Mediterranean "as deterrent to possible enemies and as a friendly sustainer of the strength and morale of NATO countries." [15] On the other side of the world, by direction of the President, the Seventh Fleet supported national policy by patrolling the waters between Formosa and the mainland of China. Its commanders, like the Naval officers who participated in the blockade of North Korea, inevitably had to concern themselves with delicate issues of policy. To some extent this growing involvement of the Navy in international affairs resulted from the world-wide deployment of its sister services. Never before in peacetime had the Navy been called upon to protect the lines of communication for so many Army units and Air Force bases in so many quarters of the globe. But the Navy's in-

[14] *New York Times,* July 16, 1955.
[15] *Semiannual Report of the Secretary of Defense, January 1 to June 30, 1953,* Washington, 1953, p. 181.

volvement also derived from the great increase in range and striking capacity made possible by the rise of naval air power.

1945–1955: The National Scene

Not only did officers acquire responsibilities throughout the world; they also performed important and increasingly complex national security functions at the seat of government. The nation was forced to maintain levels of preparedness unprecedented in its peacetime history. Military spending, which had dropped from a world war II peak of about $85 billion to $10 to $14 billion in the fiscal years 1947–1950, climbed back rapidly after the Korean affair to an average of about $40 billion in the years that followed. This permitted the country roughly to double the size of its armed forces and to embark upon an immense procurement program. Except in the case of Korea, the military power thus mobilized was not actually committed to major combat operations. This is a fact of first importance to the story. In world war II, national security planners had kept one eye riveted on the battlefield itself and had measured their success largely by the progress of the field forces. Now, however, national objectives appeared less simple and the methods for attaining them more complex. They were pursued by diplomatic action, by trade and aid policies, by propaganda, by strategic maneuvers, and by sustained technological and industrial development. Military officers were thus forced to pay closer attention to the political, economic, and scientific aspects of national security matters than ever before. Moreover, the importance of these aspects was pressed upon them at every turn by official boards, by congressmen, by community leaders, and by the authors of the innumerable critiques and post mortems on the conduct of world war II. For all these reasons the cold war provoked further growth of military concern with semimilitary functions. It was therefore no exaggeration when the secretary of the Navy concluded: "A random selection of activities undertaken by the Navy *in addition to the operation of its fleets and forces* shows a scope and diversity touching on nearly every phase of human endeavor." [16]

As the years passed—and this is perhaps the most significant

[16] *ibid.,* p. 173. Italics added.

feature of the period—the assignment of officers to these and similar functions came to be regarded as a more or less permanent feature of American government. At the same time the functions themselves became more difficult. The endless process of countering communist moves, bolstering allies, and wooing neutral nations appeared harder than defeating the Axis in war. The development of new weapons, with its disturbing impact on policy, strategy, and supply, continued at an accelerating rate. The reassertion of budget controls added another dimension to the picture. The decision-making machinery, moreover, grew more elaborate.

In adapting to this evolving situation, the executive branch not only reorganized its military establishment, a process that will be commented on below, but also spawned a number of other agencies with major national security functions. *Indeed, a key development of this period was the idea of national security as a function that encompassed the responsibilities of both military and nonmilitary agencies, and that thereby converted the military into partners in an enterprise greater than their own.* This concept of national security as a government-wide function became increasingly explicit as time passed. (We shall see it most clearly reflected in the higher military schools.) An early landmark in the process was the atomic energy act of 1946. After the enactment of this law, officers were to serve as general managers of the Atomic Energy Commission and as staff members of its Military Applications Division. They also manned the Military Liaison Committee that linked the commission to the military departments.

Even more important was the national security act of 1947. This created a National Security Council, a Central Intelligence Agency, a National Security Resources Board, and a National Military Establishment. The National Security Council was a far more formidable instrument than its predecessors, SWNCC and SANAC (State–Army–Navy–Air Force Coordinating Committee). Its statutory membership did not include military officers, but the views of the Joint Chiefs of Staff, of the individual services, and of their respective staffs were transmitted, directly or indirectly, to the council and to the planning staff that prepared papers for its deliberations. As for CIA, its first three directors were professional officers; military officers were sprinkled liberally throughout the organization; many more did business with it in the course of their daily strategic planning or intelligence duties. Officers concerned with economic mobilization also worked closely with the National Security Resources Board and its successor, the Office of Defense Mobilization, reviewing requirements, allocating scarce resources, and expanding supply.

Equally important changes occurred in the internal structure of the military establishment. The national security act of 1947 gave the Air Force parity with the other two services and brought three military departments into a weak federal union symbolized by a secretary of defense. It created a Munitions Board and a Research and Development Board within the National Military Establishment. The Joint Chiefs of Staff and their committees were given statutory recognition and a staff of 100 officers was authorized to assist them.

The interservice structure grew more elaborate each year. Following amendment of the national security act in 1949, the National Military Establishment became the Department of Defense. The secretary was provided with a deputy; three assistant secretaries for financial management, manpower and personnel, and legal and legislative affairs; a special assistant for international security affairs. The position of chairman of the Joint Chiefs of Staff was created and the Joint Staff was increased from 100 to 210 officers. But this by no means suggests the full range of interservice organization. By the end of 1952 an official directory listed about 900 different Defense Department boards, councils, committees, subcommittees and panels, not including internal committees and groups of a single military department.[17]

The functions of the Office of the Secretary of Defense were increased considerably by Reorganization Plan No. 6, in 1953. Six additional assistant secretaries of defense were provided in the fields of international security affairs, applications engineering, property and installations, health and medical affairs, supply and logistics, and research and development. The latter two replaced the Munitions Board and the Research and Development Board. Other positions established in the Office of the Secretary of Defense included a general counsel, an assistant for atomic energy, a director for guided missiles, and an assistant for special opera-

[17] Department of Defense, *Directory of Boards and Committees,* October 1952.

tions, i.e. psychological and intelligence activities. Military personnel had to deal with all of these offices; in most cases some of their number were assigned as staff members.

At the same time, assignment of officers to civilian agencies of the government became commonplace. In 1953, for example, 9 Army generals and 58 colonels were so assigned. The Navy had 9 captains in the Central Intelligence Agency, 6 in the Atomic Energy Commission, and 1 each in the Psychological Strategy Board, the Mutual Security Administration, and the Battle Monuments Commission. If retired officers, as well as those on active duty, are considered, the picture is still more impressive. Generals or admirals have headed the State Department, the Defense Department, the Central Intelligence Agency, the Tennessee Valley Authority, and the Selective Service Administration. They have held very high posts in the Atomic Energy Commission, the Foreign Operations Administration, the Office of Defense Mobilization and the Department of Justice (Immigration and Naturalization Service). In the State Department, military men have served as under secretary, assistant secretary for occupied areas, assistant secretary for the Near East, and ambassadors to the Soviet Union, Vichy France, Belgium, the Netherlands, South Africa, Paraguay, Panama, and the Philippines.[18]

Some retired officers have become presidents of civilian colleges and universities, such as Columbia, William and Mary, Louisiana State University, Long Island University, and the University of Houston. Many more have become presidents or board chairmen of major business corporations. Outstanding examples are General Lucius D. Clay of Continental Can, General Douglas MacArthur of Remington Rand, and Admiral Ben Moreell of Jones and Laughlin Steel Corporation. There is hardly a major aircraft company in the nation that does not have a retired Air Force general among its vice presidents.[19]

This chapter has examined the expansion of officers' functions primarily in terms of new high level positions in a few selected military organizations. It should be noted, however, that new de-

[18] See the Appendix for more detailed information on assignments of officers to policy and related fields.

[19] The interested reader may follow this development in the weekly "Retired Service Notes" column of the *Army Navy Air Force Journal.*

mands also have been made upon officers, many of them relatively junior, who at first glance seem to be performing *traditional* military functions. At the lofty heights of the Pentagon, it is relatively easy to see the changes that have taken place in the role of the officer corps over the last generation. It is somewhat more difficult to detect such changes at the ordinary military installation outside Washington. Yet the changes are there. The posts, bases, training stations, and camps cover more of the countryside than they did in 1935. They house far more men. The men themselves have easier access to the surrounding communities. Recently drawn from civilian life, they mingle with the civilian population more readily than the professional soldiers of the past. The existence of these small-city installations has a more pervasive impact on local housing, retail trade, roads, public utilities, sanitation, and law and order. In dealing with the civil authorities, military officers are in effect participating in intergovernmental relations that call for infinite tact, delicacy of judgment, flexibility, and courage. From a practical standpoint the commanding officer and his staff are public relations officers of first importance. Indeed, their actions and policies may fix public opinion more securely than the most carefully planned press releases of higher headquarters.

Within the confines of the post, the actions and policies of the officer corps affect not just a handful of "regulars" but the millions of adult males who must be called to active service from year to year. Here, too, lies a major public relations function; and just as many a shop superintendent had to learn that he could not approach first generation Americans as he approached their immigrant fathers, so many an old line officer has come to realize that today's draftees do not react in quite the same manner as the soldiers who elected military life 30 years ago.

Overseas, both in tactical units and in support installations, comparable burdens have been added to the traditional duties of the officer. The lieutenant in charge of a small village detachment, many miles from the systematically contrived international atmosphere of combined headquarters, is regarded as an ambassador of the United States. His conduct and bearing are scrutinized closely. Hostile elements of the population dramatize errors of omission or commission that may characterize his treatment of indigenous labor, his relations with civil authorities, his off-duty social life, or his casual remarks about local customs or institutions. Moreover, the reports that he submits to his superiors may influence official politico-military or economic-military policy more than he imagines; for just as the tradition of delegation of authority is very strong in American military administration, so also relatively great weight is placed upon preliminary analyses made by subordinate officials. This suggests once more that today's officer, wherever placed, must be prepared to recognize and to deal intelligently with many issues not strictly military in nature.

Conclusions and Prospects

The far-flung operations of military officers at mid-century may be viewed by the future historian as the start of a fundamental change in the American social order and the American political system. Alternatively, the extension of the military sphere may be regarded as a temporary expedient made necessary by the absence of an adequate civil and political service during a period of international crisis. But the thesis of this study is that the developments chronicled above can most appropriately be viewed as an inevitable consequence of America's new position in world affairs. If this assumption is correct, military officers will continue to participate in the formulation and execution of the most diverse national security policies and programs until national security itself ceases to be a paramount concern of American policy. That prospect is not now on the horizon.

It is likely, however, that the role of the military officer will continue to undergo transformations as profound as those of the last generation. This appears probable for two reasons. One is that we are likely to see a persistence and a strengthening of the forces that have created an informal federalism in the Western World. The second is that we are certain to see a continuation of the technological revolution. A single thermonuclear device of a type already tested has four times the force of all the explosives dropped by the British and American air forces in Europe during world war II. The realization that only one bomb can devastate many thousands of square miles of territory compels revision of traditional views regarding the role of force. President Eisenhower himself has confessed that he had once told a diplomat that the soldier's only excuse for living was "to regain the peace that you diplomats lost in the first place." But, continued the President, "Even if there was a modicum of truth in what I said then, there no longer is. The soldier can no longer regain a peace that is usable to the world." [20]

If, in the future, total war means total annihilation, it follows axiomatically that any officer corps that manages to survive will do so only because war has been avoided or because it has been severely limited in purpose and scope. To limit the purpose and scope of war requires the closest cooperation between military and diplomatic personnel. To attain national security objectives without resort to war requires a national strategy in which the disposition of military forces is integrated with political bargaining, policy statements, alliances, foreign economic policy, propaganda, and any and all measures that may foster the growth of friendly factions within foreign governments. In either case the role of the military officer of tomorrow will be even less conventional than the role he has played in the recent past.

[20] Remarks at the Fifth Annual Awards Ceremony of the Department of State, October 19, 1954. *Department of State Bulletin,* November 1, 1954, p. 636.

CHAPTER TWO

QUALIFICATIONS FOR HIGH LEVEL
POLICY ROLES

THE armed services are committed in their educational programs to preparing officers for the high level policy roles that were sketched in chapter one. At the same time they must continue to prepare officers for the primary duty of leading combat forces. Whether there is inevitable conflict between these tasks is a matter we shall discuss later. Our principal concern is with the manner in which the services are now preparing their officers for the policy roles. The first problem here is to identify the qualifications that seem desirable in officers who hold these positions. To be specific, what knowledge, skills, and attitudes appear especially useful for military men whose work involves important political, economic, or scientific implications?

We are aware of the presumptuousness of any effort to answer this question categorically. Its very nature precludes answers susceptible to close proof and thus encourages endless controversy. The issues involved are as old as Plato and as new as the latest studies in psychology. Moreover, the positions to be analyzed are extremely varied. Each presents a unique constellation of functions, relationships, and responsibilities. Any statement of "ideal" qualifications that purports to cover the full range of duties must be highly general. The problem is how to keep it from becoming so general that it serves no useful purpose. But when all this has been said the fact remains that the question should be answered. The services should answer it in order to derive maximum benefits from their schools. Our obligation is equally clear. Military education cannot be evaluated without some beliefs about the

27

qualities it should seek to develop. Since some standards of judgment are inescapable, they had best be made explicit at the start.

In seeking an answer to the question we employed a number of methods. We turned to relevant official statements concerning officer qualifications. An example is contained in the terms of reference of a board appointed by Defense Secretary Forrestal in 1949 to survey the service academies. This memorandum was drafted by General Eisenhower: "It is of fundamental importance that the future regular officers of the three services should possess abilities in leadership, and a basic knowledge of the techniques of modern warfare, the development of which traditionally has been among the objectives of the present system. However, in addition they must have many other qualities and talents if they are to provide the wise, balanced, and experienced direction which is required at all levels in the military forces under present-day conditions. They should have a background of general knowledge similar to that possessed by the graduates of our leading universities. They must have a firm grasp of the particular role of a military establishment within the framework of our government in a democratic society. They must be aware of the major problems of the nation which they are dedicated to serve, and understand the relationship between military preparedness and all the other elements which are also part of the fabric of real national security. In this connection they should be conscious of a responsibility toward the national economy upon which the expense of modern defense measures has such a heavy impact, and of the crucial significance in terms of security, of a healthy national economy. Finally, it is particularly important that the officers of the three services be imbued from the outset of their careers with an understanding of the concept of the national military establishments as a single integrated instrument of defense and with the sense of teamwork which must exist among the services if they are to complement each other effectively in carrying out their joint and separate missions in a unified defense structure." [1]

We also sought answers to our problem from Pentagon officers

[1] Service Academy Board, *A Report and Recommendations to the Secretary of Defense*, January 1950, p. 17. For a more comprehensive statement see Army Field Forces, *Report of Board on Army Educational System for Commissioned Officers*, Fort Monroe, January 20, 1949.

by means of a questionnaire that we designed for the purpose.[2] This was completed by over 550 officers holding responsible positions in the Office of the Secretary of Defense, the Joint Staff, and strategic and logistic planning and military assistance groups in the headquarters of the three services. Responses suggested the importance to these officers of knowledge of other services, of foreign relations, and of United States political processes and economic affairs. They also suggested the extraordinary importance of great capacity to communicate effectively, to think imaginatively and critically, to live with unsettled problems, and to mediate conflicting viewpoints. In 9 out of the 16 organizations for which results were compiled, 80 percent or more of the officers stated that ability to control service bias was more important than on a traditional military job. As another clue, we asked our respondents to think of the one individual who made the smallest contribution to the office and to state in their own words the one quality that best accounted for his inadequacy. By far the most frequent reply was lack of motivation, that is, lack of interest in the job.

To gain further insight we conducted about 300 conversational interviews with military and civilian officials, active and retired. They varied in status from a second lieutenant to a former secretary of defense. Most were or had been on duty in the Pentagon, but a good number were in other executive agencies that work closely with the armed services. The officers were asked about the qualifications they deemed essential in their own work and in the work of military subordinates, superiors, and peers. The civilians were asked similar questions about the officers with whom they were associated. Also we examined biographies, autobiographies, and military histories in an effort to identify officers who had been relatively successful or unsuccessful in national security positions.

By review of the materials summarized above and by personal reflection on the positions discussed in chapter one, we have derived some conclusions about relevant qualifications for officers

[2] Copies of the questionnaire and reports analyzing the responses are on deposit in the libraries of Dartmouth College, the Air University, the National War College, the Army War College, and the Naval War College. See also Andrew F. Henry, John W. Masland, and Laurence I. Radway, "Armed Forces Unification and the Pentagon Officer," *Public Administration Review,* Summer 1955, pp. 173–180.

who participate in the formulation of national security policies. We believe that three sets of qualifications are involved. One arises because the jobs in question demand knowledge and skill specific to the military profession. A second arises because the jobs are executive positions; as such they call for qualities desirable in all executive personnel, military and nonmilitary. A third set arises because the jobs fall into a specific category of executive positions; they are positions combining *both* the demands of the military profession *and* those of executive responsibilities, and as such they present certain peculiarities of their own. An "ideal" incumbent, in our opinion, would satisfy all three sets of criteria.

Professional Military Qualifications

The first qualification is military competence. What is meant by this and why is it placed first? The term includes the distinctive knowledge and skills traditionally expected of a member of the military profession and also the special knowledge and skills that can properly be expected of a particular officer by virtue of the type of career he has followed in the service. It includes technical knowledge about military functions, organizations, doctrine, and equipment. It includes also a knowledge of the interests and policies of the organization that an officer may represent to the outer world. When, for example, the government is judging alternative courses of action in a given situation, an Air Force adviser should be able to answer questions about the employment of air power. What can certain types of aircraft accomplish? How long would it take to get them into position? What types of support would be necessary? In other words he should be able to outline concisely the details of certain military alternatives. An ordnance officer should be able to speak authoritatively about relevant features of the Army supply system and about maintenance requirements and performance characteristics of ordnance equipment. A Naval officer should be able to contribute knowledge about the capabilities of different types of vessels, geography, climate, distance, lines of communication, and maritime strengths and weaknesses of the enemy.

Military competence is essential because in a democratic society the case for military participation in the formation of national security policy must be grounded on the assumption that professional officers have a distinctive *expertise* to contribute or that they represent distinctive points of view important to the national security that ought to be heard. Military officers who lack such an *expertise* or who are incapable of representing relevant military viewpoints have no business in such functions. There are also important practical considerations. The officer without professional competence will not be respected by military leaders. He may negotiate external settlements only to find them repudiated by colleagues in his own service. In this event he may also lose the confidence of civilians with whom he deals.

There are some civilians who hanker, foolishly we think, for officers who bear little resemblance to the professional fighting man. The military themselves do not make this mistake. The consequences of incompetence in their particular profession are so dire and visible that its official value system places an extraordinary premium on the acquisition and preservation of basic knowledge and skill. This point was made to the authors time and time again by highly sophisticated officers who had long been engaged almost exclusively in political and economic functions. It is also reflected in the general consensus among military personnel that officers operating at the highest levels should be familiar with the problems, needs, and thoughtways of men at lower echelons of command. A practice relied on to insure such familiarity is rotation in assignments. An orthodox application of the principle is found in the Army *Staff Officers' Field Manual:* "A staff officer must understand the problems of the troops. He will be better equipped to perform his duties if he has had experience as a subordinate commander." [3]

General Executive Qualifications

Officers assigned to high level responsibilities are part of the nation's largest enterprise, one with an annual budget in excess of $30 billion. As executives in this great undertaking they need many qualities desirable in managers of all large scale organizations: an ability to conduct affairs efficiently and economically, to

[3] Department of the Army, FM 101–5, *Staff Officers' Field Manual: Staff Organization and Procedure.*

inspire subordinates through leadership, to evaluate information and people, to work harmoniously with others, and to communicate effectively. The last of these skills is compounded of knowledge of the audience, knowledge of when to communicate, and skill in the use of words. Military executives, perhaps more than most, are immersed in staff duties, oral briefings, interoffice negotiations, and "position papers." He who brings in the first good draft paper often has half the battle won. These points need no elaboration here. But there are two intellectual skills and one basic attitude of the effective executive that we wish to examine in more detail.

ABILITY TO GRASP LARGE, COMPLICATED SITUATIONS

Anyone who has read testimony of ranking military officers before Congressional committees must be impressed by the variety of matters on which their opinions are sought. They are assumed to understand an astounding array of political, military, economic, scientific, administrative, and even moral issues. Further, they are assumed to understand the relation of each issue to the others. This plainly requires an ability to grasp large, complicated situations.

The skill involved here is not easily described. Colloquially, it is called the ability to see "the big picture," particularly the parts of it that lie outside an official's primary area of competence or specialization. It requires a capacity to identify major problems in their fullness and to isolate the variables or relationships most relevant to their solution. Such skill is imperative at the very highest reaches of any organization. It is highly desirable in many of the upper and intermediate level positions that are our concern here. Without it the military officer cannot assist so effectively in the solution of national security problems. For this is the skill that enables him to ask relevant questions, to expose flaws in plans, to see the relevance of apparently insignificant bits of information acquired in the past, to determine whether two recommendations are fully compatible, and to perceive not only the intended consequences of policy but the undesired consequences that many ensue. It helps him anticipate how others may react to what he proposes. It provides clues as to when to coordinate, when to seek clearance, whom to consult, and whom to keep informed.

The ability to grasp large, complicated situations can be broken down into several component skills. One is the ability to determine the relevance to one's own work of events brewing in other quarters, e.g. in the world of politics, science, or economics, or in other services, agencies, or nations. Officers who are recommending force levels, for example, should know when to seek and how to use knowledge of current American foreign policy, fiscal policy, industrial potential, or scientific research and development. A second is the ability to determine the relevance of one's own work to other parties who may be affected thereby. This requires a sense of *technical relationships,* a realization, for example, that one's decision to begin mass production of a radically new weapon may require others to revise tactical doctrine, to alter budget schedules, to postpone plans for mass production of other radically new weapons, or to reevaluate the value of overseas bases. The full technical consequences of a given decision will never be clear to any administrator, but some will always be able to sense more of the consequences than others. It also requires a sense of *organizational relationships.* It is not enough for an officer in a military aid unit to know that his proposals may affect the national debt, the logistic plans of the Navy, or trade with Spain. He should also know which officials in what other agencies will be affected. Finally, it requires a sense of *social relationships,* or an appreciation of how other persons and groups will react. Will military support to one nation antagonize another whose good will is more important? Will a plan for a large civil defense program fail because its proponents neglected the interests of state governments, labor groups, the press, Congress, or one or another set of natural scientists? Political sophistication is as desirable as technical *expertise;* and for any executive the beginning of political sophistication is the realization that there are men who may not feel as he feels, who may not dream as he dreams, or who may not pray as he prays.

A third component of ability to grasp large, complex situations is skill in dealing with "imponderables," that is, with factors that are known to be important but that do not readily lend themselves to evaluation. If there are two or more competing considerations to be balanced in arriving at a decision, how much weight should be given to each? In a decision to expand the production base, what estimate shall be placed on the often elusive factor of intentions, whether of prospective enemies, friends, or neutrals? When is it important to avoid a clear decision in the interest of keeping the future open? When is it so necessary to give direction to planning that any decision is better than no decision? These few examples suffice to suggest the importance of what is usually called executive judgment.

ABILITY TO ADAPT CREATIVELY TO CHANGING CIRCUMSTANCES

A distinctive feature of many top executive positions is that their incumbents must cope with situations that are highly dynamic as well as complicated, fluid as well as large. This is certainly true of military executives in the positions with which we are concerned. For example, diplomatic policy, which should furnish guidelines for military planning, is constantly changing as the balance of political forces changes inside foreign nations and inside the United States. Basic premises are altered within the time span of an officer's career. China, once an object of missionary zeal, becomes an enemy. Soviet Russia is transformed successively from bystander to accomplice of Hitler, suspect ally, and then menace or suspect convert. Past enemies become current partners and traditional friends draw closer or recede according to the phases of their electoral moon. The point of danger, with seemingly irresistible wanderlust, moves from the Middle East to Central Europe to East and Southeast Asia to North Africa and even to Latin America. Any move may require revised assumptions about military bases or strategic deployments. After some moves our entire military budget may be increased by a factor of four. A planner's work is never done.

Not only politics is in flux, but also technology. New weapons of awesome power appear on the horizon and become realities with equally awesome speed. In any military establishment that pretends to vitality, changes so great must produce a mental ferment comparably great. Traditional doctrines about the role of force must be reviewed. Traditional missions, weapons, tactical methods, supply procedures, and communication systems must be re-examined. How many kinds of warfare should the nation be capable of waging? At what point in weapons development should our forces give first priority to the destruction of an enemy's

34

ready air power rather than his production centers? How much manpower should be allocated to standing forces, various reserve units, and the residual labor force? These are the kinds of issues magnified by an exploding technology, and they can be resolved only by executives with a high capacity for creative adaptation.

This skill too can be broken down into component parts. One is ability to sense the rate and direction of change. In all military services, as in many other great organizations, certain men are specifically charged with projecting trends into the middle or long range future. Presumably they are chosen for this work because of their knowledge of cause-effect relations and their readiness to ask radical questions. Men are always needed who can look beyond their daily tasks, who can get a feel of the future, who can sense the shape of things yet dimly seen. But more is needed than mere awareness of the direction in which events are moving. Executives should also possess the flexibility to adjust to the requirements of the emerging situation or to "roll with the punches" of unexpected change. This is particularly true of modern military executives because they work in such a dynamic environment. There is no room today, for example, for the opposition to technological innovation that characterized the pre-1914 German General Staff. General Eisenhower noted that in world war II officers had to alter their methods, "almost even their mental processes," to keep abreast of changes wrought by modern science.[4] We would add that a similar need arises in efforts to adapt to the constant changes in diplomatic and economic affairs. In short the modern executive cannot afford obstinate, rigid, or doctrinaire attachment to the assumptions or usages of the present hour.

A third component of the desired skill is ability to capitalize on trends, to expedite them, and, if necessary, to deflect them. This should be distinguished from a capacity to adjust to the inevitable for the practical reason that existing trends may be unfavorable. The direction may be wrong or the pace too slow; and there may be nothing inevitable about either! In its most dramatic form this component has the brilliant creative quality displayed in the decision to improvise an airlift to save western Berlin from communism in 1948. Here, the executive as entrepreneur refuses to

[4] Dwight D. Eisenhower, *Crusade in Europe*, Garden City, 1948, pp. 73–75.

get bogged down in the inevitable, and instead locates the strategic factors in the situation and manipulates them to his purposes through innovations in policy and organization.

FREEDOM FROM PAROCHIALISM

Executives, almost by definition, have many contacts with the world outside their organization. Military executives are no exception. They must deal with other components of their own service, with other services, and with civilian agencies, private groups, and foreign nationals. In these associations the military executive is often called on to adjust his policies to the needs of "outsiders." For example, differences may arise over how scarce resources shall be allocated among competing claimants or over who shall command a joint or allied operation. To deal effectively with such questions it is desirable that executives have an attitude or cast of mind that can be described negatively as the absence of parochial group loyalties.

The term parochialism can be used in a general sense to signify identification with any social aggregate, from the most immediate to the nation itself, when the identification is so strong and so uncritical that a person cannot weigh either its needs or the needs of outsiders with any pretense of objectivity. In this section we shall be concerned only with parochial attitudes toward groups that lie outside the hierarchy of which an executive is part. We shall reserve until later in this chapter discussion of parochial attitudes toward authorities higher up in the same chain of command, because these often raise problems of civil-military relations peculiar to the kinds of national security positions with which this book is concerned.

The problem of avoiding parochial attitudes toward external groups is particularly serious for military executives because devotion to one's own group helps build *esprit de corps,* and the very mention of this term suggests its peculiar importance to military organizations. Parochialism may express itself as uncritical devotion to the views of earlier generations of military leaders or to particular components of an officer's own service. He may scorn all "field soldiers," "fly boys," "regulars," or members of the "black shoe Navy." He may scorn all who do not fall within one of these categories. An especially troublesome form of parochialism is service bias. In many organizations we visited, strong views were expressed about officers incapable of supporting the national interest rather than the service interest whenever the two collided. Indeed, absence of service bias has now become an official explicit criterion of fitness for appointment to the Joint Staff. Even the nation itself may be made an unduly narrow object of loyalty. Inflexible national pleading and dislike of the foreigner may spring from an exaggerated patriotism. The officer who lacks the necessary "give and take" is likely to be incapable of constructive participation in interallied operations, psychological warfare, or the administration of occupied territories. Hopelessly blinded by preconceptions, he may become needlessly involved in controversy.

We do not suggest that full impartiality is desirable or possible either in executives generally or in military executives in particular. Loyalties they must have or they could not, in large situations, distinguish relevant from irrelevant, significant from trivial, or meritorious from unworthy. But loyalty is a two-edged sword. For every element in the situation to which it may direct attention there is another element that it may hide. And when a loyalty is too parochial, it restricts executives to a very narrow range of factors in the situation, to a very narrow definition of the problem, and to a very short range view of their own interests.

Military Executive Qualifications

There remains for discussion a set of qualifications that arise out of relatively distinctive aspects of the status or functions of officers who participate in the formulation of national security policies.

VERSATILITY

In general the higher the position the wider the range of problems that its incumbent encounters. Versatility is therefore desirable in any top administrator. But it takes on special importance in the positions we are concerned with because the military services rotate officers' assignments so systematically. An officer is on the move every few years. He leaves his ship or unit for Washington or Istanbul. He may move from one executive post to a radically different one. He is always new on the job, and he does not have long to stay. If he cannot take up the reins rapidly he will not be able to take them up at all. He should consequently be a man of many aptitudes and of broad knowledge.

A military executive is fortunate if he can "switch hats" quickly as he turns from one situation to another. Sometimes he must play the judge, considering carefully different viewpoints and arriving at a decision based on the weight of the evidence. Sometimes, especially if scientific questions are involved, he may have to accept or press for a decision governed by undisputed facts or relationships. In still other situations he may have the political task of compromising rival claims to secure maximum agreement. In emergencies he may have to make peremptory decisions based upon sheer authority.[5]

The versatile military executive will also have a fairly wide range of substantive knowledge of political, economic, and scientific matters, plus an ability to absorb new data and concepts quickly. It is not necessary that every officer be equally well informed in all these fields; for any given organization can request officers with background appropriate to its needs. This is a matter of assembling a balanced team rather than trying to cram all officers full of information about all fields. Nor is it expert knowledge that is needed, but something more like the knowledge of the educated layman who understands the environment in which he has to operate. To put it another way, we are not concerned here with specialists in uniform, however essential they are to modern armed services. We are concerned with the general "line" officer who may or may not have had some specialized training, but who finds himself in a policy level position in the Department of Defense, the Joint Staff, a service headquarters, an interagency committee, or joint or combined headquarters overseas. Such an officer must frequently work with and evaluate the recommendations of different sets of experts on different aspects of national security policy. It is desirable that he be knowledgeable enough to recognize political, economic, or scientific problems when they exist, to determine when he needs additional guidance, to realize why certain action is or is not possible, to avoid recommendations whose

[5] We are indebted to Dr. George S. Pettee for these distinctions. See his *The Soldiers and the Republic,* lectures given under the Charles W. Walgreen Foundation, University of Chicago, 1954.

political or economic consequences may in the long run undermine their *military* value, and to execute faithfully the policies
and programs of higher authority.

JOB MOTIVATION

Any man in industry who transfers from the shop to the front
office may be disturbed by the sudden change of environment. He
finds himself dealing less with things, more with words. He cannot
see so readily the results of his decisions. He must adjust to a new
set of associates with new standards and customs. But to go from
command of a ship or regiment to the Pentagon is to take an even
larger step—a step large enough to raise the problem of job motivation in a peculiarly sharp form. It is therefore not trite to say
that all military executives should be so enthusiastic about their
work that they are prepared to use all the native ability and the
experience that they have. The commander of operating forces is
more likely to be endowed with adequate authority and with the
means to make it more effective. The military executive is more
likely to be hedged about with restrictions. If, like one of our
respondents, he is assigned to a committee all of whose members
have strong biases, he cannot rely on giving orders. He will have
to rely on intellectual leadership, on skill in persuading or negotiating, and on an infinite capacity to resist frustration. These are
"talkie-talkie" jobs. The men in them have got to be patient.

Moreover, most military executives know they are not going to
stay in their assignments long. More important, they often want
to return to the field. They have learned to regard command in
the field, not staff work in Washington, as the highest calling
within their profession and accordingly the most fitting object of
their ambition. Some even fear that opportunity for future advancement in grade or responsibility will be jeopardized if they
are forced to serve too long or too often as military executives.
Such fears may be exaggerated but they are not groundless. There
is ample evidence that civilian leaders of the service departments
have shared them. Directives have been issued, for example, to
protect military men assigned to the Office of the Secretary of
Defense. Promotion boards have been given special instructions
to insure that officers in certain jobs, especially in jobs outside
their own service, are not penalized for having served therein. A

highly developed sense of duty will help a professional officer overcome any negative attitudes he may have toward such positions on these or other grounds. But it will also help if he has a positive interest in the work itself.

CREATIVE SERVICE UNDER CIVILIAN LEADERSHIP

A posture of subordination to civilian authority has traditionally been expected of military officers. But mere subordination, even when supported by constitutions, statutes, or systems of indoctrination, does not bring the professional warrior into an appropriate relationship with his government. Obedience to orders lawfully issued is only one part—the negative part—of total military responsibility. The other part is the positive or affirmative duty of officers to contribute their best judgments to the decisions in which they, together with civilian leaders, participate. The simultaneous discharge of these two forms of responsibility constitutes creative service. We shall examine each aspect of this concept in turn.[6]

The principle of civilian leadership springs from the unique function and power of military forces in any society. Even non-democratic governments seek assurance that their warriors will be servants rather than masters of political policy. This is simple prudence. In democracies such assurance is also necessary to preserve popular control and individual liberties. The wisdom of maintaining civilian leadership is also suggested by a fact of intellectual and administrative life. In relation to higher political authority the military executive often plays the role of expert or specialist adviser. When this occurs it is precisely because he is an expert or specialist that his status must be less exalted. For there are other experts to be considered, and their contributions must be weighed with his by civilian superiors whose responsibilities are more general, that is, more political. These points are obscured whenever military officers do in fact have broader experience and

---

[6] We are not concerned here with the important question of the responsibility of civilian superiors to their military subordinates. We dare say, however, that in recent years political leaders, including legislators, department and agency heads, and their immediate associates, have been more remiss in their obligations to professional officers than vice versa. They have both pushed the officer into the political arena to support their positions and sucked him into peripheral duties by their own unreadiness to perform them.

better training than their civilian superiors. It would be comforting if in real life the latter could always be counted on to take the high ground appropriate to their station, or, more generally, if the principle of civilian leadership always guaranteed the wisest national security policy. Obviously this does not follow automatically. Yet the game must be played as if it did. The risks in the contrary assumption are simply too great.

Several attitudes and skills can help create a desirable sense of self-limitation within the officer corps. A genuinely professional spirit is one. We believe that the officer for whom military service is a distinct, lifetime career is less likely to meddle outside his appointed sphere than the amateur serving on a short term or part time basis. Plain old-fashioned discipline is another effective force. It is this that enables officers to obey a decision loyally after it has been made even though they argued vigorously while it was being discussed. Knowledge of and allegiance to our political system are also potential aids, though it will be seen that they do not dispose of some of the tougher issues that arise. Other relevant factors have already been suggested. Freedom from parochial loyalties is involved. Every executive knows men who are unable to identify themselves with the goals of the larger organization or who, when promoted, were unable to "grow" up to the viewpoint required by their higher status. An officer with a doctrinaire attachment to the goals of his immediate or former unit is likely to be troubled by the need to adjust to the policies of his hierarchical superiors. Finally, the sense of self-limitation may be fostered by thorough military knowledge coupled with an ability to grasp large situations. The officer who "knows his business" but who can also read himself into the larger picture will appreciate that he can never finally master the total field on which public policy is made, that his insight is at best fractional, that his perspective is only one of those on which a total national security judgment must be based. He will realize that he has less than complete knowledge, that he has less than complete responsibility, indeed that he is not supposed to have any political responsibility at all.

Few American officers will question these propositions today. But as Justice Holmes wisely said, "General propositions do not decide concrete cases." Difficult questions arise in the course of application, questions that have grown in importance since 1939 because the functions and prestige of military leaders have grown. Under what conditions, for example, should service leaders seek to deal with the Commander in Chief rather than with their departmental secretaries? Who are the properly constituted civilian leaders under our ambiguous system of separation of powers? When is allegiance due to hierarchical superiors? When to key legislators? When to the whole legislature? Ought an officer, on his own initiative, to use public statements or Congressional hearings to take issue with his superiors? What should his attitude be if he is asked to make a public statement placing his seal of approval on the policy decisions of a political executive? How long must he wait for his superiors to make up their minds? What can he properly do to influence their decisions? When do arguments become threats? It is clear that the principle of subordination to civilian leadership cannot produce unequivocal guides to action. It is not self-executing. In many cases its application calls for exquisite delicacy of judgment. As it stands it can do little more than to warn against the individual who is intolerant of all hierarchical restraints, who is overly eager to enter the larger policy arena, who is, in short, something of an administrative imperialist.

We turn now to the positive aspect of military obligation. It is desirable that the officer be prepared to put forward his point of view, to share his information, to cooperate with civilian peers as well as superiors, in a word to enter responsibly into a decision-making process in which there often cannot be hard and fast lines between the jurisdictions of military and civilian officials. This too calls for balanced judgments. On the one hand the officer should state bluntly and precisely what *military* policy he thinks will best promote national security objectives. If he knows enough about political or economic realities to realize that his position may be unacceptable, he should be prepared to propose "second best" alternatives and to identify the added military risks that they entail. But at least at the outset he should "call 'em as he sees 'em." If he does not, who will? We would not, in other words, sympathize with an officer who is so subservient or so fearful of negative reactions that his initial position is watered down to the point where it does not represent his honest convictions. Or with an officer who accepts without a murmur a policy that he thinks will

42

jeopardize national security. Such an individual would be giving service of a kind, but we do not propose to call it creative.

On the other hand the officer ought not to be so aloof or uncommunicative that he cuts off the necessary two way flow of information between himself and civilian officials. Nor should his idea of communication be to present his optimum case on a "take it or leave it" basis, or, worse yet, with a public disclaimer of responsibility if his position is not accepted. Such practices assume that policy can be divided into a set of watertight compartments one of which is labeled "purely military." If this were so it would be impossible to blend military and nonmilitary considerations at any point. Each aspect of a national security problem—military, political, economic, scientific—would have to be presented to the political branches or to the people in its pure form. But this is not necessary and only an administrative isolationist would think it is. The isolationist wishes to have nothing to do with other than military officials, possibly because he feels that exposure to their interests and motives may somehow sully his immaculate premises. He rejects the idea that policy making is a cooperative process calling for ceaseless give and take among men of different perspectives. He too is ready to serve, but not creatively.

There may actually be an affinity between the two hypothetical types sketched here: the isolationist and the imperialist. Neither is fully responsible. Though the isolationist does not appear to grasp for power, indeed though he claims he will have no part of nonmilitary considerations, he may actually subject the civilian to the most terrible pressure that an expert can bring to bear on a layman, a layman who must be presumed to care about the nation's security, and possibly a layman who cannot so easily pass the buck that has been passed to him.[7] There may even be an affinity between the two positions in the sense that both are likely consequences of a parochial outlook. Unduly narrow loyalties may dispose an officer either to dominate or to withdraw from the larger

---

[7] It is relevant to note here that the advice of military experts cannot be checked with experts outside government quite as easily as the advice of other public servants, e.g. economists, health officers, labor specialists. One reason is that members of the military profession do not have colleagues who practice their calling outside the government! A second reason is that information essential to rational judgments is often secret and therefore unavailable, even to retired officers.

arena in which he and other officials should meet in creative inter-action. In fact he is all too likely to fluctuate erratically between one course and the other. But the officer with a capacity for creative service will take a middle path between these extremes.

The Military Executive and the Combat Leader

One officer wrote us that the effort to "mass produce" military executives with the qualities discussed here "would probably ruin, or at least temporarily confuse, more potentially good commanders than it would produce good policy makers." This raises a major question. Is there inevitable conflict between the skills and attitudes outlined here and those that are desirable in a combat commander? Are the roles so different that any attempt to develop qualities appropriate to a military executive must necessarily breed out of officers essential fighting qualities on which the ultimate survival of the nation may depend?

Officers disagree widely among themselves on the point. In arguing it they often reduce it to the question of whether a good staff officer makes a good commander. The evidence cited is almost always fragmentary and anecdotal. One person points to General Eisenhower as proof that a competent officer can succeed in either type of assignment. Another points to officers who were successful in only one type or the other. A Naval captain engaged in strategic planning in the Pentagon declares that the gulf between staff and command is "largely mythical. The basic requirements for either are common sense, knowledge, understanding, leadership, and experience." But an Army colonel writes: "Command carries with it an indefinable pressure that cannot be duplicated in any staff assignment. As a regimental commander there is the constant responsibility for the lives of approximately 3,300 men. As a staff man there is no parallel responsibility." We also encountered very deep hostility among some officers toward the "staff officer type," real or imagined.[8] On the other hand the official practice of rotat-

---

[8] Here and elsewhere in our interview notes there were overtones of Riesman's contrast between "inner-directed" types, e.g. the rugged, fighting, individualistic combat commander, and "other-directed" types, e.g. the accomplished staff officer, a product of industrialized, urbanized, bureaucratic America, with its emphasis on "socialized behavior." David Riesman et al., *The Lonely Crowd, A Study of Changing American Character*, New Haven, 1950, p. 26.

ing assignments seems to assume that the same man can do well in both headquarters and the field, or at least that he can move from one to the other without disastrous consequences. The senior joint and service colleges operate on the same assumption. They do not offer one program to prospective staff officers and another to prospective commanders. They offer a single program designed to prepare men for either staff or command positions at the highest level.

It is best to rid this difficult issue of unnecessary trappings. We are not arguing a case for a semipermanent staff corps whose members might indeed lose the touch with operations required for effective performance in both staff and command positions. Nor are we attempting to determine whether any and every attribute of an effective military executive is also an attribute of an effective combat leader and vice versa. We are dealing with a limited number of qualities: military competence, ability to grasp large situations, ability to adapt to change, freedom from parochialism, versatility, job motivation, and readiness for creative service under civilian leadership. The first of these is obviously compatible with each of the two roles. We do not know for certain whether the others are. There is simply no solid evidence on the point and we are not even positive that experiments could be devised to get it. We must therefore speculate.

One line of speculation leads us to believe that the junior officer on troop duty faces a situation sufficiently different from, let us say, a junior officer in the Pentagon, that effective performance in the two cases may depend on different personal qualities. But the same line of speculation leads us to conclude that field and headquarters situations grow more alike as an officer acquires greater responsibility in either. For example, as the level of command increases, the situation faced by the commander becomes more complex and the number of variables much greater. "Purely" military considerations become less central; other considerations impinge on action, limiting the commander's freedom of choice. In short there is a steadily growing need for versatility, job motivation, freedom from parochialism, and the other qualities that have been discussed. Some of our informants have suggested that the level at which the military factor is no longer dominant in command situations is lower than is commonly believed, in the Army, for example, probably as low as the division. This implies that the conditions faced by the leader of large combat units resemble those faced by officers involved in policy issues in the Office of the Secretary of Defense, the Joint Staff, or in a headquarters such as SHAPE. We think this is the case and that it reduces the problem of role requirements to one that can be handled by correct assignment and educational policies. The implication for assignment is a rotation policy that periodically enables prospective commanders to refresh their military competence. The implication for education is a hierarchy of schools of distinctive aims. Ideally, some, designed for junior officers, would place slightly more emphasis on those special attributes useful in particular positions at lower levels of command; others, designed for senior officers, would place slightly more emphasis on qualities useful at higher levels where the requirements of headquarters and field positions tend to converge. Undergirding the whole structure would be an undergraduate education capable of supporting the missions of each of the other kinds of institutions. The chapter that follows will summarize how the armed services today try to maintain systems of military education based on the foregoing principle.

PART TWO

THE GROWTH OF MILITARY EDUCATION

FOR POLICY ROLES

CHAPTER THREE

THE ORGANIZATION OF MILITARY TRAINING

AND EDUCATION

THE provision of career officers to satisfy the pressing demands that have been discussed in the preceding chapters places a heavy responsibility on the Army, Navy, and Air Force, a responsibility that they keenly recognize. Obviously the maintenance of a high level of competence among professional officers depends on a multitude of factors, many beyond the control or manipulation of the services themselves. Basically, the quality of officer personnel depends upon the character of the American people and the elements from which that character is derived, the home, church, school, and other environmental conditions. It depends on the attitudes of the public toward the armed services, and the degree of support of their needs by the public, the Congress, and the Executive. It depends on many factors of military life, such as the social, economic, and educational backgrounds of the individuals who enter upon that life, their individual interests and motivations, the traditions, customs, and loyalties of military service, the influence of experience in a military organization upon the thought processes of these individuals, the adjustment of personal goals to those of the larger group and of the nation, the operation of the system of rewards and sanctions, and so forth.

The educational systems of the armed forces constitute only one of many influences which contribute to the character and quality of military leadership. But it will hardly be disputed in a nation that devotes much of its energy and resources to public education that they are an important factor. The armed services themselves reflect this attitude toward education. In recent years, as the services have recognized and accepted new responsibilities, they have revised existing educational programs and added many new ones as an answer to the challenges faced by officers at all levels.

In one sense the principal business of the Army, Navy, and Air Force is to teach, to teach men in the art and science of warfare. Training activities—to use the military term—constitute a large and significant proportion of the total operations of the armed services. Probably only a few laymen appreciate the tremendous range and magnitude of these activities. Most people know that the young inductee or enlistee goes through a rigorous period of basic training and usually some form of specialized training before he is assigned to a unit, ship, or station. But relatively few are informed about the variety of training and educational activities conducted at all levels by the Army, Navy, and Air Force. Within the broad range of activities, military education itself is a large and complex function, involving a variety of institutions and considerable energy and talent. Before turning to the more detailed task of describing and evaluating those programs that relate particularly to the preparation of officers for policy level assignments, it might be helpful to the lay reader to give a brief description of the over-all educational systems of the services as they now operate, prefaced by comment on the nature of the training function.

A problem of definition is involved here. Although the terms "training" and "education" as used in military parlance usually indicate two different functions, the former frequently is employed all-inclusively. In the narrower, more precise sense in which we use it here, training identifies instruction that is oriented to a particular military specialty and that is designed to develop a technical skill. It also includes tactical training of land, sea, and air units. Training thus may be given directly to the individual or to organized units and larger groups. Education, on the other hand, implies instruction or individual study for the purpose of intellectual development and the cultivation of wisdom and judgment. It prepares a man to deal with novel situations. It is usually provided in schools and is provided without regard to the student's job assignment in a particular unit. Training is job-oriented; education goes beyond the next assignment and seeks to prepare the officer for a lifetime career of service, involving ultimately the greatest responsibility that can be imposed. Actually, there is no clear distinction between training and education. The whole learning process might be thought of as a spectrum, with "pure training" (such as a simple exercise in assembling a rifle) at one end, and with "pure education" (involving the highest level of abstraction) at the other.[1] This book is concerned only with professional education of career officers, and actually only with certain aspects of that education. But an appreciation of the nature and scope of military training is relevant to an understanding of military education. The education programs of the armed services are conceptually and administratively part of the training function. The manner in which the services approach their educational responsibilities is conditioned and patterned by their experience and practices with training. Thus a summary description of the magnitude and scope of military training should be meaningful at this point.

The Range of Training Activities

Measured in terms of numbers of individuals involved, time consumed, effort devoted, and dollars expended, training is one of the most important undertakings of the armed services. In a democracy which relies to a considerable degree upon a citizen army for its security in time of crisis, this is inevitable. Much of the attention of all three services must be devoted to the training of large numbers of men who remain under arms a relatively short time. And in war, when the number of men in uniform is multiplied many times, training of necessity remains a primary preoccupation. Military training programs obviously are a reflection of the character and the requirements of the armed services themselves. Military personnel systems are essentially wholesale supply systems which identify and classify jobs meticulously and train and supply manpower for these jobs in large numbers. The purpose is to recruit, sort, and train men and to fit them into jobs.

The Army operates extensive training facilities to teach officer and enlisted personnel the special skills and knowledge required

[1] Captain William Whitson of the United States Military Academy suggested the concept of the spectrum to us.

to maintain the nation's ground forces. Much of this training is taught on the job within the units to which the soldier is assigned. But many specialized skills require classroom instruction at training installations, where courses ranging from a few weeks to more than a year are conducted. The Army School Catalog, for example, lists 43 separate schools or training organizations, with several hundred courses. The Navy likewise maintains a wide variety of training programs. Even more so than the Army, much of the training is conducted on the job, particularly on ships at sea. This situation stems from the fact that even in peacetime the Navy is largely preoccupied with the operation of its ships and supporting shore facilities. For this reason the Navy does not maintain as many separate training programs as the Army, but even so its activities in this field are extensive, involving 24 separate activities of the Bureau of Personnel and 40 schools located within the jurisdiction of other bureaus of the Navy. The Air Force places a great deal of emphasis upon training. (This is reflected, for example, in its organizational structure, which establishes the Training Command and Air University as major commands.) Basic and specialized training of enlisted personnel and pilot observer officer training constitute a large portion of this activity, but as with the other services, the Air Force conducts a wide variety of other training programs. In addition to these activities designed to provide skilled individuals in large numbers, the armed services also conduct training activities for groups, including drills, maneuvers, and exercises, in order to develop combat-ready operational units, from the platoon or smallest vessel or plane to the largest combination of forces.

Certain general characteristics stand out among these training activities. Each can be explained for our purposes in a few words. The focus in military training is on *things*, not on people. The whole purpose is to teach men to handle and care for a vast array of weapons and equipment, from the simplest firearm to the most complex weapon system. While it is clearly recognized that the highly skilled soldier-technician is the most important asset of all, his value is conceived in terms of his ability to utilize the material resources and equipment of the fighting forces. Since these resources are actually employed by organized units and groups, the emphasis in training necessarily is on the effective behavior of the individual as a part of a unit or group rather than on the individual as such.

Military training thus is geared to giving to the largest possible number of individuals the greatest amount of technical skill in the shortest period of time. Measured in terms of this clear purpose, it has been extremely successful. The Army, Navy, and Air Force can and do turn out great numbers of highly skilled technicians. They have developed a vast assortment of instructional techniques and devices by which they have reduced the training of thousands of individuals to something approaching assembly line operations.

The military place great reliance on their training programs, and these activities constitute a function that is firmly accepted as legitimate and proper. As already suggested, career officers look upon training as a primary responsibility, accepted without question. In an age of complex and ever-changing weapons, intensive and repeated training of the individual soldier, sailor, and airman, as well as of units and larger organizations, is essential and commonplace.

A corollary of this situation is that the military rely heavily on the training function and place a great deal of faith in it. Almost as a matter of course, when a complex new weapon or piece of equipment becomes available, a program to train men in its use is established. Likewise, when new tactics or strategy are developed they are tested in training maneuvers or operations. The enlisted man and the officer, short term and careerist, can expect to spend a considerable part of their careers going to school and participating in special training activities. Many regular officers serve at least one tour as an instructor in some training activity or school, and almost all are involved in one way or another in giving instruction to their men.

We are stressing here the high degree of *legitimization* of the training function by the military, and this brings us to the third general characteristic. Military training programs are highly *utilitarian*. Professional military men are called on constantly by their superiors, the Bureau of the Budget, the White House, the Congress, and the public to justify every request for funds. In doing so, they stress the need for every unit of instruction, course, or school in terms of direct utilization by the trainee on his subsequent assignment. Programs are designed and justified according to the familiar military formula of "need to know" rather than "nice to know."

Another characteristic of military training is its *uniformity*. Since programs are designed to meet the requirements of the service rather than the individual, the "standard curriculum" is employed without exception. This means that all trainees or students in a given program are subjected to exactly the same unit of instruction or course, with no deviation according to an individual's previous training or experience, and with no "electives" in the curriculum. Those charged with the responsibility of supervising and operating training programs are concerned with large blocks of manpower and with general levels of competence. Once the requirements of a particular program and the qualifications of the personnel input are determined, the program is designed in a standard form and operated on this basis.

The combination of these characteristics produces in military training a distinctive approach. The emphasis on numbers, things, utility, and uniformity puts a premium on *form* and *procedure*, rather than on the individual instructor, or even on the substance of the program. The instructor moves in and out from other assignments, but the program goes on. There is constant pressure to economize on time in order to maximize the output. The use of training aids is perfected to the very highest degree. A tremendous amount of effort is devoted to curriculum planning and to internal and external organizational and administrative matters. Instruction is highly standardized, replete with manuals, demonstration models, films, sound effects, field tests, instructors' guides, prepared examinations, and so forth. In sum, military training is a *distributive process*. It is designed to distribute to thousands of individuals the technical skills essential to the successful utilization of military weapons and equipment. It is not concerned, nor should it be, with the cultivation of knowledge, or the extension of the frontiers of human understanding.

In and about military training establishments the term "indoctrination" is given wide use. Essentially this means the application through training of standard norms and procedures. The armed forces are composed of thousands of individuals, most of whom serve for a relatively short time and all of whom remain in one assignment no more than a few years. Yet the armed forces possess an unusual degree of continuity and permanence. These characteristics are developed and maintained by means of this process of indoctrination. Individuals may change, but the accepted way of organizing the job and getting things done goes on. The training function is central to this whole situation.

Professional Military Education

While training involves all military personnel, education, in the sense used here, concerns only officers. The formal education of career Army, Navy, and Air Force officers, moreover, is very closely associated with their professional advancement. Unlike members of most other professions, in which the individual completes his formal education before qualifying for practice, the officer is given opportunity to "return to school" at regular intervals in his career, as he assumes increasing responsibility. Much of this military education has no direct bearing upon the preparation of officers for policy level assignments, which is the central concern of this book. But before proceeding to an analysis of those features and activities that are relevant, it might be helpful to give a brief outline of the present organization of the school systems for commissioned officers of the three separate services.

The organization and operation of these school systems is closely related to the size of the armed forces in general and the officer corps in particular. At the conclusion of world war II, plans were based upon total forces of about 1,000,000 men. It was assumed that about half of the officers would be regulars. But the events of the succeeding years necessitated much larger forces. By 1955 the number had stabilized at about 2,800,000, with an officer corps correspondingly larger than anticipated 10 years earlier. Congress, however, had limited by law the number of regular officers in each service. Thus it was necessary to retain a large number of reserve officers on active duty. For fiscal year 1956 the total number of officers in each service and the approximate percentage of regulars were as follows: Army, 122,200 (26 percent); Navy, 73,822 (43 percent); Air Force, 143,130 (17 percent); and Marine Corps, 18,213 (49 percent). Unfortunately the resignation rate among reserve officers on active duty has been high, leading to instability, inefficiency, and excessive costs. In 1956 Congress enacted legislation proposed by the Department of Defense increasing the statutory ceilings for regular officers to approximately 50 percent for each service. Thereupon the Army and Air Force initiated plans to offer regular commissions to reservists serving on extended active duty in order to bring the proportion of regulars in each of those services to approximately 40 percent by 1963.[2] It should be noted that the proportion of regulars increases directly with increase in rank. In this study we are particularly concerned with the educational opportunities afforded to the regulars because they are the officers who are most likely to advance to the highest responsibilities and rank.

For the fiscal year 1956, planned commissioned officer strength (excluding second lieutenant and ensign) was as follows: [3]

	Army	*Navy*	*Air Force*	*Marines*
Gen.–Adm.	494	321	443	60
Col.–Capt.	5,026	3,077	4,671	500
Lt. Col.–Cdr.	12,386	6,258	9,319	1,310
Maj.–Lt. Cdr.	17,217	12,054	22,011	2,526
Capt.–Lt.	28,500	17,684	38,707	3,949
1st Lt.–Lt. j.g.	19,645	17,086	63,699	4,218

These figures reflect a slight downward trend in the number of Army officers, relative stability in the Navy, and an increase in the Air Force. When the Air Force attains its planned 137 wing goal in 1957, it will require an additional 27,000 officers.

PRECOMMISSIONED MILITARY EDUCATION

The armed services draw their junior officers from a number of different educational sources. West Point, Annapolis, and (after 1959) the new Air Force Academy provide only a small portion of the total requirements. Until 1959 the Air Force will continue to secure up to 25 percent of the graduates of West Point and Annapolis. The Reserve Officer Training Corps programs main-

---

2 For detailed information on the size and structure of the officer corps see House of Representatives, 84th Congress, 2d Session, Subcommittee No. Two of the Armed Services Committee, *Hearings on Armed Forces Regular Officer Augmentation*, May 1956.

3 *Army Navy Air Force Journal*, 19 February 1955, p. 3779.

tained in several hundred colleges and universities are the largest single source. Selected honor graduates of ROTC units are given regular commissions, but the vast majority serve only several years on active duty as reservists. The Army also offers regular commissions to selected graduates of several military colleges, such as the Virginia Military Institute. Still another source is the officer candidate program (OCS), relied upon in peacetime only when the principal sources fail to meet requirements. The Navy and the Air Force also operate aviation cadet programs. All services commission men directly from the ranks, and offer commissions to some individuals directly from civilian status, notably doctors and chaplains. The Marine Corps commissions from a variety of sources, including the Naval Academy, ROTC units, an officer candidate program, and a special platoon leaders' course. The following tables show the relative standing of these sources:

Input of Army Officers
(fiscal year 1956)

USMA	325
ROTC (distinguished military graduates)	551
ROTC (other)	10,770
OCS	1,088
Direct appointments	504
U.S. Army Reserve and National Guard	2,206
Nurses and women medical specialists	405

Input of Naval Officers
(fiscal year 1956)

USNA	462
NROTC (regular)	1,157
NROTC (contract)	1,258
OCS	2,522
Aviation officer candidate	965
Reserve officer candidate	379
Limited duty officers	191
Naval aviation cadets	1,059
Integration program	225
Direct procurement	2,228
Voluntary recall USNR	711
To USN-temporary (pilot)	303
Augmented from inactive reserve	152

Input of Air Force Officers
(fiscal year 1956)

USMA	141
USNA	169
ROTC (distinguished honor graduates)	188
ROTC (other)	10,612
OCS	500
Aviation cadet	2,800
Ranks	400
Direct (including recall)	770
From Army (engineers on duty with AF)	430
Medical	2,317

GRADUATE OFFICER EDUCATION

The Army School System. Except for OCS graduates, the new Army second lieutenant does not begin his full time military schooling until after he has received his commission. Whether he has graduated from the Military Academy or the ROTC program, he attends the 9 to 16 week basic course at the school maintained by his branch. The Army is organized into 16 branches: 3 combat arms (armor, artillery, infantry), 7 technical services (Army Medical Services, Chemical Corps, Corps of Engineers, Ordnance Corps, Quartermaster Corps, Signal Corps, and Transportation Corps),[4] and 6 special staff services (Adjutant General's, Chaplain's, Finance, Judge Advocate General's, Military Police, and Women's Army Corps). Each of these branches operates its own schools. The short basic course prepares the young officer for duties and responsibilities as a platoon leader. All newly commissioned regular officers of the Infantry, Armor, Artillery, Corps of Engineers, and Signal Corps must complete either the Army Ranger or the Army Airborne course prior to their first assignment. A few special cases may elect Army aviation and bypass ranger or airborne training.

After a period of two to five years of service with troops, the young officer attends the company officer course at his branch school, preparing for duties at company and battalion levels. All regular officers and reserve officers remaining on duty attend this course, varying from 12 weeks (Chaplain's Corps) to 36 weeks (Artillery). Subsequently, after more troop duty and a total of 5 to 12

---

[4] The Corps of Engineers and the Signal Corps also are classified as combat arms.

Figure 1

ARMY SCHOOL SYSTEM

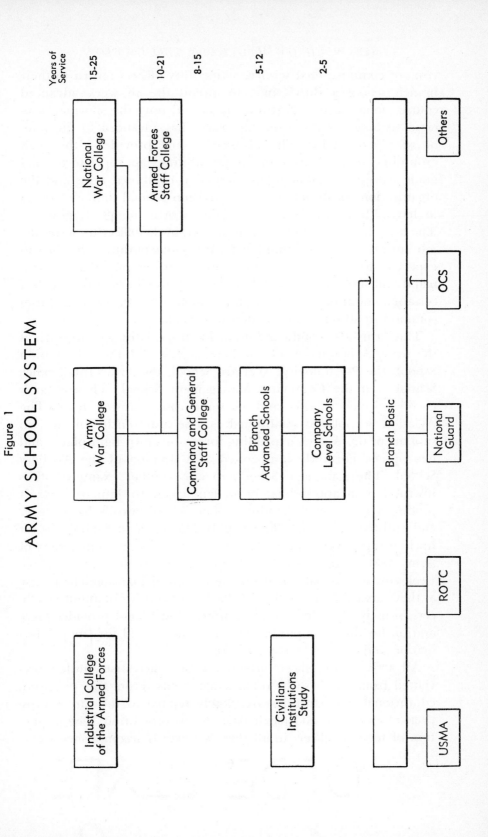

Years of Service

National War College	15-25
Armed Forces Staff College	10-21
	8-15
	5-12
	2-5

Industrial College of the Armed Forces

Army War College

Command and General Staff College

Branch Advanced Schools

Company Level Schools

Civilian Institutions Study

Branch Basic

USMA   ROTC   National Guard   OCS   Others

years of commissioned service, active duty officers return to their branch school a third time, to attend the 16 week advanced course. Some have opportunity to attend only the shorter "associate" course. By this time the officer has advanced to the rank of captain or major. The advanced course provides a thorough grounding in the duties and responsibilities appropriate to field grade officers. It includes instruction in combined arms and the organization and functions of the division general staff, and varies in length from 16 weeks (Chaplain's Corps) to 38 (Engineers). The branch courses do not attempt to train the officer for a specific job but rather prepare him for the full range of duties that he can expect in his career within his branch, with emphasis upon command and staff functions. All of the branch schools also provide a certain amount of instruction in common subjects, covering duties common to all officers regardless of branch.

The Army also conducts courses in 16 specialist schools, such as the Army Aviation School, the Language School, the Information School, the Psychological Warfare School, the Army Intelligence School, and the Command Management School. These schools enroll selected officers and in some cases enlisted men. The Aviation School was established as a separate entity in 1953 in support of the Army's expanding force of its own light planes and helicopters. Formerly it operated as a division of the Artillery School. The Language School, to cite another example, offers instruction in approximately 30 languages. In January 1955 it produced its 15,000th graduate. The school enrolls both officer and enlisted personnel. The Supply Management School was set up in 1954 to raise the management practices of commanders of Army posts, camps, arsenals, hospitals, and so forth. The three week course was patterned on the advanced management course at the Harvard Business School. Each class consists of about 50 officers, principally colonels. The Information School provides preparation for duties as public relations officers, and for troop information and education assignments.

All active duty officers attend the branch courses, unless prevented from doing so by other assignments. From this point on, educational opportunities are closely related to the career prospects of an officer, and particularly to his promotion. The promotion of regular officers in all three services is accomplished in accordance with a selective process regularized in the officer personnel act of 1947. This provides for consideration of all officers for promotion to higher grade at periodic intervals and for the systematic separation or retirement of those who are not advanced.

In the Army each branch of the service maintains its own promotion list. A percentage of the total strength is designated for each grade. When an officer is promoted he goes to the bottom of the list in the new grade. Second lieutenants are promoted after three years of service, or sooner if vacancies exist in the grade of first lieutenant. Promotions to the grades of captain, major, and lieutenant colonel are considered no later than upon the completion of 7, 14, and 21 years of service, respectively. Selection boards are convened for this purpose. Promotions may be made in less time when vacancies occur in the next higher grade. Officers in the grades of first lieutenant to major who are passed over for selection for promotion become "deferred officers." These are considered a second time by the next selection board. If passed over a second time, these officers are eliminated from the active list and are either retired or separated 13 months after the date on which they would have been promoted at the first selection. If an officer is within two years of qualifying for retirement he may be retained in the service until he is so qualified. The officer personnel act also authorizes the services to make temporary promotions, depending upon requirements for officers of higher rank. Promotion to the grade of colonel and higher depends upon the existence of vacancies as well as upon selection by a board. Lieutenant colonels who are not advanced in grade upon completion of 28 years of service are retired. Colonels and brigadier generals not selected for promotion are retired after serving 5 years in grade, but not until they have completed 30 years of service. Major generals are retired after 5 years in grade if they have completed 35 years of service. There are certain exceptions to these regulations.

It should be noted that separate boards are convened to select officers for promotion and for school attendance, and that the standards employed for the two purposes are not the same. The promotion boards are concerned principally with an officer's performance, with accomplishments so far in his career, and his prospects for the future. The school boards, while examining these factors, are concerned with the pattern of an officer's career and the need to round out his knowledge and experience. Selection for the advanced schools does not necessarily indicate that the officer will subsequently be promoted, although generally it enhances his chances for promotion.

Officers of all branches with 8 to 15 years of service, usually in the grade of major or lieutenant colonel, and under 41 years of age are eligible to attend the regular course of the Command and General Staff College at Fort Leavenworth. Approximately half of all regular officers are selected for this opportunity. Successful completion of the course greatly enhances prospects for further advancement and responsibility in the Army. Officers do not apply for Leavenworth, but are considered automatically as long as they remain in the "eligibility zone." Leavenworth takes an officer beyond his own branch, providing advanced instruction in the employment of all of the arms as a combined team. The officer is prepared for duty as a commander and a general staff officer at division, corps, and army levels, and at comparable levels in the communications zone. The Command and General Staff College is concerned with "how the Army fights." For most officers, this is the last educational opportunity, and graduates are presumed to be qualified to command any Army ground unit, or to act as general staff officers.

The Army War College is the senior institution within the Army educational system. It now prepares officers for "the highest command and general staff positions in the Army, and for such high level positions within the Department of Defense or other governmental agencies as the Army might be called upon to fill." Eligibility requirements are 13 to 21 years of service, rank of lieutenant colonel or colonel, and completion of or constructive credit for the regular or associate course at Leavenworth.

The Navy School System. Army officers belong to a branch, one of the 3 combat arms or 13 technical and administrative services. Naval officers are either "line" or "staff." The former make up the majority of all officers; these are the officers who may exercise military command. The rule is that unrestricted line officers are the only officers assigned to command at sea. Restricted line officers, such as EDO (engineering duty only) and certain other specialists, may command shore stations. Staff officers are members of the 7 corps (Supply, Medical, Nurse, Dental, Civil Engineering,

Figure 2

NAVY SCHOOL SYSTEM
(for line officers)

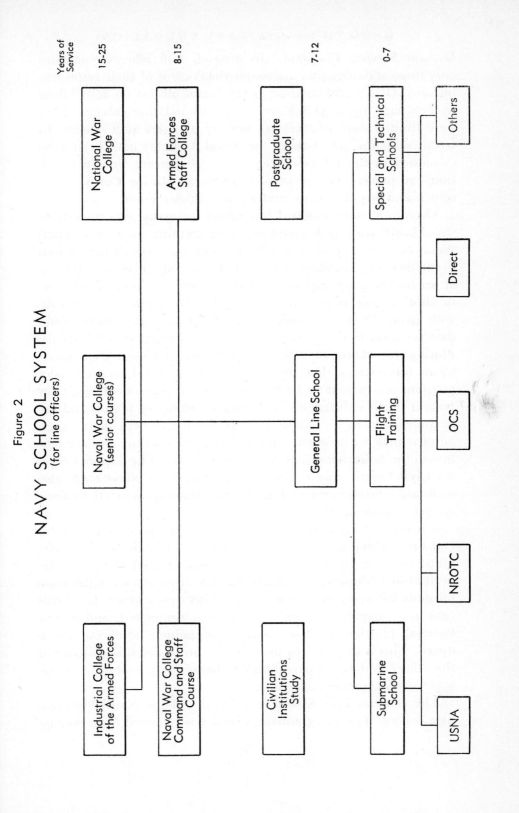

	Years of Service
National War College	15-25
Armed Forces Staff College	8-15
Postgraduate School	
	7-12
Special and Technical Schools	0-7

Industrial College of the Armed Forces

Naval War College (senior courses)

Naval War College Command and Staff Course

Civilian Institutions Study

General Line School

Flight Training

Submarine School

Others

Direct

OCS

NROTC

USNA

Medical Service, Chaplain). In general, staff officers command only those activities that are under the control of their respective bureaus. Of a grand total of 73,115 Naval officers on active duty in February 1954, 51,838 were unrestricted line officers, 3,814 were limited duty line officers, and 17,463 were staff officers. In recent years the graduates of the Naval Academy have been commissioned in the following categories: 40 percent line (nonaviation), 20 percent line (aviation), 9 percent Marine Corps, 6 percent Naval Supply Corps, and 25 percent Air Force.

The newly commissioned line officer normally goes directly to sea. Aboard ship he is given intensive training under the supervision of more experienced officers, rotating through the various departments of the ship. If he is a regular officer, he will remain at sea for six years, unless he is accepted for aviation, submarine, or another type of special duty. Prospective aviators go immediately from the Naval Academy, the ROTC, or the officer candidate program to the Naval Air Training Command at Pensacola, Florida, for about 18 months of training. To meet its requirements for aviators, the Navy also operates a Naval aviation cadet program. Entrants must have completed two years of college. They remain in an enlisted status during the training period and are commissioned in the Naval Reserve when they win their wings. Submariners are accepted after two years of sea duty and are sent first to the Submarine School at New London. The Supply Corps, the Civil Engineering Corps, and the other staff officer corps also maintain educational and training programs appropriate to their special requirements.

It is now anticipated that most line officers will attend the General Line School after five to seven years of commissioned service. Until the year 1956–1957 this school was utilized to fill out the professional education of officers who had been given regular commissions following experience as reservists in world war II. At this time the program for these officers was completed, and a new General Line curriculum on the postgraduate level was introduced. This is designed to broaden the professional knowledge of the officer and to prepare him for higher responsibilities as he approaches command assignments.

The General Line School is a division of the Naval Postgraduate School. The Postgraduate School was removed from Annapolis and reestablished at Monterey, California in 1951 as an independent institution with its own superintendent, and with authority to confer bachelor of science, master of science, and doctors' degrees in engineering and related subjects. It consists of three main divisions: the General Line School (which already had been established at Monterey in 1948), the Engineering School (also at Monterey), and the Intelligence School (located in Washington). The Engineering School is geared principally to the needs of the technical bureaus, providing advanced instruction in engineering and scientific subjects at Monterey or at selected civilian institutions. The Intelligence School provides instruction in all phases of intelligence, including foreign area and language study. These two schools, as well as such others as the Submarine School and the Supply School, are essentially for officers assigned to duty in their respective functional areas.

As in the Army, attendance at the advanced Navy schools is closely related to promotion. The Navy introduced the practice of "promotion up or selection out" long before it was applied to all services in the officer personnel act of 1947. In general its promotion system is similar to that of the Army, already described. Except for advancement from ensign to lieutenant junior grade, which comes by the end of three years, all promotions are made on the basis of selection by boards. Consideration for promotion to lieutenant, lieutenant commander, commander, and captain is made on or before completion of four, four, five, and three years in the next lower grade, respectively. Promotions may be made only when vacancies occur in the higher grade. Promotion to the grade of captain requires a minimum of 18 years of commissioned service. In 1955 the Navy reestablished a prewar practice of requiring written examinations of officers coming up for promotion to all grades from lieutenant junior grade through captain. Those officers who have attended certain schools or who have completed equivalent correspondence courses are exempt from this requirement. Officers may prepare for the examinations by study of suggested manuals and texts.

Unlike the Army, a Navy selection board, when it passes over an officer, may recommend that he be retained on active duty in his present grade if this is in the best interest of the service. A special feature of the Navy's promotion policy provides for the designation of a line "running mate" for each staff officer; no staff officer can be promoted until his line running mate is promoted also. Regulations concerning promotion and retirement of senior officers are similar to those of the Army. A captain, for example, who is not selected for promotion to rear admiral is retired upon the completion of 30 years of service.

After completion of shore duty, and at least a second period at sea or equivalent duty for specialists, the Naval officer is eligible for the Command and Staff Course at the Naval War College in Newport. By this time he is a lieutenant commander or commander. This course emphasizes the operational functions of command and the organization, functions, and procedures of operational staffs.

After a minimum of about 15 years of commissioned service, Naval officers in the grade of commander and captain are eligible for one or both of the two senior courses now conducted at the Naval War College, the most advanced educational opportunities offered by the Navy. Attendance at these courses is on a selective basis.

Marine Corps Schools. Although the education and training program of the Marine Corps does not fall within the terms of reference of this study, a brief outline of the program will fill out the picture of the over-all school system here. The Marine Corps operates an integrated school system at its training center at Quantico, Virginia. Upon receiving his commission as a second lieutenant, the new officer attends the 21 week Basic School, similar in general purpose to the basic course in the Army branch schools. As a captain or major the ground or aviation officer attends the Junior School, to prepare for command of a Marine battalion or squadron, and for staff duty at the levels of regiment or group and division or wing. The Junior School course is nine months in duration. Subsequently, as a lieutenant colonel or colonel the officer attends the Senior School, also a nine month course, in which emphasis is placed upon the latest doctrines and techniques of amphibious warfare, with particular attention to the coordinate employment of air, naval, and ground forces. Presumably all Marine officers attend these three schools.

The Marine Corps also makes extensive use of the regular and specialist schools of the Army, Navy, and Air Force for both general educational and specific training assignments of its officers. It relies upon the service and joint war colleges for the preparation of its officers for policy level duties.

The Air Force School System. Within the Air Force, the training function is the responsibility of the Air Training Command, and the education function is the responsibility of the Air University. The former is divided into three training air forces employing 42 bases and providing training for both officers and enlisted personnel. In June 1955, about 53 percent of all Air Force officers were "rated," that is, they were qualified pilots or observers. This was an increase from 51 percent a year before. The Technical Training Air Force produces skilled technicians and operates officer candidate schools. The Flying Training Air Force provides individual instruction for pilots, navigators, bombardiers, and radar observers. The Crew Training Air Force trains rated pilots and observers in first-line combat aircraft. The Air Training Command gives the officer, either rated or nonrated, his initial skill, and trains him in additional skills as required, both as an individual and as a member of a combat or supporting unit. Altogether the Air Force lists in its personnel classification system over 200 officer and over 300 airmen specialities.

The Air University, located at Maxwell Air Force Base, Alabama, is concerned with professional education as distinguished from technical skill. It combines within one command institutions comparable to those of the Army and Navy, but which in those services remain under different administrative or supervisory authority. The first of these is the Squadron Officer School, a constituent unit of the Command and Staff College, and roughly comparable to the company officer course in the Army branch schools, or the Navy's General Line School. Officers selected for attendance must be in the grade of lieutenant or captain, have not less than one nor more than six years of commissioned service, and be under 35 years of age. This is the first course that does not train the officer as a specialist. Rather it prepares him for duties relating to the command and operation of the lowest organizational unity, the squadron. Upon graduation the officer is reassigned to one of the major commands of the Air Force. Ideally the Air Force would like every regular officer and reservist on extended active duty of more than four years to attend the Squadron Officers Course. Actually the present annual capacity of three classes of 750 students each will permit only a minority of the eligibles to have this experience. Priority is given to regular officers and to reservists who expect to spend a career on active duty.

The Air Force promotion system is similar to those of the other services, and likewise bears upon attendance by officers at advanced schools. Second lieutenants must be promoted to first lieutenant by completion of three years of service or be dropped from the service. First lieutenants must be considered for promotion to captain by completion of seven years of service, captains to major after 14 years, and majors to lieutenant colonel after 21 years. As in the other services, an officer who is passed over the second time must be separated or retired, unless within two years of retirement age. Lieutenant colonels may be considered for promotion to colonel an unlimited number of times, but must be retired if not selected by completion of 28 years. Likewise, colonels must be retired after 30 years if not selected for brigadier general or after 5 years in grade, whichever is later. Because of increased requirements for officer personnel brought about by the expansion of the Air Force since 1950, many officers of this service have been promoted to higher temporary grade in advance of permanent promotion.

After about 10 years of service (no less than 7, nor more than 13) the Air Force officer may be nominated by his command to attend the Command and Staff School, another unit of the Air Command and Staff College. By this time he is in the grade of major or lieutenant colonel. To attend he must be under 38 years of age. This school is roughly comparable to the regular course at Leavenworth and the Command and Staff Course at Newport. It deals with Air Force operations at the wing, group, and numbered air force levels, and its mission is to prepare officers for command of wings and groups and for staff duties associated with numbered air force air divisions and wings. Until 1954–1955 this was a five and a half month course; it is now a nine month course. Ideally, the Air Force would like to have about 60 percent of all career officers, regulars and reservists, attend, but it is far from this goal. For all but a small percentage, this is the terminal educational opportunity.

The Air University conducts a variety of educational programs

Figure 3

AIR FORCE SCHOOL SYSTEM

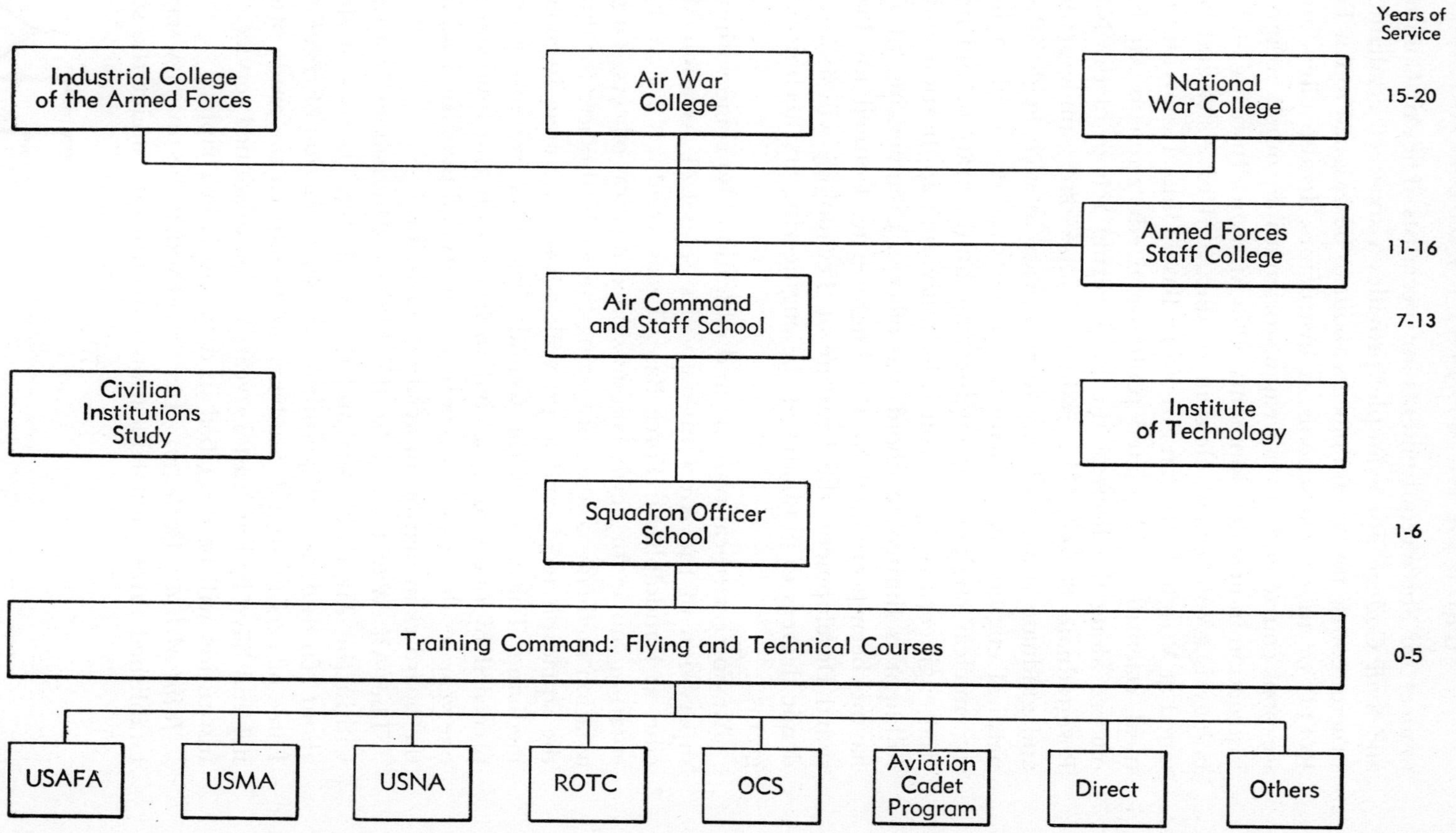

Years of Service	
15-20	Industrial College of the Armed Forces — National War College — Air War College
11-16	Armed Forces Staff College — Air Command and Staff School
7-13	Institute of Technology
1-6	Civilian Institutions Study — Squadron Officer School
0-5	Training Command: Flying and Technical Courses

USAFA USMA USNA ROTC OCS Aviation Cadet Program Direct Others to meet Air Force requirements for specialists. The Air Command and Staff College, for example, provides a six week academic instructor course for certain officers about to be assigned to Air Force ROTC or to service schools as instructors. It also offers an air weapons course and other weapons orientation courses to provide instruction in new developments. The Air Force Institute of Technology is a constituent element of the Air University and is situated at Wright-Patterson Air Force Base, Ohio. It provides technical, scientific, and related professional education to Air Force officers, along the lines of the Engineering School of the Navy's Postgraduate School. The resident course offers undergraduate and graduate courses of one to two years in such fields as aeronautical engineering, armament engineering, electrical engineering, nuclear engineering, engineering administration, and industrial engineering. Admission is by individual application and enrollment is limited to about 350 officers. Commencing in 1956, having been accredited by the Engineering Council for Professional Development, the Institute of Technology will award academic degrees to graduates of the engineering and technical programs.

Air Force medical training and education also come within the supervision of the Air University. Its School of Aviation Medicine, at Randolph Air Force Base, Texas, conducts a 3 week orientation course for newly commissioned medical officers, a 9 week aviation medicine course, preparing the medical officer for duty at the squadron level, and a 47 week advanced course in aviation medicine. The latter is the second phase of a five year program preceded by one year at a civilian institution and followed by a one year residency and two years of supervised practice, leading to the board examination in aviation medicine.

The Air War College is the highest educational institution within the Air University and the Air Force. Its present size of about 160 students will permit only a small fraction of regular Air Force officers to attend. Students are usually in the grade of colonel and have had at least 12 years of commissioned service. This institution will be described in detail in later chapters.

Joint Military Colleges. After world war II the military services established three joint educational institutions, under the supervision of the Joint Chiefs of Staff. The Armed Forces Staff College, at Norfolk, Virginia, offers a five month course, twice yearly, with an enrollment of about 125. Its purpose is to prepare officers for duties on joint and combined staffs. It is attended by selected officers of the three services with a minimum of about 10 years of service. Generally speaking, but not uniformly, the students are slightly older and more experienced than those at the Command and Staff Schools.

The Industrial College of the Armed Forces, in Washington, enrolls about 120 selected officers, usually with a minimum of 15 years' service, and civilians from the Department of Defense and other agencies. Its 10 month program is concerned principally with all phases of the national economy that bear upon economic readiness for war and with high level joint and combined planning and operations.

The National War College, also in Washington, was designed as the nation's highest military school. The student body is composed of about 105 officers, usually with a minimum of 15 years' service, and civilian representatives of the Department of State and other executive agencies. The 10 month program is designed to prepare its graduates for joint high-level policy and command and staff responsibilities, and for strategic planning duties with the separate services. The National War College is thus of primary interest in this book, and is considered at length in later chapters, as are the two other joint colleges.

In addition to participating in these joint schools, the services also have established the practice of assigning selected officers to the institutions of the other services, both as students and, in smaller numbers, as staff members. At the service war colleges the annual quota for representatives of the other services is about 8 to 10 each, and at the command and staff level about 4 to 8. All three services also send officers on an invitational basis to the military schools of certain allied nations, particularly the United Kingdom, Canada, and France. While the total number of American officers attending school abroad is by no means as great as the number of allied officers coming to this country, the number of American officers in senior schools is larger than the number accepted here. Several Americans, for example, attend the Imperial

Defence College, the highest British military educational institution.

In 1951 the United States, upon the urging of General Eisenhower, who had recently assumed the supreme command of allied forces in Europe, participated in the creation of the NATO Defense College in Paris. This new international school was established to prepare officer representatives of member nations of the North Atlantic alliance for duty at SHAPE and other NATO commands. The college now conducts a five and a half month course, twice annually, with an enrollment of 50 to 54 students ("members") in each session. The course is concerned with the principal factors, nonmilitary as well as military, involved in the defense of the North Atlantic region, with the problems of developing NATO defense forces, and with the organization and procedures of NATO commands and staffs. The United States is represented at the command level, on the faculty, and by about 8 students in each class.

Educational Opportunity and Career Development

All three armed services regard the education of a regular officer as a continuous process, extending throughout his professional career and consisting of actual experience on a variety of assignments supplemented by formal educational opportunity. They look upon their educational systems as devices for appropriate instruction at progressively advanced stages in the officer's career, preparing him for higher levels of responsibility. The underlying assumption is that since the lifetime career of a single officer is not long enough to permit him to serve in all of the multitude of functional areas within his service, let alone those of the sister services, the educational programs should be utilized to round out his experience, and provide him with at least the bare essentials, and a basic understanding of these areas, so that he is prepared for any eventuality. This requirement of the educational systems has become increasingly significant, as the weapons and organizational and management problems of the armed services have become more complex.

Actually, only the Army comes close to achieving this goal. All of its regular officers can expect to attend the branch schools, and at least one specialist school. About half are selected for the regular course at the Command and General Staff College, and about 10 to 15 percent for the Army War College. Attendance at Leavenworth (or constructive credit) is a prerequisite for selection for the Army War College. Virtually all officers advancing to general rank are graduates of the Command and General Staff course, or have constructive credit for the course, and many are graduates of the Army War College or one of the other senior joint or service War Colleges. The majority of these officers will have spent a total of two years in advanced education, and some of them three years, a period similar in length to that required for postgraduate work in other professions. The difference, of course, is that professional military education is experienced at intervals over a period of 15 to 20 years, rather than at one time.

The Navy's Command and Staff course and the senior courses at the Naval War College are not large enough to permit the same proportion of Naval officers to have a similar educational experience. Enrollment in the Command and Staff course, for example, has not exceeded 150 students per year. The Navy does not require graduation from this course (or an earlier junior course) as a prerequisite for the senior courses at the Naval War College, or for the joint or other service colleges.

Ideally the Air Force would like to send all of its officers to the Squadron Officer School, about 60 percent to the Command and Staff School, and up to 25 percent to the Air War College. A large integration of officers into the regular Air Force at the end of world war II created a "hump" in the officer structure and a corresponding problem in getting the desired percentages through the career schools. Until the officer procurement program is stabilized the above goals will not be met. A study made in 1953 of selected Air Force officers in the grades of lieutenant colonel, colonel, and higher who were holding key positions revealed that about one third had attended one of the senior joint or service colleges. Thirteen percent had attended the National War College or the Industrial College, 14 percent the Air War College (a few of these had also attended the National War College), and 4.8 percent either the Army War College or the Naval War College. At the Command and Staff course level, 17.3 percent had attended the Air Force course at Maxwell, and 17.8 percent the Army course at Leavenworth. Slightly under 8 percent of these officers had attended the Armed Forces Staff College.[5]

A cursory examination of the educational experience of officers promoted to general or flag rank in the six year period between January 1948 and January 1954 indicates that about 58 percent of the Army officers were graduates of one or more of the senior joint or service War Colleges or foreign equivalents. The comparable figures for the Navy and Air Force were 39 percent and 68 percent.[6] In other words, among officers who advanced to high rank, the Air Force had provided opportunity for attendance at the highest schools for about two thirds of its officers, the Army for almost 60 percent, and the Navy for almost 40 percent. For the most part these officers had attended these schools since world war II. In other words, in the Air Force there was a fairly high correlation between selection for the joint and service War Colleges and selection for promotion. Although opportunity for an educational experience at the highest level was limited, the Air Force was making the most of it for its prospective generals. In the Navy, on the other hand, there was not this same degree of connection between attendance at one of the colleges and promotion. More recent promotions suggest that the Navy is providing increased educational opportunity for its superior officers. Of the 39 captains selected for rear admiral in July 1955, 17 were graduates of the National War College, 10 of the Naval War College, and 2 of the Industrial College.[7]

The promotion systems of the armed forces provide for retirement of officers who are not advanced beyond certain rank levels. The operation of this selective process, coupled with competitive selection for attendance at the advanced schools, results in a higher level of educational experience in the upper ranks than among military officers at large. The selective processes, moreover, favor combat arms, line, and rated officers as well, since it is from among these officers that the Army, Navy, and Air Force promote a larger proportion to general and flag rank and thus to the highest command and executive responsibilities. Within the frame of reference of this study, in which the focus of attention is upon precisely

---

[5] T. R. Ford, *Service School Attendance by Key Air Force Personnel*, Officer Education Research Laboratory, Air Research and Development Command, Maxwell AFB, February 1955.

[6] From the *Army, Navy*, and *Air Force Registers* for 1954.

[7] *Army Navy Air Force Journal*, June 30, 1955, pp. 1921, 1927.

those senior officers who are most likely to hold positions involving policy formulation, this situation increases the significance of military education. These officers are most likely to be represented in the student bodies of the military schools that are examined in the most detail here—the senior joint and service colleges.

The Dimensions of Military Education

In conclusion, it is seen that these education programs of the armed forces constitute a large public enterprise. In addition to the regular courses outlined above, most of the schools conduct related activities, such as shorter "associated" courses for reserve officers, correspondence courses, and special programs for officers from allied nations overseas, and, in several cases, publication of a magazine.

This brief account suggests the range and variety of educational opportunities available to officer personnel. In terms of the number of people involved as well, this is an impressive undertaking, although the totals are far less than those in strictly training activities. The Army characteristically has the largest number of officers in school at a given time, but the Air Force is pressing close behind for this distinction. For fiscal year 1955, for example, the Army planned to assign about 47,000 officers to its schools for courses of varying length, and in addition 3,800 officers to schools of other services and to joint and foreign schools and the NATO Defense College. At the same time, plans provided for 860 officers in civilian colleges, 443 in civilian industrial training programs, and 6,804 officers of other services and of allied nations and civilians attending Army schools. The support of Army service schools required a total of 6,274 officers, 16,497 enlisted men, and 7,213 civilians, as of September 1955. This included direct support of the schools, related Army post activity, Department of the Army and other administrative supervision, the Army's share of the support of the joint colleges, and resident liaison duty with foreign schools.[8] The programs of the other services were proportionately large.[9]

[8] *A Review of the Army School System,* Department of the Army, Office of the Assistant Chief of Staff, G-3, 25 August 1954.

[9] For a summary of educational opportunities available in the armed services, see American Council on Education, *Your Life Plans and the Armed Forces,* Washington, 1955.

CHAPTER FOUR

THE EVOLUTION OF MILITARY

EDUCATION

PRESENT day military schools and colleges are the products of more than a century of experience. Throughout most of their history the armed forces have prepared officers for the military aspects of their careers. They have stressed the technical knowledge relevant to military operations and the skills and attitudes expected of the military leader. Yet throughout this history there has been a slow but steady broadening of the formal education of the soldier and sailor. This trend was promoted during the nineteenth century by a few leaders who emphasized the *professional* aspects of a military career, as distinguished from the purely technical. It paralleled the beginnings of graduate and professional education in civilian institutions. Later it was supported by those who saw need for greater understanding of the relationship of military affairs to other factors in our national society. Some progress along these lines had been made before the outbreak of the second world war. Since the war these trends have come to fruition in the military schools and colleges of today. The purpose of this book is to describe and analyze these postwar developments, but since they are derived from earlier experience, we turn first to a brief sketch of the historical evolution of military education in the United States.

Pre-Civil War Developments

Prior to the civil war, professional military education was limited almost exclusively to the two academies—the Military Academy at West Point, established in 1802, and the Naval Academy at Annapolis, founded 43 years later. These two institutions served as a primary, but by no means the sole, source of regular Army and Navy officers.

The Military Academy was the first school of technology in an English-speaking country, and was one of the nation's principal sources of trained engineers. The solid foundations of the Academy were constructed by Sylvanus Thayer, who was appointed superintendent in 1817. Thayer, a graduate of Dartmouth College as well as of the academy (class of 1808), and a man of scholarly interests, devoted two years to travel and study of military education and practice abroad before assuming his duties. Already an admirer of Napoleon, he was most favorably impressed by the French military schools with their emphasis upon a rigidly prescribed course of study.[1] The West Point molded by Thayer in the 16 years of his superintendency established a firm pattern that has prevailed to this day. Thayer created the office of the commandant of cadets, with responsibility for the discipline and military training of the cadets, organized the corps into tactical units under cadet officers as a device for promoting qualities of military leadership. He inaugurated a stern disciplinary system, divided classes into small groups on the basis of merit, and introduced a marking system based on a daily grade for each recitation. Thayer's strict disciplinary methods brought him into conflict with President Andrew Jackson, culminating in his resignation. It has been suggested that the practices introduced by Thayer at West Point contributed to the development of a gap between the officers of the regular Army and the broad current of Jacksonian democracy, resulting in the relative isolation of the military from the democratic spirit of the age.[2]

Thayer instituted other reforms at the academy. He organized the Academic Board and instituted the well-known honor system. He also enriched the academic fare. When he assumed office, instruction was given in mathematics, English, natural philosophy (the sciences), drawing, and French. He added chemistry, general history, moral philosophy, law, geography, and ethics. The emphasis remained upon military subjects, particularly military en-

---

[1] It is interesting to note that Saint-Cyr was established by Napoleon about the same time that the Military Academy was founded.

[2] Pendleton Herring, *The Impact of War,* New York, 1941, pp. 35–38.

gineering. Dennis Hart Mahan, a brilliant young officer brought to the academy by Thayer following several years of European study and observation, was chiefly responsible for building up the program in engineering. He served at West Point from 1830 to 1871. His civil engineering text became standard in other institutions during his time. The first professors of engineering at Harvard (1849) and at Yale (1852) were West Point graduates. The term *civil engineering* was first employed to distinguish it from military engineering, out of which it developed.

On the eve of the civil war the West Point curriculum provided instruction in mathematics, the physical sciences, civil and military engineering, military tactics and gunnery, and in English composition, French, Spanish, rhetoric and ethics, constitutional, international, and military law, and history. Instruction in history, law, and ethics was delegated to the chaplain, "in addition to his other duties." [3] In the summer of 1860 a joint Congressional-military committee, headed by Senator Jefferson Davis, a graduate of the academy and former secretary of war, spent seven weeks at West Point examining the entire operation of the institution. The committee submitted a report of several hundred pages and a bill incorporating its recommendations, but in the growing crisis on the eve of war no legislative action was taken. The suggested changes called for higher admissions and performance standards, and the introduction of a five year course of study. Generally the committee found the instruction well suited to the training of the junior officer, but lacking in preparation for higher levels. It recommended the establishment of the office of chaplain and that of professor of ethics and English letters and the addition of five assistant professors to give increased instruction in English, geography, history, and law. The committee also found the library deficient in historical works and literary magazines and reviews. It suggested that cadets be permitted to use library books in their own rooms. [4]

Until Secretary of the Navy Bancroft established the Naval Academy by administrative action in 1845, the training of midshipmen was accomplished on shipboard and at Naval stations.

---

[3] John D. F. Phillips, "The Course in Social Sciences at the United States Military Academy," *Assembly*, October 1950, pp. 1–4.
[4] 36th Congress, 2nd Session, Senate Misc. Doc. No. 3, December 1860.

The inadequacies of this method were long apparent, but Congress had failed to respond to earlier requests for a permanent Naval school. Those who planned the Naval Academy consciously modeled their program upon the Military Academy.[5] Commander Buchanan, the first superintendent, was like Sylvanus Thayer a strict disciplinarian. He introduced the use of demerits and the daily recitation and grade. The curriculum emphasized mathematics, science, seamanship, navigation, and tactics. The French and Spanish languages also were taught. Various miscellaneous courses were grouped together in the Department of Ethics, including English grammar, rhetoric, geography, history, moral philosophy, natural, constitutional, and international law, and naval law. As at West Point, instruction in these subjects, such as it was, was handed over to the chaplain.

Prior to the civil war a number of other educational institutions in which military training was required were established by individuals who had been associated with the Military Academy. The first of these was Norwich University, founded in 1819 in Norwich, Vermont as the American Literary, Scientific and Military Academy. This was followed in 1839 by Virginia Military Institute and in 1842 by the Citadel. The courses of study were similar to the West Point program. Some graduates of these schools entered the United States Army as regular officers.

Civil War to First World War

Following the civil war the academies became more deeply rooted as permanent features of the Army and Navy. In the case of West Point, Congress by law recognized the fact that it had been training not only engineers, but officers for all branches of the Army, by providing that the superintendent might be selected from any arm of the service. There were no significant changes in the curriculum and the methods of instruction that had developed before the war, however. Mathematics and engineering dominated the course of study throughout the nineteenth century.

As a result of passage of the Morrill act in 1862, military train-

[5] The archives of the Naval Academy contain a detailed report to Secretary Bancroft on the Military Academy prepared by Samuel Marcy, subsequently an instructor at the Naval Academy, following an extended visit to West Point in July 1845. Extensive use was made of this report in plans for the new school.

ing in civilian institutions was extended very considerably. This act, which authorized the donation of federal lands to the states and territories for the establishment of colleges for instruction in agriculture and mechanical arts, specified that military training should be offered. In 1866 Congress provided for the detail of Army officers to the land grant colleges as professors of military science and tactics. The compulsory feature of the military training was introduced by the states. This was a reserve program; it was not designed to produce regular Army officers.

At the Naval Academy after the civil war the prewar pattern was continued, with emphasis on the preparation of midshipmen for early assignments. Some observers suggested that Annapolis should attempt more than this, perhaps giving some attention to theoretical science and literature. But this was firmly resisted. A board of visitors headed by Rear Admiral John Dahlgren, for example, declared that "the first requisite—failing in which all the work of the Academy will be only lost time—is, that its graduates shall be qualified to enter upon the varied and responsible duties of active service in the grade to which they are admitted." The board proposed that the study of rhetoric as a special branch be discontinued, and that physical geography, history, ethics, constitutional, international, and naval law should no longer be taught by textbook, but rather by "familiar lectures." It recommended that the time thus gained be used "in giving increased attention to branches having a more immediate bearing upon the active duties of naval life." [6] That the Naval Academy still regarded such subjects as composition, rhetoric, ethics, history, and law as marginal is suggested by the fact that these and other miscellaneous courses continued to be grouped together in a single department. By 1876 this Department of English, History, and Law was giving about two or three hours of instruction each week in each of the four years at the academy. This general pattern prevailed for the next half century.

The most significant development in military education during the period between the civil and first world wars was the introduction of instruction at what might be called the postgraduate level. Of special importance was the establishment of the Naval and

[6] United States Senate, 39th Congress, 1st Session, Ex. Doc. No. 53, June 11, 1866, pp. 2–3.

Army War Colleges and the Army Command and General Staff School. By the 1880's the armed forces had slowly emerged from the depths to which they had been permitted to fall after the war. The United States was now turning from its preoccupation with internal affairs and was feeling the first stirrings of a sense of great national power. Within the services new technological developments in warfare, including use of more complicated weapons and of new tactics and supply practices to employ them effectively, necessitated more thorough preparation of officers. In the Army this was reflected in the growing strength and independence of the separate branches of the service. It also was accompanied by the development of a number of special schools, the forerunners of the present branch schools. These included the School for Application of Light Artillery, established at Fort Riley, Kansas, in 1869, and the School for the Application of Cavalry and Infantry, opened in 1881 at Fort Leavenworth.[7]

About the same time an intellectual awakening stimulated a few serious-minded officers to consider the requirements for a well-qualified professionalized corps of officers. They saw need for theoretical and scholarly study of the role of military power and for the development of career officers prepared not only in the technical aspects of military affairs but in the higher arts of strategy and warfare. In 1875 the secretary of war dispatched one of these imaginative officers, Brigadier General Emory Upton, a former instructor at West Point, on an 18 month trip around the world to study military instruction and schools abroad, particularly German schools. Upton reported that although the Military Academy provided superior preparation for the newly commissioned officer, the Army, except in the artillery, did not provide officers "the means of acquiring a theoretical and practical knowledge of the higher duties of their profession." He accordingly proposed the establishment of infantry and cavalry staff schools and of a war college, along the lines of those he had observed in Europe.[8]

In spite of the foresight of Upton, the growth of the branches retarded development of an Army-wide approach to officer educa-

---

[7] As early as 1824 an Artillery School was set up and in 1826 an Infantry School, but these subsequently were discontinued.

[8] James C. Shelburne, *Factors Leading to the Establishment of the Air University*, doctoral dissertation, University of Chicago, 1953, p. 34.

tion. Upton's dream of a war college, as a center of the intellectual consideration of the art and science of war, was realized first by the Navy, which was the cosmopolitan and worldly-wise service at that time. Within the Navy a concern for more adequate professional education likewise had been demonstrated by a small group of imaginative officers. They expressed themselves through the meetings and publications of the Naval Institute, which was founded in 1873 for "the advancement of professional and scientific knowledge in the Navy." The first annual prize essay contest of the Institute, in 1878, was on the subject of naval education.[9]

The leader in the advocacy of a postgraduate program was Captain (later Rear Admiral) Stephen B. Luce, who previously had served four tours at the Naval Academy and also had established a shipboard training program for enlisted personnel. Overcoming heavy odds, Luce in 1884 secured appointment from the secretary of the Navy as head of a special board to consider a postgraduate course for officers of the Navy. The establishment of the Naval War College at Newport, Rhode Island, with Luce as first president, followed. The purpose of the War College as outlined in the report of the board was "that there might be a place where our officers would not only be encouraged, but required to study their profession proper—war—in a far more thorough manner than had heretofore been attempted, and to bring to the investigation of the various problems of modern naval warfare the scientific methods adopted in other professions." The purpose was to prepare officers for the higher branches of their profession, and in the science and art of war.[10]

The Naval War College during its first 25 years was not generally accepted throughout the Navy. It was only through the determined efforts of its faithful supporters that it survived a precarious existence, in spite of the world-wide fame of its most noted president, and lecturer, Alfred Thayer Mahan. Various attempts were made to abolish the school or to move it to Annapolis, where

[9] Second honorable mention in this contest was won by Commander Alfred T. Mahan's entry, and this was his first published work. *United States Naval Institute Proceedings*, Vol. v, 1879, pp. 345–376. See also William H. Russell, "Seventy Five Years of Progressive Naval Thinking," *United States Naval Institute Proceedings*, October 1948, pp. 1251–1261.

[10] Quoted in Albert Gleaves, *Life and Letters of Rear Admiral Stephen B. Luce*, New York, 1925, pp. 175–176.

it would become a postgraduate course at the Naval Academy, or to Washington, where it would serve as a planning agency. Enrollments were low and the principal instruction was given during six summer weeks to the officers of the fleet while it was stationed at Newport. The first annual course was not established until 1911, and then enrolled only four students. Writing of this period of the Naval War College's history some years later, Admiral William V. Pratt declared: ". . . The College was tolerated, but was not looked upon as being one of the most essential features of the Navy." [11] The insecurity of the Naval War College was in large measure due to the failure of the Navy to accept the broad interpretation of the purpose of education that had been eloquently expressed by Luce and Mahan. Moreover the relationship of this institution to the organization and operations of the Navy was not clear. The Navy was still dominated by its separate bureaus. It had not yet thought through the concepts and principles of overall administration and operation and of the relationship of fleet operations to factors outside the Navy itself.

In the Army, on the other hand, the establishment in 1901 of the Army War College and subsequently of a coordinated system of schools came about as an integral part of sweeping reform of the service, of which Secretary of War Elihu Root was the principal author. Root became secretary in 1899 at a critical stage in the Army's growth and development. The war against Spain had revealed serious weaknesses in organization and personnel. New responsibilities in the Philippines, including military government and colonial administration, imposed heavy burdens upon a frail structure. Root's greatest contribution was the creation of the General Staff and the structural reorganization of the Army, but the Army War College occupied an important role in his scheme.

[11] Admiral W. V. Pratt, "The Mission and the Work of the Naval War College," 1926, in *The United States Naval War College, A Staff Study*, Newport, 1954, Appendix C, pp. 4–5. For interesting commentaries on the obstacles that faced the Naval War College within the Navy, see the reports of the secretary of the Navy, Josephus Daniels, for 1916 and 1919. In the latter Daniels declared that whereas the Navy had developed the training and performance of its officers for the performance of their duties on board a particular ship to "a high state of efficiency, . . . with which we may well be proud," "the study of problems in connection with the many possible conditions that would exist in time of war or threatened attack, and practice in solving these problems have not kept pace with the study and solution of problems arising in the single ship." *Report of the Secretary of the Navy, Miscellaneous Reports*, 1916, pp. 48–50; 1919, p. 92.

He was strongly influenced by an account of the German General Staff published in London by Spencer Wilkinson, and by the earlier report of General Emory Upton, who had recommended a general staff and the systematic extension of military education.[12] The Spanish war indicated that Upton's proposals were even more relevant than when he had first made them more than 20 years before. Although officers in the lower ranks had performed creditably, those "at the higher levels were almost completely unprepared to handle the problems of sudden mobilization, training, and the widespread deployment of military forces." [13]

The Army War College was established in 1901 to remedy this situation. Root and the first commandant, Brigadier General Tasker Bliss, considered it an interim staff agency to do advanced planning for the Army as well as a school to prepare for high level command and staff positions. After the passage of the Army Reorganization Act of 1903 and the creation of the General Staff, the college became primarily an educational institution, but it continued during the period before the world war to engage in planning activities in association with the General Staff. After the war it was concerned with the broad operations of field armies and the higher levels of the War Department, and stood out as the senior school in the Army's educational system. Until its operations were suspended in 1940 it occupied the imposing structure in Washington for which Elihu Root had laid the cornerstone in 1903.[14]

The Army Command and General Staff School at Fort Leavenworth, Kansas was another product of the reforms developed under Root's leadership. This school had its beginnings as the School of Application for Infantry and Cavalry in 1881. In 1902

[12] Spencer Wilkinson, *The Brain of An Army,* London, 1890. Root had Upton's *The Military Policy of the United States* published as a government document (Washington, 1912) and supplied a preface in praise of Upton.

[13] Department of the Army, Office of the Assistant Chief of Staff, G-3, *A Review of the Army School System,* unpublished staff study, Washington, 1953.

[14] This building is now the home of the National War College. In the rotunda is a plaque commemorating Root's role in the establishment of the Army War College and the erection of the building. Looking ahead in our story for a moment, it is interesting to note that the Army War College as established by Elihu Root bore a relationship to the Army similar in character to that of the National War College as established following the second world war to the total military establishment. A principal purpose of the former was to overcome the parochial view of the separate branches and to support *Army-wide* strategic planning. A principal purpose of the latter was to overcome parochialism of the separate services and to support truly *national* strategic planning.

it was reopened after the Spanish war as the General Service and Staff School and assumed an important role in the development of the Army's regular officer corps. Instruction in basic subjects was delegated to post schools, and this new school of combined arms concentrated on preparation for higher command and staff responsibilities. In 1904 the course was extended to two years. During the first world war graduates of the school filled many important command and staff positions.

The reforms of the Root period also included an extension and improvement of the Army's branch schools. In the 10 year period after 1901 the following schools were established or reorganized: Engineers, Infantry, Ordnance, Quartermaster, Artillery. At the Military Academy, although there was no change in the basic structure of the curriculum during this period, individual courses of study were improved and brought up to date and the standards of admission were raised. Through the support of Theodore Roosevelt, Elihu Root, and others, a large scale building program was undertaken at West Point. The Navy, emphasizing training with the fleet, did not attempt to match this Army school system, although in 1909 it did establish at Annapolis a postgraduate school as a division of the Naval Academy, offering courses in ordnance, mechanical engineering, radio, shop management, naval architecture, and civil engineering.

In looking back over the evolution of military education in the nineteenth century, one is impressed by the record of leadership of a handful of men, particularly Sylvanus Thayer, Dennis Mahan, George Bancroft, Stephen Luce, Tasker Bliss, Alfred Thayer Mahan, Emory Upton, and Elihu Root. These individuals were motivated by a conviction that the professional officer corps required a high level of educational achievement, over and above military training. They believed firmly that scholarship should be applied to the art and science of military affairs, and that military schools, designed for this purpose, should prepare officers for higher responsibilities. There was, moreover, a striking continuity among them and the institutions with which they were associated. Thayer, Dennis Mahan, Bliss, and Upton had engaged in serious study of European military practices and education before making their important contributions to American military education. European influences also led to the improvement of graduate and professional education in this country during this same period. The West Point of Thayer and Dennis Mahan, which drew heavily from European practices, served as the model for the new Naval Academy created by Secretary of the Navy George Bancroft, who also was a distinguished scholar and statesman. Upton taught at West Point before he was selected by the secretary of war to travel round the world and make a study of foreign military education. Stephen Luce, commandant at the Naval Academy and founder of the Naval War College, was influenced by Upton, as was Elihu Root some years later. Luce turned to the Army for Tasker Bliss as the Naval War College's first instructor in tactics and strategy. Bliss went on to a distinguished career in the Army and was selected by Root to organize the Army War College as its first commandant. He returned to the college again in 1909 before becoming assistant chief of staff and ultimately chief of staff of the Army. Alfred Thayer Mahan, who made his fame at the Naval War College, was the son of West Point's Dennis Mahan, and the namesake of Sylvanus Thayer.

Officer Education in the Interwar Years

Following the first world war the service schools were reopened on a peacetime basis and patterns were established which prevailed during the interwar years. The Army, in keeping with its established practice, maintained a more elaborate and comprehensive school system than the Navy, which continued to emphasize the primary value of shipboard experience. At West Point this was a period of slow but significant change. After the civil war, with the establishment of the land grant colleges and the accelerated development of private institutions of higher learning, the Military Academy had tended to withdraw upon itself, cherishing its traditions and customs. Criticism of the academy, particularly of the alleged narrowness of its program and the authoritarianism of its methods, was common. The academy, in turn, became more introspective and unduly conservative in outlook and procedures. By the first world war, West Point reached the nadir of its development.

In the twenties the situation was somewhat improved, commencing with a review of the curriculum during the superintendency of Douglas MacArthur immediately following the war. The Academic Board restated the academy's mission to be "to give, in addition to that character building for which it has long been famous, and in addition to the necessary military and physical training, such a combination of basic general and technical education as will provide an adequate foundation for a cadet's subsequent professional career." [15] The four year course of study, which had been set aside during the war, was reinstituted. Under the leadership of Lucius Holt, who had come from Yale University in 1910, the time devoted to English was doubled, permitting more attention to the study of literature, and instruction in economics and government was introduced. At first this additional work was given in a combined Department of English and History, but in 1926 a separate Department of Economics, Government, and History was established. Subsequently, under the effective leadership of Herman Beukema, further changes were made in the social sciences, but within the same over-all allotment of time. Colonel Beukema introduced instruction in Far Eastern history, comparative government, and international relations. Likewise, during this period, more time was devoted to military history by the Department of Military Art and Engineering.

Commencing about 1927, and at first on a small scale, the Military Academy developed the practice of sending officers selected as instructors in English, foreign languages, and the social sciences to civilian institutions for graduate study. Until after world war II most of this work was accomplished during the summers and at night.[16] Beginning in 1925 cadets were permitted to compete for Rhodes Scholarships. Altogether thirteen West Point graduates received Rhodes Scholarships between 1925 and the outbreak of the second world war. In 1925 the Military Academy was listed by the Association of American Universities as an approved technological institution, two years later it was admitted to membership in the Association of American Colleges, and in 1933 Congress

[15] Cited in Herman Beukema, *The United States Military Academy and Its Foreign Contemporaries,* West Point, 1944, p. 43.

[16] The scientific departments profited from the graduate education program of the Corps of Engineers and, to a lesser extent, of the Signal Corps. The officers of these branches usually were sent to civilian engineering schools for graduate training. Many of the instructors in the scientific departments at the academy had been so schooled.

authorized the Military Academy (as well as the Naval Academy) to confer the degree of Bachelor of Science upon its graduates. In part this authorization was sought to facilitate the enrollment of increasing numbers of regular officers in civilian universities for graduate study, particularly in the sciences. Thus in the two decades prior to the second world war the Military Academy turned increasingly to a broad educational program planned as preparation for a professional military career rather than merely for the initial duties of a young officer.

During the interwar years the Military Academy was the principal but not sole source of Army officers. Regular officers also were commissioned from the several civilian colleges and universities that were conducted as military institutions, including the Virginia Military Institute, Norwich University, the Virginia Polytechnic Institute, and Texas A and M. ROTC instruction was provided in the 52 land grant institutions, but all but relatively few of the graduates of this program were commissioned as reserve officers on inactive duty. Approximately 100,000 of these men were called up during world war II. The Army branch schools, having demonstrated their value during the first world war, were extended and placed on a regular basis. These schools were concerned with instruction in the procedures and tactics of their respective branches. Courses ranged from six weeks to nine months in duration. On the eve of world war II there were 19 of these branch schools.

The Command and General Staff School occupied an important position in the Army during the interwar years. The faculty produced a complete series of military texts, based upon American practice, and Leavenworth became the recognized source of Army doctrine and procedure. The course of instruction was one year in length, except for the years 1927–1936, when it was extended to two years. It prepared officers for duty at division, corps, and army levels of operation, and dealt exclusively with professional military subjects. Attendance at Leavenworth usually was a prerequisite for assignment to the Army War College, the Army's senior school, and for promotion to high rank. Many of the regular officers who were to distinguish themselves in the second world war attended the college during this period. The one year course was divided into two major parts: preparation for war and conduct of war. The first covered the functions and operations of the four "G's" (personnel, intelligence, operations, and logistics). The second involved preparation of war plans for hypothetical situations. The college equipped officers for command and staff duty in large units at the level of the army and above, for the General Staff in the War Department, and for the Office of the Assistant Secretary of War (Procurement).

The principal air arm of the armed forces during the interwar years remained a part of the Army, although the persistent demands of air officers throughout this period was reflected in organizational changes culminating in the establishment of the autonomous Army Air Forces in 1941. The growth of air operations naturally produced new training programs. Naval pilot training was conducted at Pensacola, Florida, Army training at Randolph and Kelly Fields. The Air Corps also conducted two technical schools, an engineering school, and a School of Aviation Medicine.

In the field of officer education, as distinguished from training, the Air Corps also set out on its own, although air officers were regularly assigned to the Army schools, particularly Leavenworth. As early as 1920, a separate air service school was established at Langley Field and this grew eventually into the Air Corps Tactical School, which was removed in 1930 to Maxwell Field, Alabama. The school was closely identified with advocacy of air power and is credited with a decisive role in developing, teaching, and defending the strategic and tactical concepts and doctrines employed by the American forces in the second world war. Because the Army schools taught that the air arm should be utilized principally in support of ground operations, Air Corps officers were generally critical of these schools and proud of their own Tactical School.[17]

Another important innovation that broadened professional military education was the creation of the Army Industrial College in 1924. This was part of a larger plan, undertaken pursuant to the national defense act of June 4, 1920, to adapt the military services to the kind of warfare fought by great industrial nations. Other elements of the plan were the vesting of mobilization duties in the

[17] James C. Shelburne, *Factors Leading to the Establishment of the Air University, op.cit.,* Chap. v.

assistant secretary of war for procurement and the creation of the Army and Navy Munitions Board. The entire program rested on three widely shared convictions: that success in combat depended more than ever on prodigious quantities of matériel, that adequate supplies could be secured only by general mobilization of the national economy, and that effective mobilization required close teamwork between *specially prepared* military personnel and private citizens.

Bernard Baruch, head of the War Industries Board, suggested a mobilization school. In 1920 Secretary of War Newton D. Baker wanted to establish a training program at Fort Belvoir, Virginia, but funds were not available. The assistant secretary of war therefore instituted apprentice or on-the-job training for officers in his planning branch. It was soon decided that this device was inadequate. It did not reach enough officers, and those it did reach were torn between their duties as students and the demands inevitably made on them to take part in the regular work of their office. At the same time officers of the Ordnance Department started to press for a more organized educational program. A special course was instituted at the Army War College. The Navy had already begun to send officers to the Harvard Business School and by 1923 the Army had decided to send eight to the next class. But the War Department had in mind something more specific than general business training. Early in 1924, therefore, it opened its own Industrial College to educate officers "in the useful knowledge pertaining to the supervision of procurement of all military supplies in time of war and to the assurance of adequate provision for the mobilization of material and industrial organization essential to war-time needs." [18] Control of the school rested with the assistant secretary of war since he, rather than the General Staff, had statutory responsibility for procurement and mobilization.

The first class started with nine Army students, including one from the Air Service. The next year a group of Naval officers was added. Beginning in 1929 a few officers of the Army combat arms were assigned, and about this time Industrial College students started to attend lectures at the Army War College. The first Naval officer was added to the faculty in 1931. In 1941 a Marine Corps officer served briefly as commandant. Thus the Industrial College

[18] General Order No. 7, War Department, February 25, 1924.

became in large measure a joint military school. In 1939, at the peak of its prewar development, its 62 students included 12 Naval and Marine Corps officers, 9 from the Army Air Corps, 8 from the Army combat arms, and 33 from the Army technical and administrative services.

In the 1930's the Industrial College also began to provide direct staff services to the War Department. Drawing on their own research, students and faculty commented on or actually helped prepare mobilization plans. As war approached the school geared itself more closely to immediate needs of the government. Staff and faculty worked at revising the annexes of the War Department's 1939 mobilization plan. One of its new units, the Economic Warfare Information Section, was later transferred bodily to the Office of the Administrator of Export Control.

Following the first world war the Navy gave considerable thought to its educational program. A special board, composed of Captains Dudley W. Knox and Ernest J. King and Commander William S. Pye, was convened in 1919 for this purpose. The board favored greater educational opportunities for Naval officers, pointing out that whereas the Navy had limited the education of its officers to preparation for the lowest commissioned grade, there now was need for periodic instruction throughout the career. While recognizing the validity of the traditional Navy emphasis upon learning by doing, the board stressed the value of a firm educational basis upon which to build the structure of practical experience. Accordingly it recommended that the Naval officer receive formal educational preparation for each of the four major phases of his career. The first phase was identified as "inferior subordinate." For this duty the officer is prepared by the Naval Academy. The second phase, "superior subordinate," involves duty as head of a department on shipboard. The board recommended attendance at the General Line course between five and ten years after commissioning (preferably after five years) preparatory to this phase. The third phase, "commanding officer," consists of command of a single ship. Attendance at a junior course at the Naval War College between the tenth and twentieth year of commissioning was recommended prior to advance into this phase. The final phase, "flag officer," involving command of a group of ships, should be preceded by attendance at the senior course at the Naval War College, after the twentieth year and preferably in the grade of captain.[19]

There were some parallels between developments at Annapolis and those at West Point in the interwar years. But in general the changes made at the Naval Academy, except in the area of Naval science and supporting technical subjects, were more modest; they aroused considerable opposition; and some important ones did not last. One noteworthy development was that during much of the period the work in English and history was under the supervision of a civilian department head. A course in advanced literature was added. The scope of the work in naval history was broadened. A course in government was added; so was a course in economics, but the latter was later dropped. Except during the years 1932–1937 English and the social sciences remained associated in a single department.

The situation at the Naval Academy during this period was the cause of concern to some observers. Boards of Visitors pointed to the relatively limited attention directed to the nontechnical side of the curriculum. In 1923, 1924, 1931, and 1933 the board proposed a study of the problem. In 1933 a strongly worded minority report was filed by Admiral William S. Sims, always an outspoken critic of those things which he found unsatisfactory. "The Naval Academy," he declared, "does not provide either educational or technical instruction to the degree required 'to mold the material received into educated gentlemen'. . . ."[20] Indeed some of the liberalizing changes made during the era may well have been influenced by the recommendations of Boards of Visitors. But traditional, conservative views were dominant by the late 1930's. For example, Rear Admiral David Sellers, superintendent in 1937, declared that ". . . success or failure in battle with the fleet is in no way dependent upon a knowledge of biology, geology, ethics, social science, the literature of foreign languages, or the fine arts."[21] Accordingly, the emphasis continued to be placed upon mathematics, engineering, and naval subjects.

A comprehensive study of the Naval Academy curriculum was

[19] "Report and Recommendations of a Board Appointed by the Bureau of Navigation Regarding the Instruction and Training of Line Officers," *United States Naval Institute Proceedings,* August 1920, p. 1265.

[20] United States Naval Academy, *Report of the Board of Visitors,* 1933, pp. 8f.

[21] Kendall Banning, *Annapolis Today,* New York, 1938, p. 73.

made in 1939 by Captain W. W. Smith at the direction of the superintendent. His report declared that the mission of the academy is to turn out officers who can perform "all the duties of junior officers." He concluded that the curriculum was too crowded, but the changes that he recommended had to do almost entirely with engineering and the sciences. He suggested that the study of American government should be dropped, since the midshipmen had studied civics in high school, and that the time saved be assigned to another department, or to international law or military geography. The Smith report vindicated the Naval Academy's conviction that its central purpose was to prepare midshipmen for the duties of junior officers, and that this mission still required a heavy emphasis upon mathematics, science, and engineering.[22]

In 1925 Congress authorized a Naval ROTC program. The following year units were established at 6 institutions (California, Georgia Tech, Harvard, Northwestern, the University of Washington, and Yale). By the eve of the war, in 1941, the number had been increased to 27. Graduates were commissioned in the Naval Reserve but were not required to serve on active duty. A small number of reserve officers, mostly those commissioned in the Supply Corps, were permitted to apply for active duty, and of these many transferred subsequently to the regular Navy. As in the case of the Army program, NROTC graduates were called to active duty during the emergency of the second world war, and some of them elected to transfer to the regular Navy.

Beyond the undergraduate level, the Navy during the interwar years accepted the Knox-King-Pye recommendations in principle but applied them to relatively few officers. This was due to restrictions imposed during the twenties by economy, and subsequently in the thirties to the shortage of line officers produced by the rapid expansion of the Navy. Most regular officers during their first shore duty attended the General Line course, conducted by the Postgraduate School at Annapolis. This course of one year was concerned entirely with professional naval subjects. Some officers proceeded immediately upon completion of this course to a second year of study at a civilian school of engineering or to the Navy aviation, submarine, or torpedo school. After about 15 years of rotat-

22 The report of Captain W. W. Smith on the Naval Academy curriculum, directed by a letter dated 28 July 1938, is on file in the Library of the Academy.

ing between sea and shore duty, selected officers, usually of the rank of lieutenant commander or commander, attended the junior course at the Naval War College. A smaller number of the regular line officers attended the senior course after about 20 years of service.

At the Naval War College increasing emphasis was placed on the training of officers for command and staff duties at sea. The junior course was designed to prepare officers for staff duties, dealing in problems of tactics and minor strategy. The senior course was concerned with "grand tactics," that is, fleet operations. In spite of the efforts of Admiral William C. Pratt, president of the college in the late twenties, and others to broaden the course of study, emphasis during the interwar years was placed largely on the conduct of maneuvers which tested and retested various tactical procedures and doctrine, looking toward fleet action. According to a recent Naval War College staff study, the college "prepared its officers to fight battles rather than wars." [23] During this period the college was closely associated with the fleet, developing tactical doctrine for fleet action. The staff study concludes that in this respect "it became unduly rigid and doctrinaire." Studies at the strategic level were conducted by means of "operations problems," during part of which the officers moved model ships on the linoleum floor of the large game room at the college. Much attention was devoted to the battle of Jutland. As the staff study indicates, "the War College could not forget that 'Jellicoe was the only man who could have lost the war in an afternoon.' " The emphasis upon "grand tactics" was also due to another situation. Because relatively few officers during the twenties and thirties attended the intermediate programs that had been proposed by the Knox-King-Pye board, those in charge of the college believed that they were not adequately grounded in fundamentals. The result was that the senior course devoted considerable attention to instruction that otherwise would have been offered earlier in an officer's career. The situation was not entirely one-sided, however. Some of the strategic concepts that were employed in the Pacific in 1942–1945 were conceived at the college in the years before the war.

[23] Naval War College, *Staff Study, op.cit.*, p. 13.

Characteristics of Prewar Education

What conclusions can be drawn from this brief survey of the evolution of military education before we proceed to a survey of the contemporary situation? In the first place, military education, including advanced education, had become well established as a regular and legitimate function of the armed services. In the nineteenth century, European influences played an important part in this process. The Army developed an elaborate and carefully integrated school system, extending from the Academy, through the specialized branch schools, to the Command and General Staff School at Leavenworth, and on to the Army War College. The Navy had nothing as elaborate, but in its Naval Academy, postgraduate school, specialized schools, and Naval War College, it had a school system of somewhat similar outline.

Yet the Army and Navy exhibited distinctive attitudes toward education. Education, as distinguished from training, occupied a more important role in the scheme of things in the Army than in the Navy. This was due in considerable measure to the inherent differences in the two services themselves. The focus of attention in the Navy was concentrated upon the handling of ships. Whether at war or in peace, the Navy had to operate its vessels, and it always insisted that the best teacher was experience itself. So, as indicated throughout this chapter, the Navy very properly emphasized shipboard training. The Naval Academy was regarded as preparatory to the young officer's early duties at sea. In spite of the early establishment of the Naval War College and the leadership of Luce, Mahan, Sims, and others, the Navy was slow to accept a concept of education, as contrasted with training. Nor did the Navy feel the need of an elaborate intermediate school system. The recommendations of the Knox-King-Pye board in 1919 were implemented only in part in the interwar years. Except for the Naval Academy, the Navy looked upon education as a substitute for actual experience. And because in peacetime ships were available, officers could gain this experience in handling ships and engaging in fleet maneuvers at sea rather than in schools ashore. It should be pointed out, however, that as early as 1864 the Navy instituted written examinations as a part of its promotion system, encouraging self-instruction and -preparation by its officers.

The Army, on the other hand, regarded its educational system as a means to prepare the officer in peacetime for the situations that he would face in war. Since war situations did not exist, schools were necessary. Moreover the peacetime Army, to a much greater degree than the Navy, was a relatively small cadre which would become the core of a vastly larger citizen army in time of mobilization. Therefore its officers had to be prepared to assume the command and staff responsibilities of units much larger than could be assembled in peacetime. The schools provided the opportunity to teach the basic concepts and doctrines that made possible the management in wartime of large units throughout which regular officers would be widely dispersed.

The difference in approach of the two services involved more than the difference in their peacetime situations. As early as the time of Sylvanus Thayer, the Military Academy began to point its educational program toward the professional career of the officer, as contrasted with his next duty assignment. The Navy, even in its attitude toward the Naval War College as late as the interwar period, appears to have regarded the school experience as training directly related to specific duties.

There was still another characteristic difference between the two services. To a much greater degree than the Navy, the Army used its schools as a means of testing its officers and screening them for greater responsibilities. Assignment to the more advanced schools was on a progressively more selective basis. Many of the officers who were selected for important commands in world war II and who subsequently distinguished themselves in these assignments came to the attention of their superiors at the Army schools.[24] In the Navy this selective process was more likely to operate at sea.

Finally it should be noted, and this is particularly relevant to the theme of this book, that those responsible for military education, in defining the responsibilities of the professional officers, did so in terms which remained very largely purely military. Thus even at the highest levels, the two War Colleges were focused sharply upon command and staff responsibilities. These responsi-

[24] Among them Dwight Eisenhower, who drew the attention of General George Marshall at the Infantry School.

bilities were not yet generally perceived to include concern for broader considerations at the national and international levels, particularly of political and economic factors. This situation is not surprising in the light of the environment in which the schools operated. As suggested in chapter one, the nation as a whole was slow in appreciating the intimate relationship between military and nonmilitary factors in our national life.

There were a few developments before the second world war, however, that pointed the way to more recent policies and practices. The start made toward extension of the instruction in the social sciences at the Military Academy was small but it represented an important attempt to break away from the established pattern. At higher levels the establishment of the Army Industrial College added an important new dimension to officer education. The initiative for this came largely from civilians and from the technical services rather than from the line of the Army, and numerous officers felt that the school lacked prestige. But in any case this was a significant undertaking, providing between 1924 and 1940 about 800 officers, including Dwight D. Eisenhower and Henry H. Arnold, with an opportunity to study the relationship of military strategy to the national economy.

Perhaps the most significant developments occurred at the Army War College during the thirties. Increasingly the curriculum of the college reflected a growing concern for problems of national policy, insofar as these related to the conduct of war. Committee studies were undertaken on such topics as organization of nations for support of wars and for national defense, national objectives in wars, coordinated use of armed forces and economic forces in war, and the influence of public opinion on the conduct of war. Attention was given to the problem of coordinating foreign and military policies.[25] Committees in 1939 and 1940 recommended a council for national defense, composed of the President, Vice President, secretary of war, secretary of the Navy, chief of staff, and chief of naval operations, to coordinate national policies. The 1939 committee proposed also that a College of National Policy and Defense be established, "the faculty and students of which would be drawn from both civil and military departments of the

[25] Chronicle of the Army War College, Vol. 3, in National War College Library.

government to study problems of coordination between civil and military matters." [26] Numerous other committee reports urged that closer relations be established between the State Department and the Army and Navy for the purpose of "coordinating diplomatic action with the means available to support it." Thus the Army War College, sheltered from the prevailing isolationist forces of the times, which restrained even Franklin Roosevelt, was ahead of the government in addressing itself to the problem of providing adequate institutional arrangements for the proper coordination of national security policy formulation. The college also during this period initiated a thorough reconsideration of United States military government principles, organizations, and procedures, preparing the way for new doctrines that were applied after the outbreak of war. [27]

A number of relatively minor developments at the Army War College might also be noted as evidence of an emerging awareness of the need to widen the curriculum. In 1935, for example, an informal course on "foreign news" was introduced, "to encourage habits of careful but rapid newspaper reading and prompt evaluation of the information in its relation to international affairs in general and the manner in which it might or might not affect the present and future of this country." The course consisted of brief semiweekly student presentations by five different student groups, each one responsible for a different foreign area. Representatives of the Department of State addressed the Army War College, and a few Foreign Service officers were enrolled in each class. Also, occasional lectures were delivered by historians and other scholars, including Samuel Flagg Bemis and the late Edward Mead Earle.

At the Naval War College the principal area of interest outside the study of naval strategy was international law, carrying on a tradition going back to the earliest days. Each year, the college published its "Blue Book," a compilation of the cases, documents, and situations utilized in the course of study. For many years this volume was prepared by George Grafton Wilson, and later by Judge Manley O. Hudson, professors of international law at Har-

26 Army War College, *Course in 1938-1939, Analytical Studies,* Report of Committee No. 6, 24 February 1939, in Army War College Library.
27 Edgar L. Erickson, *An Introduction to American Military Government—Civil Affairs in World War II,* unpublished manuscript, Office of the Chief of Military History, Department of the Army.

vard University.[28] The Naval War College also scheduled occasional lectures by representatives of the Department of State and other civilians, and, like the Army War College, it enrolled a few Foreign Service officers.

Thus, in conclusion, we find throughout the evolution of military education a persistent effort on the part of a few creative leaders to go beyond the training of highly skilled and strongly motivated combat soldiers and sailors in order to emphasize the "professional" aspects of a military career, and to dignify the systematic, scholarly study of military affairs. Steady progress was made. Yet during much of this history, and particularly within the Navy, these individuals had to struggle against entrenched conservatism to win acceptance of their ideas and proposals.

[28] Naval War College, *International Law Documents,* Washington, Government Printing Office, annual series, under varying titles, commencing in 1894. See also Rear Admiral Thomas H. Robbins, "International Law Is No Dead Letter," *United States Naval Institute Proceedings,* May 1956, pp. 491–495.

CHAPTER FIVE

EDUCATIONAL DEVELOPMENTS DURING

THE SECOND WORLD WAR

THE American experience in the second world war, which drastically changed the role of the United States in world affairs, naturally made a heavy impact upon professional military education, particularly after the conclusion of hostilities when there was time for reflection and the making of new plans. Officers had found that the management of fighting forces on a global scale was an even more complex undertaking than they had anticipated, involving unforeseen dimensions in depth and breadth. They were confronted with a range and variety of responsibilities far beyond their expectations, as already described in the first chapter of this book.

Between 1940 and 1945 the existing educational facilities of the armed forces were focused upon immediate requirements. Emphasis was shifted to specialized training of large numbers of men for specific duties in an emergency situation.[1] Education, as contrasted with training, was greatly curtailed or suspended altogether. At the undergraduate level, the courses at West Point and Annapolis were compressed and accelerated. The Army retained the ROTC program, but relied principally upon officer candidate schools for the production of thousands of junior officers. It also instituted the Army Specialized Training Program, in which enlisted men between the ages of 18 and 22 were given training in such fields as medicine, dentistry, engineering, psychology, and foreign areas and languages at a large number of civilian colleges and universities. This program was not for officers

[1] See for example Robert R. Palmer, Bell I. Wiley, and William R. Keast, *The Procurement and Training of Ground Combat Troops,* Office of the Chief of Military History, Department of the Army, Washington, 1948.

or officer candidates. While it demonstrated the practicability of specialized training of this sort, the program was hampered from the start by opposition within the Army and because poor use was made of the knowledge and skills of the graduates. The Navy utilized civilian institutions during the war for a variety of officer candidate programs, of which the V-12 was the largest. This was designed to provide the requisite education for subsequent officer training. Graduates of the V-12 program were qualified to go on to officer candidate schools. The Navy program was more flexible than the ASTP, tended to stay closer to normal college requirements, and usually retained men in school somewhat longer. The Navy also managed to assign graduates with more success than the Army.[2]

The principal wartime programs were, of course, beyond the undergraduate level. The Army branch schools and other specialized schools in both services turned out large numbers of graduates quickly and effectively. At the Army's Command and General Staff School approximately 1,800 officers, including AAF, Navy, and foreign personnel, were put through a shortened course in preparation for command and staff duties. The Army War College and the Air Tactical School were closed even before the United States entered the war because experienced officers could not be spared from other duties. Subsequently the AAF operated a Staff Officers' Course, roughly comparable to Leavenworth, in association with other training programs conducted by the wartime AAF School at Orlando, Florida. The course at the Army Industrial College was first shortened in 1940, deactivated the following year, and reinstituted in 1944. Although earlier plans had called for the Naval War College to be closed in wartime, Rear Admiral E. C. Kalbfus, its dedicated president, succeeded in persuading the Navy to keep it open. A five month course at the command and staff level was conducted, principally for reserve officers.

Area Studies

In spite of the wartime emphasis upon specialized training, two developments were initiated during this period that were to fore-

---

[2] Henry C. Herge, *Wartime College Training Programs of the Armed Services,* American Council on Education, Washington, 1948.

shadow postwar practices. One was the provision of systematic instruction in foreign areas and languages, international affairs, and related matters. This was accomplished principally in programs set up to equip officers for military government and similar duty abroad. Even before Pearl Harbor, Major General Allen W. Gullion, then the judge advocate general of the Army, had proposed that special training be provided in military government. In the spring of 1942, after General Gullion became provost marshal general, his office established an Army-operated school of military government, on the campus of the University of Virginia. Subsequently civil affairs training schools were conducted by 10 civilian universities, under contract with the Army. The Charlottesville school prepared officers for military government duties at the staff level, the CAT schools for duties in field operations. The latter accordingly placed greater emphasis upon foreign area and language instruction.[3] The Navy also established a school of military government and administration, first at Columbia and then at Princeton, and assigned some officers to the Army civil affairs schools.

At the end of the war the Army Air Forces set up still another program, the Post Hostilities Staff Officers Course, conducted by the AAF School at Orlando from May to September 1945. While the Army military government schools were designed to train officers for specific military government duties, the AAF course was based upon the proposition that all officers in the occupational forces in Europe, regardless of function, should understand the history, politics, and economics of the European countries, particularly Germany. It followed the general pattern for area courses that had been employed in the civil affairs training schools.[4]

During the war the armed forces partially met the demands for competent personnel in fields beyond conventional military affairs by commissioning civilians already skilled in appropriate specialties. Although most of these individuals subsequently returned to their normal occupations, the need for their knowledge and skills remained, throwing a new burden upon regular officers. The sit-

[3] Charles S. Hyneman, "The Army's Civil Affairs Training Program," *The American Political Science Review*, April 1944, pp. 342–353.

[4] Historical Office, Army Air Forces Special Staff School, *A History of the AAF School, 29 October 1943–2 September 1945*, 1946, Vol. II, pp. 153–162, in USAF Historical Division Archives, Maxwell AFB, Alabama.

uation was soon reflected in plans for postwar military education, as we shall see below. The AAF Post-Hostilities Course, for example, was first proposed by Lieutenant General Carl Spaatz, commanding the United States Strategic Air Force in Europe, in a communication to General Henry Arnold, chief of the Air Forces. General Spaatz envisaged the course as one for regular officers about to be assigned to occupation duty to replace temporary officers.

The Army-Navy Staff College

A second wartime educational development that dramatized a new dimension of permanent consequence—a joint approach—was the establishment in June 1943 of the Army-Navy Staff College. The idea for such an institution originated with officers on the staff of General Arnold, who emphasized the need to prepare officers for command and staff duties with joint commands, and to develop new ideas for the employment of all arms and services in joint operations. Officers on General Marshall's staff elaborated upon the proposal. Although the Navy was at first cautious, ANSCOL, as it was known, was finally set up by the Joint Chiefs.

Throughout most of its existence, the college was located in the Army War College building, now the home of the National War College. It conducted a 21 week course, commencing with instruction at the Air Forces School of Tactics at Orlando, the Command and Staff School at Fort Leavenworth, and the Naval War College at Newport, and followed by two months in Washington. Various classes also visited the Artillery School at Fort Sill, the Infantry School at Fort Benning, the Navy Yard at Boston, the Submarine School at New London, the Seabee Training School at Quonset, and the Amphibious Training Base at Norfolk, to observe equipment and training procedures. Throughout the program emphasis was placed upon logistics, the exercise of command, and the unified employment of arms. During the Washington phase past operations of the war were analyzed, and the students, organized in committees, went through all of the requirements of planning and conducting a major amphibious operation involving participation of sea, land, and air units. In all, 12 classes of 30 to 40 each, composed of Army, Navy, Air, and Marine officers, completed the course. Several representatives of the State Department were enrolled in each of the last five classes. Most of the students were in the grade of colonel or captain in the Navy.

ANSCOL is important to our story for a number of reasons. In addition to providing meaningful training for officers about to assume responsibilities in joint operations, the school demonstrated the value of a joint effort of this sort, in which officers of all services with varied backgrounds came to know and understand each other. Moreover the commandant, Lieutenant General DeWitt, and his faculty were to assume a leading role in the preparation of plans for postwar officer education at the joint level, providing the initiative for the deliberations that led to the establishment of the National War College.[5]

Thus two principal developments in postwar military education had their beginnings during the war. Both are directly relevant to the theme of this book. One was the conscious effort to prepare professional officers to deal with political, economic, and other considerations beyond conventional military affairs. This is now reflected at all levels of military education. The other development concerned the relationship of military education to the larger problem of unification of the armed forces. It involved the concept that military educational programs, commencing with the academies and extending up through the senior schools, should be so designed and integrated as to contribute to common attitudes and understanding among Army, Navy, and Air officers.

[5] Commander T. A. Brown, "ANSCOL at the Naval War College," *United States Naval Institute Proceedings,* March 1946; W. T. Turner, "The Army-Navy Staff College," *American Foreign Service Journal,* March 1945, pp. 20–21.

CHAPTER SIX

UNDERGRADUATE MILITARY EDUCATION

IN THE POSTWAR DECADE

As the end of the war approached, responsible military agencies began to consider postwar educational requirements in the light of wartime experiences, and to make appropriate plans for the future. They wished not only to restore the regular schools on a peacetime basis, but to redesign these schools and to provide new ones in which to apply the lessons learned in the war. Among other things, they favored preparation for a broader range of military responsibilities. Forces generated outside of the military circle also influenced these plans. The war had caused many people to think seriously about the role of the military and the education of career officers. It moved professional military men out of the shadows of relative obscurity in American society and politics into the center of the stage. Millions of people were thrown into intimate association with them, either as bearers of arms themselves, as temporary government administrators, or as industrialists, college administrators, journalists, labor leaders, clergymen, and others doing business of one sort or another with the Army and the Navy. Among those brought into government service were a large number of highly qualified individuals, including such men as Henry Stimson, Frank Knox, John McCloy, James Forrestal, Ferdinand Eberstadt, and Robert Patterson, who concerned themselves with problems of the military services, including military education.

Organized planning for postwar military education was initiated as early as 1944. It reached a climax in the twelve months commencing with the victory in Europe in the spring of 1945. The basic pattern of military education prevailing today took shape by the end of 1946, although changes have been made since that time.

Further changes may be expected to take place constantly, since this is a field that must adjust to new circumstances and requirements.

The planning process was initiated and carried forward separately by the Army, Navy, and Army Air Forces (after 1947, the separate Air Force). At the joint level, plans were formulated by direction of the Joint Chiefs of Staff. Procedurally it was handled by a series of *ad hoc* boards and committees. Among the broad range of topics that were reviewed, we shall examine here two areas of special concern in this book. The first of these, the education of candidates for careers as regular commissioned officers, is the subject of this chapter. The second, the advanced education of officers at various stages of their professional careers, is considered in chapters seven and eight.

The Academies Reconsidered

West Point and Annapolis are among the most firmly established institutions in American society, deeply rooted in history, reinforced by colorful tradition and custom, and supported by an intensely loyal body of graduates. One would not expect that they could be easily changed. That the question of their role and purpose was opened at all was due largely to creation of a third service, the Air Force. Once the question of armed forces unification was raised, the door was open to related inquiries. Should there be three separate academies or should they be combined into a single military school? Should there be any academies or should prospective regular officers receive part or all of their undergraduate education at civilian institutions? Some individuals—and these were mostly outside of the professional military circle—entertained some doubt concerning West Point and Annapolis. They argued that too many academy graduates went on playing the Army-Navy game throughout life, suggesting that the long-established traditions and customs of the two institutions created attitudes and encouraged behavior that obstructed full and effective interservice cooperation. They proposed that unification of the armed forces should include the undergraduate education of future officers as well as high level organizational arrangements. Others declared that West Point and Annapolis were too narrowly

106

based upon scientific and military subjects and that teaching methods were too rigid.

During the winter and spring of 1943–1944 the notion that the first two years of instruction at the military academies might be offered in a single institution, to provide a common approach and point of view, and possibly to reduce costs, circulated in Washington. For example, Secretary of the Navy Frank Knox in March 1943 named a board, headed by Rear Admiral William Pye, the same officer who had served on the educational review board of 1919, to make a comprehensive study of the entire field of Naval education. The board was instructed to explore among other matters "the question of carrying on preliminary education in established colleges rather than at the Naval Academy," and to consider "the relative merit, advantages, and disadvantages of a single institution for preliminary training of war officers—Army, Navy, and Air—followed by extensive specialized training in the assigned branch." The board rejected both of these propositions in no uncertain terms, devoting a major part of its report of over 100 pages to justification of an enlarged four year Naval Academy. It reasoned that while any one of many technical schools and colleges could provide a proper scholastic education, "none . . . can provide the equivalent training, discipline, and indoctrination and character building." Indoctrination, it contended, is effective in proportion to the earliness of the age at which it starts and the length of time it continues.

As for sending prospective officers of all services to a common academy for the first two years, the board admitted that the idea had "popular appeal" but argued that it had several very definite disadvantages. A combined academy would be too large. Much of the program of the first two years had to be geared to the unique needs of each service. The case for a common basic program was "based upon a misconception of the course as a purely educational rather than a functional educational and training course," and upon the failure "to realize that divergent paths after college tend to divergent interests and points of view and that it is these interests and points of view . . . that lead to differences of opinion and so-called service rivalries." The board declared that "no effective coordination is possible except through mutual understanding which can only begin when each individual concerned is well indoctrinated in the ways and methods of his own branch." [1] Undoubtedly these sentiments received widespread support within the Navy as a whole.

The situation within the Army was similar. A few high-ranking officers did indicate that they might favor change in the organization of the Military Academy.[2] But at no time did the Army propose the establishment of a single service academy, or basic alterations in the program at West Point. The Army position actually was fixed by decisions reached at West Point toward the close of the war. In mid-1944 the superintendent appointed a special committee to consider the postwar curriculum. Its report was approved by West Point authorities in August 1945. The committee stated that among its "basic assumptions" were the premises that the mission of the Military Academy would remain "unchanged," and that the program of instruction, which had been condensed to three years during the war, would return to a four year basis.[3] A special board of consultants, headed by President Karl Compton of the Massachusetts Institute of Technology, endorsed wholeheartedly the principle that West Point should be a four year undergraduate institution.

A few months later Major General Maxwell Taylor, then superintendent of the Military Academy, told a Congressional committee that "no one who has been closely connected with or in a position of responsibility in connection with West Point" has favored making the Military Academy into a two year postgraduate school for cadets who had graduated from a unified service academy or a civilian institution. He stated that "we must have these young men in their formative years if we are to implant the principles in them which we try to implant." [4]

1 *Report of the Board to Study the Methods of Educating Naval Officers*, appointed 3 March 1944, typescript, dated July 1944, in Naval War College Library. Proposals for change in the academy were still offered, however. The so-called Jacobs-Barker plan providing for two years of NROTC followed by three years at the Naval Academy was under consideration in the summer of 1945. See *Memorandum from the Holloway Board to the Secretary of the Navy, Study of Proper Form, System, and Method of Instruction of United States Naval Officers of the Post War United States Navy*, 15 September 1945.

2 See for example, the off-the-cuff testimony of General Brehon Somervell, House of Representatives, 78th Congress, 2d Session, Select Committee on Postwar Military Policy, *Hearings*, 1944, pp. 112, 117.

3 *Post War Curriculum at the U.S. Military Academy*, West Point, 1945, p. 10.

4 House of Representatives, 79th Congress, 2d Session, Subcommittee on Appropriations, *Hearings*, 27 May 1946, p. 619.

Within the Army Air Forces, however, there was a disposition to try something new. Air officers, as already suggested, had been somewhat critical of the educational systems of the other services. They were proudly unhampered by tradition. This situation was reflected in ideas about an air force academy.

The idea of a separate academy had been suggested as far back as 1918. But the first study of postwar education representing the Army Air Forces view, prepared in September 1944, linked the new academy with a "combined services academy." It proposed a common two year academic program in a single institution for cadets of all three services, followed by two years at West Point, Annapolis, or the new Air Force Academy. The memorandum stated that the combined academy was "strongly advocated as tending to bring about" a common standard of scholarship and discipline, common military vocabulary and grounding in the customs and traditions of all the military services, the early recognition of the importance of interservice teamwork in modern warfare, reduction of unhealthy rivalry and interservice friction, and the weeding out of the undesirable or the unsuited.[5]

The Army and the Navy continued to oppose proposals to require two years of education in either civilian institutions or a combined military academy before enrollment in the service academies. Yet they were faced with the fact that West Point and Annapolis were not large enough to produce sufficient numbers of officers, and that enlargement of these institutions was not feasible. The Navy's answer to this challenge was its now famous Holloway plan, devised by a board headed by Rear Admiral James L. Holloway, Jr., at that time assistant chief of the Bureau of Naval Personnel. The heart of the Holloway plan was the proposal to procure regular officers from the Naval ROTC programs in civilian colleges and universities, as well as from the Naval Academy. Students in the "regular" NROTC program would be selected on a competitive basis, prior to entering college. They would receive a stipend of $50 per month plus the cost of books, tuition, and laboratory fees. It was anticipated that junior officers drawn from this source would equal in number those who had graduated from the Naval Academy. After two or three years of duty NROTC

[5] Memorandum for the Chief of Staff, *System of Education for Career Air Force Officers*, 4 September 1944, in Air University files.

"regulars" who so desired and who were selected would have opportunity of making a career in the Navy; others would be commissioned in the Reserve. The Bureau of Naval Personnel calculated that this arrangement would provide an adequate number of junior officers on active duty at any one time; would reduce the proportion of such officers embarking on a permanent Naval career, thus lessening forced attrition of older officers under the promotion system; and also would create a continually replenished reservoir of well-prepared reserve officers. Legislation incorporating the NROTC provisions of the plan was passed by Congress and became law in August 1946.[6] Twenty-five additional units were established, bringing the total to 52. The first class of Holloway plan NROTC candidates was screened early in 1947, entered colleges and universities the following September, and was commissioned in the reserves in 1951. Thus the Navy moved promptly to secure adequate numbers of officers, and at the same time retain the essential character of the Naval Academy. It gave an ingenious answer to those who had felt that a civilian college education would produce a less narrowly technical and less authoritarian officer. Instead of giving the *individual* officer part of his education at a civilian school and another part at the Naval Academy, it decided to educate one part of its officer *corps* at civilian schools and another part at the Naval Academy. In other words, by broadening the base from which the entire body of Naval officers was recruited, it sought to meet the demands of its critics without altering the traditional role of Annapolis.[7]

The idea of some sort of change in the role of the academies was not eliminated, but the initiative for keeping it alive rested with civilian officials, including President Truman. James Forrestal indicated in his journal as early as July 30, 1945 that the President favored "a common basic and beginning education for

[6] Rear Admiral James L. Holloway, Jr., "The Holloway Plan—A Summary View and Commentary," *United States Naval Institute Proceedings*, November 1947, pp. 1293–1303. See also Bureau of Naval Personnel, *The Navy Plans the Peacetime Education of Naval Officers* (1946, no date specified).

[7] Changed circumstances have altered somewhat the Navy's purpose for the NROTC program. Because of the increased size of the Navy beyond levels anticipated in 1946, the Navy would like to secure a larger supply of career officers from among NROTC "regulars" than the approximately 10 percent who have requested transfer to permanent status.

110

all officers, Army, Navy, and Air Force, on the general thesis that modern war is a composite and not separate business. I told him that his views fitted in to a large extent with our own thinking on postwar education. . . . So far as West Point and Annapolis are concerned, he said he regarded them more or less as finishing schools . . . for . . . specialized training." [8] Neither the President nor any civilian official in the Pentagon, however, pressed for a change at this time.

The question of the academies was raised again in connection with the unification issue when Congress considered the national security act of 1947. During hearings by the House Committee on Expenditures in the Executive Department, several members expressed dissatisfaction with arrangements at West Point and Annapolis, suggesting that they obstructed complete interservice cooperation and provided unnecessary duplication. Of particular interest was the testimony of Secretary of War Patterson and Chief of Staff Eisenhower. Secretary Patterson responded that "a good deal can be said for the view that . . . there would be value in giving the men from [West Point and Annapolis] a year at the other institution," but that this could not be accomplished within the four year program because "the people in charge of the curricula . . . think they have all they can do . . . to cover the ground they think they have to cover." Patterson declared that he personally did not see any pressing need for an air force academy.

General Eisenhower made a spirited declaration supporting greater cooperative effort between West Point and Annapolis. "It is very difficult," he testified, "when you have kept services apart and you wait until men are over 30 before they begin to meet and know each other . . . to develop the kind of team play that applies on one of the Knute Rockne football teams. What we must do is promote and adopt every method that gets us all together from the time we are kids." He went on to say: "If I had my way, . . . I would trade classes between Annapolis and West Point and I would make every class going through Annapolis do

<hr />

[8] Walter Millis, ed., *Forrestal Diaries*, New York, 1951, pp. 88–89. For Mr. Truman's attitude on the broader question of armed forces unification see *Memoirs by Harry S. Truman*, Vol. Two: *Years of Trial and Hope, 1946–1952*, New York, 1956, pp. 46f.

a year at West Point, and do the same for West Point through Annapolis." At a later point in his testimony he added: "It isn't a case of a cadet coming to Annapolis and learning so very much about the sea, or vice versa, but they will learn to be friends and they will learn that the other fellow does not wear horns and a tail, and that is what we are trying to promote early in the lives of these people who are all trying to work for their country and maintain security." But then General Eisenhower proceeded to explain: "When you get a new idea in this world, then the technicians and all the administrators go to work, and on this one [Admiral Nimitz, chief of Naval operations, and I] decided we were licked temporarily, but I don't believe we are licked permanently."

Before this same House committee, General Spaatz, commanding general of the Air Forces, was questioned about an air force academy. He responded that "there had been some talk about the necessity for a third academy . . . ," and added his personal view that "if such an academy were established, . . . it should be an Air Academy." But he went on to say that there would be no need for this, if the Air Force could get sufficient officers from West Point and Annapolis.[9]

In retrospect, these reservations about the need for an air force academy and indeed about the entire system of separate academies appear to be no more than scattered expressions of doubt. Yet they prompted Army and Naval authorities to restate their determination to retain West Point and Annapolis in their present forms. Their case rested principally upon two points. First, that the academies, by exemplifying the ideals of the services, set standards for other service personnel—a standard not only for professional competence but of personal character and of loyalty to service and country. And second, that other systems of preliminary education might not motivate young men to seek permanent careers in the services. In contrast the academies were "known quantities," having the proved capacity to inspire large numbers of graduates to become career officers.[10]

[9] House of Representatives, 80th Congress, 1st Session, Committee on Expenditures in the Executive Department, *Hearings on HR 2319*, April–July 1947, pp. 55, 71, 157, 299–310, 332–333, 343–344.

[10] See for example the case for the Naval Academy in Admiral Holloway's article in the *Naval Institute Proceedings* for November 1947, *op.cit.;* Admiral Holloway

Plans for an Air Force Academy

In the face of this reasoning, and with no evidence that the Army was prepared to support radical changes in West Point, ideas about a combined service school began to appear increasingly utopian. By this time, moreover, the Air Force had been established as an independent service, and this situation stimulated hopes for a separate air force academy. An officer who served in personnel planning in Air Force headquarters during this period reported to us that although consideration was still given to several alternative possibilities, "everyone knew that the final recommendation would be for a regular air force academy."

It is not surprising that the Air Force wanted its own academy. Air officers, at last possessed of their own separate service, naturally looked to an academy as a further symbol of their independence. Moreover, the Air Force required a permanent and adequate source of regular officer personnel. It felt that it could not count on West Point and Annapolis for this purpose since the Army and Navy declared that they required the full output of the two academies to fill their needs. The Navy particularly was reluctant to let Annapolis graduates volunteer for the Air Force. It had its own air arm to staff. This was a time when relations between the Navy and Air Force were severely strained. In 1949 arrangements were made whereby up to 40 percent of the graduating class at West Point and 7 percent at Annapolis could volunteer for transfer to the Air Force. Some consideration was given to the possibility of enlarging West Point and Annapolis to satisfy the needs of all three services, but this solution was ruled out because of the limitations imposed by the physical sites of these academies, and because of the high cost involved. Thus both the Army and Navy looked with favor upon the creation of an air force academy.

Active planning for an academy by the Air Force was initiated shortly after the establishment of the Air Force as a separate service in September 1947. The following month, in response to a

---

later elaborated on this theme by stating that only highly motivated men would elect a life featured by "long periods of separation from hearth and family . . . living in restricted space afloat, eternal vigilance in the face of weather, and highly variable and dangerous operating conditions." *Statement of the Superintendent to the Board of Visitors, United States Naval Academy*, April 2, 1949.

request by Congressman Kilday of Texas for support of his bill for an academy at Randolph Field, the Air Training Command was directed to prepare a proposal, including flying training as an integral part of the curriculum. Although the Air Force did not initiate the Kilday bill, it turned to it as a means of securing a larger number of academy-trained officers.

The Air Force was unable to win the approval of the Truman administration for its plan for an academy of its own, however. For one thing, the President had no enthusiasm for a new, separate academy. The Bureau of the Budget also held things up. As early as 1944 the budget director, Harold Smith, had favored a combined services academy.[11] In June 1948 Acting Director Frank Pace, Jr. rejected the Air Force report favoring the Kilday bill and declined to support legislation in Congress. He stressed the desirability of an over-all study of the existing service academies as well as a thorough study of the functions, organization, size, and training program of the proposed air force academy, before undertaking the creation of a third institution. He also suggested the preparation of a single omnibus bill for all three academies. The opposition of the Budget Bureau to separate legislation for an air force academy continued for several years. At the same time, the proposal to draft a uniform legislative pattern for all of the academies in turn produced friction within the services because of the disinclination of West Point and Annapolis to risk the loss of certain favorable features of the existing patchwork of laws.

Acting in response to Mr. Pace's suggestion, Air Force headquarters turned to the Air University for a thorough study concerning a new academy. In August 1948 a preliminary conference of Air Force officers and civilian educators was held at Maxwell Field. This group recommended that the academy be an undergraduate institution with a five year course of instruction, the first two years of which should consist of subsidized education at selected civilian institutions, and that pilot training should not be included. The chief of staff, General Vandenberg, approved the recommendation that pilot training be excluded, but directed

---

[11] See his statement prepared for the House Select Committee on Post War Military Policy in *Hearings, op.cit.,* p. 303.

that plans be based upon a four year course. He rejected the recommendation that officer candidates first attend civilian institutions because he felt that this training would vary too much, that the cadets would be less amenable to the disciplinary training essential to any military organization, and that there would be no initial motivation for a service career.

To carry out its planning mission, the Air University set up an Air Force Academy Planning Board composed of 23 officers. The board undertook a comprehensive and detailed study of its assignment, including extensive studies of West Point and Annapolis and numerous civilian institutions. It consulted over 60 civilian educators, many of whom came to Maxwell Field, and prepared detailed memoranda. The board also sought the ideas of officers in the three services through correspondence and interviews.[12]

By January 1949 this planning board had completed the draft of a detailed study. This called for a four year air force academy, with an enrollment of 2,500 cadets and a faculty of approximately 260. The selection and admission of cadets would be basically similar to procedures at West Point and Annapolis, and the organization of the cadets for military training and indoctrination also would be similar. Flight training, as directed by the chief of staff, would be postponed until after graduation on the grounds that its inclusion would interfere with the basic educational preparation of the cadets.

The board's report justified the establishment of an air force academy on the grounds that the Air Force was "the only branch of the nation's armed services lacking a center for the education of its future leaders in the intricacies of its own particular field." It pointed out that the Air Force faced a serious problem due to the fact that the educational prerequisites for commissioning had to be lowered during and following the war in order to secure the necessary number of officers, and that consequently the number of officers without a college education was disproportionately large. It declared that the supply of regular Air Force officers from West Point and Annapolis, provided by agreement with the Army

---

[12] This group was headed by Lieutenant Colonel (now Colonel) A. E. Boudreau, whose association with the planning project continued throughout its history. He became the first assistant dean of the faculty of the new academy.

and Navy, and from the aviation cadet program, the Air Force ROTC, and officer candidate school fell 50 percent short of the requirement.

The board rejected two alternative solutions. It stated that procurement of larger numbers of graduates from West Point and Annapolis was not feasible. It turned down the suggestion that the education of future Air Force officers could be given as effectively and economically at selected civilian colleges and universities. These institutions, the board declared, do not grant a degree on the basis of courses of study needed by future air officers. "More important to the Air Force, civilian colleges are unprepared to accept the responsibility of weeding out the students lacking the traits of character, qualities of leadership, and amenability to discipline that are essential to an efficient officer corps. Furthermore, civilian colleges, with their diversified interests, are unprepared to face the problem of instilling in segments of their student bodies, the enthusiasms for a career in the military services and establish the basic principle on which the desired background may be built. By placing students in the military environment of an academy devoted to a single aim and objective, the maximum training may be given in discipline and leadership and those lacking the requisite traits and abilities can be eliminated." [13]

Accordingly, the mission of the academy would be to provide an assured and constant source of approximately 50 percent of the annual regular officer replacement requirements; to provide these officer replacements with the requisite educational background essential to career service in the Air Force; and to provide a nucleus around which an adequate officer corps may be built in time of war or national emergency. This study included detailed plans for the curriculum, including descriptions of separate courses for a four year program. It stated that the curriculum was designed "to provide such a program of education as would enable every Air Force officer, regardless of his specialty, to represent the Air Force advantageously in any educated group, at home or abroad, socially or officially." The study explained that the underlying concept was that a "major purpose of education is not only to educate the air cadet, but to develop in him deeply-rooted hab-

[13] Air Force Academy Planning Board, *A Plan for an Air Force Academy* (three volumes), Headquarters, Air University, January 1949, Vol. I, pp. 3-6.

its of learning, an unswerving sense of honesty, and a definite and constructive loyalty to his country and to the Air Force. This will give the Air Force an officer corps that will always be culturally up-to-date and ever on the frontiers of knowledge and thought, thereby providing far-sighted leadership in the furtherance of our national security."

The planning board's final report, consisting of three bound volumes of detailed plans and course outlines, was ready by January 1949. But at this point further progress toward the establishment of an air force academy was delayed temporarily by events brewing in a wholly different quarter. As a part of its investigation of the executive branch of the government in 1948, the first Hoover commission established a task force on national security organization, headed by Ferdinand Eberstadt. This group, among other things, looked into military education and recommended to the commission that "efforts be made throughout the entire educational process to instill a stronger sense of interservice unity." With respect to an air force academy, it pointed out that creation of such an institution would "fix for an indefinite future an important element in the pattern of military officer education." Accordingly it proposed that a thorough examination be made of "possible means of securing a period of joint education and training at the undergraduate level for prospective officers of the Army, Navy, Air Force, and Marine Corps, as well as a survey of possible alternatives to the establishment of an air academy." [14]

The Service Academy Board

Although the Hoover commission itself made no comment one way or the other upon this recommendation, the task force report contributed directly to the sort of thorough evaluation of the service academies that the Bureau of the Budget had wanted. On March 14, 1949, shortly after he had submitted his letter of resignation and two weeks before he actually left office, Secretary of Defense Forrestal established the Service Academy Board, "to recommend that general system of basic education which . . . is

[14] *Task Force Report on National Security Organization* (Appendix G), prepared for the Commission on the Organization of the Executive Branch of the Government, January 1949, pp. 17–18, 82–84.

best adapted to provide all three services with a sufficient number of young men qualified to meet the needs of the regular armed services."

The creation of the Service Academy Board was part of the broad review of interservice problems that culminated in enactment of amendments to the national security act in August 1949. In January Secretary Forrestal had called General Eisenhower back to Washington from Columbia University to advise him on reorganization plans and related matters.[15] Eisenhower drafted the terms of reference of the board, and served as its vice chairman. The board was headed by Robert L. Stearns, president of the University of Colorado, and included four other civilian educators, all of whom already were familiar with the problems of military education from previous experience. The three service representatives were Major General Bryant E. Moore, superintendent of the Military Academy, Rear Admiral James L. Holloway, Jr., former superintendent of the Naval Academy and author of the Holloway Plan for Naval officer education, and Major General David M. Schlatter, former deputy commandant of the Air University.[16]

In the terms of reference of the board, Secretary Forrestal stated that a decision already had been made in the Department of Defense to support legislation authorizing the establishment of the Air Force Academy, "since there can be no question concerning the need for an expansion in the capacity of the present academy system and since West Point and Annapolis cannot for physical reasons be expanded substantially beyond their present size." [17] But he added that "this legislation [would leave] unanswered many fundamental questions concerning the kind of basic education which career officers of the three services should receive and the role of the three academies in providing it." Mr. Forrestal suggested that although the board should give full recognition to the fine traditions and splendid contributions to military leadership made by the existing service academies, it should not allow

[15] Walter Millis, ed., *The Forrestal Diaries*, pp. 540, 547.

[16] Service Academy Board, *A Report and Recommendation to the Secretary of Defense,* Washington, January 1950.

[17] The Department of Defense announcement of the appointment of the board also contained the information that the department would support legislation for the Air Force Academy. *New York Times,* March 6, 1949.

the distinction of the service rendered by these institutions in any way to interfere with its freedom of recommending changes in their roles. He requested the board to consider "the role of the three government academies and the relationship which should exist between them," and to make a preliminary report on this issue by April 1 so that appropriate provisions could be incorporated in the proposed legislation authorizing the third academy. He also asked it to consider the "desirable percentage of governmental academy graduates in the regular officer corps."

The board turned promptly to its task and in a first report, submitted in April 1949, recommended that an air force academy be established without delay. It based its conclusion both on a general defense of the academy system and on an examination of the particular difficulties faced by the Air Force in recruiting career officers. The academies were justified on the same grounds advanced earlier by Admiral Holloway, now a member of the board. The report contended: "They set a pattern for reaching . . . the highest professional standards," and they secure "an early devotion to a military career." Moreover, "It seems unlikely that the excellence achieved in the ROTC programs would be maintained without this benchmark of comparison." It was also concluded that the four year pattern was highly appropriate. The board felt that "approximately one half of the career officers" of all services should be graduates of such academies. It then noted that only one tenth of the Air Force's officers were academy graduates, and that this figure could not be increased to the preferred ratio "through any desirable expansion of the present service academies." Next the board stated, with only General Eisenhower withholding his concurrence, that a separate air force academy should be established *even if* it were possible to expand West Point and Annapolis to meet the needs of the Air Force.

How did the board reach this decision? We have learned from several members that all of the civilian members were predisposed to recommend the establishment of a combined services academy for officer candidates of all three services, followed by attendance at West Point, Annapolis, or the new air force academy, but that they all turned around 180 degrees when they gave serious study to the issue. They have suggested that General Eisenhower, who was serving in a civilian capacity as a university president, experienced the same change of mind. The three military members from the very outset firmly urged the continuation of the two academies as they were and the establishment of a third institution for the new sister service.

By the time this preliminary recommendation favoring the early establishment of an air force academy had been made, Louis Johnson had succeeded James Forrestal as secretary of defense. He found the recommendation contrary to his own views. Unlike his predecessor, he believed that unification of the services could be imposed by direction. Moreover, he was convinced that inter-service rivalries could be traced in considerable degree to the academies. So he held up the legislation for the academy and in May directed the three service secretaries and the Joint Chiefs of Staff to reply to his suggestion that "one of the principal means of accomplishing unification lies in revising the basic education and training of officers at the service academies." He explained his own preference for a common, basic education for all men at the same school, followed by specialization at separate schools or by specialization in some particular area common to all the serv-ices, such as procurement, intelligence, or industrial mobiliza-tion.[18]

Secretary Johnson's position created genuine alarm among many officers in the Pentagon and at West Point and Annapolis. During the summer of 1949 all forces were mobilized to justify the present role of the academies. At the Pentagon, in response to Secretary Johnson's request, the Joint Chiefs of Staff prepared a highly comprehensive and forceful memorandum on behalf of the traditional system of education.[19] Five alternative plans were considered *and rejected.* This report was transmitted to Secretary Johnson in August 1949 *through* the three civilian secretaries, each of whom indicated agreement with its conclusions. At the Pentagon, in other words, Secretary Johnson was faced with a united opposition.

During this summer the Service Academy Board buckled down to its long-term job. In June it had created panels or task forces

[18] Memorandum from the secretary of defense to the secretaries of the Army, Navy, and Air Force and to the Joint Chiefs of Staff, 13 May 1949.

[19] The full memorandum, transmitted August 9, 1949, is reproduced in Service Academy Board, *A Report and Recommendation to the Secretary of Defense,* January 1950, Appendix B. It was based on the work of an *ad hoc* JCS committee, com-posed of Admiral Fechteler, USN, General Edwards, USAF, and General Brooks, USA.

of experts in six areas: science and engineering, social sciences, language and area studies, teaching and testing methods, physical education, and military education. Interim reports were submitted in August; and three of the panels came to the same conclusion as the Joint Chiefs of Staff. The engineering and science panel commended the academy system for developing a sense of obligation and warned against trifling with a great national asset. The panel on teaching and testing methods denied that service rivalries originated at West Point and Annapolis. The panel on military education, with only Admiral Raymond A. Spruance (Ret.) dissenting, stated that the "present system of proven value should not be discarded for a new untried system." All three panels reiterated their conclusions in final reports, submitted in November 1949. On this occasion they were joined by the panel on social sciences, which argued that service needs were sufficiently distinctive to warrant separate schools. With such views from its own consultants, the great majority of whom were civilian educators of considerable stature in their respective fields, and with the Joint Chiefs and service secretaries already on record, it was inevitable that the Service Academy Board would reject decisively the suggestions of the secretary of defense and all other proposals for fundamental change in the academies. The board submitted its final report in December 1949. It endorsed "the integrity and the service identity" of West Point and Annapolis, and recommended that a parallel air force academy be created. In defending its recommendation the board analyzed four other alternatives and pronounced them inadequate.

Establishment of the Air Force Academy

The Air Force, anticipating that the final report of the Service Academy Board would be as favorable as its first recommendation, had in the meantime speeded up plans for the establishment of its academy. Activity took place on several fronts. In November 1949 Secretary of the Air Force Symington appointed a board, headed by General Spaatz, to recommend a site for the new school. By the following autumn, after preliminary surveys of 354 sites and visits to those considered best, the board recommended a final list of seven possibilities. In December 1949 Lieutenant General Hubert R. Harmon, an officer with a long interest in educational matters, was appointed to the new office of special assistant to the chief of staff for air force academy matters, in the Pentagon. Assisted by a staff of two or three officers from the Maxwell planning group, General Harmon was responsible, as a part time duty, for promotion of the subject within the Department of the Air Force, the Department of Defense, and the government at large. Across the Potomac, at Bolling Field, a new planning group was constituted, with the mission of continuing curriculum planning and related matters. It was anticipated that these officers would serve on the first faculty of the academy, which would be started on an interim basis in a short time.

During the following stage of development the planning group evolved an expanded philosophy of the academy program. Without rejecting the ideal of the broad general education built into the curriculum by the Maxwell Field planners with the encouragement of civilian consultants, the Bolling group now placed emphasis upon the unique mission of the school as a source of *Air Force* officers. It was felt that the Air Force could not justify the establishment of another academy before the Congress unless it could demonstrate that no other school was doing what was required. Thus, while time to be devoted to the social sciences was increased, greater attention was given to those aspects of the program that were designed to develop a professional sense of "airmanship" and to make the potential officer air-minded. Upon orders of Secretary Symington, the decision to delay flight training until after graduation was reversed, and plans were made for the inclusion of a limited pilot training program. It was reasoned that every graduate of the Air Force Academy, while not necessarily committed to further training as a pilot, should at least go as far as observer training so that he would have sufficient comprehension of the requirements and processes of flight. Secretary Symington's decision, which was supported by the top Air Force officers, was made after he had learned that Congressman Vinson, the most influential member of Congress on matters relating to military affairs, felt that an air force academy could not be justified unless it included plans for flight training.[20]

As a result of this study, detailed plans for the academy were

[20] William Y. Smith, Captain, USAF, *The Air Academy: The Growth of an Idea,* unpublished seminar paper, Harvard University, Summer 1953, pp. 3–31.

soon available. If given authorization, and the necessary funds, the Air Force could have activated an interim academy on short notice. But in spite of the positive and emphatic endorsement by the Service Academy Board, further delay was encountered. The report of the board, though submitted at the close of 1949, was not finally approved by Secretary Johnson until the summer of 1950. Although he endorsed the report, the secretary of defense remained unsympathetic to the creation of an air force academy. Undoubtedly estimates that the cost of construction would reach $150 million or more influenced this attitude. Soon the Korean crisis pushed the project into the background. Each year the Department of Defense asked Congress to authorize the academy, but Congress failed to act. The delay appears to have been caused by various factors in addition to cost. The Budget Bureau's demand for an omnibus academy bill and other attempts by this agency to coordinate legislative proposals dealing with academy and ROTC matters met with stiff opposition from the Army and Navy, which wished to avoid raising the issue of changes at West Point and Annapolis. In Congress, conflict over the location of the air force academy loomed ominously in the background. Moreover the lingering controversy between the Navy and Air Force over roles and missions, revealed anew in the public display of acrimony during the hearings on the B-36 bomber in 1949, probably stimulated further caution in the executive branch and Congress on this far-reaching proposal. Likewise, the shocking news in August 1951 that approximately 90 cadets, including a large number of football players, had been dismissed from the Military Academy for violation of the honor code hurt the cause of an air force academy as well as that of West Point. President Truman, for one, was deeply disturbed by this affair and seriously considered appointing a Presidential commission to evaluate the whole question of the academies and of the proper education of career officers in a democratic society.[21] Thus the climate was not yet favorable to action. The Bolling planning group was dissolved and the affairs of the proposed academy were left in the hands of two or three officers in General Harmon's Pentagon office.

In spite of the delay, the Air Force was even more determined to secure its academy. From 1950 on, Congress annually increased

21 *New York Times,* August 11, 1951.

the authorized strength of the Air Force. As new units were activated, new bases brought into operation, and other programs accelerated, the demand for regular Air Force career officers became
more acute. During the Korean conflict the Air Force had been
obliged to recall many world war II fliers, and the experience was
not an altogether happy one for either these officers or the Air
Force. New arrangements were made to secure up to 25 percent
of each graduating class at West Point and Annapolis on a voluntary basis, but this left the Air Force far short of its requirements.[22] Moreover both the Army and Navy favored an air force
academy, to eliminate this demand upon their own limited supply
of academy-trained regulars. Consequently a renewed effort was
made to secure approval. When General Harmon reached retirement age in February 1953, he was immediately recalled to active
duty to continue for an additional six months as special assistant
on air force academy matters so that he could participate in the
further development of plans.

Following the change of administration in March 1953, the prospects for an academy picked up quickly. The Eisenhower administration's "new look" placed even greater emphasis upon air
power. For a time the new secretary of the Air Force, Mr. Talbot,
questioned proposals for an interim academy and for preliminary
land surveys as excessive in cost. Also John A. Hannah, on leave
from the presidency of Michigan State University as assistant secretary of defense for manpower and personnel, was lukewarm to
the measure. Even after reading the Stearns report he felt that
civilian colleges could meet the educational needs of the services
by providing "a desirable variety of background, training and
experience, and often a high degree of specialization." But in
the course of time, according to his own testimony, Dr. Hannah
became "convinced of the wisdom of establishing an air force
academy, believing it to be necessary from the standpoint of national defense and wholly desirable from an educational point
of view." [23]

Once approval was secured within the Department of Defense,

[22] Air Force officers also were assigned to the faculties and staffs at West Point and
Annapolis on a proportional basis.

[23] House of Representatives, 83rd Congress, 2d Session, Committee on Armed
Services, *Hearings on HR 5337*, pp. 2975–2985; Senate, Committee on Armed Services,
pp. 3–13. (January 13, February 18, 1954.)

the way was clear to proceed. On May 21 Secretary Talbot reported that President Eisenhower gave the project his "enthusiastic" support. Subsequently the President stated that he had believed that the Air Force should have an academy once it had been proved that West Point and Annapolis could not be enlarged sufficiently.[24] On that same day, May 21, the chairman of the House Armed Services Committee introduced a bill prepared by the Air Force and the Department of Defense. General Harmon was again recalled to active duty in November, after only a few weeks of inactive status, and final plans were made for Congressional approval.

The academy bill moved along fairly rapidly. Short hearings were held before the Armed Services Committees in January and February 1954. Dr. Hannah stated frankly that he had changed his mind. He explained, "Before I came to this post I weighed West Point and Annapolis solely on the basis of educational grounds." That, he now felt, had been "a mistake." For, "While there are some things they may not do as well as our good civilian institutions . . . they do one thing much better and that is they do instill in their students . . . a loyalty to the service, a loyalty to the government, an appreciation for ethics and integrity to a degree beyond what we do at our civilian institutions."

A few members of the House committee questioned whether Dr. Hannah's second thoughts had been as sober as his first. Representative Bennett still felt that civilian education would be more desirable and that the development of loyalty and integrity could be taken care of at advanced military schools. Representative Durham asked why, if the academies developed such strong career motivation, did so many of their graduates resign. Representative Hardy asked whether both West Point and an Air Force Academy would be required in an age of guided missiles and unpiloted aircraft. Despite such statements, the committee approved the bill without a dissenting vote. The House then voted 329 to 36 in its favor, after a small economy-minded group that expressed concern over the cost had failed in an effort to recommit.

The legislation cleared the Senate with similar ease. Only Senator Gore spoke in opposition. He wanted Congress to create an air academy in which all air training—for the Navy, Marines, and

[24] *New York Times*, May 22, 1953, January 13, 1954.

Air Force—would be consolidated; and he felt that this should be but the first step toward creation of one unified Defense Academy for all services. He argued that Congress, instead of coming to grips with the problem of unified training, was giving the Air Force a school simply because the other services had theirs. He stated, "We are in an age in which aerodynamics, hydrogen weapons, and atomic weapons will some day force unification. This bill flies in the teeth of unification." Senator Saltonstall, chairman of the Armed Services Committee, admitted that Senator Gore had raised a fundamental question as to "the whole basic foundation of the educational system of the military." But, he said, "I think the system which the President and the present Secretary of Defense favor is a better system. There will be three football games instead of two football games (Laughter)." [25] The Senate, upon the recommendation of the Committee on Armed Services, amended the bill to permit up to 12.5 percent of the graduating class of each of the three academies to volunteer for another military service, including the Marine Corps. Annapolis graduates entering the Marine Corps would not be included in the Naval Academy quota. The committee report declared that this arrangement "would contribute to both the efficiency and unification of the services in the interests of the national defense." [26] The arrangement would go into effect upon the graduation of the first Air Force Academy class, at which time the present agreement whereby 25 percent of the Annapolis and West Point graduates may enter the Air Force is expected to terminate.

The bill then passed by voice vote. Minor difficulties were encountered in conference, but the bill was signed into law by President Eisenhower on April 1, 1954. In its final form the act authorized an expenditure of $126 million for construction of the academy, of which one million was for the purpose of modifying facilities on an existing Air Force base as a temporary site.

Passage of this legislation by the Congress was facilitated by the manner in which the question of the location of the new school was handled. Following Congressman Kilday's 1947 bill providing for an academy at Randolph Field, in his home state of Texas,

25 83rd Congress, 2d Session, *Congressional Record*, Vol. 100, Part 2, March 8, 1954, pp. 2796–2808.

26 Senate, 83rd Congress, 2d Session, Committee on Armed Services, *Report No. 1041, Providing for the Establishment of an Air Force Academy*, March 3, 1954.

more than 70 bills naming locations in 20 different states had been introduced. The Air Force's 1954 bill simply directed the secretary of the Air Force to determine the location, but authorized him to establish a commission to advise him in making the selection. This provision was amended by the Senate to require the secretary to accept the unanimous decision of the commission, but to permit him to choose between three recommended sites in the event the recommendation was not unanimous. As events turned out, the commission was unable to reach unanimous agreement, and Secretary Talbot designated a site at Colorado Springs, Colorado, probably thereby selecting a location that had been preferred by the Air Force for some time.

The Air Force Academy was activated officially at its temporary site, Lowry Air Force Base, Denver, on August 15, 1954. President Eisenhower designated his West Point classmate General Harmon the first superintendent. Plans were announced at this time for the opening of the academy with a single first year class of 300 cadets on July 1, 1955. Each succeeding entering class would be limited to this size until the permanent site was fully occupied. Then regular classes of 625 would be admitted.

The three academies, of course, are not the only source of military officers. In the period since world war II and particularly since the Korean conflict, the ROTC programs have played a more significant role than formerly in undergraduate military education. While they are still identified by the term "reserve," they now constitute the principal source of junior officers for all three services. The operation of the selective service system usually necessitates that ROTC students, who are deferred while in college, must go on active duty upon graduation. The Navy, with its Holloway Plan, and the Air Force, following changes instituted in 1952, now would like to procure up to 50 percent of their career officers from their ROTC programs. The ROTC units still operate under the reserve provisions of the national defense act of 1916, however. In chapter twelve we examine certain features of the ROTC programs.

Thus the organizational pattern of undergraduate preparation for a military career in the last decade represents no basic change from the prewar situation. Although various schemes were put forth at the end of the war for the integration of the two military academies, at least for the first two years, or for attendance at civilian institutions prior to more specialized work at the academies, none of these materialized. Rather the academies were continued as before as four year undergraduate institutions, and a third academy was added by the Air Force. With the extension and strengthening of the ROTC programs, civilian colleges and universities were now called upon to play a larger role in the education of active duty officers, but, as before the war, the greater proportion of these officers will not make a career of the military service.

CHAPTER SEVEN

POSTWAR PLANS FOR ADVANCED

MILITARY EDUCATION

CONCURRENT with developments concerning the service academies, described in the last chapter, the armed services also formulated plans to strengthen educational opportunities for career officers at higher levels.

Service Plans

The Army Air Forces was the first to initiate serious study of this matter. Suggestions for a separate three level school system for air officers had been made within the Air Corps as early as 1940. Wartime experiences and growing dissatisfaction with existing Army schools further convinced the AAF that it needed its own comprehensive educational program. In January 1944, as part of the planning for the organization and composition of postwar air forces, the AAF Training Command prepared a study on education and training requirements. This was based on the assumption that the armed services would be reorganized into a single department composed of three autonomous, coequal services, and that the air arm would have complete responsibility for training its own personnel. It recommended an integrated school system, starting with a two year combined services academy, enrolling candidates for commissions in all three services, followed by a two year air force academy, three air force schools at progressively higher levels, various technical courses for specialists, and finally a "combined services war college" at the highest level. In September 1944 these features were included in a more elaborate plan prepared by the assistant chief of the Air Forces staff for operations, commitments, and requirements, and submitted by the commanding general of the Air Forces to the War Department. Under this plan the highest air force school, termed the "Air College," would be the equivalent of the Army Command and General Staff School. The War Department was urged to establish three additional schools related to joint employment of all arms and services. These would be, first, a joint war college, enrolling carefully selected officers from the three services with 15 years of service, secondly, a new Industrial College at the same level, enrolling selected officers who would not attend the war college, and thirdly, an Army-Navy-Air Staff College, to prepare officers for duty on joint staffs at the highest levels.[1] The Army-Navy Staff College, which had been operating for more than a year when this report was submitted, already had set a precedent for joint institutions of this sort.

The following month the AAF submitted to the War Department a revised plan for an integrated school system, incorporated into a single command organization to be called the Army Air Forces University. This would include basic and advanced tactical schools, a command and staff school, a school of technology, and an air college. It was stated that the university would be "similar to a civilian university, in containing several distinct schools and in providing progressive stages of instruction commensurate with the student's experience, ability, and length of service." The AAF plan emphasized the need to control the flow of officers through these schools at appropriate stages in their career development. The War Department approved this plan, and the AAF school was activated in November 1946. The following March it was designated the Air University.[2]

In the Navy, plans for a regular educational program for officers also were taking shape. The Pye board, as indicated in the preceding chapter, was appointed by Secretary Knox to make a comprehensive study of the entire field of Naval education. Like its predecessor in 1919, the Knox-King-Pye board, this group recommended that the Navy operate a more highly developed school system, providing educational experience at regular intervals in

[1] Memorandum for the Chief of Staff, 4 September 1944.
[2] James C. Shelburne, *Factors Leading to the Establishment of the Air University*, doctoral dissertation, University of Chicago, 1953.

the officer's career. Specifically, the board recommended that the General Line School, the Command and Staff Course, and the Naval War College be enlarged, and that attendance at these schools play a greater part in each officer's career. All officers should attend the General Line School after 7 to 11 years of commissioned service. The purpose of the General Line School should be to prepare the officer for duty as head of a department on board ship or of an administrative unit on shore, and as a commanding officer of a small ship or aviation unit. The board recommended that 50 percent of all officers of the rank of lieutenant commander attend the Command and Staff Course, to be conducted at the Naval War College. Likewise, at least half of the officers reaching the grade of commander should attend the regular course at the college, in preparation for duty as commanding officers of capital ships, commanders of groups of small ships or aircraft, or as chiefs of staff. The board also proposed an advanced course at the Naval War College, for a select group of senior officers immediately prior to assignment to important commands in the fleet. The final recommendation is of particular interest in the context of this book. Going beyond regular Naval education, and citing the need for appreciation of the relations of national policy, international policy, and military force, the Pye board proposed the creation of a College of National Defense, enrolling students from the War Department, the Departments of State, Commerce, and the Treasury, and committees of Congress, as well as from the Department of the Navy.[3]

Joint Plans

No action was taken on the Pye board's recommendations while the war continued. But in the meantime plans were taking shape in the other services and at the joint level. As these plans progressed they inevitably became associated with the unification issue—that is, the larger problem of the organization of the armed services. Discussions of unification had been initiated as early as the 1920's and the question had been under periodic review by the War and Navy Departments since 1941, with the Army more

---

[3] *Report of the Board to Study the Methods of Educating Naval Officers,* appointed 3 March 1944 (Pye report).

or less favoring a single military establishment and the Navy hold-ing back.[4] In April 1944 the Joint Chiefs had established a Special Committee for Reorganization of National Defense, headed by Admiral James O. Richardson, USN (Ret.), and composed of rep-resentatives of the Army, Navy, and Army Air Forces. The com-mittee spent a full year in extensive study, involving visits to all the major commanders and their staffs in the European and Pa-cific theaters of operation. At the suggestion of Lieutenant Gen-eral John DeWitt, commandant of the Army-Navy Staff College, it gave some consideration to problems of military education. Its report, which was submitted in April 1945, included comment on military education. With the exception of the chairman, the com-mittee unanimously favored a single department of defense. The majority report placed heavy emphasis upon the necessity for close teamwork between the Army and Navy, and declared that following the reorganization of the military establishment "there must follow joint education and training of the armed forces aimed to develop in all ranks and ratings a knowledge and under-standing of the capabilities and limitations of each other, with-out which no form of organization can be effective." It declared that without exception the senior officers who testified before it "placed great emphasis on this point." Accordingly it urged that joint education and training be provided at the junior, inter-mediate, and advanced levels in the officer's career.[5]

Following receipt of the Richardson report the deputies of the Joint Staff delegated to General DeWitt and his staff at the Army-Navy Staff College the responsibility of drawing up a plan on postwar joint education. The directive to General DeWitt as-sumed that after the war the Army and Navy would be reorgan-ized into a single department, or, if that were not accomplished, the Joint Chiefs or a similar agency would continue to coordinate their activities. The Army-Navy Staff College responded in June

[4] See Lawrence J. Legere, Jr. (Major, Infantry, USA), *Unification of the Armed Forces*, doctoral dissertation, Harvard University, 1950; also Ray S. Cline and Maurice Matloff, "Development of War Department Views on Unification," *Military Affairs*, Summer 1949, pp. 65–74.

[5] Report of the Joint Chiefs of Staff Special Committee for Reorganization of Na-tional Defense, in United States Senate, 79th Congress, 1st Session, Committee on Military Affairs, *Hearings on Department of Armed Forces and Department of Mili-tary Security*, October–December 1945, p. 411.

1945. Its paper was further developed by the Joint Secretariat and approved by the Joint Chiefs the same month, as the general plan for postwar joint education of the armed forces. This was a comprehensive document, reflecting the thinking of many individuals in both services, as expressed, for example, in testimony to the Richardson board, and formulated in the educational plans of the separate services. Because it was to have an important bearing on the pattern for the establishment of the postwar education, it is reviewed here in some detail.[6]

The plan first outlined the basic considerations underlying the recommendations. It declared that the war had demonstrated the need for "common indoctrination, mutual understanding, and good will between components of the armed forces. These are best developed by close association in planning, training, and education." While declaring that the first consideration remained the "production of competent ground, sea, and air force officers," it endorsed the Richardson committee recommendations that joint education and training should be provided at the junior, intermediate, and high levels. It stated that the war also demonstrated that logistics and operations are inseparable and that the logistic problems involved in joint operations should be emphasized in joint education. The plan declared that "Joint education on the highest level must provide a study of the related interests and activities of the other government departments and agencies which contribute to the war effort," and pointed out the need to prepare military officers and representatives of the Department of State for the important function of coordinating national policies with the activities of the armed forces.

To accomplish these objectives the Joint Chiefs proposed a far-reaching program of joint military education commencing after 6 years of commissioned service with the assignment of substantial numbers of officers to courses of instruction in schools of a service other than their own. This would be continued after 12 years of service by cross-assignment of officers to the command and staff courses of the other services. At each of these two stages officers of the other services would constitute at least 30 percent of the en-

[6] Joint Chiefs of Staff, *General Plan for Postwar Joint Education of the Armed Forces,* 22 June 1945, mimeographed, in National War College Library.

rollments. At the command and staff level it was proposed that officers complete the course in their own service before being eligible to attend a school of another service.

At the highest level, the Joint Chiefs urged a joint approach, already demonstrated by ANSCOL and suggested as a permanent arrangement by Air Forces and Navy planners. They declared that "common indoctrination cannot be provided at a high level college conducted by any one component since each will be engaged primarily in its own field. No one component has paramount interest in joint action, and the doctrines and teachings of one component should not be permitted to predominate in the formulation of common doctrine. A joint institution in which all components have equal interest is essential." Accordingly they proposed the permanent establishment of an Army-Navy College, located in Washington and concerned with "a broad appreciation of the inter-relationship between national and international policy and the military force by which such policies are sustained and enforced." This institution should provide instruction in social, political, and economic affairs, and should maintain close liaison with the various departments of the government. The course of study, requiring one year, should embrace subjects of broad national interest related to the conduct of total war as well as the higher aspects of joint action. The Joint Chiefs also suggested that if and when the State Department established its own college for Foreign Service and departmental officers, this institution should be located in close proximity to the Army-Navy College, "preferably under the same roof," and that subjects common to both should be studied in common. They also proposed that the Industrial College be reestablished as a joint rather than an Army school. The responses to the Joint Chiefs' plan from the Army, Navy, and AAF all were favorable. All accepted the basic philosophy and recommendations.

Later Service Plans

After V-J Day the services stepped up planning for postwar education. The Navy, with the report of the Holloway board in September 1945, was the first to prepare a definite plan. As indicated above, this was concerned primarily with the undergraduate

134

level. But the board also considered the advanced education of commissioned officers. Reiterating firmly an established principle, the Holloway board declared that "the professional development of the naval officer consists first of experience at sea . . . ," but it also recommended that officers be given more opportunity for formal education. Specifically, it proposed that the General Line School be opened in temporary quarters pending the preparation of a permanent site at Monterey, California, and that the Command and Staff Course be located at the Naval War College, at Newport.[7] The focus in Navy planning remained sharply fixed upon the development of the officer's professional skills. The Holloway board did accept the recommendations of the Joint Chiefs for joint education, including the establishment of a joint war college at the highest level. But except for the relatively brief reference in the Pye report to a College of National Defense, neither the Pye nor the Holloway board had anything to say about the need to provide a wider understanding of developments outside of the conventional professional field, such as national and international affairs. In this respect the Navy presented a marked contrast to a growing trend in the Army.[8]

The Army's major postwar study of officer education was prepared between December 1945 and February 1946 by a special board headed by Lieutenant General Leonard T. Gerow, at the time commandant of the Command and General Staff School. This board was strongly influenced by the Joint Chiefs of Staff plan for joint education. It also was influenced by the current thinking in the Army that each officer should have a better understanding of all aspects of Army operations, beyond the scope of his own particular branch, and also that he should be better prepared in areas outside of conventional military affairs. Yet at the same time, it was impressed with the demands of technological de-

---

[7] *Memorandum to Secretary of the Navy, Study of the Proper Form, System, and Method of Instruction of United States Naval Officers of the Post War United States Navy,* 15 September 1945 (Holloway report).

[8] The Holloway report was the last general study of Naval education until the summer of 1956, when a committee headed by Rear Admirals Weakley and Daniel reviewed Naval officer graduate education. This committee was concerned, among other things, with the problem of adjusting increased demand for well-qualified officers with the limited availability of officers for assignment to educational programs. As this book goes to press, the report has not yet been approved by the chief of the Bureau of Naval Personnel and the secretary of the Navy.

velopments upon the officer, necessitating a more thorough knowledge of his own particular field of responsibility. It resolved this difficulty by proposing an elaboration of the educational opportunities within each of the three arms, the Ground, Air, and Service Forces, as well as a more highly integrated school system for the Army as a whole.

The basic plan was simple. In the Ground and Service Forces, the officer, after commissioning, should go to basic school in his branch, and subsequently, after several years in the field, to advanced branch school. Later he should attend the Ground College, or the Service College, depending upon his service arm. The former should provide an understanding of the Ground Forces as a whole, the employment of ground units on the division and corps levels, and the coordination of these units with air, naval, and service forces. The latter should perform the same function for the Service Forces, and should give instruction in budgeting, management, mobilization, and the organization of the War Department and other agencies of the government. These colleges would be at the level of the prewar Command and Staff School.

With respect to the Air Forces, the Gerow board in effect endorsed the plans that already had been established by the AAF. These provided for a separate school system for air officers parallel to the Army school system, organized within the Air University. An Air Tactical School, preparing officers for duty at the squadron level, would correspond to the advanced branch schools. There would also be an Air Command and General Staff School, and an Institute of Technology for specialized training. At the top would be an Air War College, corresponding to the proposed Ground and Service Colleges.

The Gerow board devoted considerable attention to joint military education, showing the impact of the war experience upon Army thinking. It recommended that the Command and Staff School at Leavenworth in effect be replaced by a joint Armed Forces College, and the Army War College by a joint National War College. The board proposed that subsequent to attendance at the Ground, Air, or the Service Forces College and duty in the field, the officer should be assigned to the Armed Forces College, which would be an extension of the wartime Army-Navy Staff

College. Here he would learn about the combined employment of air, ground, naval, and service forces.

At the highest educational level, the Gerow board elaborated upon the Joint Chiefs plan for joint education. It extended the number of proposed joint colleges from three to five, and grouped them together to form a National Security University. It declared: "Close and definite coordination is required on the highest military educational level. This should be accomplished by the establishment of a National Security University . . . [which] will be interested in all problems concerning the military, social, and economic resources and foreign policies of the nation that are related to national security. The scope of that interest will be limited only to the extent of military concern. . . . The purpose of the institution is to assure the development of officers capable of high command and staff duties in connection with prevention of war, preparation for and prosecution of war on a global scale, and the execution of the responsibilities of the Armed Forces subsequent to hostilities."

The board proposed that the university be composed of five colleges. These would be:

1. An administrative college, with the mission of providing joint instruction to insure proper allocation of manpower and efficient methods of administration and over-all management of military personnel and civilians under military control.

2. An intelligence college, to insure effective over-all organization and operation of intelligence and counterintelligence.

3. A national war college with the mission of providing instruction to insure the nationally efficient development, organization, and employment of armed forces and the utilization of the nation's resources to support those forces in the furtherance of national policy. The national war college would take over the mission assigned to the Army War College before the war. Accordingly the board recommended that the Army War College need not be reopened and its facilities should be made available to the National Security University.

4. An industrial college, to insure the most efficient mobilization and demobilization of our industrial resources and to study other nations' industrial capabilities for war.

5. A State Department college, to be closely coordinated with the four military colleges.[9]

One thing stands out clearly in these postwar plans—in the minds of those who drafted them, preparation for command in combat remained the basic purpose of military education. A later Army review board put this succinctly: "The objective of the Army school system," it declared in 1949, "can be stated concisely. It is to prepare an officer to perform effectively those duties to which he may reasonably expect to be assigned in war, with emphasis on the art of command."[10] The Navy's Pye board used a similar definition. The objective of Naval education, it declared, is "to obtain the best officer material, and to equip it by education and training for the most effective performance of its future duties, . . . and especially to produce an adequate number of highly selected officers capable of exercising high command in time of war, with skill, imagination, and determination. . . . All naval education and training should stress the development and practice of combat leadership."[11] These statements might suggest that the focus was entirely upon military matters. Actually the services, particularly the Army and the Army Air Forces, recognized at the close of the war in 1945 new and challenging responsibilities, adding unexpected dimensions to the traditional definition of military affairs. The significance and meaning of these responsibilities were being driven home to many previously unsuspecting officers in Germany, Japan, and elsewhere around the globe. Patently, these broad responsibilities called upon the services to do more than prepare their officers for combat. This situation was reflected in the various reports that we have reviewed in this chapter, particularly in comments on the need for better understanding of such areas as logistics, intelligence, personnel management, budgeting, communications skills, the operations of other government agencies, civil affairs, public relations, and international affairs. It was reflected also in the emphasis upon the

[9] Report of War Department Military Education Board on Educational System for Officers of the Army, Washington, April 1946 (Gerow report).

[10] Report of the Department of the Army Board on Educational System for Officers, 15 June 1949 (Eddy report).

[11] Report of the Board to Study the Methods of Educating Naval Officers (Pye report), op.cit.

development of executive talents, such as "initiative, resourcefulness, and mental capacity," "leadership and the power of decision," and "constructive thought to ensure constant appreciation of, and adjustment to, the trends which may affect warfare of the future." (These excerpts are from the Gerow report.) These demands posed new problems for military education in the postwar years.

Lastly, throughout these plans for postwar education there runs a persistent emphasis upon the need for greater understanding of joint operations and the capabilities and limitations of the other services. The joint approach in education found its most advanced expression in the plans for the National War College, the Industrial College, and the Armed Forces Staff College. The Joint Chiefs plan and the Gerow report also proposed that joint education below the senior levels be accomplished by the exchange of students among service schools. This arrangement was also satisfactory to the Navy. Air Forces officers were disposed to go further, as we have seen in their proposal for a combined services academy. The demand for an appreciation of joint operations, it should be noted, extended beyond the services themselves, to include other agencies of the government, as represented in the proposal for the National War College.

CHAPTER EIGHT

POSTWAR DEVELOPMENT OF THE SENIOR

JOINT AND SERVICE COLLEGES

IT HAS BEEN NOTED in previous chapters that the wartime experience impressed upon the armed services the importance of educational preparation for high level responsibilities involving non-military considerations, and also of preparation for joint military planning and operations. All three services officially endorsed these concepts. The National War College, the Industrial College of the Armed Forces, the Armed Forces Staff College (all joint institutions), and the Army, Naval, and Air War Colleges (service institutions) are now the principal military schools designed to accomplish these purposes. The story of the establishment of the joint institutions and of the evolutionary changes that have been made in the service institutions in recent years reflects the response of the armed services to the wide range of tasks that they are now being called upon to perform. It also casts some light on the progress of armed forces unification since 1947.

The National War College

Even before the Army's Gerow report was filed in February 1946, the Joint Chiefs initiated steps to transform the wartime Army-Navy Staff College into a permanent high level joint institution, as proposed in the Joint Chiefs plan for postwar joint education. Conversations with representatives of the Department of State resulted in agreement by State to participate in the joint institution rather than to establish a State Department college within the proposed National Security University. Plans were already well advanced within the State Department by this time for

140

its own Foreign Service Institute. On February 4, 1946 the War, Navy, and State Departments together announced the establishment of the National War College.[1] By this time General Eisenhower, Army chief of staff, had approved the Gerow report, recommending that the Army participate in the National War College and that the Army War College not be reopened. The scheme for a National Security University was not realized, but two of the proposed five units came into being, that is, the National War College and the Industrial College of the Armed Forces. The latter was established in April 1946 when the old Army Industrial College was reestablished as a joint school. The joint Administrative and Intelligence Colleges, as well as the Department of State College, were not established.

With the transformation of the Army-Navy Staff College into the National War College and the focus of the latter upon politico-military affairs, there remained need for another institution to fulfill the original mission of ANSCOL. This situation was foreseen by the Gerow board, which had recommended an Armed Forces College to prepare officers for joint staff assignments, as described above. Subsequently the Navy approved this recommendation, and in August 1946 the school, under the name Armed Forces Staff College, was established at Norfolk, Virginia. Thus the plans for joint military education culminated within one year after the war in the creation of three new joint institutions, the National War College, the Industrial College, and the Armed Forces Staff College.

At first the services regarded the National War College and the Industrial College as higher institutions than their own war colleges, with respect to both the course content and the experience levels of the students. The National War College was planned to stand at the top of professional military education, capping the educational experience of a relatively few carefully selected officers. It was to provide an understanding of the relationship of military factors to a broadening range of political, economic, social, and scientific affairs, both national and international. This purpose, moreover, was to be accomplished with a clear emphasis

[1] The text of the press release is given in *Department of State Bulletin,* 17 February 1946, p. 250. The evidence suggests that the approach to State was conducted orally with the secretary or assistant secretary for administration.

upon a joint approach. Subsequent events have resulted in the "up-grading" of the service war colleges so that they have been given equal status with the National War College.

Leadership in creation of the National War College rested with the Army, and primarily with General Dwight Eisenhower. As chief of staff, General Eisenhower converted the concept of the college into a going proposition, providing the vision, broadmindedness, and energy to get it underway. It was his suggestion that the Army make available its prize piece of real estate, the Army War College building in Washington. Army leaders generally were inclined toward a relatively advanced degree of armed forces unification, and thus toward joint officer education. The Army Air Forces also emphasized the importance of joint educational experience. It was favorably disposed toward unification, probably with the self-assurance that air power would play the dominant role in the integrated military establishment. The Navy on the other hand, while agreeing to the establishment of the National War College and providing the first commandant, Vice Admiral Harry W. Hill, was at most lukewarm in its feelings, as it had been at first when ANSCOL was proposed. True, the Navy Pye board had suggested a joint college, and the Eberstadt report on unification had proposed joint training. But this approach did not prevail throughout the Navy. In the nineteenth century the Navy, unlike the Army, had a more realistic understanding of the relationship of military power to diplomatic policy. But at the conclusion of world war II the Army had become even more deeply concerned with the growing intimacy of military and nonmilitary factors in national and international life. This difference, in part at least, reflected the different characteristics of the two services. In the nature of things, the Navy accomplishes its mission in peace and war "at a distance." That is, the Naval officer is at sea in his ship; he has fewer contacts outside of the regular line of Naval operations with problems ashore involving dealings with agencies of his own or foreign governments or dealings with civilian society. At the end of the war, in marked contrast to the Army, fewer Naval officers had been drawn into responsibilities outside of conventional professional fields. Whereas the Army during the immediate postwar period was deeply involved in the multitude of political, economic, and social problems arising out of its huge administrative responsibilities in Germany and Japan, the Navy had only modest experience along this line, except in the special case of the Pacific islands. Moreover the organization of the Navy Department, in which operations were headed up in the Office of the Chief of Naval Operations while the bureaus handled matters of procurement, finance, and so forth, traditionally had tended to detach the general line officer from experiences involving a "civilian" dimension. As we have seen in chapter one, it was not until the Navy became involved in the formulation of postwar policies as a consequence of its participation in the State-War-Navy Coordinating Committee that this situation began to change.

The first detailed plan for the National War College was contained in the Gerow report. The mission of the college would be "to provide instruction to insure the nationally efficient development, organization, and employment of armed forces and the utilization of the nation's resources to support these forces in the furtherance of national policy." It would prepare commanders and key staff officers for the highest echelons of the armed forces, qualify officers for participation in the formulation of national policy, and foster understanding and coordination between the armed forces and other agencies both government and civilian. The board anticipated that graduates "will exercise a great influence on the formulation of national and foreign policy in both peace and war." [2]

The idea of a joint college of this nature was not new. There was already the example of British experience. In 1927 similar considerations had led the British government, as a by-product of plans for a single Ministry of Defence, to establish the Imperial Defence College for "the training of a body of officers and civilian officials on the broadest aspects of imperial strategy." [3] As already noted in chapter four, a student committee at the Army War College as early as 1939 had recommended the establishment of a College of National Policy and Defense, drawing faculty and students from both the civil and military departments of the govern-

[2] *Report of War Department Military Education Board on Educational System for Officers of the Army,* Washington, April 1946 (Gerow report).

[3] T. S. Chegwidden, "The Imperial Defence College," *Public Administration,* Vol. 25 (1947), pp. 38–41.

ment to study problems of coordination between civil and military affairs.[4] Experience with the British during the war further stimulated the interest of American officers and civilian officials alike in the organizational arrangements of the British government for the formulation of national policies. Responsible leaders in the United States, like the British before them, linked an educational program common to all services and departments with consideration of permanent coordinating machinery. They concluded that while the separate services should continue to train officers in staff work and in the strategy, tactics, and organization of their own services, the interrelated nature of high level responsibility called for further preparation in broader problems of national security. The wartime Army-Navy Staff College had been a step in this direction.

The Gerow report and other statements defining the purpose of the National War College make it clear that the separate services anticipated that this institution would meet their requirements with respect to the preparation of officers for politico-military assignments at the highest levels. To a degree its output would be supplemented by the Industrial College of the Armed Forces, for it was planned that ICAF students would attend a considerable number of lectures on national and international affairs at the National War College. This was before the Truman Doctrine and Marshall Plan, the North Atlantic Treaty and the mutual defense assistance program, the Korean conflict, and the rapid defense build-up of 1950–1953. These subsequent events and other factors had a marked impact upon the educational programs of the separate services, and particularly upon their War Colleges. The result, as already suggested, was to alter the relationship between these service colleges and the National War College.

The Air War College

The change was first apparent at the Air War College. This institution, as it is presently situated in the Air Force educational system, is not the school that was projected by AAF planners in 1944–1945. At that time the Air War College was expected to

[4] Army War College, *Course 1938–1939, Analytical Studies*, Report of Committee No. 6, 24 February 1939, in Army War College archives.

concern itself almost exclusively with military problems directly related to the employment of large air units.[5] It would not devote much attention to national and international affairs, although it would not neglect these matters.[6] Two principal developments have taken place to alter this situation. In the first place, the Air War College has been elevated to a higher position in the educational system than was initially anticipated. Secondly, the curriculum has come more and more to include a broader focus upon all nonmilitary considerations, with increasing emphasis upon international relations and current world affairs.

These changes at the Air War College were part of the same process that caused the Air Force to alter its initial concept of a combined services academy in favor of a separate air force academy. After 1947 the Air Force was an independent service, proud of its position and motivated by strong convictions concerning the strategic employment of military forces. Increasingly it felt the need for officers qualified to represent the Air Force in negotiations with the other services. These and related considerations naturally led to an upgrading of its own senior educational institutions. At the same time similar changes were taking place at lower levels within the Air University, resulting in the strengthening of the Command and Staff School within an enlarged Air Command and Staff College.

The Army War College

Parallel forces were at work within the Army. In 1946 the Army deliberately had decided not to reopen its War College, and had turned over the building to the National War College. From the start the decision was questioned in the War Department. Some felt that the Command and General Staff School would be unable in the time allowed to cover adequately the full range of Army functions, particularly at the highest levels. Subsequent developments strengthened this conviction. Leavenworth found that to provide adequate instruction on functions at the War Department level, it was necessary to divide the class into four groups

[5] Report of AAF Educational Conference, Maxwell Field, 18–20 February 1946.
[6] Memorandum by Lieutenant General Muir Fairchild, 29 March 1946, Air University archives.

for the last 10 weeks of the 40 week course, giving each group instruction in only one of the four principal areas. This arrangement was regarded as unsatisfactory. Various solutions were proposed, including the establishment of a second, higher level institution at Leavenworth.[7] In August 1947 a War Department review board headed by Lieutenant General Wade Haislip looked into the Army school system. It concluded that a "gap exists in general staff instruction, except in the joint phases, at the highest War Department, theater, and zone of interior levels. . . . The present system does not provide adequate instruction for officers . . . at these higher levels." The board suggested that the gap "might best be closed by the establishment of an Army war college," and proposed that this matter be reconsidered.[8]

This recommendation was not followed immediately, however. It appears that the Army chief of staff, General Eisenhower, was not yet convinced of the need to reopen the college, nor was his successor, General Bradley. But in June 1949 a special board on the educational system for officers, headed by Lieutenant General Manton Eddy, commandant of the Command and Staff School, and consisting of the commandants of the other principal Army schools, strongly urged that the Army War College be reestablished. It is clear that the Eddy board was thinking in terms of filling the "gap" and not of adding new areas to the curricula of the Army schools. It endorsed the National War College, but pointed out that because of its mission the National War College had to concentrate on global strategy and related political and economic affairs, leaving insufficient time to teach to Army, Navy, and Air Force officers the details of their own services. The board declared that the Army officer, in view of this situation, should come to the National War College already knowing the capabilities and limitations of his own service, and its organization, administrative techniques, and strategic powers. Otherwise, he is not able to make his full contribution in the "common solution of military problems of national and international scope." The board concluded that the Army War College should be reestablished to provide integrated instruction for selected officers in

[7] *Survey of the Educational Program of Command and General Staff School,* 1947 (Henry report), in Command and General Staff College archives.
[8] *A Review of the Army School System,* Department of the Army, Office of the Assistant Chief of Staff, G-3, 25 August 1954.

the duties of commander and general staff officer above the field army and equivalent zone of interior activities.[9]

A decision finally was made in January 1950 by the Department of the Army to reopen the Army War College, and in August the first class convened at Leavenworth, where the college was located on a temporary basis. The following year it was relocated at its permanent home at Carlisle Barracks, Pennsylvania.

The reports of the Haislip and Eddy boards indicate that these groups did not anticipate that the Army War College would duplicate the program of the National War College. Within a relatively short time, however, the Army took steps that made at least some duplication of the program at the National War College inevitable. Only a few Army officers could attend the two highest joint schools, the National War College and the Industrial College, annually (about 30 to 35 each). This meant that many well-qualified officers would be unable to go beyond the Army War College. If the latter were regarded as a subordinate institution, this might reflect adversely upon such officers. The Department of the Army, in approving the Eddy report, stated that "attendance at either of these two institutions *ipso facto* will not be given more weight than attendance at the Army War College when selecting officers for promotion or high level positions." It also directed that greater emphasis would be placed on the joint aspects of all military operations at Army schools, "with due caution that courses currently given at the joint schools are not unduly paralleled or overlapped." [10] These actions suggest that even at this time it was recognized that the curriculum of the Army War College, since this would be the highest school for most officers, would have to go into some of the areas taken up at the National War College, even though the Army War College presumably was to prepare officers for duty primarily within the Department of the Army.

The first commandant of the Army War College, Lieutenant General Joseph Swing, was convinced that the curriculum should include a very considerable amount of instruction in political and economic affairs, of the sort developed at the National War

[9] *Report of the Department of the Army Board on Educational System for Officers,* Washington, 15 June 1949 (Eddy report).

[10] *Memorandum,* Modification of the Department of the Army Board on Educational System for Officers, 11 October 1949, in Command and Staff College archives.

College. A study made at the Army War College under his direction concluded that the Army required over 700 officers in the grade of colonel and above qualified for assignment to policy level positions. Although some doubters protested that the college had enough of a job to do in covering topics more directly connected with the operations of the Army ("closing the gap," to use the description of the Haislip and Eddy boards), it was decided in the Department of the Army that the college should go into national and international affairs. Accordingly the curriculum was devised so that about four of the nine months are devoted to this area of study.

Subsequently the statement of the mission and objectives of the college was revised, removing language that might have been given a restrictive interpretation. It was indicated that the college was concerned with the preparation of selected officers for duty at the highest levels to which they might be assigned in the Army, including high level joint positions. Also the chief of staff, General Collins, issued a circular in which he declared that any impression that Army officers, even though having graduated from the Army War College, must attend the National War College or the Industrial War College in order to gain maximum recognition in the Army, was "contrary to the approved position of the Army War College as the senior institution in the Army's educational system. . . . So far as the Department of the Army is concerned," General Collins said, "graduates of the National War College, the Industrial College of the Armed Forces, and the Army War College will receive equal consideration for high command and staff positions." [11]

The Naval War College

The change in the organization and content of instruction at the Naval War College has been even more striking than that at Maxwell Field and Carlisle Barracks. This story is complicated by the fact that the Naval War College has conducted concurrently at least three separate programs, each for a different group of students. Moreover, to further complicate the picture, there have

[11] Department of the Army, Circular No. 16, 3 March 1952.

been frequent changes in the composition of all of the courses and classes.

The Navy's Pye board in 1944 had recommended greater emphasis upon officer education, with enlargement of the regular course at the Naval War College. It recommended that at least 50 percent of all officers reaching the rank of commander should attend this course and that it should prepare officers for command of major ships, command of groups of smaller ships or aircraft, or as chiefs of staff of such units. The Pye board did not exclude some attention to nonmilitary matters, for it declared that the course should "ensure a knowledge of international relations, [and] international law," as well as strategy, tactics, and logistics, and familiarity with "the broad aspects and trends of history, particularly naval, military, and diplomatic history." But it felt that these nonmilitary subjects should receive subordinate consideration. They should be covered in greater detail, it suggested, at a proposed joint military-civilian College of National Defense.[12] This interpretation of the Naval War College's role and of its relationship to the joint war college prevailed when the institution was reestablished on a peacetime basis following the war. The Navy took the position that it should not be concerned with the provision of more than marginal educational opportunity for its officers in broad problems of national and international affairs, and that insofar as Naval officers received such opportunity, this should be as students at the National War College.[13]

The first postwar courses at the Naval War College were concerned for the most part with the development of the professional competence of officers in operational planning and the exercise of operational command. Initially, two courses were conducted, the senior and junior. These were almost identical, the principal difference being in the age and rank of the students. The senior course was composed of captains and commanders, the junior course of commanders and lieutenant commanders. In 1950, the junior course was redesignated the Command and Staff Course, and the similarity with the senior course ended. Henceforth it

[12] *Report of Board to Study the Methods of Educating Naval Officers,* 1944.
[13] See Rear Admiral James L. Holloway, Jr., "The Holloway Plan—A Summary View and Commentary," *United States Naval Institute Proceedings,* November 1947, pp. 1293–1303.

corresponded roughly with the Army's Command and General Staff School.

In 1947 a second senior course, in logistics, was undertaken at the Naval War College. This came about as a consequence of the belief within the Navy that wartime experience had demonstrated need for more systematic education in this field than previously had been available. During 1945 serious thought had been given to the concept of a separate Navy logistics school, but this approach was rejected in favor of a separate logistics course at the Naval War College. The purpose of the course was to prepare trained logisticians for logistic operations billets. But the decision to establish the course at the Naval War College rather than as a separate school resulted from the conviction that logistics could not properly be considered in a vacuum, divorced from other functions, especially command. As initially organized, the logistics course was concerned principally with such matters as base operations, mobile logistic support afloat, personnel and matériel distribution and control, and transportation.

The Navy's preoccupation with professional Naval affairs at the Naval War College appears to have been derived from a variety of factors. It was certainly in keeping with the traditional Navy emphasis upon the command function, and the concept that the purpose of its educational system was to prepare an officer for his next higher level of responsibilities. At the college this meant preparation for command of larger vessels and groups of vessels or aircraft, and related staff duty. Following the war responsible Naval officers were impressed by the tremendously increased technological complexity of naval operations, which greatly increased the range of understanding required of the commander. Most officers below the senior levels had spent the greater part of the war years in a relatively narrow area of operations, that is, they had gained experience with a particular type of sea or air operation or some supporting activity. But the Navy, more than the other services, is organized on a task force basis, involving coordinated use of its different components, including land forces— the Marines—as well as sea and air forces. Command of such coordinated forces requires an appreciation of the capabilities and limitations of each of the elements. Consequently the year of study at the War College was looked upon as the first opportunity for most officers to gain an appreciation of the Navy outside of their own areas of specialization, the first opportunity, for example, for a submariner to learn about the methods and problems of naval aviation. Even the most superficial treatment of the wide scope and rich variety of activities within the Navy, it was felt, left precious little time to consider political, economic, and social problems. This situation was compounded by the fact that very few Naval officers before and during the war had had the opportunity for formal educational experience after commissioning, except in certain technical fields. Whereas officers coming up to the comparable level in the Army would have attended the Command and Staff School, this usually was not so in the Navy. Thus it was felt that the senior courses at the Naval War College had to be utilized to make up this deficiency.

Lastly it appears that the Navy attitude toward officer education in the interlude before the Korean war reflected its approach to the issue of unification. Throughout this sometimes bitter controversy the Navy was on the defensive, fighting to retain control of those functions deemed essential to the accomplishment of its mission, sensitive to preservation of its prerogatives and its traditional values. While endorsing plans for joint education, the Navy did not share the enthusiasm of the Army for the new joint schools. It never contemplated doing away with its Naval War College. It felt that the Navy's schools had a big enough job to do preparing officers for responsibilities within the Naval service. It was uncertain about assignment of its officers to positions on joint agencies above the operational level. Accordingly it did not recognize a need to provide educational preparation for such assignments. While the Navy went along with plans for the National War College, many officers felt that that institution gave the Naval officer information on nonmilitary subjects that he did not need to know and too little information on professional subjects that he did need to know. In view of the operational responsibilities of the Navy it is easy to see why this attitude prevailed.

Forces were soon set in motion, however, that were to modify this traditional concept of Naval education in general and the program of the Naval War College in particular. The effect of these was first felt in the logistics course. Almost as soon as it was established, this course began to move away from the initial emphasis upon the production of logisticians. For reasons of administrative facility the new course was scheduled concurrently with the regular course, now identified as the strategy and tactics course, and students in the logistics course participated in some of its program. Likewise strategy and tactics students partook of some of the instruction in logistics. Thus there began a process of integration of the two courses. The transition was due to several factors. There was a growing conviction at the college that logistics could not be learned apart from the larger context of naval operations. It was felt that all Naval officers should have an understanding of the significance of the logistical dimension in planning and conducting naval operations. And lastly, the course in logistics was not popular. The subject matter was technical, detailed, and dry; moreover, most Naval officers did not wish to be tagged as specialists in logistics.

By 1950 the emphasis in the logistics course had shifted from the training of logisticians to the preparation of officers for command and staff positions, but with a greater appreciation of the logistics factor. Accordingly the integration of logistics and strategy was stressed and the name of the course was changed to strategy and logistics. At the same time greater attention was given to the treatment of logistics in the strategy and tactics course. Consequently the common core of the two courses increased annually. By 1953 it amounted to about 80 percent of each course. At that time it was decided to merge the two into a single course in naval warfare. In the process of putting the two together, however, it was found that the remaining logistics content in the strategy and logistics course was too technical and too detailed for the single course. Accordingly it was redesigned, to put the logistics content into proper relationship to the command function. Thus the original purpose in establishing the logistics course at the college was abandoned in favor of a broader approach to logistics in which it is no longer regarded as a special function, but rather a dimension of all naval activity with which *all* officers must be cognizant. Moreover, the instruction is no longer directed toward what the Navy calls "consumer logistics," that is, the actual handling and utilization of matériel and personnel, but goes beyond these matters to consider the larger, more complex problems of "producer logistics," and of the relationship of supply to questions of economic capabilities, political implications, and over-all national strategy.

While these changes were taking place in the logistics course, others were altering the strategy and tactics course. The first postwar president, Admiral Raymond Spruance, rejected a narrow interpretation of the college's role. During his administration, consideration of political and economic factors was incidental to naval areas of study, but it was by no means neglected. Lecturers at this time included professional historians and social scientists, and a number of representatives of the Department of State. Beginning in 1946 the student body included one Foreign Service officer, and subsequently a Foreign Service officer was appointed to the staff.

By 1953–1954 the common core of the two courses (strategy and tactics, strategy and logistics) had come to include considerable attention to questions beyond the basic professional level, dealing with broader problems relating to sea power and to over-all national and military strategy. For the most part these topics were not organized into separate units of the curriculum, but were scattered throughout the year, in the form of lectures on such matters as American foreign policy, the Soviet Union, and current national or international affairs. Several days each were devoted to international law, preserving the customary Naval War College interest in this field, and to military government. In the spring an entire week was devoted to the formulation of global strategy for the United States, during which reserve officers and civilian guests of the college participated in the program. As long as the college felt that it had to provide systematic coverage of basic professional subjects, however, its consideration of these broader topics perforce was limited.

Increasingly there was pressure to alter this situation. The Navy found itself pulled more and more into responsibilities far beyond conventional naval affairs. This process was accelerated with passage of the national security act of 1947, bringing about an increased number of arrangements requiring the assignment of Naval officers to joint agencies. It was stimulated further by ratification of the North Atlantic Treaty and the erection of NATO and other interallied regional groupings. The United States Navy assumed major responsibilities for the leadership of the NATO commands in the Mediterranean and Atlantic. It felt a critical increase in the demand for more highly qualified commanders, planners, and other staff officers to represent it in joint, interdepartmental, and interallied committees, boards, headquarters, and other agencies. The Navy had come into this business reluctantly at first. But once involved it realized that it must do a job, or suffer the consequences by failing to justify itself in a highly competitive arena. More than the other services, the Navy felt a greater gap between responsibilities of this type and its regular operations. For officers trained for command at sea, assignment to a joint or interdepartmental committee offered novel features for which they not infrequently felt inadequately prepared.

Although no officers suggested that there was any less need for professional naval competence, a feeling spread that perhaps the Navy should devote more attention to the preparation of officers for these unconventional assignments. Admiral Robert Carney, chief of Naval operations, 1953–1955, for example, declared that there was need for greater knowledge of international affairs within the Navy.[14] Both Admiral Carney and his chief of personnel, Admiral Holloway, stressed the importance of assigning the best-qualified officers to the Joint Staff and comparable activities, and also the value of the senior schools. It is interesting that these trends, which constituted something of a deviation from the traditional Navy position, should originate at such high levels. These are precisely the men who are exposed to the difficult, perplexing, and sometimes frustrating problems of policy formulation and administration that do not arise aboard ship. By virtue of their daily duties they appreciated the importance of high level staff organization, manned by well-qualified personnel.

The Naval War College felt these pressures to broaden its program. They were reinforced by members of the faculty who had come from Washington or overseas assignments with the feeling that they should have been better prepared for these jobs. In response to this situation the then president of the college, Vice Admiral Richard Conolly, in 1953 personally negotiated authority from Admiral Carney and Admiral Holloway to establish a two year course of study. Admiral Conolly, like Admiral Carney, had commanded United States Naval forces in the Mediterranean.

14 *New York Times,* July 26, 1953.

He also had been naval advisor to the Council of Foreign Ministers and the European Advisory Commission. He argued that the demands for basic professional education on one hand, and of broader preparation in national strategy on the other, rendered it impossible to accomplish the mission of the college in less time. Accordingly he proposed that the strategy and tactics and strategy and logistics courses be merged into a single first year course in naval warfare and that a second year course dealing with higher level strategy be established. Recognizing that the Bureau of Naval Personnel would not increase the total number of officer students assigned to the college, he suggested that the total remain the same, and that some officers attend only the first year, some only the second, and some both. Those taking only the first year course would be lower ranking commanders. At least some of them might return for the second year at a later date. Those who would attend only the second year course would be high-ranking captains, presumably those who would be selected for advancement to flag rank fairly soon. The group attending both years consecutively would be composed of younger captains and older commanders.[15]

Admiral Conolly proposed that the first year course remain essentially the same as the combined strategy and tactics and strategy and logistics courses, with some consideration of international relations, foreign policy, and national strategy. The emphasis would remain at the basic professional level. The second year course would include more detailed study of the political, economic, and military aspects of national strategy, the formulation of national policies, foreign areas, and current international affairs. It would devote major consideration to war planning, and to military command and decision. In the thinking of Admiral Conolly and others responsible for planning the two year sequence, this would be a temporary arrangement. They believed that by increasing enrollments in the Command and Staff Course, the need to provide instruction at the basic professional level in a senior course at the college would decrease, and that accordingly in about

[15] Undoubtedly prestige was a factor also in Admiral Conolly's plans. A study about this time indicated that no members of the Annapolis classes of 1922 to 1925 inclusive who had attended the Naval War College had attained flag rank in contrast to 36 who had attended the National War College. See also Captain Grenville A. Moore, "The Naval War College Takes a New Look at Its Courses," *United States Naval Institute Proceedings,* December 1955, pp. 68–73.

ten years the first year course in naval warfare could be terminated. The college could then devote all of its energies to a single senior course preparing officers for the highest responsibilities offered within the Navy.

Thus the interpretation of the role of the Naval War College and of its relationship to the National War College that had been proclaimed in 1946 (although perhaps not fully accepted in spirit) was, by 1953, officially rejected. Now the Naval War College was declared to be on a par with the National War College. As at the Army War College, the change in the concept of the role of the Naval War College was accompanied by corresponding changes in the curriculum. Although the Navy felt that it could not decrease instruction in naval subjects, by use of the device of the partial two year program it was able to introduce a new course of study in which considerable attention was devoted to national and international affairs and other strategic level factors. In both courses, to be sure, the college still declares that the purpose is the preparation of officers for higher command. The changes that have taken place do not represent any deviation from that well-established purpose, but rather a different interpretation of the nature and scope of the functions and responsibilities of higher command.

The Industrial College

These developments relating to the National War College and the service War Colleges were paralleled by others affecting the purpose and status of the Industrial College of the Armed Forces. The old Army Industrial College was reconstituted as an inter-service school in April 1946. In September 1948 it was placed under the supervision of the Joint Chiefs of Staff. The mission of the school and its place within the armed forces remained a subject of frequent debate.

Several major issues were involved. First, there was the question of how to modify the program of the school in the light of the lessons of world war II. Agreement was widespread that professional officers required an understanding of the supply factor that was considerably broader than any that had been imparted by the prewar Army Industrial College. Second, there was the question of how to convert the college from an Army enterprise into a joint institution. This also reflected wartime experience. And both issues, it should be noted, were similar to those that arose in connection with the creation of the National War College. In each case it was felt that career officers needed to be "sensitized" to areas of national policy of great concern to them and to the civilian leaders of the country. It was also felt that men drawn from different services, with different customs and interests, should be given a common educational experience.

The parallel extends to still another issue, namely how to sustain the status or prestige of the schools as the senior educational institutions of the armed forces. But here the problem of the Industrial College becomes more complicated than that of the National War College, for the Industrial College had to compete for prestige not simply with the service war colleges but with the National War College itself. The problem with which it grappled was not so much one that set one service against another, but rather one over which each service was divided internally. Planning and conducting combat operations had long been regarded as more "important" than *supporting* combat operations. Strategists and field commanders had long enjoyed greater prestige than supply officers. This was not an official doctrine but rather an implicit premise of military administration. On the other hand the supply function was of great importance in the scale of values of civilian industrialists and service secretaries. Inevitably they lent strong support to the Industrial College. This led to differences of view over the appropriate locus of administrative supervision over the college, and over the appropriate relationship between strategy and supply.

Pressure to reopen the Army Industrial College built up in 1943 as the Army developed demobilization plans. Even at that early date there was concern for the broader problem of educating officers in the supply field after the war. As in 1923, some Army officers suggested that industrial courses should be conducted at the Harvard Business School. But Under Secretary of War Robert Patterson vetoed this suggestion quite firmly. Instead he proposed reinstituting the Army Industrial College. Late in 1943 the War Department convened an *ad hoc* board, headed by Major General Oliver T. Echols, a graduate of the college, to advise in the matter. The board agreed with Patterson. It also proposed that the student body of the Industrial College should include civilian administrators and that the college should maintain a staff of research specialists, partly military, partly civilian. This latter point reflected the advice of Colonel Francis H. Miles, Jr., recorder of the board and prewar commandant of the Industrial College. He had made the same suggestion in 1939. Miles' influence was also apparent in two other recommendations made by the Echols board. One was that supervision over the college should be transferred to the General Staff. The other was that the commandant be of general officer grade. Both proposals were designed to increase the prestige of the school within the service. Miles told the board that it had had an "uphill fight" to obtain equal ranking with the Army War College.

The *ad hoc* board then proposed that its own membership should be broadened and that it should continue its study. The group was therefore reconstituted in January 1944. Its senior officer now became Lieutenant General DeWitt, commandant of the Army-Navy Staff College. Two Naval officers were added. Bernard Baruch and John Hancock provided civilian representation. At this time, also, the Industrial College was reopened on an interim basis to offer short courses on contract termination and surplus property disposal. For the first time, civilians were included in the student body.

With the passage of time and the broadening of the membership of the planning groups, the terms of reference of the problem began to expand. Military officers realized that the vast majority of men in uniform were in supply and administrative work, and that the success of combat plans frequently hinged on supply factors. Many of them also realized the profound effect that supply plans could have on the economic order of the nation. This was particularly clear to those who held key positions in the Army Service Forces—a great many of whom, incidentally, were graduates of the prewar Industrial College. No longer, they felt, was it enough to train officers merely in procurement problems and in the preparation of the mobilization plan itself. It was necessary to expose them to all aspects of war economy.

The terms of reference began to broaden in another sense also; that is, the problem began to be seen as an interservice rather than Army one. Even before the war the Industrial College had taken on some of the aspects of a joint school. Naval officers were now participating in planning the institution's future. Moreover, as 1944 went on, the Joint Chiefs of Staff became increasingly concerned with joint education, and suggestions began to be heard that an industrial college be considered one of the components of a larger system of joint education. A new planning group was therefore required, one on which the Navy would sit as a full partner rather than an invited guest. The secretaries of war and of the Navy each appointed an individual to work out a precept for a joint board to study the entire question. These individuals, Brigadier General Donald Armstrong and Rear Admiral Lewis Strauss, concluded that the military establishment had to lift its sights on the nature of education in the supply field. As a means to this end it was proposed that two entirely different types of courses be given. The first was a junior course for supply specialists, particularly procurement officers, which might be taken at a civilian university. The second, to be taken after a long interval of practical experience, was a senior course that marked a much greater departure from the prewar program of the Army Industrial College. It included the study of total requirements for global war and the human and material potential available, both here and overseas, to meet them. In suggesting such a division Armstrong drew heavily on recommendations made by Colonel Miles and his staff in 1939 and repeated by the Echols board in 1943.

Following the submission of this precept, the secretaries of war and of the Navy appointed a joint board, headed by John Hancock, to make more precise recommendations. In June 1945, at the first meeting of the board, General Armstrong stated that he assumed the postwar school would be a joint institution.[16] A week later the Joint Chiefs of Staff study of postwar education made the same recommendation. By December a Naval officer had been assigned to the school as assistant commandant; and in April 1946 the name was officially changed to Industrial College of the Armed Forces.

But while these steps were being taken, two other issues arose.

[16] The United States Joint Board on Postwar Joint Army and Navy Training in Industrial Mobilization consisted of four civilians and nine officers equally divided among the three services. It met in June, July, and October 1945 and submitted its report in February 1946.

One was the question of who should exercise staff supervision over the school. On this there was general agreement. The Hancock board, the Richardson committee of the Joint Chiefs of Staff, and the ANSCOL study of postwar education had all recommended that the Industrial College be under civilian supervision. The latter had stated that if a single defense department were created, the school should be controlled by the under secretary of defense. This agreement reflected the long-standing belief that military supply problems were of peculiarly great interest to the civilian leaders of the armed forces. It was at variance, however, with the suggestion of the Echols board a few years earlier.

The second issue, which was more troublesome, concerned the Navy's position toward the college. The Army had taken the lead in the reinstitution of the school, just as it had in the creation of the National War College. This was quite natural because it had managed the prewar Industrial College and because its Army Service Forces had had to cope with supply problems of extraordinary magnitude during the war. The Navy, as suggested earlier, was generally less enthusiastic about joint institutions at this point. Moreover, it had a particular problem in the case of the Industrial College because it made a much sharper distinction than the Army between "producer" and "consumer" logistics. The former, which involved contacts with civilian industry, was regarded as a field for officer specialists and for civilians. The latter, which involved distribution to the fleets, was regarded as a field for general line officers. It was considered to be a function of command that had to be closely associated with fleet operations in general. During the meetings of the Hancock board General Armstrong noted that the Navy was considering establishment of its own supply course at the Harvard Business School. He was delighted at this move because it was apparently intended that this would be a junior course for supply specialists, much like the program he had proposed in the precept for the Hancock board. He was greatly distressed, however, when the Navy reworked its plan and proposed instead to give a course in "consumer" logistics, and to give it at the Naval War College instead of at Harvard. The Industrial College course, under this arrangement, was to become a prerequisite for the Naval War College course, which to Armstrong seemed to reverse completely the status relationships he was striving to establish. The Navy, however, was merely following the recommendation that its own educational planners (the Pye board) had made the preceding year. The Pye board had noted that logistics had acquired "an importance out of all proportion to our prewar conception," and had proposed that the Naval War College provide adequate instruction in the subject. The acceptance of this proposal and the subsequent history of the logistics course at Newport have been discussed above.

The first regular postwar course of the Industrial College of the Armed Forces began in September 1946. The broadening of its mission was concealed by the retention of the word "Industrial" in its title. This was actually a misnomer, because the curriculum had been expanded to include study of the requirements of allies and of the civilian population, price control, shipping, manpower availability, foreign resources, economic warfare, research and development, and combined supply operations. When the full meaning of this new focus became clear, questions arose as to the appropriate relationship between the Industrial College and the National War College, and the Joint Chiefs of Staff began to have second thoughts on the question of who should supervise the institution. Both issues were soon intermingled with the darker question of the prestige of the school.

The national security act of 1947 placed the Joint Chiefs of Staff on a statutory basis and led to the development of a more highly organized Joint Staff. One component of the latter was the Joint Logistics Plans Group, which had a natural interest in the Industrial College. In 1948 the Joint Chiefs of Staff endorsed a proposal made by its own study group that the Industrial College come under its jurisdiction, as the National War College and the Armed Forces Staff College already were. But the national security act of 1947 had also opened up other alternatives to JCS supervision. One was supervision by the Munitions Board, an interservice agency within the National Military Establishment. Another was supervision by the National Security Resources Board, a Presidential level agency concerned with industrial mobilization. The latter suggested that the secretaries of war and of the Navy appoint an *ad hoc* committee to examine the problem. This committee consisted of the under secretaries of the Navy and the Air Force, the assistant secretary of the Army, the deputy commandant of

ICAF, and the deputy chairman of the Munitions Board, Lieutenant General Leroy Lutes.

In the debate that followed, the proponents of supervision by the JCS argued that logistics training ought to be more closely related to strategic training, and that if the Industrial College acquired a status under the JCS comparable to that of the National War College, its prestige would be raised. The proponents of civilian supervision argued that the Joint Chiefs would "downgrade" the school, would not require the services to assign a reasonable proportion of their ablest officers to it, and would generally treat it as a "stepchild." General Lutes, incidentally, argued this point most forcefully and if the Office of the Undersecretary of Defense had existed at that time it is quite possible that the Industrial College would have remained under civilian control. But this possibility did not exist. The alternative of control by the Munitions Board was opposed by officials at the Industrial College because they feared the school might degenerate into a mere training ground for a specific staff agency. Moreover, some of them felt that the school should be supervised in the same manner as the National War College. In May 1948, therefore, the *ad hoc* committee reluctantly recommended that jurisdiction be transferred to the JCS.[17] Defense Secretary Forrestal concurred and a charter was issued to the school by the JCS in September 1948—a charter placing it on precisely the same level as the National War College.

But this did not alter the *de facto* status of the institution. The commandants and deputy commandants of the Industrial College almost invariably were of lower rank than their counterparts at the National War College. Its students also tended to be relatively junior, and this, plus the fact that so many of them were supply specialists, meant that they made a much poorer showing on the promotion lists. Finally, its inferior physical facilities were a standing reminder of its actual place on the scale of values.

Doubts and misgivings over the prestige of the Industrial College increased in 1949. By this time Louis Johnson had replaced James Forrestal as secretary of defense. Johnson endorsed his predecessor's decision. But he also asked the Joint Chiefs of Staff to

[17] The suggestion was made at one point that this be for a trial period of one year, but the Joint Chiefs objected to such an arrangement.

obtain periodically the views of the Munitions Board on the "progress" of the Industrial College; and he conveyed to them his belief that the courses of the Industrial College and the National War College should be "further integrated."

This last point had been inserted at the specific request of authorities at the Industrial College. But it naturally commended itself to civilian secretaries. Many of them had concluded that it was the senior *line* officer rather than the supply specialist who most needed a knowledge of the economic aspects of national security. Johnson and others felt that the National War College curriculum devoted far too little attention to such matters. Suggestions were made that selected officers should be given the opportunity to attend both the National War College and the Industrial College, or that all graduates of the National War College should be required to take a summer course at the Industrial College after finishing their own program of study. In any event it was felt that the programs of the two schools should be tied together more closely.

These views were not received enthusiastically at the National War College. Its deputy commandant specifically objected to increasing the time devoted to logistics or to requiring students to take summer work at ICAF after completing their own course. But Secretary Johnson, together with General Lutes of the Munitions Board, continued to press the issue. In July 1949 Lutes proposed to the Joint Chiefs of Staff that the two schools be integrated within a single National Security University. The Joint Chiefs replied that any further integration beyond what was currently recommended by the commandants or what "may be recommended by them in the future" was not desirable. It was impossible, they argued, to educate every officer in all subjects in the limited time that the services could spare for schooling.

The concern of Johnson and Lutes did, however, lead to the appointment by the Industrial College and the National War College of committees to review the possibility of establishing closer relationships between the two schools. The committees noted that the schools had been physically proximate since 1946, when the Industrial College had moved from the Pentagon to Fort McNair. There was some interchange among the students on a social and recreational level. The schools exchanged syllabi and tried to coordinate starting and graduating dates. More important, Industrial College students attended about 70 percent of the National War College lectures. National War College students, on the other hand, attended relatively few ICAF lectures. The major change that grew out of these discussions was the addition to the program of each institution of a common problem in strategy and logistics. This made its appearance during the 1950 academic year. Briefly, it required students of the two schools to meet together in committees and to test the feasibility, from the supply standpoint, of a hypothetical war plan.

In the next few years, however, even these slight relationships grew more tenuous. Between 1950 and 1955 the number of National War College lectures attended by the Industrial College decreased from 125 to 91. In 1953, at the request of the War College, the common strategy-logistics problem was discontinued. Throughout this period the commandants of the Industrial College continued to be concerned with the prestige of the school; and on several occasions the plea for a National Security University was revived. The Joint Chiefs of Staff, however, continued to respond negatively to this latter suggestion.

Thus by 1953 these parallel developments—those on one hand affecting the relationship of the National War College to the service War Colleges, and those on the other hand affecting the status of the Industrial College—had created considerable apprehension at both of these institutions. In that year, acting upon the advice of his Board of Consultants, the commandant of the National War College, Lieutenant General Harold Craig, USAF, urged the Joint Chiefs to establish a board composed of distinguished individuals to review higher military education. At the same time the Joint Chiefs were aware of the demands of the Industrial College for an improved position. After some delay the chiefs finally approved the establishment of a review board. But instead of directing it to make an over-all investigation of higher military education, as had been hoped for by General Craig and the National War College consultants, they turned the recommendation around and asked the board to review only the National War College and the Industrial College. This board, headed by President James P. Baxter of Williams College, was established in April 1854 and reported the following January. Discussion of the deliberations and report of the Baxter board and of the broader question of the status of the joint colleges is reserved for a later chapter, following more detailed examination of their operations and of the operations of the service War Colleges.

PART THREE

UNDERGRADUATE EDUCATION: PREPARING

FOR A MILITARY CAREER

CHAPTER NINE

THE MISSION AND ORGANIZATION OF

THE SERVICE ACADEMIES

IT IS NOT the immediate purpose of the service academies to prepare officers for policy level positions in the government. Yet our study would be seriously incomplete without an analysis of these historic institutions. Though only a small fraction of all military officers are academy graduates, most academy graduates devote their careers to the military profession, while most nonacademy officers do not. In the Navy the percentage of academy graduates among regular officers is particularly high. It is lower in the Air Force than in the other two services only because the rapidly expanding Air Force had no academy of its own until 1955. All services hope to secure about 50 percent of their future regular officers from the academies. In all services, moreover, the percentage of academy graduates tends to increase as rank increases; it is highest among generals and admirals. Finally, we found a significant concentration of academy men in precisely those policy level positions with which this study is concerned.[1]

For many of these officers, especially those not eventually selected for a senior military college, the service academy provides the most complete nontechnical education that they will get during their careers. For all of them this experience comes at an age when they are still relatively impressionable. Even if this were not so, the academies would warrant close examination because

[1] For example, of the Pentagon officers who completed the questionnaire discussed in chapter two, and who held the grade of colonel or its equivalent, 58 percent were academy graduates. The breakdown by services was: Navy, 99 percent; Army, 67 percent; Air Force, 19 percent. The only non-Annapolis man among the Naval officers, appropriately enough, served in the Reserve Officers Branch in the Office of the Secretary of Defense.

they are peculiarly the repositories of service ethos. It is at their academies that the services define the ideals to which they expect their officers, from whatever source derived, to aspire. Here they formulate the standards of excellence suggested by their corporate experience. Here they confront the prospective martial leader with the great models of the past. Hopefully and prayerfully the desired characteristics of heart and mind are laid before young men, and every incentive and contrivance that can be imagined is employed to encourage them to follow.

West Point and Annapolis are national landmarks visited each year by countless Americans. They are provided with impressive, if sometimes overcrowded, physical structures. Bancroft Hall at the Naval Academy has been called the world's largest dormitory. The massive buildings that overlook the Hudson River at West Point rival those of any campus in the land. Both schools enjoy not merely the facilities customarily expected at great colleges, but also those specialized features necessary to accomplish their particular missions. The Military Academy holds field maneuvers at the West Point reservation at Camp Buckner. Though the Naval Academy lacks a modern airfield, it has access to seaplanes as well as to yawls, yachts, and smaller craft based on the Severn; warships are made available for summer training cruises. The new Air Force Academy, which will be located permanently near Colorado Springs, will be comparable to its sister institutions in all these respects. It has a magnificent natural setting on the eastern slope of the Rockies, with a fine climate and ample room for expansion. In the interim the Air Force Academy continues in temporary facilities at Lowry Air Force Base in Denver.[2]

Student bodies at the academies are comparable in size to those of many liberal arts colleges. West Point has about 2,500 cadets. The Air Force Academy will ultimately be of the same size but it plans to build up to full strength over a period of several years. The Naval Academy will have about 1,000 more students than the other two. The number of midshipmen at Annapolis has increased from 2,700 in 1946 to about 3,700. This reflects the desire of the Navy to draw a relatively large percentage of its career officers

[2] The Air Force Academy was only one year old at the time this book was completed. Our comments on it are based upon this single year, as well as upon such plans or trends as we have observed.

from Annapolis. It has also, one must add, placed a strain on the physical facilities at Annapolis.

Instructional staffs, exclusive of the many overhead or supporting personnel, number over 300 at West Point and well over 400 at Annapolis. The Air Force Academy is starting with a smaller number but this will expand as the size of the student body increases.

Mission

It is with these basic ingredients—physical facilities, students, and staff—that the service academies attempt to accomplish their missions. Precisely what those missions should be has long been a subject of discussion and argument in military circles. In essence the question has been whether the academies should equip men for the relatively specific duties that will confront them *soon* after graduation, or whether they should equip them for the broader responsibilities that may confront them *later* in their careers. Few thoughtful officers have fled to either extreme. But over the long sweep of history some have placed more emphasis on the desirability of a relatively technical program that would graduate trained junior officers; they have been more content to leave preparation for higher responsibilities to advanced military schools, self-education, or practical experience. Others have emphasized the desirability of a relatively general education that would serve as a foundation for an officer's long term career; they have been more content to leave preparation for the specific technical duties of a junior officer to on-the-job training or additional specialized training after graduation.

Needless to say, neither group has won a complete victory. Nor have the compromises reached been exactly the same in all services. The Navy states the official purpose of Annapolis to be the provision of "Graduates who are capable junior officers in whom have been developed the capacity and foundations for future development in mind and character, leading toward a readiness to assume the highest responsibilities of citizenship and Government." The Army omits the adjective "junior." It states: "The mission of the United States Military Academy is to instruct and train the Corps of Cadets so that each member will have the qualities and attributes essential to his progressive and continued development throughout a lifetime career as an officer of the Regular Army." The Air Force uses similar language. Each Air Force cadet should graduate "With the qualities of leadership and the knowledge required of an officer in the United States Air Force, and with a basis for continued development throughout a lifetime of service to his country, leading to readiness for responsibilities as a future air commander."

It is clear from these statements that all three academies hope to lay a foundation for the future growth of their graduates. It also appears that the Naval Academy's mission makes the most explicit reference to the preparation of students for the earlier phases of their careers.

The official missions do not specify any particular *kind* of career for which the academies are to develop men. They do not, for example, indicate that the goal is preparation of future staff officers, engineers, troop commanders, intelligence experts, or any other specific category of men. But it quickly becomes apparent, at least at the two older academies, that special emphasis is indeed placed on the development of a specific category, namely prospective *combat commanders,* men who can "fight the fleet" or lead regiments in battle. This *de facto* mission, which is of considerable importance from the point of view of our study, manifests itself in many ways. West Point's Tactical Department, Annapolis's Executive Department, and the Air Force Academy's airmanship divisions stress those qualities of leadership that are deemed especially relevant to the exercise of command. The models held up to the students are those of great combat leaders of earlier years; the flags, songs, mottoes, and customs are associated with battle. Moreover the students expect upon graduation to be assigned to "line" activities rather than to technical or administrative work. At the Naval Academy, only those 5 or 6 percent of the graduates who are physically disqualified for line duty, usually because of inadequate eyesight, may be commissioned in the Supply Corps.[3] West Point graduates must spend two years in one of the combat arms before they may request transfer to a technical or administrative service. Moreover mem-

[3] Others may request transfer to the Supply Corps or to the Civil Engineer Corps after 18 months of duty as line officers.

bers of the Tactical Department at West Point ordinarily represent only those branches in which a cadet may be commissioned upon graduation. At the Air Force Academy all cadets who are physically qualified will graduate as rated navigators and will enter pilot training immediately after graduation. Nearly all of the officers in the airmanship training divisions are rated pilots or navigators.

Organization and Control

In the discharge of their missions all three academies are governed directly by the headquarters of their respective services. Major policy matters, such as Congressional relations, drastic revision of programs, or the selection of superintendents, are likely to be handled personally by the chief of staff of the Army, the chief of air staff, or the chief of Naval personnel respectively, the latter presumably in close cooperation with the chief of Naval operations. Routine supervision is in all cases delegated to staff units in each headquarters. It is probably accurate to say that the affairs of the academies are more likely to engage the personal attention of the very highest military leaders than the affairs of any other service schools, with the possible and by no means certain exception of the service War Colleges.

Nor are military leaders the only ones who follow academy affairs. Each school has a devoted and influential body of alumni. Each school is a federal instrument in which many private citizens and public officials take a proprietary interest. Public reaction to the violation of the honor code at West Point in 1951 was stronger than it would have been to a similar violation at a private college or even a state university. It is but another aspect of this widely shared sense of involvement or ownership that the academies at various times have been exposed to strong external pressure in such matters as the standards of discipline imposed on cadets, entrance requirements, architecture, the discussion of controversial political issues, and the fortunes of football teams.

We do not suggest, however, that the academies have little freedom to manage their own affairs. The Military Academy seems to be given considerable latitude in matters of educational policy. The Naval Academy is influenced somewhat more by higher authority, but careful inquiry will often disclose that regulations emanating from Washington have actually been drafted at Annapolis. At the time of this writing the Air Force Academy is controlled more closely than the other two because the major policy issues that inevitably arise in the formative years of such a school naturally engage the attention of departmental officials in Washington. But the Air Force Academy, too, will probably acquire greater freedom as the years go by. At all academies the superintendents are high-ranking officers known personally to and trusted by their service chiefs. Their institutions are not routinely involved in those great battles over program and resources, especially money, that expose the policies of other military agencies to searching inquiry by central authority. For many practical purposes, therefore, they may be said to enjoy a status of substantial autonomy modified by countless inspections.

Academic policy at West Point and Annapolis is determined by the superintendent and his Academic Board.[4] The superintendent is cast in a multiple role. He is at once a college president, a military commander, a post commander, and the custodian of a national monument. He greets a constant flow of very important visitors. He supervises innumerable support installations such as hospitals, hotels, theaters, churches, laundries, bands, motor pools, preparatory schools, and machine shops. Though most of these functions are delegated to others, he retains a final responsibility that adds to his total burdens and that may distract him occasionally from his primary task. Since the close of world war I, superintendents have invariably been general or flag officers. In marked contrast to the presidents of civilian colleges, they rarely hold office for more than three or four years; sometimes their terms are as short as one or two years. In this limited period some superintendents have made notable contributions to their institutions. Others have proved to be square pegs in round holes. Moreover brevity of tenure can limit the effectiveness of even the most dynamic superintendent. He is a transient; it is always problematical whether he has the intimate knowledge, at least at the start, to ask the right questions. His status is in some respects comparable to that of a political minister who assumes control of a department of professional civil servants. If he has in mind far-

[4] Air Force Academy organization differs sufficiently to warrant separate treatment below.

reaching changes, he may be dissuaded by the thought that he will not be around long enough to see them through. If he makes them anyhow, he has no assurance that they will be continued by his successors. This means he must make a conscious effort to guard against undue preoccupation with management details, athletics, and the social and ceremonial aspects of his task at the expense of educational policy.

The Academic Board is essentially a committee of department heads presided over by the superintendent. At West Point the superintendent is assisted by a dean of the Academic Board; the dean is a general officer who must previously have served as the head of an academic department. The superintendent of the Naval Academy is aided by a secretary and an assistant secretary of the Academic Board. At both academies these officials have a coordinating rather than a command relationship to the academic departments, and in actual practice much of their time is devoted to personnel and other administrative matters. All regular voting members of the Academic Boards are officers.[5] Frequently they work through standing or *ad hoc* committees. Certain of their powers—for example, their authority to recommend whether students deficient in their work should be dismissed—rest on statutes of long standing. Others derive from regulations approved by the secretaries of the service departments.

At Annapolis this collective body is empowered to prescribe, subject only to the approval of the secretary of the Navy, such matters as the subjects and arrangement of the course of instruction, the textbooks to be used, the system of examinations, and entrance requirements. These powers are vested in the entire board, not in the superintendent. The latter, however, is entitled to three votes on the board. More important, he has the influence that flows from his personal qualities and from Naval customs regarding seniority and status. It does not follow that other members of the board must sit back quietly to await his pronouncements. Debate can be vigorous and the superintendent's views do not always prevail. But all members, including the superintendent, have one common bond that does not exist at West Point: they are

[5] The assistant secretary of the Academic Board at Annapolis is a civilian who also serves as educational adviser to the superintendent. He does not have a vote on the Academic Board.

assigned to their positions for only a few years. Other things being equal this decreases the likelihood that they will develop different institutional interests.

At West Point the Academic Board is recognized by statute and its members have permanent tenure. Officially they are appointed by the President of the United States. In practice the President relies heavily on recommendations made at successively lower echelons the most important of which is often the Academic Board itself. The great majority of members are West Point graduates. They may come from a wide variety of stations within the Army; they may be recruited directly from civilian life. Most often, however, they are selected from among those officers who are already serving, or who have earlier served, on the faculty. The board is authorized to determine the time allocated to each department, to conduct and grade examinations, to grant diplomas, to recommend students for commissions, to recommend textbooks, and to recommend, through the superintendent to the Department of the Army, changes in the course of study or methods of instruction. The superintendent has a vote on the board and in case of a tie his vote is the deciding factor. The board as a whole is clearly a very powerful body. Its members constitute a category of officers whose special status is recognized in law and custom. They stand at or very close to the top of their particular career ladder. They see superintendents come and go. Some of them may be senior to the superintendent in point of service.[6] Others have influential classmates or friends in the Pentagon. It is not too much to say that over any considerable period of years the integrity of West Point rests in the hands of this body.

The powers of the Academic Boards and the relatively autonomous status of the academies within the services give these schools a certain amount of protection against crude political interference. Indeed, it appears that a reason for the original grant of authority to the Academic Boards was a desire to ward off politicians who sought to "pressure" the War and Navy Departments into admitting or graduating students who were incapable of

---

[6] In 1955 almost half of all members had been general officers in the past. Fully half had been graduated from West Point earlier than the then Army chief of staff, General Maxwell Taylor, '22.

meeting prescribed standards. "Home rule" also operates as a defense against other types of hasty or ill-considered suggestions. The academies, as public institutions, are "fair game" for all critics and all those who would peddle educational nostrums to superintendents and secretaries of military departments. In this situation the authority of an Academic Board may serve as a useful anchor to the wind. The danger of the system is the converse of its virtues. It may insulate the schools not only against unwholesome pressures from the outside world but against the most necessary and proper proposals for change. This depends on whether the board members in any given era are able to resolve difficult questions of policy or whether they become deadlocked, thereby freezing the *status quo* and relinquishing effective power to the individual academic departments.

The statute creating the Air Force Academy gave the secretary of the Air Force great latitude in determining its basic structure, and he in turn has permitted academy officials to experiment with a relatively distinctive organization. The academy has both an Academy Board and a Faculty Council. The council is limited to academic and instructional matters and is only advisory to the Academy Board; but its recommendations may be expected to carry weight if made by substantial majorities. The council is composed of the dean of the faculty and the heads of all academic departments. These are expected to be permanent personnel. The dean is its presiding officer and is authorized to cast a second vote to break ties. Neither the superintendent nor the commandant of cadets is a member of the council. Each is, however, a member of the more powerful Academy Board. The name "academy board" was chosen in preference to "academic board" to make plain that its jurisdiction extended both to the airmanship and academic programs; in other words its interests are academy-wide. Unlike the Academic Boards at West Point and Annapolis, the Academy Board is *not* composed of department heads. It is a 10-member body consisting of the superintendent, the commandant, the dean, the directors of the three airmanship divisions (military, flying, and physical training), and the chairmen of the four academic divisions (humanities, social sciences, basic sciences, and applied sciences). Within the Air Force Academy the board is the final authority on educational policy. The superintendent is the presiding officer and has one additional vote to break ties.

The organization appears to strengthen the position of the superintendent, the dean, and the commandant. A calculated effort seems to have been made to avoid undue concentration of power in the permanent department heads either individually or collectively. Except on curricular matters and on matters governed by statute, the Academy Board is merely advisory to the superintendent. The board's decisions on curricular matters may be submitted by the superintendent to the Department of the Air Force for review. Also, the superintendent appoints for a term of two years the academic division heads, who constitute 4 of the 10 board members. The fact that these division heads rotate, and that each represents several departments, is expected to decrease the expression of departmental vested interests in board meetings. The board is also evenly divided with respect to permanent professors (academic division heads and the dean) and transient officials (superintendent, commandant, and airmanship directors). However, the dean is the only person who will serve on the board longer than a few years. He is clearly expected to have major responsibility for educational leadership. Department heads are responsible to him in the line of command. In consultation with them, and within policies prescribed by the superintendent, he may establish academic and faculty policies in such areas as organization, curriculum development, personnel, instructional standards, scheduling, and examinations.

The main burden of conducting the work of the academies inevitably falls upon the regular departments of instruction. At West Point there are 13 such departments, each established by statute:

Tactics	Mechanics
Military Topography and Graphics	Physics and Chemistry
	English
Ordnance	Law
Military Art and Engineering	Social Sciences
Mathematics	Foreign Languages
Electricity	Military Hygiene

At Annapolis there are 11 departments, each established by order of the secretary of the Navy:

178

Executive
Seamanship and Navigation
Ordnance and Gunnery
Marine Engineering
Aviation
Mathematics

Electrical Engineering
English, History, and
    Government
Foreign Languages
Hygiene
Physical Education

At this writing the Air Force Academy has 16 academic departments grouped into four divisions under the dean, plus three airmanship divisions under the commandant:

Basic Sciences Division
Mathematics
Graphics
Chemistry
Physics

Social Sciences Division
History
Economics
Political Science
Military History
Psychology

Applied Sciences Division
Mechanics
Electrical Engineering
Thermodynamics
Aerodynamics

Humanities Division
English
Foreign Languages
Law (including Logic)

At West Point and Annapolis it is apparent that some departments actually constitute combinations of disciplines that would enjoy separate departmental status at most civilian institutions. For example, the Electrical Engineering Department at Annapolis, which is actually misnamed, conducts instruction in physics and chemistry as well as electrical engineering and electronics. The Social Sciences Department at West Point teaches government, history, economics, and geography. To understand this tendency to combine disciplines one must appreciate that the academies ordinarily offer but one or a few introductory courses in a given field of learning, and that these courses may take but a single semester or a part of a semester. In other words the time allotted to a field does not always seem to warrant giving it separate departmental status. "Holding company" departments also make it easier to shift instructors from one field of knowledge to another during the year and thus to make full use of their time. In addition such departments may help in tying together related courses. The Air Force Academy, on the other hand, is less inclined to combine disciplines

179

in this way. Instructors' teaching loads are evened out in part by offering courses to half of the student body in the first semester and half in the second. It is expected that the division chairmen and the dean will assist in tying together related departments.

Any observer from a civilian college is quickly struck by the number of nonteaching or administrative personnel in each department at West Point and Annapolis. Rarely does a department head conduct classes. One result is that the Academic Board, which effectively controls educational policy, contains no teachers. At West Point many departments have both a head and a deputy head who do not teach. At Annapolis, besides the department head and his executive officer, many departments utilize a civilian faculty member largely for administrative purposes.[7] At the Air Force Academy, department heads and their deputies are expected to carry at least a one-fourth teaching load. At all academies operating groups or committees are created to plan and supervise each course for which a department is responsible. This heavy administrative superstructure is a consequence of the requirements of military organization, of the nature of the curriculum, and of the pedagogical methods and theories of these schools. The latter two topics will be discussed in the next chapter.

It is not easy to generalize about the role of the department head at the academies. At West Point his influence is relatively great. He is not merely a "commanding officer," but also a permanent official with considerable substantive knowledge and skill. At the Air Force Academy the department head is also a permanent official, but he does not sit on the Academy Board and his jurisdiction is more often confined to a single field of learning. He will, however, have command authority within his department. At Annapolis the situation can vary widely. The head of a department like Seamanship and Navigation, though a transient, will have superior technical knowledge of his subject. On the other hand the head of a department like English, History, and Government may lack equally specific qualifications. The influence of department heads will also vary with their personal interests and administrative

[7] For example, preparing recitation and room schedules, assigning instructors to sections, examining textbooks, supervising the training of new instructors, and coordinating the preparation of examinations.

styles. Some concern themselves with the finest details of substantive policy. Others supervise their staffs in only a very general way, that is, by signing orders, performing ceremonial duties, and insuring that the departments do not stray too far from the primary mission of the academy.

Faculty

The ability of the academies to produce graduates who will eventually contribute effectively to national security policy depends in great part on the competence of their faculties. At West Point the faculty is composed almost wholly of military personnel.[8] These are drawn from a variety of sources. The largest group consists of regular Army officers who are themselves West Point graduates and who have had from 4 to 12 years of active duty. Army reserve officers and Air Force officers (many of the latter are also West Point graduates) are two other important components; together they have constituted as much as 50 percent of the teaching staff.[9] There are also a few Naval and Marine Corps officers, some of whom come to West Point under an exchange-of-instructors agreement with Annapolis. One or two Latin American officers have been utilized to teach foreign languages.

Each officer holds an academic rank, e.g. instructor, assistant professor, associate professor, or full professor. Academic rank depends not on military rank but on the particular duties that the officer performs. In the English Department, for example, the title of associate professor has been conferred on a major while his military superior, a lieutenant colonel, held the lower academic title of assistant professor. In Mathematics, officers of grades ranging from first lieutenant to lieutenant colonel have been lumped together in the rank of instructor. At the top of the hierarchy, however, academic status and military status harmonize more closely. Here there are about 20 officers who are both full

[8] A few civilians are employed in the Foreign Languages and Physical Education Departments.

[9] In 1955 there were 85 Air Force officers at West Point, 25 at Annapolis. This liberal sprinkling reflected the fact that the older academies allocated up to one fourth of their graduating classes to the Air Force. When the Air Force Academy becomes fully operative, the number of Air Force instructors at West Point and Annapolis may be expected to decrease to not more than 5 percent of the total faculty at each institution.

professors and colonels.[10] Congress has provided most of the departments with two full professors. One of the incumbents is designated as the department head; the other is usually his deputy. Both hold permanent appointments and only rarely does an incumbent resign before reaching retirement. Except for reserve officers, most faculty members are assigned for three or four years. Some return for a second tour later in their careers, a practice that Boards of Visitors have sought to make more common. Difference in tenure, coupled with differences in age and military rank, sometimes create a wide gap between the permanent professors and other members of a department.

The Air Force Academy began with an exclusively military faculty. Eventually some civilians may be added, especially in Foreign Languages. The full professors initially assigned were given probationary terms of three years. In the future it is expected that full professors will receive permanent appointments and that most other faculty officers will rotate. The normal tour in the latter case will be four years, though some officers may be retained longer. There are 20 positions for the rank of permanent professor and one for the dean. The academic rank of other faculty members is based on earned degrees and teaching experience.

At Annapolis the composition of the faculty is markedly different. Civilians have occupied a permanent position on the teaching staff since the founding of the school. Today they constitute almost half of the instructors, though they are by no means distributed uniformly among the departments. In a typical recent year no professional department employed civilians.[11] In Marine Engineering, civilians constituted only about 16 percent of the staff. In Electrical Engineering about 40 percent of the staff was civilian. On the other hand the figure ranged from 70 to 75 percent in the Department of English, History, and Government, in Mathematics, and in Foreign Languages.

Like West Point, Annapolis utilizes Air Force officers as instructors. Proportionately the number has been far lower than at the Military Academy. On the other hand many of the line officers

---

[10] A newly appointed full professor may start as a lieutenant colonel and receive a promotion after a period of years. A few full colonels have also been assigned as associate professors but it is expected that this practice will be discontinued.

[11] The "professional" departments are Aviation, Executive, Ordnance and Gunnery, and Seamanship and Navigation.

on its staff are Naval aviators. In addition there are about two dozen Marine Corps instructors. An important distinguishing aspect of the Annapolis faculty is that no officer, not even the department head, has permanent tenure. Moreover officers do not bear conventional academic titles. Many civilians, on the other hand, do hold permanent appointments, including the "senior professors" (usually one per department), the professors, and the associate professors.

Faculty members at the academies also vary greatly in academic background and in the manner in which they are recruited. Recruitment is a particularly serious problem for West Point and the Air Force Academy because the career officers on whom they rely so heavily are not primarily trained as academicians. At West Point the need for professionally competent teachers is met partly by providing selected officers with a year or two of graduate work in appropriate subjects prior to their assignment to the Military Academy, and partly by giving them an intensive preparatory course during the summer of their arrival. The young men who have just come from graduate school, although not seasoned scholars and rarely experienced teachers, often have a distinct *élan* and display great enthusiasm for their work. The program of graduate study began on a very limited basis before world war II. It has become much more extensive since the war but still does not extend to all officer instructors. Some departments rely upon it more than others. In the Mathematics Department, for example, half or more of the staff will have taken no graduate program *in mathematics*.[12] In the case of military art there are no civilian schools at which instructors can obtain degrees. The department therefore seeks older and more experienced officers who have graduated from a military school at the command and staff level. For equally understandable reasons graduate degrees are less common in the Department of Topography and Graphics. On the other hand most instructors in such subjects as physics and mechanics hold graduate degrees, normally the master's. In the English Department every officer has had some graduate work. In 1955–1956 half held a master's degree; four held Ph.D.'s. In the same year all officers in the Social Sciences Department had had

---

[12] Some of these, however, may have advanced degrees in engineering sciences, and all are exposed to "refresher" courses at West Point before they assume their duties.

some graduate work; 30 out of 32 either held a master's degree or lacked only the completion of a thesis to acquire it. Frequently one or two members of this department hold Ph.D.'s and up to 50 percent may be working toward Ph.D.'s. At this writing both permanent professors were former Rhodes scholars. A number of others have served in the department from time to time. Advanced work is taken in such institutions as Columbia, Harvard, Oxford, Princeton, Pennsylvania, Stanford, and Yale.

In many cases West Point uses a distinctive method to select its instructors. Staff members attempt to identify cadets who display unusual aptitude for a particular subject. These cadets are sometimes called in just before graduation and sounded out informally about their attitude toward a future teaching assignment. A roster is kept of those who express interest. When a vacancy exists the department in which it occurs prepares a panel of names for the appropriate career branches in Washington. If none of the officers on the panel is available, the career branches may make their own suggestions, but these in turn may be vetoed by West Point. In many other cases officers take the initiative themselves by requesting assignment to West Point, a practice specifically authorized by Army regulations. Departments also receive "tips" or suggestions from other officers in the service. Finally, the Adjutant General's Office prepares lists of men who have appropriate academic qualifications.

After an officer has been selected for assignment to West Point, arrangements may be made for him to go to graduate school. This depends on a number of factors. Not all departments are equally insistent on graduate study. Not all branches are equally prepared to lose an officer for so long. Lack of funds can be an insuperable obstacle. If the officer does go to graduate school, the appropriate department at West Point selects the school and determines the general nature of the studies to be taken. Breadth rather than depth is sought because the officer may have to teach different subjects in what would ordinarily be regarded as different departments. Most graduate programs are one or two years in length, depending again on the availability of funds and other factors. Ordinarily, therefore, officers cannot complete the requirements for a Ph.D. Prestige aside, some departments feel that actual possession of the Ph.D. is pointless because the student will often have completed all the work required except for a specialized doctoral dissertation.

We asked close acquaintances at some graduate schools to comment frankly on the performance of these officers. Invariably the response was that they worked harder than civilian graduate students, that they were at least as able as other special groups of more mature students, that they never fell near the bottom of a class, and that a very small minority stood near the top of a class. The general response was highly favorable.

Supplementary training does not end when an officer reports to West Point. Departments have orientation programs, refresher courses, prelesson staff conferences, and so on.[13] Many officers take special work at summer schools or at Columbia University during the academic year. The Department of Social Sciences sends instructors to the University of Beirut to equip them to teach the history of the Near East. It has also sent them to Southeast Asia to equip them to teach the history of the Far East.

It must be emphasized that these practices, especially the policy of sending men to civilian graduate schools to prepare them for a specific teaching assignment, are not commonly employed by military schools at higher level. Most officers sent to civilian universities are being prepared for specific operating duties, sometimes quite technical, in the service at large. The schools either recruit instructors who have learned from experience, or, quite commonly, press into service recent graduates of their own who show special aptitude for the course. But for many reasons these two devices are less relevant to West Point. Its students are much younger, and it seeks to give them important elements of a liberal education. Parts of the program consist of subjects with which the average career officer does not necessarily become familiar in his work, and consequently is not equipped to teach. Also, while advanced military schools are obviously unique in their missions and programs, some departments at West Point are sufficiently

---

[13] In the English Department, a day or two before the lesson, instructors may convene to discuss it. For example in a lesson on Chaucer the officer in charge of the meeting may outline the author's life and works, discuss the background of *The Canterbury Tales,* and go through the lesson in detail pointing out passages and clearing up textual questions. The Mathematics Department conducts both a course in teaching method and a refresher course in substantive mathematics. The latter lasts two years and consists of about 120 lengthy lessons. Topics, textbooks, and procedures are identical to those covered or used by cadets.

like those at civilian colleges to be subjected to pressure to conform to standards accepted by the larger academic profession; and these standards almost invariably include graduate training for instructors. For all these reasons it is absolutely essential that special training in advance of assignment be given to many of the career officers on whom West Point relies so heavily. The only practical alternatives would be to rely on a faculty composed largely of civilians and reserve officers taken from the teaching profession, or to abandon all efforts to give a liberal education.

Much that has been said here applies to the new Air Force Academy as well. The Air Force has realized the need for special qualifications in the instructors it has assigned to the older service academies. Indeed, Air Force members of certain departments at West Point and Annapolis have sometimes been better qualified, in terms of prior formal schooling, than their Army or Naval colleagues. More important, however, are the standards used by the Air Force in recruiting the nucleus of its own academy faculty. As of 1956 the group selected consisted entirely of officers. Many were career officers; some were civilian teachers who had been recalled to active duty since the Korean war; none had been commissioned specifically for this assignment. Except in the Graphics Department nearly all academic instructors held graduate degrees; 25 percent held doctor's or professional degrees; others were working toward them. The average college level teaching experience was over five years. This included teaching at civilian colleges, service academies, and in AFROTC programs. A significant number of the original appointees had taught at West Point. West Point backgrounds were particularly common among the 15 acting professors; 12 had taught at the Military Academy and 11 were alumni. A smaller number had taught at Annapolis.

In recruiting instructors in the future, the Air Force Academy plans to select officers who are under 30 years of age and have had about five years of active duty. They will be sent to graduate school for one or two years. The Air Force apparently has less difficulty in securing funds for this purpose. It is also hoped that special educational opportunities can be given to men already on the staff. Many will enter "off duty" programs at the University of Denver. Exceptionally capable instructors, half way through their tour of duty, may be permitted to volunteer for an additional year of graduate work to complete the requirements for a Ph.D.; they will then return to the academy. Finally, it is hoped that permanent professors may be allowed leave of absence every five years to attend a senior military college, to work for a Ph.D. if they don't already have it, or to serve in a relevant Air Force position outside the academy.

Faculty practices at the Naval Academy differ somewhat from those at the other two schools. Instead of using military instructors with some graduate training and/or teaching experience, Annapolis relies on a combination of civilians who are making a lifetime career of the academic profession and officers who vary widely in their special preparation to teach given subjects. We shall consider the officers first.

Annapolis has been less aggressive than West Point in seeking out particular officers to teach particular subjects. Each year, of course, departments list the number of vacancies they anticipate and the subjects that prospective instructors will teach. In a number of cases they also outline the special qualifications they desire. In a few cases—for example, in Foreign Languages—they may list the actual names of former midshipmen whom they would like. But this latter practice is less common than at West Point.[14] Moreover there are fewer direct contacts between individual academic departments at Annapolis and assignment officers in Washington. Instead the secretary of the Academic Board, who functions as a kind of dean of the military faculty, deals with the Bureau of Naval Personnel. It is part of the same pattern that when an officer is ordered to duty at Annapolis he is assigned to the *Naval Academy* and not to any particular department therein. Assignments to particular departments are made by the secretary of the Academic Board on behalf of the superintendent. Our attention was called to a few cases in which officers were not assigned to the departments that they were best qualified to serve.

The superintendent and his secretary of the Academic Board take greater initiative in the selection of the more senior officers, especially the captains who are to serve as department heads. They are particularly concerned with the personalities, seniority, and

[14] A former senior professor in one department told us that he used to request officers by name but stopped when he found that the particular individuals desired were often unavailable.

general service reputation of these men. Assignments to the Naval Academy, and particularly assignments to the position of department head, are regarded as desirable shore billets. Many officers specifically request such duty. Department heads are almost always graduates of the Naval Academy who have had about 20 years of active service. Though not always members of the same graduating class, most of them will have lived together as midshipmen for at least a year. There seems to be some tendency to let each graduating class get a "crack" at Annapolis assignments as its turn comes around.

Relatively few Naval officers, senior or junior, are sent to graduate school *immediately before* they start teaching at Annapolis.[15] All have college degrees; about 70 percent are graduates of the Naval Academy. Some, but not many, have had graduate training in the particular fields they are destined to teach.[16] At this writing there are signs that the situation may be altering, but it is too early to say to what extent. An increase in the proportion of Naval aviators and NROTC graduates on the faculty is resulting in more officers with special educational preparation. Some officers are also coming to Annapolis after completing scientific or technical education at the Navy's Postgraduate School. The superintendent is pressing his personnel needs on the Bureau of Naval Personnel more vigorously than some of his predecessors.

Past Boards of Visitors have so often called attention to the need for more graduate training that it is reasonable to inquire why the situation has not altered in any material respect over the years.[17] One may speculate that department heads at Annapolis are less concerned to request advance training for their instructors than department heads at West Point. They are temporary officials

[15] An exception must be noted in the case of some Naval officers who are scheduled to teach foreign languages. These men may be sent to Middlebury College or to Europe for special training during the *summer* preceding their assignment to the Foreign Languages Department.

[16] Advanced training was more common among Air Force officers at Annapolis. In a recent year such training had been taken by four out of five of them in the Department of Electrical Engineering; all three in the Department of Mathematics; two out of three in the Department of English, History, and Government; and both in the Department of Foreign Languages. Also, graduate schooling was more common among Naval reservists than among "regulars."

[17] See, for example, the reports of the Boards of Visitors for the years 1939, 1944, 1946, and 1947. Particularly sharp criticism was voiced in a minority report submitted in 1940 by Representative Melvin J. Maas.

themselves, and they have much less opportunity to develop a vested interest in the maintenance of departmental academic standards. The permanent civilian staff can develop this interest but, as will be noted below, it does not have much voice in such matters of policy. Moreover, its very presence tends to reassure Naval officers that the problem of providing technically qualified personnel has already been solved. Finally, it is probable that Naval authorities in Washington are less responsive to this need than their counterparts in the Army. As noted in chapter three, younger line officers of the regular Navy rarely have the opportunity of remaining ashore for the sustained period necessary to take graduate work in, let us say, economics and to complete a tour of duty at the Naval Academy. Moreover such a pattern of assignments might well jeopardize their future advancement. The whole career plan is built around the idea of frequent rotation, especially in shipboard assignments. This is by no means an arbitrary device. It reflects the very structure of the Navy. While the Army is divided into a relatively large number of combat arms and technical and administrative services, the Navy has only a few specialists' corps on the one hand and the "line" on the other. The line officer must therefore be something of an engineer, an ordnance officer, a communications officer, a navigator, and so on. He must be familiar with many different types of combatant ships, supporting forces, and supporting installations. It is difficult indeed to give the younger officer a minimum competence in all these matters and still make him available for an extended assignment to the world of education.

The Naval Academy, accordingly, has had to improvise. All new instructors participate in an instructor training program in the summer before they start teaching. Many departments offer "refresher" courses. Such courses, however, often include indoctrination in departmental policy and teaching techniques as well as drill in the subject matter. In other words there is a great deal to cover in a short time. Moreover some officers do not report for duty until the school year is almost under way. New officers are also helped as they go along by elaborate daily lesson outlines or "gouges" prepared by departmental staffs. The "gouges" may summarize the material to be presented, indicate points that deserve emphasis, and suggest questions to be asked. Finally, as at West Point and the Air Force

Academy, many officers attend summer school or evening classes at nearby civilian universities.[18]

Seldom has the new officer much time to digest and apply such supplementary training. The younger ones are usually assigned to Annapolis for two years; captains and more senior commanders for three years. The brevity of the tour, like the lack of special preparation, has long attracted the attention of Boards of Visitors. It also has its critics at the Naval Academy itself. One of them asked us to "Imagine a destroyer flotilla headed by a college president who rotated every three years. Imagine further that each destroyer in the flotilla is commanded by a dean who rotates every three years. Imagine, finally, that many of the executives within each destroyer are professors who rotate every two years. There you have, in reverse, the USNA."

This comment exaggerates the case somewhat because a number of department heads and higher administrative officials may be serving their second tour of duty. It should also be noted that there is rapid turnover among the younger instructors at the other academies and among nearly all officials at more senior service schools. At Annapolis, moreover, the presence of civilian instructors relieves the situation. In the "nonprofessional" departments the net effect is that some officers serve essentially as administrators and as examples to the midshipmen of the personal standards and service ideals that the Navy seeks to inculcate. But such instructors lack the sense of deep personal involvement in their subject matters that prompts a civilian educator to contribute to knowledge in his field, to keep abreast of the literature, or even to belong to the relevant learned societies.

Unlike the career officers at the academies, most of the civilian instructors are devoting their lives to teaching. About 60 percent, however, have also had prior military service as officers in the Naval Reserve. The bulk of these were employed after 1940, when the Naval Academy suddenly doubled its civilian staff to make its officers available for sea duty. They were commissioned as reserve officers for the duration of the war and many stayed on in a civilian capacity when the war ended. Most civilians have at least a

[18] Maryland, Georgetown, Catholic University, George Washington, or American University. At West Point it is likely to be Columbia; at the Air Force Academy it is likely to be Denver University or the University of Colorado.

master's degree prior to their appointment. Since 1949 possession of a Ph.D. has been a prerequisite of promotion to the grade of full professor. About one third of the civilians now have this degree; many others are working toward it. In some departments one third or more of the civilians are graduates of normal schools or have taught in normal schools or in secondary schools. We have, incidentally, been struck by a similar phenomenon at other military schools and we have speculated inconclusively as to whether it is related as cause or effect to the great interest in teaching methods at these institutions.[19]

In the past the Naval Academy did not always adopt aggressive recruiting practices in filling civilian vacancies. Sometimes it relied on official placement offices of teachers' agencies, professional societies, and universities. Sometimes it limited its search to individuals who had written in to inquire about possible openings. Recently, however, Annapolis has advertised its vacancies more widely. Promising candidates are invited to the Naval Academy for an interview that includes an informal subject matter examination. Nearly all new appointments are made at the level of assistant professor. Salaries are roughly comparable to those at many other eastern colleges. Appointments are for a limited period of time, but once appointed a man can usually count on staying at Annapolis for a good number of years. Rarely since the war has reappointment been refused.

Civilian faculty members write professional books and articles. They attend the annual meetings of their professional associations, and some hold high office therein. Only occasionally do they win renown as research scholars or as great lecturers because the methods of Annapolis, deriving from its mission, do not place a great premium on either function. Time is of the essence for students; much has to be covered. Inevitably emphasis is given to careful preparation, precise administration, and refined teaching techniques.

Though some civilians at Annapolis disagree with us on the point, we believe there are aspects of their status that may inhibit

[19] It may also be of interest that 15 of the first group of officers assigned to the Air Force Academy enrolled in a program leading to a doctor's degree in education; 4 of the first 6 officers assigned to the History Department either were graduates of teachers' colleges or had taught in them or in secondary schools. A few West Point instructors have also worked toward a doctor's degree in education.

their effectiveness. One is that they have had less influence on academy-wide educational policy than professors have had on university-wide educational policy at many civilian universities. Within a given department they may have an important voice in curriculum planning, promotions, and other matters of deep interest to them; this naturally varies a little with different department heads and senior professors. But because no civilian teacher serves as head of a department, none sits on the Academic Board.[20] Even professors of great experience and technical *expertise* have their performances evaluated by officers who in many cases are transient amateurs. This, of course, is common practice in military administration; it is not common practice in the academic profession. In the past civilians were not always regarded as absolutely equal partners in the Annapolis enterprise.[21] Today they do not always enjoy all the personal opportunities and prerogatives of other college teachers. Their work is more closely supervised. They have less freedom in arranging their own schedules. Since advanced elective courses are not permitted, they do not often develop a master-apprentice relationship with gifted students. Since most of their energies are given to introductory survey courses, they have less opportunity to develop their personal interests. As generalists rather than specialists they may give introductory work in widely separated fields, such as English and economics. Leaves of absence for research or advanced study are less common than at civilian colleges.

All these matters were noted by Boards of Visitors prior to world war II. But the position of the civilian faculty was not materially improved until the war itself suddenly forced a great increase in its numbers. One immediate result was the creation in many departments of the position of senior professor. This enabled department heads to deal with their enlarged staffs through

20 Two civilian professors, Dr. C. Alphonso Smith, followed by Dr. Carrol S. Alden, served as head of the English, History, and Government Department between 1917 and 1941. But this practice, apparently instituted at the insistence of Navy Secretary Josephus Daniels, was later discontinued.

21 Commander Leland P. Lovette, USN, tells a story of long ago that suggests the point we wish to make. Professor Lockwood, a member of the first faculty of the Naval Academy, was once hung in effigy by some midshipmen. In the ensuing court martial an ingenious defense counsel argued that the culprits had not insulted a superior officer because Lockwood was merely a civilian employed by the Navy to teach, and thus in the same category as a steward or paymaster. Proceedings were quashed. See *School of the Sea*, New York, 1941, pp. 75–76.

an experienced member of the civilian faculty. Soon after the war another major civilian post was created, that of educational adviser to the superintendent.[22] A third step, taken after long discussion of faculty morale by the Board of Visitors in 1948, was the creation of an Academic Council. This consists of five civilian professors and five Naval officers, each representing a different department. Its presiding officer is the educational adviser to the superintendent. It may study and make recommendations on all matters of educational policy. Also, in the postwar period Vice Admiral James L. Holloway, then superintendent, sought to encourage research by the civilian staff and to increase opportunities for leaves of absence. In 1956 for the first time the commencement procession was led by members of the civilian faculty garbed in academic gowns. One civilian now sits on each of the important committees on the curriculum, entrance requirements, scheduling, and civilian faculty problems; certain other committees have greater civilian representation. Sabbatical leaves for study and research have been authorized.[23] But change comes slowly and reforms instituted by one superintendent are not always preserved intact by his successors. The Academic Council has not yet become a major center of educational policy. The approval of the Navy Department must be obtained whenever funds are required to help civilians travel to professional meetings. Frequent references are made to the desirability of exchange arrangements with professors at civilian universities. But proponents rarely recognize the practical difficulties of such arrangements. Few senior faculty members at other colleges are likely to seek opportunity to teach numerous small sections of an introductory course; few junior faculty members could afford to spend a year or two away from their own institutions in order to perform such work. Better prospects exist for exchange professorships with advanced military schools such as the

[22] Creation of such a post had been urged by prewar Boards of Visitors to provide continuity above the departmental level of the Naval Academy.

[23] Regulations approved by the Navy Department in 1956 state: "Sabbatical leave for study and research may be granted to civilian faculty members by the Chief of Naval Personnel on recommendation by the Superintendent when, in the opinion of the Navy Department, such leave would result in the improvement of education at the U.S. Naval Academy. Unless otherwise specifically provided, such leave shall be granted at full pay for one-half year or at one-half pay for an entire year." *Policy Regarding Pay, Promotion, and Tenure of Office of the Civilian Faculty at the United States Naval Academy*, Annapolis, 1956, p. 6.

Naval War College, the Naval Postgraduate School, or even the National War College or the Industrial College of the Armed Forces. These possibilities, however, have not really been developed. Indeed, it is our general impression that the Naval Academy can profitably continue to experiment with measures designed to release the creative energy that lies within its permanent staff.

The Selection of Students

The attributes of entering midshipmen and cadets suggest not only the general standards of achievement that academy authorities should expect but also the special interests and disinterests of the students with whom they must deal. Moreover the characteristics of these young men at entry probably affect their performances in later life as profoundly as any formal education they receive, either at the academies or at the senior colleges. The subject therefore deserves much closer study than we have been able to give it. We do, however, have some confidence in the few generalizations that follow.

Entering students are more broadly representative of American society than their counterparts at many eastern residential colleges. They are more representative socially as well as geographically. For example there is no marked concentration of young men who have attended fashionable private preparatory schools. Nevertheless it is not accurate to say that the students constitute a true cross section of the American people. Very few are Negroes or sons of laborers; only about 5 percent are sons of farmers. Quite a few, 25 percent of the West Point class that graduated in 1955 and 14 percent of the same Annapolis class, are sons of service personnel. In the case of West Point, where we have fuller information, the 1955 percentage is fairly typical of recent experience. It is also higher than the comparable percentage for the latter half of the nineteenth century. Again, at West Point about one third of the entrants are the sons of business executives and professional people. About one fourth are the sons of craftsmen, salesmen, clerks, enlisted men, and smaller independent merchants. Members of the Catholic faith are well represented; at Annapolis, for example, they constitute 30 percent of the student body.

Such a population might well be a little more conservative in

194

its political orientation than the average young American male. We have some testimony from instructors at the academies that this is so, and we have no testimony that it is not so. But we also have no substantial evidence on the point.

The entrants tend to be healthier and more vigorous than the average college freshman. Dr. Arlie Bock, professor of hygiene at Harvard University, has noted that men of rugged physique (mesomorphs) predominate.[24] This attribute probably results not only from the entrance requirements of the academies but from a tendency of such types to be attracted to the service schools and from the selection practices of congressmen.[25] At entry the average cadet or midshipman is also older than the average college freshman. He has had more education. Roughly half of all entrants have already taken a year or more of college work. Many others have supplemented their regular secondary school courses with other forms of special preparation. Their scores on the college board scholastic aptitude tests are higher than those of college freshmen. This is especially true of mathematical aptitude tests, at which they do much better than on the verbal tests. Their verbal aptitude is a little above average, but it is lower than that of freshmen at some of the very best liberal arts colleges.

It would seem that entering cadets and midshipmen are qualified mentally for a relatively rigorous educational program. There is little doubt, however, that the quality would be still higher if military careers were more attractive to American youth. This is a matter that has concerned the academies in recent years. All of them have undertaken public relations programs to sustain the level of applications for admission. Speeches have been made, literature mailed, parent forums created, and cadets and midship-

[24] In an unpublished memorandum for the panel on physical education of the Service Academy Board, 1949, Dr. Bock made other points of potential significance, but we relegate them to this footnote because many specialists feel they are not supported by adequate evidence. He states that muscular development is less prominent among sensitive, intelligent, and creative persons, and that such persons tend to reject hard physical work, sports, or drastic forms of exercise. He asserts they are often better suited for scientific research and other "high level" military duties. He suggests that the academies review their physical requirements, now designed to recruit prospective combat leaders, in view of the changing functions of the professional officer corps. His views stem from recent medical, anthropological, and psychological research, some of the inferences from which are highly controversial.

[25] The reluctance of some members of Congress to restrict entrance to the academies to "bookworms" or "bright boys" became apparent during the hearings on the Air Force Academy bill in 1954.

men dispatched on "good will" missions. Strenuous efforts have been made to build winning football teams that will attract public attention. Entrance requirements have also been simplified. There has been a growing reliance on college board aptitude and achievement tests. The only secondary school courses required by all three academies are English and mathematics through plane geometry. West Point permits applicants to take a college board achievement test in social studies if they have not had a course in United States history. In the postwar years Annapolis ceased to require secondary school courses in chemistry, physics, and trigonometry. It found that many high schools did not offer these subjects annually and that civilian colleges, as well as West Point, were tending to impose fewer such specific requirements on applicants.

There is also little doubt that the quality of entrants would be higher if Congress permitted a genuine competition for appointments. The present competition is limited and unsystematic, startlingly so considering that the prize is in effect a four year national scholarship covering all expenses. In the case of 61 percent of the nominations at Annapolis and 85 percent at West Point, members of Congress simply designate a preferred candidate who is appointed if he can pass the official entrance requirements. He does not have to excel; he does not have to beat competitors. All he has to do is pass.[26]

The Air Force Academy has won legislative authority to use a different selection system for its first four years. Here, each member of Congress designates as many as 10 candidates for each vacancy, and all candidates from any given state are considered to be in competition with one another. But unless Congress renews this authority after 1959, the Air Force Academy will automatically revert to the system used by its sister institutions.

[26] Some members of Congress give examinations before they name the principal and alternates from their districts. But no one knows to what extent they bind themselves by the results. Some have frankly confessed that they do not.

CHAPTER TEN

THE CURRICULA AND INSTRUCTION OF THE

SERVICE ACADEMIES

IT WAS our original intent to examine only the social sciences and humanities at the service academies because we believed these subjects to be particularly relevant as a foundation upon which officers could later build in an effort to prepare themselves for policy level positions. We soon found, however, that the place of the social sciences and humanities could be understood only in terms of other requirements, and that the work in other areas, coming during a formative period in the life of a prospective officer, had too great an impact on his motivation, his interests, and his outlook to be ignored in our study. We have therefore attempted a general analysis of the curricula.

Courses of instruction at the service academies are both longer and more intensive than those at most liberal arts colleges. Cadets and midshipmen attend from 25 to 30 percent more classes during the academic year. They must also take two months of practical training each summer. The latter requirement in effect adds a fifth year to the total course. About half or slightly less than half of this rigorous program is devoted to the subjects that are traditionally associated with a liberal arts education. This is a direct result of the multiple objectives of the service academies. Their stated aim is not only to produce educated men but officers who can eventually assume the responsibilities of leadership in air, sea, or land warfare. To accomplish their goal they deem it necessary to provide instruction in no less than four areas, three of which have no exact counterpart at many civilian institutions. These

197

areas, all very closely interrelated and often mutually supporting, are:

1. Character building. This is designed to develop certain values, motives, and personal habits deemed desirable in officers.

2. Military, naval, or air science. This is designed to provide substantive knowledge and skills specifically related to an officer's chosen profession.

3. Basic engineering. This is designed to prepare the ground for intelligent use of military equipment or apparatus but often has applicability to other professions as well.

4. Liberal arts and sciences. This is designed to lay a foundation for the development of officers as human personalities, citizens, and public servants.

Before these programs are discussed in detail, three general warnings must be issued. The first is that the curriculum of the Air Force Academy continues to undergo substantial modifications; the most recent changes were made in 1956. The second is that the missions of the three schools are not identical; therefore their curricula cannot be expected to be identical. The Naval Academy, in particular, seeks to produce more fully qualified junior officers than its sister institutions. Many of its graduates go directly to sea while graduates of the other two academies receive intensive schooling after graduation. The third point is that since each academy uses different categories to describe its curriculum, we have found it necessary to adopt our own terminology in order to make comparisons. No academy organizes its work on the basis of all the terms or concepts employed here. We are also certain that no academy would agree completely with the manner in which we have distributed parts of its program over the areas defined above.[1]

Character Building

Character building, the first and most important area to be discussed, is least closely related to particular courses of instruction; to be more accurate it is related to *all* courses of instruction. This

---

[1] For example, we have classified as "engineering" some work that might just as appropriately be regarded as an integral part of military, naval, or air science. Similar difficulties arise in attempting to determine whether given courses should be categorized as "engineering" or as "basic science," or whether studies in military law, psychology, and history are better categorized as "social science" or "military science."

is the phenomenon that distinguishes the service academies most sharply from civilian institutions. At the academies the desire to build character is more than a vague hope; it is a firm determination. They undertake the job with greater confidence, with the unequivocal support of all officialdom, and, most important of all, with infinitely greater system. Use is made of every kind of condition, precept, example, and incentive that Plato so long ago prescribed for men whose way of life must be that of a camp.

The image of the good man, the ideal military leader, is itself drawn in considerable detail. He is a highly motivated person, determined to devote his life to his country through a career in the armed forces. He is crisp, firm, dignified, and loyal to his calling and to his comrades. He performs zestfully the work expected of him. He abhors indifference or lethargy in the path of duty. He is a team player, unselfish and reliable. His sense of honor induces him to keep faith, to strive for truthfulness, sincerity, and straightforwardness in all things. Deceit, quibbling, or evasiveness he regards as impermissible. He is obedient to orders, prompt, and courageous, both physically and morally. He respects rank and its privileges and responsibilities. He honors the age-old traditions of his profession.

The work of developing responsible leaders starts immediately upon entry into an academy. The new cadet or midshipman does not begin by attending classes but by spending a summer in preliminary training. He is introduced into the discipline and routine of military life, with its courtesies, ceremonies, and responsibilities. He learns to take orders, to work fast, and to keep fit. At West Point this regimen has become known as "beast barracks." The term itself suggests that it is something of a shock treatment designed to impress the new cadet with the break that he has made with civilian life, to eradicate any sloppy habits he may have acquired, to give him the confidence that comes from facing and conquering reasonable hardship, and to knit him together more closely with his classmates, who undergo the same experience.

None of the academies grants its students leaves of absence in the first year, except for Christmas vacation in the case of the Naval Academy. It is felt important to guard them against unsettling exposure to the outside world. Upperclassmen have four weeks' vacation each summer. But even at the Air Force Academy, which is inclined to be less severe in these matters, there is little opportunity for such time-honored collegiate pursuits as bull sessions, burning the midnight oil, having a beer with the boys, or just loafing around campus. The student is a member of the armed forces subject to military law. His daily life is planned with infinite care. Up about six o'clock, he follows a schedule that tells him when to eat, study, change his clothes, go to formation, go to class, clean his room, stand inspection, drill, play, and sleep. His wristwatch is less a convenience than a necessary instrument of survival.

An elaborate system of self-government enables each man to exercise leadership and thus to develop maturity and responsibility. The student bodies are formally organized into military units. The Air Force Academy has its wing of cadets, the Naval Academy its brigade of midshipmen, the Military Academy its corps of cadets. The officers of these units are upperclassmen selected on the basis of aptitude and other factors. New students serve in the ranks in accordance with the principle that he who wishes to rule must first learn to obey. Upperclassmen also help supervise summer training, intramural athletics, and other student activities. Under their tutelage the plebe is kept on his toes. He learns the ethical credo of the institution. He also memorizes bits of lore and meaningless answers to irrelevant questions. He discovers that it is not his to reason why, that it is bad to be a "lone wolf," and that cheering at athletic events is a duty as well as a joy. Cruder forms of hazing, however, are prohibited at all academies. Moreover, there is no social snobbery. Young men of varying origins are knit together into a group with a remarkable *esprit de corps*.

In their efforts to make leaders of cadets and midshipmen academy officials rely mainly on the massive social pressure that students can exert on each other rather than on their own disciplinary powers. Such pressure is made particularly effective by the pervasive system of self-government that has been described above and by the almost compulsive gregariousness of the students themselves. One formal instrument of social control has often played an important part. This is the aptitude rating system. As it worked in the past, each student evaluates the leadership potential of certain other students at fixed periods. The particular criteria he is asked to keep in mind varied at the different institutions. They included such qualities as ability to elicit group cooperation, firmness, enthusiasm, and thoughtfulness. The important point is that the rating scale forces comparative judgments. Some name has to be put at or near the top, some name at or near the bottom, and the other names in between.[2] Each individual receives a composite score based on all the ratings he has received. Those who do poorly are counseled and guided by commissioned officers. In extreme cases they may be dismissed for "lack of aptitude for the service." In all cases the aptitude rating is transformed into a grade which plays a part in determining a student's class standing.[3]

A psychiatrist at one of the academies told us that the rating period is a time of heightened tension and stress in the student body. This is deemed a small price to pay for the information about his own deficiencies that a student may obtain from his company officers, the experience he receives in the art of judging men, and the incentive afforded him to conform to group norms. Men who know that they are on trial before a jury of their peers will govern themselves accordingly.

Physical education and athletics also contribute to the larger character-building program. Great emphasis is placed on them. Participation is compulsory; the observer is quickly struck by the number of sports offered and by the high quality of the facilities and equipment provided. The service academies invest more time and money in such activities than do civilian colleges of comparable size because they expect greater dividends. They hope to develop those special qualities regarded as essential in a fighting man: an aggressive competitive spirit and the strength and endurance to surmount severe physical hardship. Students at all academies therefore participate not only in recreational sports such as golf but in the more rugged physical-contact sports such as football or wrestling. Moreover, each man is required to play on a team. A third or more are members of varsity or plebe squads that take part in intercollegiate competitions. The others take part in the serious and highly organized business of intramural competitions. Their performance is observed by civilian coaches and commissioned officers. At West Point undesirable traits of players, cadet coaches, cadet officials, and even "benchwarmers" may be called

---

[2] Each student is rated by a commissioned officer as well as by his peers.
[3] The weight given to the aptitude rating may increase as the student progresses from his first to his final year.

to the attention of a tactical officer whose duty it is to eradicate them.

In singling out the physical education and athletic programs at this point, we do not wish to suggest that they are the only subjects of instruction that are intended to contribute directly to character formation. Opportunity is taken in all classes, drills, maneuvers, and cruises to provide practical experience in the exercise of approved personal virtues. Special work in military psychology and leadership, though designed primarily to develop substantive military knowledge and skills, constantly presents relevant moral themes. For example, in the course given at West Point the very first principle of leadership is said to be, "Take responsibility for your actions regardless of their outcomes." Courses in naval and military history present the great captains of the past not merely as skilled practitioners but as bearers of those personal attributes that have always been revered by men of arms. Moreover the *methods* as well as the subjects of instruction are intended to build character. The famed system of daily recitation and grading, instituted by Thayer and only recently modified, is defended on disciplinary as well as intellectual grounds. It is believed to develop a sense of responsibility, a habit of meeting commitments faithfully. In a sense the entire atmosphere and tone of the academies are planned to support their principal aim. From the moment he takes his oath of office a midshipman or cadet is surrounded on all sides by monuments, relics, trophies, buildings, and pictures that remind him what manner of man he must be. It is the duty of *every* instructor to set the example in his class and to erase faults where he finds them. A student does not enter a different world when he goes from the drill field to the desk.

Though every officer at the academies has a serious obligation to contribute to the character-building program, special responsibility is vested in the commandant of cadets or midshipmen.[4] The commandant at West Point heads a Department of Tactics whose mission is stated to include the development of "character" and "qualities and attributes of leadership." The commandant at

[4] The commandants also direct much of the practical military training. At the Air Force Academy and West Point they have an additional responsibility for physical education. At Annapolis and West Point they have an additional responsibility for instruction in military psychology and leadership.

202

Annapolis heads an Executive Department which exists "to prepare midshipmen, mentally, temperamentally, psychologically, and through indoctrination and the development of character, for the exercise of command." The prestige of a commandant is greater than that of heads of academic departments and probably second only to that of the superintendent. At Annapolis and the Air Force Academy this is acknowledged by regulations that authorize the commandant to preside over the governing board in the superintendent's absence. At West Point and the Air Force Academy the commandant's billet is the only one except the superintendent's and the dean's that may be filled by a general officer. Moreover, the commandant shares with the superintendent the special attitudes and interests of a transient military executive, while the dean's background and duties are more likely to equip him with attitudes and interests similar to those of the permanent heads of departments and permanent academic professors.

Each commandant has a battery of commissioned officers to assist him in supervising the student military organizations. A particularly heavy responsibility rests on the roughly two dozen company officers, or "tacs" as they are called at West Point. They are constantly on duty in the barracks and on the drill and athletic fields. They provide guidance to student delinquents and advice to student officers. They maintain discipline and monitor many extracurricular activities and organizations. Each of these men has strong views about the importance of his work. If pressed, more than one will admit that the academic programs in arts, sciences, and engineering could be accomplished as well at many civilian colleges. Some will even concede that the program of military studies could be carried on as well at officer candidate schools or comparable institutions. But not so the character-building program. "That," in the words of one of them, "is the primary reason for the existence of this school." Another one raised with us the question of what Annapolis can give a man that he cannot get elsewhere. He answered his own question, simply but with deep conviction: "Bancroft Hall." [5] A West Point tactical officer

---

[5] The same point was made by Rear Admiral Wilson Brown, superintendent, to the Board of Visitors in 1940 when he stated, "Character and general aptitude for the service are emphasized even more strongly than the mental facility to learn."

told us, "The academic people are their teachers; we are their fathers." We have also been told that the latter remark distorts by exaggerating the relative influence of each group of officers on the students. Certainly some students develop mixed feelings toward those who conduct official inspections.

A rough but important clue to the value placed on many Army and Naval activities is the percentage of academy graduates assigned to them. In the Tactical and Executive Departments the percentage is relatively high. We were also told that the Executive Department receives the first opportunity to select from the pool of junior officers assigned to the Naval Academy. We have not confirmed this but we are impressed that such a story circulates. Impressive evidence can also be found in the attainments of athletic and physical education instructors whose work, as noted above, is believed to have particular relevance to the character-building program.[6] Similarly, although this is admittedly an impressionistic observation, the facilities and equipment available for athletics seem superior to those available for many purely academic purposes. The Service Academy Board's panel on physical education concluded that the programs at West Point and Annapolis surpassed almost all such in civilian colleges. It is difficult to see how a comparable verdict could have been passed on the libraries of the service academies or on the office space then available to the teaching staff. All these things indicate *de facto* values of an institution.

Under these circumstances it would be unnatural if there were not occasional conflicts between the commandants and their staffs on the one hand and the academic staffs on the other. If the academic staffs pile too much work on cadets or midshipmen, the company officers are likely to be the first to hear about it. There is bound to be some competition for the time and interests of the students in any event simply because the program is so crowded

[6] For example, of the eleven men listed as coaches in a recent Annapolis catalog, one had formerly coached a world championship crew, one had coached a major professional football team, one had played second base on a team in three world series, one was a former world record holder in a track event, and two were former presidents of national intercollegiate coaches' associations in their respective sports. In other words these men were not simply adequate; they stood near the very top of their professions. It is not easy to say what would constitute equivalent attainment in the case of academic professors, but surely not many of those at the academies hold comparably lofty positions in their specialities.

and all authorities are equally persuaded that their part of the program has overriding importance. We do not wish to exaggerate this problem, first because a moderate amount of competition may be a sign of high morale and pride of work on all sides, second because we also encounter evidence of strong support by each group for the program of the other. Similarity of status may also promote cooperation. At Annapolis both the heads of the academic departments and the members of the Executive Department are temporary appointees; all other things being equal this common bond simplifies the relationship. At West Point the heads of the academic departments are permanent, the members of the Tactical Department temporary; in this situation cooperation is more dependent on deliberate efforts on both sides and therefore varies more with personalities.

The gulf may also narrow if subordinates on the two sides resemble one another in background. Here again, West Point's problem is more difficult than Annapolis's because the entire group of academic instructors contains relatively more men who made good academic records as cadets and who were sent to graduate school at civilian institutions. The Tactical Department refers to itself proudly, though with some exaggeration, as the only self-perpetuating oligarchy of "goats." The gap widens if a larger percentage of tactical officers are drawn from the ranks of troop leaders, especially those who have served in combat. For there is sometimes an implicit bond among men who have come under enemy fire and have survived. Their spiritual fraternity may lack even the semblance of form but it is not on that account less real. Its gates are guarded by the few who have not merely fought but have held in their hands the lives of other fighting men. No one who has not seen battle may enter. Sophisticated academic department heads at West Point have avoided the creation of such a psychological barrier by securing officers who have served meritoriously with troops as well as with books. Their beribboned instructors are most likely to be able to communicate effectively with the Tactical Department and with the cadets who already know what must come first in their scheme of things. The academic instructors themselves help immeasurably by assisting in the summer program, on the athletic field, and in extracurricular activities.

We come now to that part of the service academy programs presented in separate academic courses in a formally organized curriculum. In brief outline, these courses at each of the academies are as follows:

Subjects of Academic Instruction [7]

MILITARY ACADEMY

Freshman Year
Mathematics
Military topography and graphics
English composition
Foreign language
Military hygiene

Sophomore Year
Mechanics of fluids
Mechanics of solids
Electricity
Military instructor training
Geography
U.S. and foreign government
European history
Far Eastern history
Military hygiene

Junior Year
Mathematics
Physics
Chemistry
Foreign language
English literature
Military psychology and leadership
Military topography and graphics
Military hygiene

Senior Year
Military engineering
Military history
Elements of economics
Economics of national security
International relations
Ordnance
English literature, composition
Law (elements; constitutional; military)
Military psychology and leadership
Military hygiene

NAVAL ACADEMY

Freshman Year
Mathematics
Chemistry
Marine engineering (descriptive geometry; engineering drawing)
Foreign language
English composition and literature

Sophomore Year
Electrical engineering
Marine engineering (fluid mechanics; thermodynamics)
U.S. government
Principles of economics
Speech
Ordnance and gunnery
Mathematics
Naval leadership
Hygiene

[7] As offered in 1955–1956; the Air Force Academy curriculum was approved in this form in 1956.

Junior Year	*Senior Year*
Mathematics	Naval tactics and operations
Physics	Naval history; research paper
Marine engineering (materials; naval machinery)	Composition and literature
Modern European history	Marine engineering (naval construction; internal combustion engines)
U.S. diplomatic history	
Geography	Electronics
Foreign language	Aviation
Aerodynamics	Naval organization and administration
	Military law

AIR FORCE ACADEMY

Freshman Year	*Sophomore Year*
Mathematics	Mathematics
Chemistry	Physics
English composition	English composition and literature
Logic	
Geography	History of Western civilization
Graphics	Psychology

Junior Year	*Senior Year*
Mechanics and materials	Thermodynamics
Electrical engineering	Aerodynamics
English literature	Aircraft design appreciation
American history	Isms and international economics
Principles of economics	
Economics of national security	Comparative government
U.S. government	International relations
	Foreign language
	Law
	Military history

Military, Naval, or Air Science

Each student gets an introduction to knowledge and skills that ordinarily cannot be acquired at civilian colleges except insofar as they are provided in ROTC courses. Much of this work is administered by the commandants though certain academic departments play important supporting roles, especially at the Naval Academy. It is given some attention in every academic term and absorbs almost all the time of the summer months. The first step is to give cadets and midshipmen an idea of the conditions under which fighting men live and work. Learning is from the ground up. It proceeds from the simpler duties of the individual airman, sailor, and soldier to the over-all structure of the armed forces. In the course of their summer cruises, for example, midshipmen stand watch, scrub decks, fly in torpedo planes, clean boilers, and overhaul machinery. Each man spends some time in navigation, gunnery, engineering, and communications. West Point cadets acquire basic knowledge of combat arms, supporting services, and major components of other services. In the summer they visit warships, observe amphibious training, and visit Air Force bases and centers. The Air Force cadet likewise gets a basic knowledge of operating and support commands, and an introduction to troop, air-borne, amphibious, submarine, and joint operations. Annapolis, it should be noted, does not send midshipmen to installations of the other services in the summer; instead it instructs them in the amphibious and air problems of its own service.

The Naval Academy has been concerned with aviation since the first world war. Emphasis on it has increased in recent years. But no effort is made to produce pilots; prospective Naval aviators go to Pensacola upon graduation. In the second world war, West Point actually engaged in pilot training, but this was discontinued after the war because it encroached too much on the remainder of the curriculum. Planners of the Air Force Academy took careful note of this experience. Their original impulse, as noted in chapter six, was to omit or to limit severely the amount of practical flight instruction. They were unable to maintain this position because of actual or anticipated criticism from congressmen and the public. The problem was how to make a convincing case for the expenditure of large sums of money for an Air Force Academy that did not take to the air. The compromise reached at the opening of the school provided each cadet with training leading to the wings and the aeronautical rating of an observer (navigator). He received only a limited indoctrination training in piloting an aircraft. In practice more than two thirds of his navigation training consisted of ground instruction. Even this compromise solution placed a heavy burden on the rest of the curriculum. In the future, moreover, the academy may be subjected to pressure to provide more flight instruction. In 1956 its first Board of Visitors recommended a program of pilot training in light aircraft.

At all three academies students are instructed in the principles and use of weapons, and in the direction or maneuvering of forces and equipment. Annapolis is distinguished from the other academies by a much greater use of classroom recitation time for such subjects. It provides academic courses in seamanship, naval tactics and operations, air operations, ordnance, and gunnery. At the Air Force Academy most of the work in analogous areas is given in afternoon drills and in the summers. West Point stands about halfway between the other two schools in this respect. It provides academic courses in map reading and ordnance. Its ordnance work, however, emphasizes design, engineering, and production problems rather than the technique of using weapons. In general West Point devotes less *total* time to the operational aspects of military science than the other two schools.

The academies also provide work in administration, leadership, instruction technique, military law, and military history. Some of this, as will be evident, might appropriately be regarded as part of the social sciences program but we prefer to treat it at this point. One major generalization that can be made about these fields is that both West Point and the Air Force Academy, particularly the former, devote considerably more classroom time to them than Annapolis; in this respect the situation that exists with respect to operational training is reversed.

Law is studied because officers are often required to prepare or investigate charges or to serve as trial counsel, defense counsel, members of courts-martial, or members of boards of inquiry. At West Point this instruction is given by a separate department whose staff consists of lawyers and members of the bar. The course includes not only military law but also elements of criminal law, constitutional law, the rules of evidence, and those aspects of civil law that an officer may find useful in advising enlisted men when qualified lawyers are unavailable. The Air Force Academy's approach is roughly similar but instruction in military justice is part of the airmanship program rather than the academic program; as such it is under the jurisdiction of the commandant of cadets. The Naval Academy's program is much shorter.

Courses in military psychology and leadership were introduced into West Point and Annapolis shortly after world war II, probably as a result of the changing composition of the armed forces. The increase in the educational level, technical skill, and demands or expectations of fighting men put a premium on a sophisticated understanding of human relations. The armed forces turned to professional psychologists for help in designing courses that had special application to human problems likely to be encountered by junior officers. At West Point the pressure to include instruction in this subject came directly from General Eisenhower, who, as chief of staff, asked the superintendent to provide work in "practical or applied" psychology. At both the older academies the instruction is given by the Executive or the Tactical Department, assisted by some professional psychologists. Concepts and theories of human behavior are studied for the "payoff" value they may have to a young officer who must help his men adjust to one another, to him, and to the requirements of service life. Leadership is understood in the context of the relationship of commander to subordinate in small face-to-face groups. At West Point distinct subunits cover basic psychology, principles and techniques of leadership, and military instruction and training. At Annapolis psychology and leadership are merged in a much shorter course. At the Air Force Academy the study of psychology and leadership is about the same as at West Point but more emphasis appears to be placed on "pure" rather than "applied" psychology.

The military and naval history courses, which are highly regarded by the students, are a kind of capstone of the work in military, naval, or air science. They also support the work in liberal arts, especially the study of national policy and history. As noted earlier, they make important contributions to the program of character formation. But their major function is to introduce the student to the evolution of his service and to the development of its higher doctrines. At West Point and Annapolis great battles are examined in terms of the strategies that set the stage, the tactical plans and decisions of commanders, the use of new technical devices, and so forth. Since leadership is a prime element in any battle or campaign, study is made of the principal commanders involved. At West Point this is a broad-gauged course ably administered by the Department of Military Art and Engineering. The framework is naturally the field of ground warfare but air and naval participation are studied to widen the students' perspective. Attention is directed to parallel political, scientific, economic, and social events. Annapolis's course, administered by the Department of English, History, and Government, is considerably shorter but its place is secured by a small band of civilian professors who continue to dedicate scholarly lives to research in the field. It too reaches out to explore more general topics such as disarmament, blockades, joint operations, bases, lifelines. Throughout runs the theme that control of the seas has been of decisive importance in time of peace and war. The Air Force Academy has the shortest military history course. At the time of this writing its content and departmental status had not yet been finally determined. Topics that may be included are great military leaders and thinkers, evolution of weapons, command, strategy, joint operations, military policy, and principles of war. About half of the course will be devoted to the history of air warfare, but the time available will be insufficient to study specific battles in great detail. At all academies, it should be noted, there is a missionary aspect to military history courses. Among other things they are designed to make a student proud of the past achievements of his service, confident of its central importance, sensitive to the consequences of failure to provide the national resources necessary for its support, resolute to maintain its claims in the face of competing demands, and determined to follow a lifetime career in its ranks.

Engineering

It is sometimes said that the service academies are engineering schools. This is untrue. But introductory courses in the various branches of engineering, civil, mechanical, and electrical, have long occupied a large part of their teaching time. Distinguished civilian engineers often serve on Boards of Visitors. Administrative officials often compare and contrast their curricula with those of engineering schools. Some of the methods and concepts that they employ are familiar to engineering institutions. One illustration, small perhaps, but of interest, is the frequent use they make of the term "humanistic-social" to designate subjects other than mathematics, the natural sciences, or the engineering disciplines. The point is that this term, which is standard usage for the American Association for Engineering Education, would be regarded by most liberal arts colleges as a fusion of two distinct areas of human knowledge. The liberal arts college regards the humanities and the social sciences as two of the three main pillars

211

of a general education, the third pillar being the natural sciences and mathematics. The engineering school often regards them as a single residual or "all other" category in an otherwise technical education.

At the Naval Academy most engineering courses are administered by the Departments of Marine Engineering and Electrical Engineering, but courses with some engineering content are also taught by the Departments of Mathematics, Aviation, and Ordnance and Gunnery. At the Military Academy engineering courses are taught by the Departments of Electricity, Ordnance, Military Art and Engineering, and Military Topography and Graphics. The major components of this program at both institutions, as well as at the Air Force Academy, are revealed by the curricular outlines set forth earlier in this chapter.

One significant generalization that can be made about this work is that the Air Force Academy devotes considerably less time to it than its sister institutions. Another is that each academy seeks constantly to apply general engineering principles or techniques to the special problems of its parent service. In addition each academy offers one or more engineering courses concerned almost exclusively with service matériel. The Air Force Academy has a single short course on aircraft design. The Naval Academy has courses that deal with boilers, machinery, internal combustion engines, and ship construction and stability. The Military Academy has courses that deal with armaments, vehicles, bridges, roads, fortifications, and so on. Some of this work actually goes beyond principles of design and construction to a consideration of operating techniques and might therefore be regarded as part of the work in military, naval, or air science. The main emphasis, however, appears to be on engineering.

Mere enumeration of these topics helps explain why so much attention is given to engineering at the service academies. The world of combat is peculiarly a world of physical means. The younger officer has always to deal with highly complicated apparatus. The senior officer must be competent to direct and evaluate the technical work of his subordinates. Increasingly, he is also called on to administer research and development programs or to accept or reject the far-reaching proposals that flow therefrom.

In the case of West Point and Annapolis there are also important historical reasons. Until about 1870 West Point made its reputation in the world of education and industry by the quality of its civil engineering courses and the technical competence of its graduates. The Corps of Engineers was universally esteemed as the intellectual elite of the Army and as a major contributor to the development of the American nation. As late as 1956 it furnished a significant number of the department heads that shaped the curriculum of the Military Academy.

In the case of the Naval Academy the historical factors are more complex. The advent of steam in the nineteenth century led to a separate corps of engineer officers in the Navy and a separate program for cadet engineers at Annapolis. The rise of these specialists produced a crisis over command at sea. By sending his crew aloft the captain of a sailing ship had at once controlled the movement of his vessel and confirmed his authority over his men. He united in his person the knowledge necessary to navigate, propel, and fight the ship. The coming of steam and the rise of a separate corps of officers who alone understood its mysteries, by destroying this unity of knowledge, threatened to destroy unity of command. Engineer officers had their own ideas about speed, repairs, conservation of fuel, and strain on machinery. A captain without the technical competence to question their judgments was in the position of a dog being wagged by his own tail. By the turn of the century the line officer had no alternative but to eliminate the specialist at sea and to become something of an engineer himself. The place to start was at Annapolis; the place to continue was at postgraduate school. Only seven years elapsed between the demise of the corps of engineers (1899) and the start of postgraduate instruction in engineering for line officers (1906).

The hold of engineering at the academies may also reflect national attitudes.[8] We value technical skill. Our military men are not content to be mere manipulators of equipment; they feel they must know why it works as it does. The price paid for this attitude has of course mounted rapidly in recent years. As each

[8] It is interesting in this respect to note that the engineering department retains greater autonomy in the British Navy; the line officers' technical qualifications are correspondingly less. American officers tell the story of the British captain who is asked what kind of engines his ship has and replies, "I believe they are steam engines."

new technical breakthrough occurs our academies are determined to teach at least the fundamentals of the subject. This creates constant pressure to expand the engineering side of the curricula. The availability of postgraduate courses does not relieve the situation because instructors in engineering at the academies argue that officers will be unable to complete advanced work within the time normally allowed unless they have had an adequate technical education at the undergraduate level.

Liberal Arts and Sciences

We have defined liberal arts and sciences narrowly to include only basic courses at the academies that are also found at most nonspecialized undergraduate schools. These are mathematics, physics, chemistry, communication arts, the humanities, and the social sciences. Even under so narrow a definition all three academies spend more time on arts and sciences than on either engineering or military subjects. Moreover the absolute amount of instruction they provide is much closer to the amount provided by civilian colleges than one might suppose, because their total educational programs are unusually long. But at no academy do the arts and sciences as defined here constitute more than about two thirds of all instruction given during the academic year. At Annapolis they constitute less than one half. It has the shortest program, shorter than West Point's because it devotes more time to naval science than West Point does to military science, as those terms are defined here. The Air Force Academy has the longest program, longer than West Point's because it devotes less time to engineering as defined here. At both West Point and Annapolis, mathematics and the natural sciences together constitute the largest component of the program; at the Air Force Academy they constitute the smallest.

Mathematics, physics, and chemistry are not simply the natural basis of the extensive work in engineering; they are also regarded as essential to professional competence in the field. Study is constantly directed to practical military applications, for example, in trajectory, turbines, gyroscopic action, or explosives.[9] West Point's

[9] Sciences that appear to have less immediate relevance—for example, biology and geology—receive much less attention.

214

program in mathematics is exceptionally long; half again as long as Annapolis's.

Again history supplies an explanation. The need to train artillerists and engineers in mathematics was a premise of undergraduate military education in the Napoleonic era. It was an important reason for the founding of West Point. Today the Department of Mathematics at the Military Academy is the beneficiary of this great tradition. One cannot visit it without feeling that here is something more than an aggregate of teachers, pupils, and textbooks; here is the citadel of an ancient faith. We also encountered a contention that mathematical and scientific studies are uniquely conducive to rigorous analytical thinking.[10] Clarity of thought, ability to reason logically from given premises, and ability to order data systematically are much prized by professional officers. Many mathematicians and natural scientists at the academies are sincerely convinced that their subjects are especially likely to develop such capacities, or at least more likely to develop them than a study of Latin, lyrics, or law.

There is a prevailing misconception that work in the humanities and in such communication arts as composition and speech is virtually nonexistent at the academies because they are primarily technical schools. The truth is that no academy offers less work in these subjects than is ordinarily *required* of a student at a civilian college; the Air Force Academy offers substantially more. But it is not easy to determine how much time is spent on the humanities proper because the communication arts, for accounting purposes, are lumped in with them instead of being regarded as tools that support all parts of the curriculum. The practical effect is to overstate considerably the time devoted to the humanities. The same practice prevails at civilian colleges and a similar distortion results; but the consequences are more serious at the academies because the absence of free electives makes the official allocation of time a more important and controversial matter.

The Air Force Academy devotes more time to English than the other two schools. It is also the only institution that provides a separate course in logic.[11] Originally it had planned a required

---

[10] This argument is also used in defense of work in engineering.

[11] The course in logic includes the study of propaganda, fallacies, semantics, syllogistic reasoning, and scientific method. West Point includes some logic in its first year English course.

course in fine arts, but this has been converted into an optional course for students who demonstrate unusual proficiency in English. All academies include a little instruction in fine arts in other courses. The literary masterpieces that their students analyze are comparable to those studied at better civilian institutions, and many of the instructors assigned to this work are highly competent.

Concern for the professional relevance or applicability of subject matter is less obviously present in this part of the curriculum than in any other. But it is not wholly absent. By occasionally using literature to support the work of character formation, the academies follow a path that Plato pointed out long ago. Some literary works may be selected for their martial themes. Instructors may draw principles of leadership from the experience of characters in fiction. The impulse to relevance also appears in the growing attention given to speech, parliamentary law, conference procedure, and similar subjects useful to graduates who may become negotiators or spokesmen for military units interacting with the outer world.[12] Emphasis on composition in part reflects the growing importance of memoranda, orders, staff studies, and correspondence in large scale organization. It also reveals that the academies, like civilian colleges, are struggling against what they deem the semiliteracy of high school graduates. In this struggle there are some hidden traps of which the academies may well be wary. Despite their prodigious efforts there are always some "old grads" who complain that newly commissioned lieutenants and ensigns can neither read nor write. Such alumni opinion carries more weight at the academies than at civilian institutions. The danger is that literature courses may be denuded of genuine literary content in a futile effort to establish levels of proficiency in writing and speech that are satisfactory to every kibitzer in the Pentagon and in the field.

Foreign language study at the academies cuts across the communication arts, the humanities, and to some extent the social sciences. West Point and Annapolis require two years of study of one of a number of modern languages, including Russian; the student may make his own selection. At the Air Force Academy language study was originally intended to be optional. Partly as

[12] The Naval Academy has conducted an excellent program in after-dinner speaking since the 1920's.

a result of external pressure it now requires each cadet to take work in French or Spanish, but the course is slightly shorter than at the other schools. Additional languages may be offered in the future. At all academies it is the spoken language that is emphasized, though advanced sections may study literary works of high quality. Special work is made available at some academies to those who hope ultimately to qualify as interpreters or attachés. Relevance may also be sought by study of the literature or phraseology of foreign armed forces.

The social sciences are of special interest to us because the amount of attention given to them may indicate the academies' sensitivity to the challenge posed by the growing employment of officers in policy level positions within the government. We are therefore impressed by our finding that the social sciences have increased in importance in undergraduate military education. In the nineteenth century, West Point, like many civilian colleges, offered only a little history and less geography. Each was taught intermittently; each was frequently the responsibility of a chaplain also burdened from time to time with the teaching of grammar, rhetoric, logic, morals, and law. Today, even if one excludes the work in military history, law, and the more practical or applied aspects of psychology, no academy offers less instruction in the social sciences than is ordinarily required of a civilian undergraduate. The Naval Academy, whose program is by far the shortest, offers the equivalent of four single semester courses in its work in European history, American government, principles of economics, American diplomatic history, and geography. The diplomatic history course devotes a brief period to systematic analysis of international relations.

The Air Force Academy stands at the other extreme. Its original program provided the equivalent of about thirteen single semester courses in social science; in a sense this field was the major beneficiary of the decision to curtail academic courses in engineering, air science, and to some extent natural science. In 1956 the program was cut back to the equivalent of about ten single semester courses.[13] These provide work in the history of Western civilization, Oriental civilization, American history, American and foreign government, international relations, geography, basic

[13] The largest reductions were made in history and international relations.

217

psychology, principles of economics, the economics of national security, international economics, and "isms." The latter is a very short course on economic aspects of fascism, communism, socialism, and capitalism. Optional courses in the history of the Middle East, the history of Latin America, and United States diplomatic history are provided to cadets who pass qualifying tests in required history courses. An optional course in American political thought is being planned for cadets who demonstrate proficiency in American government. Such options reflect in part the influence of the Social Science Department at West Point.[14]

West Point provides the equivalent of slightly more than seven single semester courses in the social sciences.[15] The topics covered are similar to those at the Air Force Academy, though considerably less time is devoted to history and a little less time to basic psychology and government. Cadets who pass appropriate qualifying examinations take optional courses in Russian, Middle Eastern, or American diplomatic history. Over the years the Social Sciences Department has shown much vitality. Its course on the economics of national security has had considerable influence at other institutions.[16] In the first class year selected cadets undertake "operation statesman," a seminar in which they prepare policy papers on problems of American foreign policy, following the model of the Brookings Institution studies.[17] The better students in this class are selected to attend the annual Student Conference on United States Affairs, cosponsored by the department and the Cadet Forum. SCUSA has been held at West Point since 1949 and has established a notable reputation in the collegiate community. It provides a well-organized program of lectures, round table discussions, and plenary sessions lasting several days. Student delegates come from more than fifty ranking colleges, and senior participants from the academic profession and public service also are

---

[14] A number of the first social science instructors at the Air Force Academy had earlier taught at West Point, and authorities at the latter institution were consulted at various stages of Air Force Academy planning.

[15] As at the other academies, elements of social sciences are also included in law, military history, literature, and foreign language courses. For example, the senior English course at the Military Academy is in effect a course on contemporary social issues.

[16] See George A. Lincoln and others, *The Economics of National Security*, 2d edition, New York, 1954. This text was written by members of the Department of Social Sciences at the Military Academy.

[17] The Air Force Academy plans a similar project.

invited. The guest speakers usually include men who have served in the highest military or civilian posts. The Air Force Academy also plans a student conference.

To those civilian social scientists who are skeptical of all military education we can say with conviction that the substantive content of the academies' work in the social sciences is as rich as the content of their own courses. Syllabi are well designed; the texts are standard works in the field. It is true, however, that lack of time plus the desire to range over a broad area forces the academies to move from topic to topic more rapidly than most civilian colleges. They are also required to be more selective in the choice of subject matter. West Point and Annapolis, for example, do not provide much work in domestic American history. No academy gives courses in anthropology or sociology, although Colonel Lucius Holt made an eloquent plea for the latter at West Point many years ago. Not even the Air Force Academy requires all students to take a course concerned primarily with the history of social or political speculation.[18] Moreover the problem of time is only one aspect of a larger problem of status or prestige. Words must be chosen carefully here. We are not saying that the social sciences have no prestige at the academies. Our point is that there are very great pressures on the curricula of these institutions; that no field of learning can be certain that its battle for recognition has been finally won; that the recognition given to the social sciences has come fairly recently; that it varies today from academy to academy; and that certain special problems complicate efforts to maintain the status of the social sciences at any such school.

Consider, for example, the case for industrial geography or economic mobilization. It can be argued quite logically that knowledge of these subjects is important because outer limits of military power are set by the availability of resources. It can be argued that international relations or American diplomatic history should be taught because those who employ military power ought to understand the national policies that it serves. But both propositions may seem less obvious or more "theoretical" to the midshipman than the contention that knowledge of ferrous metals, oil, or alloys is useful to a young engineer officer aboard ship. A

[18] Elements of the history of ideas are included, however, in certain other courses —for example, in history or literature.

second difficulty is that such subjects, except as they involve the student's general responsibilities as a citizen, seem to him to deal with issues that will confront him only in the long distant future when he has risen to exalted status in his profession. In a word, scientific, engineering, and military studies appear to deal with matters that are visible, tangible, and immediate; the social sciences with matters that are invisible, intangible, and remote. A third difficulty is that the social sciences, to the uninitiated, seem not to require such a large substratum of specialized knowledge. Understanding of them appears to lie open to any man of common sense.

Unless real counterpressures are built into the system, this can result in an unfavorable climate of opinion. Some will conclude that "all this stuff" should be picked up by self-study in later life. Others will conclude that a little social science is useful as a kind of finishing touch or polish for the officer or gentleman, a nice extra like ballroom dancing, but not to be confused with "professional"—that is, highly relevant and important—subjects.[19] Where such attitudes exist the social sciences will be threatened by any report from the field that newly commissioned officers are lacking in some technical skill. Such attitudes also will communicate themselves to students. Cadets and midshipmen have a clearer vision of where they are going than civilian undergraduates; they respond more quickly to cues about what is important and what is not. Their scale of values may reveal itself even in the nicknames they bestow upon departments, however affectionately. They are sensitive to such subtle indices of importance as the percentage of academy graduates, line officers, or men with outstanding combat records assigned to given departments.[20]

The status of the social sciences at Annapolis is complicated by factors that do not exist at the other academies. One is that the

[19] It is well to record here our misgivings about the use of the term "professional departments" at Annapolis. It refers to Seamanship and Navigation, Ordnance and Gunnery, Aviation, and the Executive Departments. We think it cannot fail to have unfortunate effects on "nonprofessional" departments and on midshipmen. If the adjective "professional" is to be used at an undergraduate institution, it should designate any subject that may prove valuable to the generality of students in their later careers. A decision to call a subject "nonprofessional" should also be a decision to exclude it from the curriculum. But better that the term not be used at all.

[20] The percentage of academy graduates in the Department of English, History, and Government at Annapolis has sometimes been far lower than in any other department at the school.

career system of the Navy makes it necessary to instruct every student thoroughly in subjects like marine engineering and gunnery. Another is that the head of the Department of English, History, and Government holds office for only a few years. Even with the best of will he cannot provide the kind of sustained leadership within the Academy *and within the service* that was provided for over two decades by Colonel Herman Beukema of the Department of Social Sciences at the Military Academy. A third difficulty is that the social sciences are only part of a larger department that includes literature, naval history, and composition. This arrangement can be defended on the ground that it facilitates integration of related subjects. But the history of the academies suggests that something more is involved. In the 1920's West Point split its English and History Department into a Department of English and a separate Department of Economics, Government, and History, the forerunner of the present Social Sciences Department. This was both accompanied and followed by a marked increase in social sciences instruction. In 1932 Annapolis created a separate Economics and Government Department to parallel its English and History Department. This also was accompanied by a marked increase in social science instruction.[21] A few years later a new superintendent, Rear Admiral D. F. Sellers, initiated steps to reverse these decisions. Admiral Sellers stated: "No other argument has ever been heard than the general statement that the knowledge of economics and government contributes to the cultural background of a well-educated man. Turning specifically to the case of a naval officer and particularly an ensign afloat, we find that however well versed an officer of the navy may become in the subject taught him with reference to the 'government of the United States' or 'the great powers of world politics,' he is very strictly prohibited by naval regulations from expressing any opinion whatsoever that he may have formed on these subjects as a result of this study." [22]

Admiral Sellers had come to Annapolis fresh from his position as commander in chief of the United States Fleet; his views were

[21] At the same time the Department of Seamanship was merged with the Department of Navigation. This was accompanied by a decrease in time allotted to the military studies program.

[22] *Report of a Board Appointed to Consider and Make Recommendations with Respect to the Adequacy of the Curriculum at the Naval Academy to Meet the Needs of the Fleet,* Annapolis, October 5, 1937.

speedily accepted. The new department was abolished and the social science program drastically reduced. Economics disappeared from the curriculum and was not restored until after the second world war.

It does not follow that administrative parity for the social sciences automatically results in increased emphasis. But separate departmental status assures an independent voice and vote on the Academic Board. Other things being equal, the more the board is weighted on the side of science and engineering, the more difficult it is for the social sciences (and the humanities) to prosper. From this standpoint the Faculty Council and the Academy Board at the Air Force's institution are better designed than the governing boards at West Point and Annapolis because at the Air Force Academy the number of members representing the social sciences and humanities is the same as the number representing the basic and engineering sciences. Separate departmental status may also be important as a symbol of professional identity and integrity. It signals the presence of specialized knowledge and of trained men who are its creators and custodians. Other things being equal, it sustains the morale and initiative of the social scientist and advises laymen that his needs must be given serious attention. Obviously there may be situations where no such contrivance is necessary to maintain status. We do not think such conditions yet obtain at all academies despite the very real strides that their social science programs have made in this generation. Although no responsible official at Annapolis would today subscribe to the position taken by Admiral Sellers in 1937, some could ponder with profit the diametrically opposite position taken by the Board of Visitors in 1946: "The duties of a naval officer now transcend the walking of the quarter deck. Naval assignments today include responsibility not simply in the field of combat, but also in the vast area of logistics, procurement, mobilization, and international diplomatic and economic policy. Our naval officers will fill constantly increasing responsibilities as naval attaches abroad, on the staff of the United Nations organization, and at international conferences dealing with weighty diplomatic and economic questions. . . . We feel that the present curriculum can be strengthened in directing the midshipmen's thoughts along these lines."

The System of Instruction [23]

The system of instruction at the academies is as distinctive and important as the content of the curriculum. It includes an almost completely prescribed course of study, close supervision of students' work, a concern for uniform and fairly frequent grading, and extraordinary devices to help all men assimilate the great quantity of material placed before them.

No academy permits its students any substantial freedom of choice in the selection of subjects.[24] Cadets and midshipmen may not decide whether they wish to major in mathematics, economics, physics, or some other discipline. A subject is not included in the curriculum unless it has been determined to be "essential" to all. Although entering students vary widely in educational background and interests, there is a general assumption that they should receive the same education. For most practicable purposes, therefore, the elective principle gives way to the principle of relevance and unity. Modest variations have nevertheless been permitted. Sometimes, as in foreign languages, options are dictated by the needs of the services for men with a variety of linguistic abilities. A few options are given to students who are already well prepared in a given subject; this was noted in the discussion of the curricula of West Point and the Air Force Academy. A more common practice is to give superior students advanced work in the same subject. West Point and the Air Force Academy usually assign students to sections in accordance with their grades in a given subject.[25] The membership of sections is changed periodically as students' averages rise or fall. Top sections, which may include up to 20 or 30 percent of a class, often complete the required work more rapidly and move on to other topics. At West Point, for example, the top sections in mathematics spend more time on differential equations, less on calculus; in freshman English they take what almost amounts to a separate course. Several other de-

[23] The following is based principally on present and past practice at West Point and Annapolis. The Air Force Academy appears to have adopted a number of the same methods but has also expressed a determination to be more flexible. As will be noted, the other academies also continue to experiment with changes in method.

[24] The Air Force Academy originally planned to offer cadets a choice between foreign languages and aircraft design but this option was abolished in 1956.

[25] Random sectioning has been used in some of the social science and English courses at West Point.

partments excuse the top sections from review examinations to make more time available for advanced work. At the Air Force Academy, students who are especially proficient in mathematics take an accelerated course that permits them to go on to such topics as mathematical statistics. An analogous program is contemplated at Annapolis. The Naval Academy has never applied the principle of sectioning by merit across the board. But in three or four courses students have at times been divided into an "A" group and a "B" or advanced group.

About 1953 there was pressure at both Annapolis and West Point to introduce greater flexibility into the prescribed program. A committee of the Academic Council of the Naval Academy recommended that abler language students be allowed to read masterpieces in the original instead of taking the regular comparative literature course. This proposal was rejected by the Academic Board. At West Point the challenge to the prescribed curriculum was more serious. The Academic Board was asked by the Board of Visitors to study the advisability of introducing two or more majors at the end of the first or second year. One professor at the Academy suggested that West Point award two degrees, a B.S. to students specializing in science and engineering, an A.B. to those specializing in humanities and social sciences. Many practical problems were raised by these proposals. Numerous electives cannot be added without deleting present courses, each of which has staunch defenders. To modify the program of the last two years is to call into question the program of the first two years. If a student can avoid later work in engineering it is harder to contend that he should take so much preparatory work in mathematics. If some electives turn out to be easier than others, grades may no longer reflect ability and effort.

Additional reasons were also found for rejecting elective majors. It was felt that such a system would require a more specialized faculty, introduce a divisive influence into the corps of cadets, and circumscribe unduly the future development of each student. The last two points are related. Together they raise the spectre of career specialization.[26] Laymen will better appreciate the intensity of feeling on this subject if they remember that it threatens to

[26] See the discussion, earlier in this chapter, of cadet engineers and cadet midshipmen at Annapolis.

reopen century old debates over the proper relation of the combat arms to the supporting components, over promotion rates, indeed over the structure of the Army itself, that is, whether there is to be a single united army composed of several branches or only an aggregate of separate branches loosely termed an army but possessing separate career systems and relatively unresponsible to central controls of a chief of staff.

There is another moral as well. The fact that the proposal for majors was analyzed in terms of its career implications suggests once again the preoccupation of the academies with the vocational relevance of their work. The instinctive assumption is that education must and will have a direct bearing on subsequent duties; the conclusion is that if premature career specialization is undesirable, it should not be encouraged by the creation of a two track system at the undergraduate level. A civilian college, on the other hand, may support elective majors not because the fields chosen by students may be useful to them later (often the college has no idea what they will do later), but on the simple theory that a student benefits from intensive work in a field of special interest to him regardless of whether he later embarks on a career to which it has direct application. In principle, at least, the utility of elective majors can be argued without even raising the question of future vocations. Not so at the academies.

Some consequences of the prescribed curriculum now deserve closer examination. The absence of electives is resented by some students; conceivably it may discourage applicants to the academies. It also inhibits curricular change. When students are free to select courses, decisions about the allocation of instructional time and staff are to a great extent made automatically, in other words through the free market of student choice. When the curriculum is prescribed, such decisions must be made by central authority. Each change requires not only rescheduling and transfer of personnel, but, because something must be deleted, an explicit debate over educational priorities. This is a nerve-racking business that cannot be indulged in too often. The net effect is that change comes more slowly. When the curriculum is prescribed, each department also finds it necessary to prepare a persuasive case for its work. Since this case is often made in terms of its relevance to later studies or to students' future careers, the effect is to make the curriculum more vocational. Often under a prescribed curriculum important new material can be introduced only if it is added to an existing required course. The result is that all courses tend to swell with content; the pace of work quickens in order to "cover the ground"; and a variety of devices, discussed below, are introduced to help students adjust to the rapid tempo.

To some extent the academies compensate for the absence of electives by a very wide range of extracurricular activities. These include numerous clubs that support closely the more organized work of the classroom. For example, members of the Foreign Relations Club at Annapolis meet weekly to hear speakers; they also have their own reading program.[27] The Cadet Forum at West Point sponsors an ambitious program of voluntary seminars that meet weekly under the direction of a faculty member.[28] This program fills a real need and student interest in it has been remarkably high. But here, as in the case of other extracurricular activities, the final limiting factor is time.

A second feature of the instructional system is close supervision of student work. This is made easier by the small size of classes. Large lectures are by no means unknown but they are used sparingly.[29] Long periods of self-directed study are impracticable because of the numerous classes and other fixed commitments on the schedule. Sometimes the study period is a free hour sandwiched between two classes. At Annapolis, where students must form and march to and from each class, part of the hour is lost. Substantial independent projects are also the exception rather than the rule, although both West Point and Annapolis require monographs or research papers that may range from 10 to 20

---

[27] The popularity of this club attests the special interest in foreign affairs at Annapolis. Such interest is also developed by the required course in diplomatic history, advanced voluntary work in foreign languages, summer cruises to foreign ports, and the annual visit to Annapolis of naval attachés of foreign powers. The Library also reserves its highest priority for books in the field of international relations.

[28] Seminar topics at West Point have included moral and political philosophy, the great faiths, strategy, causes of war, the novel, creative writing, the history of maps, mobility of forces, armaments regulation, and the security problems of different regions of the world.

[29] Special lecture series bring distinguished outside speakers to the academies. The Annapolis series consists of some two dozen talks, primarily for the senior class, often on some foreign affairs topic. The West Point series consists of a larger number of lectures sponsored by particular departments and designed to support instruction currently being given to different classes.

typewritten pages in length; at Annapolis the best of these are published. The Air Force Academy plans a comparable project. Libraries play a far smaller role at the service academies than at civilian colleges; indeed the relative unimportance of the library may be regarded as a distinctive feature of their instructional systems.[30]

Nearly all instruction takes place in sections of from 12 to 16 students. These small classes, made possible by ample personnel and funds, are the envy of many civilian educators. Ideally they maximize each man's opportunity to participate in discussion, to state and defend a position, and to develop poise and fluency in the expression of his views. We were impressed by the relaxed atmosphere and the free exchange of ideas that prevailed in top or "savvy" sections of certain English and social science courses. But small sections also make it easier to check up on students, to drill them, and to pour content into them. This is still one of their primary functions in many courses. Each man must be prepared to recite daily in each class. This does not mean he is actually questioned or graded each day, though in some courses he is. It does mean that he will be questioned or graded quite often. The "study and recite" system has been modified to the greatest extent in the social sciences and the humanities. In fields where it is still employed it is sometimes associated with the conspicuous formalism of an earlier day. Questions and answers may follow one another as in a catechism. Students may repeat bits of data they have memorized.[31] Not too long ago one of the academies tried to teach administration by having instructors read aloud certain portions of official regulations. The ritual of the blackboard is no longer typical but it persists in a few strongholds. West Point was the first American school to make systematic use of blackboard and chalk in classrooms; its Mathematics Department led the way. In a current class in mathematics cadets proceed to numbered blackboards (odd numbers, one problem; even numbers, another). Each man marks off his domain with a ruler and

[30] Physical facilities are in some cases inadequate; staffs are too small; the per capita expenditure on books is pitifully low; collections are spotty in fields like philosophy, sociology, anthropology, economics, and domestic politics. One library closes at 6:15 p.m. because students are rarely able to use it in the evening!

[31] Here again slang terms used by students are often revealing, e.g. "spec," meaning to memorize verbatim, or "poop," indicating the material to be memorized.

writes his name neatly in its upper right-hand corner. Answers to problems are underscored with two lines in red chalk. With most of the class thus occupied, two students stand at attention in front of the instructor's desk and respond orally to questions about the assignment. Then some who have been at the boards are asked to explain their work. Each proceeds according to a set formula that runs something like this: "Sir, I am called upon to solve the following problem. . . . My method has been. . . . My results are. . . ."

Because grading is frequent there is a tendency to break subjects down into component parts, a knowledge of which can be tested in a short quiz. The grave danger here is that a course will be so fragmented that the student fails to acquire a sense of the unity of the subject. His quiz grades have great weight in the determination of his final grade. He therefore has less incentive to carry over his knowledge from one part of the course to the next. This may affect his study habits, causing him to read for detail rather than for broader themes. Some departments at West Point try to meet this problem by consolidating a series of "written general reviews" in the last days of a course, thereby creating a kind of *de facto* final examination. The Naval and Air Force Academies normally provide final examinations of two or more hours.[32]

Both the fragmentation of knowledge and formalism in classroom technique result in part from the desire to supervise students very closely. It is easier to discover whether work has been done and lessons absorbed if courses are divided into small units and if instructors follow a methodical routine in class. Conversely, in departments that do not convert classes into policing or drilling operations, students are more often encouraged to think in large terms and to advance their own views.

A third feature of the system is the desire to minimize the subjective element in grading. At West Point this is related to the importance of class standing at graduation. Top-ranking cadets are free to select not only the combat arm of their choice but their first station within that arm; the "goats" take what is left. At all academies class standing determines the order of precedence

[32] But no academy gives comprehensive examinations in which a student must show his understanding of several related courses.

among graduates commissioned on the same date. Men nearer the top of their class may also have first call on desirable living quarters or other perquisites. The emphasis on uniform and fair grading has pervasive consequences. As noted earlier, it strengthens the case for a single uniform curriculum. It also strengthens the case for frequent quizzes on the theory that a student should not be penalized unduly for one "off day." It makes it harder for teacher and student to maintain a free and easy relationship. It requires elaborate bookkeeping, now done primarily by business machines. It generates measures to minimize the effects of a particular instructor's methods or attitude. Instructors are often shifted to new sections every seven or eight weeks, sometimes more frequently. By staff conferences and staff lesson notes they are briefed in advance about what they are expected to cover in class. We do not suggest that the teacher is rigidly bound by instructions. He has more leeway than outsiders (and some superiors) might suppose. But in the last analysis he must face the controls imposed by his own conscience. His conscience tells him that his students may be put to a competitive disadvantage if he plays the prima donna or if he lets them wander all over the lot in class. An unduly sensitive conscience may cause him to restrict class discussion in subjects where such discussion is vital to the point where he nullifies the major advantage of small sections. A conscience of any kind prods him to adhere to the procedures and standards of his department head. Finally, the quest for equity affects the nature of examinations. In the past it discouraged the use of essay questions because they were harder to evaluate. It encouraged the use of true-false, multiple choice, and other forms of objective questions. Recently departments have come to rely much more heavily on essays, but even so it is necessary to guard against adopting questions simply because they are easy to grade. The temptation, by no means limited to military academies, is to confine the inquiry to whether the student understands what the textbook said. When this happens accuracy, meticulousness, and clarity of memory tend to be rewarded more than critical ability or imaginative thought.

One last feature of the system that deserves attention is the amount of assistance given to the students. Instructors dig out the important points in each assignment in order to hammer away at them in class and in laboratory.[33] Explicit and detailed instructions are given. Elaborate manuals and syllabi direct attention to key facts or concepts. Little is left to chance. Midshipmen on summer cruise complete journals containing highly detailed questions about the ship's equipment, organization, and procedures. A cadet's history notebook consists of a series of flags or blinker lights signaling the presence of names and dates to be remembered, central themes or relationships to be grasped, or provocative or penetrating questions to be asked. Laboratory apparatus and even athletic equipment is carefully laid out in advance to avoid waste time and motion. In a few courses as soon as a student finishes a quiz he proceeds to a bulletin board on which the "approved solutions" are posted. Review sessions are frequent. Departments offer extra instruction in the late afternoon or evening to those who are failing in a subject. This is sometimes supplemented by an organized coaching system operated by the students themselves with the support of company officers.

All such devices are a natural response to the challenge of how to teach courses very rich in content in a very short time. Where men must advance with one eye always on the clock there is an inevitable tendency to remove some of the boulders along the highway to knowledge, to seal off some of the side roads, and to give the panting runner an occasional whiff of oxygen.

At various points we have suggested reasons why the service academies have evolved a distinctive system of instruction. Two summary observations must now be added. One is that the less liberal remnants in the system assume the existence of a student body younger, less well informed, and less intelligent than actually exists at any academy today.

Some methods used in military, naval, and air science instruction are shaped by techniques used to train enlisted men of widely varying abilities.[34] In certain other courses, where methods have persisted over generations, they reflect an era in which students

[33] In answer to a point made by the Service Academy Board's panel on science and engineering, the superintendent of the Naval Academy stated that laboratory sessions were designed for demonstration rather than experimentation.

[34] ROTC programs have also been affected by this.

were younger, primary and secondary schools less advanced, and requirements for entry into the academies less exacting.

The other observation is that method is heavily influenced by curriculum. In introductory mathematics, natural science, and engineering courses there is often a greater presumption that questions can have a single determinate answer. Such answers cannot be argued about; they can only be found. In military science the approved technique has traditionally been drilled into men on the training field lest they find themselves helpless on the battlefield. There is a presumption that some responses must become automatic when the issue is life or death. A revealing incident occurred when the Service Academy Board's social science panel noted that to develop a skeptical, inquiring mind in future officers might breed indecision. In a superintendent's copy this passage was underlined in red and the word "yes" written in the margin. Scientific and military studies occupy a prominent place in all the curricula. Methods thought to be appropriate to them have spilled over into the humanities and social sciences, whose problems are somewhat different and whose instructors are only now beginning to evolve techniques better suited to their needs.[35]

[35] At Annapolis the advanced literature and composition course provides an outstanding example of such evolution. Each instructor remains with his class throughout the semester; he has considerable freedom in selecting the masterpieces it is to study; and he need give but a few one hour essay examinations during the course.

CHAPTER ELEVEN

AN EVALUATION OF THE SERVICE

ACADEMIES

Two difficulties stand in the way of a balanced evaluation of the service academies. One is that they were not created to prepare officers for policy level positions in the government. It is true that their literature and statements frequently suggest such an obligation. West Point acknowledges a duty to prepare cadets for ultimate "responsibilities of the highest order in the Department of Defense." The Naval Academy speaks of ultimate readiness to assume "the highest responsibilities of citizenship and Government." The Air Force Academy proposes to give each cadet a basis for "continued development throughout a lifetime of service to his country." But these phrases denote only special aspects of the total purpose. The pressing obligation of the academies is to provide the armed forces with men who can train and lead *operating* forces. Some distortion may therefore follow when evaluation is based on the partial perspective of this study. We have tried to keep this to a minimum.[1]

The second difficulty is inherent in any critique. A desire to be helpful rather than merely pleasant leads to a stress on shortcomings. We wish to make plain, therefore, that we have no desire to

[1] But apparently not with complete success. One officer who has himself been a great force in the liberalization of a service academy commented as follows on a draft of our manuscript: "To my doubtless over-sensitive soul there appears to be a subtle implication that the policies and methods of the independent liberal arts colleges are the natural ideal of all education, and that service academies, engineering schools and teachers' colleges which deviate therefrom are in some way missing the mark rather than consciously aiming in a slightly different direction. In some respects the aims of the service academies might better be compared with those of medical schools or theological seminaries which also are attempting to prepare young men for a lifetime career of dedicated service."

engage in destructive criticism of these great institutions. Though we shall not tarry long over their achievements, we do not minimize them. It means much, after all, to have academies that year after year produce loyal servants of a democratic society. Never have the men of West Point or Annapolis threatened to set themselves up as a "state within the state." It means much also that cadets and midshipmen acquire a certain civic dedication not always noticeable among more self-indulgent college youths. It is this civic dedication that inspires a readiness to sacrifice material benefits, to endure personal restraints and hardships, and to put the lifetime service of the state ahead of personal aggrandizement. The virtues of Sparta as well as of Athens have a place in a good society. If the academies do not wholly neglect Athens, they surely deserve high praise. Uninformed critics may be startled, perhaps embarrassed, when confronted with some hard statistics about these schools. Midshipmen and cadets do significantly better than average college freshmen on the graduate record examinations administered by the Educational Testing Service. From 1923 to 1956 West Point cadets won an average of one Rhodes scholarship each year. In many years they won three or four. Only three institutions of higher learning in the United States could boast a better record. Civilian colleges do not even pretend to compete with the academies in the development of essential military competence, and such competence, as noted in chapter two, is an important criterion of effectiveness in policy level positions. Whether they can compete with the academies in the development of other essential skills and attitudes is probably an irrelevant question, because most civilian colleges cannot take the indispensable first step of motivating their students to seek a military career. The college senior, unlike the high school senior, can visualize fairly clearly a number of career alternatives. His knowledge and his tastes have developed to the point where he has a surer sense of the kind of life he wants to lead. Rarely is it a military life, especially in a time of full employment. Given the nature of American society, the absence of a feudal tradition, and the powerful hold of materialistic values, military life has relatively few attractions. Even the academies would like to hold more of their students than they do. We believe that under present conditions any attempt to staff our large armed forces without drawing upon service academies would inevitably result in lowering professional standards in order to fill quotas. The only kind of society that can safely do without academies is one in which the military profession occupies such a dominant role that it can command the pick of the nation's youth for the officer corps. For better or worse America seems to have no choice but to accept these historic institutions and to lend them every encouragement as they seek to do a progressively finer job.[2]

The reader may well ask at this point how the academies' undisputed record of achievement, and particularly the scholastic prowess of their students as reflected in nation-wide tests, can be squared with the numerous criticisms made in this book. We think there is no problem here. The truth is that the academies, in their effort to keep abreast of the growing responsibilities of career officers, have already modified organization, methods, and curricula in many of the ways suggested here. Like many engineering and professional schools they have made a decision to sacrifice some degree of immediate technical skill in the hope of building more lasting assets. That decision has not affected adversely the intellectual capacity of their students, at least if the statistics we have seen are correct. We do not think that further evolution in the same direction will prove harmful, but to the contrary.

Obstacles to Further Evolution

It may be well, however, to summarize at this point some of the obstacles to further evolution. First, weapons grow more complex daily. This creates a demand for a more technical curriculum. In recent years the academies have adapted their programs to the advent of aviation, electronics, nuclear power, and other wonders of the modern age. Second, applicants to the academies seem to have a somewhat greater interest and aptitude for technical and mechanical matters. Third, because the academies are public, national institutions, they must appear to be "tending to business." A curriculum believed to have inadequate technical content is vulnerable to criticism by Congress, by the American people, and by officers who retain reservations about all education

---

[2] This does not dispose of the question of whether each service should maintain its academy in splendid isolation from the other two academies. We shall return to this issue in the last two chapters.

that is not somewhat vocational in nature. As a result of such criticism the Air Force Academy converted a course in aircraft design from an optional to a compulsory, though considerably shorter, course. Fourth, the commandants and their staffs are extremely influential agents at the academies, and important aspects of their programs are necessarily designed to prepare students for combat leadership rather than to interest them in policy level assignments in the service. These officials emphasize general military proficiency, physical fitness, and rugged competitive sports. Their aptitude-rating systems are pointed toward predicting the performance of officers in junior command and staff positions. The illustrative materials and concepts of their military psychology courses tend to assume an officer who is dealing with small face-to-face groups rather than one exercising high executive leadership. Many of the character traits that they seek to develop, though also relevant in an executive context, are necessarily the virtues of the fighting man.

A fifth obstacle to further evolution is the prescribed curriculum. This intensifies competition for teaching time, with the result that a premium is placed on courses that can be shown to be relevant to known future tasks. The search for relevance produces the characteristic rush of the academies from basic theory to applications: from physics to firepower, from mathematics to mechanics, from engineering to naval machinery, from chemistry to gasses, from psychology to leadership, and from economics to national logistics. The premium on relevance may help to explain the magnificent physical equipment available for some of the work —for example, in electricity at West Point or marine engineering at Annapolis.

Sixth, the purpose of the academies is clearly defined. Some civilian educators have commended and envied this clarity of purpose. But the causes and consequences of such clarity deserve close scrutiny. The academies have a better vision of their goals because their graduates enter but one profession. Knowing this profession, they find it easier to prescribe a study program and to insist that most courses have demonstrable "payoff" value. Military and technical courses seem to them to meet this specification. Seventh, not only do the academies know the future business of their graduates, but a central part of that business has always been war. Men who prepare other men for modern war are not likely to leave the form of preparation to chance or mere surmise. The grave responsibility they bear is not conducive to that relaxed or skeptical attitude toward learning which often nourishes the soil of liberal education. It is more likely to lead to an insistence that highly specific kinds of knowledge are essential and that the necessary skills be driven home to the student until they become part of his instinctive responses. Such views affect intermediate level schools to a greater degree, but the academies are not wholly uninfluenced by them.

For all these reasons the academies move cautiously in adjusting their programs to the developing pattern of national security assignments. This is particularly true of Annapolis. The Naval Academy's work in character building, science, and engineering will stand an officer in good stead throughout his entire career. But the phrase "junior officer" appears in literature and speech at the Naval Academy more often than at the other two schools. Some officials of the Bureau of Naval Personnel speak of "the immediately employable ensign." The Pye board contended that the Naval Academy should equip an officer "for the first period of his career." [3] This does not mean that Annapolis is concerned only with the immediate future of its students. We are dealing with a relative matter, not an absolute one; it is a question of more or less; it is a question of the rate of change in the orientation of an institution, not of the direction of change. For our purposes the important point is that the earlier period of an officer's career is one in which he is less likely to hold policy level positions, and therefore one for which officials are less likely to prescribe highly intensive training in the humanities and social sciences.

But one must not overlook factors that differentiate the Navy's problems from the Army's or the Air Force's. Men at sea must carry with them an impressive amount of technical *expertise*. For many years sea captains contended that such *expertise* could be developed only on ships. It required a whole generation of argument plus a technological revolution to get a Naval school founded, covertly at that, in 1845. For still another generation the school had to fight for its life, and to survive it had to serve the eminently practical

[3] *Report of the Board to Study the Methods of Educating Naval Officers,* appointed 3 March 1944.

purpose of training junior deck officers. The system of transient department heads has helped perpetuate this tradition. Fresh from the sea, they remain responsive to fleet needs.[4] For equally understandable reasons the Navy was slower than the Army to establish intermediate professional schools. It has also clung to the tradition of the versatile line officer, adept at engineering, navigation, gunnery, and other matters. These last two factors combine to place a heavy load on Annapolis, a load that can be carried by a four year curriculum only if the social sciences and humanities are pruned to a minimum.

Areas for Improvement

How can the academies lay a better foundation upon which the services can subsequently build in their efforts to prepare officers for policy level positions? Part of the answer lies in a more liberal curriculum. The academies realize this. That is why they have improved their programs in the social sciences and humanities since world war II. But the pressure to give a relatively technical education remains strong for reasons outlined above. The academies are grimly determined not to waste time. There is no danger that they are going to convert cadets and midshipmen into dilettantes. The real problem is one of avoiding a superficial definition of the practical. The real danger is that the student will be burdened with details that he may soon forget or never use. This is a problem common to all schools, especially professional ones. Somehow a line must be drawn between what is best accomplished on the job and what is best accomplished in class. Every day the professions grow more complex and technical. Every day selected professional men in the fullness of their careers are promoted from specialized jobs into the ranks of executive leadership. Both developments have convinced certain professional schools, wisely we think, that they must do more to develop critical standards, to enlarge social vision, and to create an appetite for further study. There is no reason why this need impair the quality of their total programs. On this point we can do no better than to repeat the conclusions of a report published by the American Society for

---

[4] On the other hand it has also been argued that this system helped keep Annapolis sensitive to changing technological conditions.

Engineering Education in 1956, following a careful study of this matter. Its basic findings were:

"1. That engineering educators throughout the country are in nearly unanimous agreement that their students would profit—as professional men, as citizens, and as individuals —from a fuller acquaintance with the resources of the humanities and social sciences.

"2. That a sizeable number of these same educators are honestly fearful that attempts to incorporate into already overcrowded curricula a substantial program of humanistic-social studies may either jeopardize the quality of the technical education, or lead to superficiality in the treatment of the humanities and social sciences; but

"3. That some thirty or more of our leading engineering schools have demonstrated such fears to be groundless by developing carefully planned programs that provide a sound introduction to the humanities and social sciences while simultaneously reinforcing the student's engineering training." [5]

In the case of both Annapolis and West Point we believe the technical emphasis in the curriculum may discourage applicants who are otherwise very able and who would like to enter a service academy. It also seems to be unjustified in the light of experiences and policy decisions of the services themselves. Many men have risen to great heights in the services without having studied some of the more technical courses that are now declared to be essential at the academies. ROTC programs do not require a comparably full range of engineering, military, scientific, and mathematical studies. When the services were compelled to justify their academies after world war II, they did not base their ultimate defense on the indispensability of certain technical studies; they based it on motivation, character, and other intangibles. We think their instinct was sound. One academy authority has even stated that he would prefer a classical education as provided at Oxford coupled with a military training program. Without endorsing quite so detached a view, we suggest it provides a useful counterweight to premature practicality.

[5] American Society for Engineering Education, *General Education in Engineering, A Report of the Humanistic-Social Research Project,* Urbana, 1956, p. vii. The Massachusetts Institute of Technology has developed a particularly outstanding faculty and program in the humanities and the social sciences.

What would a more liberal curriculum require? An obvious answer is that more time would have to be allocated to nontechnical subjects. But this leaves open the question of how profitably the time available for such subjects will be used. We have already stated our belief that the content of most courses at the academies does not suffer by comparison with the content of similar courses at good civilian colleges. We are struck, however, by the fact that certain kinds of topics consistently receive a little less attention than others. For example, there is much discussion of public policy, especially foreign policy, but less discussion of the underlying processes and mechanisms of social change. The values or ideals for which men strive are explored, but less thoroughly than more tangible matters such as geography, resources, or governmental structure. Something important was lost when the old nineteenth century courses in moral philosophy fell into disrepute at the academies. An appropriate substitute has not yet been found. Again, while students are exposed to many of the great ideas and doctrines of Western man, they rarely have opportunity to wrestle with them as they should. The work is more likely to enable a student to identify social theories than to manipulate them. It is also true that many students, even without formal courses in sociology or anthropology, come to learn of the existence of social strata, professions, and cultures with customs and standards other than his own. We think this invaluable discovery might be planned more systematically. Many devices generate a commendable *esprit de corps* at the academies. But the other side of *esprit de corps* is exclusiveness or guild solidarity. Many devices encourage cadets and midshipmen to distinguish themselves from outside groups, including other services and the civilian populace. This makes it more essential that they become aware of the problem of stereotyped thinking and that they become adept at the art of "reading themselves into the other fellow's mind." Perhaps the best way to summarize these observations is to say that the academies, as they move forward, will have to continue to experiment with courses and extracurricular activities that do more to disturb the student, shake his complacency, force him to think in large, theoretical terms, and make him aware of the sources of his deepest convictions.

In terms of the allotment of time to different areas of knowledge, we feel that the curriculum of the Air Force Academy is well balanced; half of the academic work is devoted to the humanities and social sciences, half to the basic and applied sciences. The Military Academy increased substantially the liberal content of its program between the 1920's and the end of the second world war. There has been no significant change since. We agree with the conclusion of its 1952 Board of Visitors that West Point should go further. It would be presumptuous to submit a blueprint or a timetable. Yet we cannot resist comment on the extraordinary place given to mathematics, however liberal, in the West Point curriculum. The subject receives almost as much attention as literature and all the social sciences together. The virtues of mathematical training are undeniable. The point is that in a world of finite time and resources a price must be paid for all skills. We think this price is too high. Certain other requirements at West Point also suggest imbalance. For example, the course in graphics is allotted as many hours as the entire Department of English. This situation would surely be modified in any determined effort to shift the balance of the curriculum further to the nontechnical side. So would the amount of emphasis now given to other engineering or preengineering subjects.

Annapolis's curriculum might be liberalized somewhat by transferring to the summer cruises part of the work now given by the Seamanship and Navigation, Ordnance and Gunnery, Aviation, or Marine Engineering Department during the academic year. This may be the outcome of a general review of the curriculum contemplated by the notably dedicated leadership of the Naval Academy as this book goes to press. But there are many difficulties in trying to make a cruise serve some of the purposes of a classroom. We think a more radical step would be necessary to make substantially more time available for history, international relations, comparative government, psychology, or English. This would be to defer until *after graduation* some of the work now given in "professional" subjects during the academic year. We cannot specify how much time this will take; we suspect that it would not be less than three months. This suggestion may seem to fall into the category of nice but utopian. But two points, one practical and one logical, should not be overlooked. The practical point arises in connection with the Navy's declaration that midshipmen must join the fleet immediately upon graduation. The truth is that many of them do not. In the mid-1950's up to 50 percent of a graduating class was composed of men who continued in school in order to qualify as Naval aviators, men who entered the Marine Corps, and men who entered the Air Force. The latter group will dwindle as the Air Force Academy builds up to full strength. The Naval aviation group is expected to expand. The Bureau of Naval Personnel has testified that it plans to send 50 percent of future graduates into Naval aviation. These officers will take over a year of technical and aviation training at Pensacola and Corpus Christi. A smaller number of men will continue to receive commissions in other services and in the Supply Corps.[6] But the Naval aviation program alone stands as an answer to the argument that it is utterly impracticable to lengthen preparatory training.[7] It is already being lengthened. One must, however, acknowledge the advantages of having officers start their useful service as soon as possible. Among other things it lengthens their period of total active duty. This, however, can better be accomplished by requiring midshipmen to enter and thus to graduate from Annapolis at an earlier age. The average age at entry (about 19) is unnecessarily high. This will be elaborated on later. First we must dispose of the logical point. The Naval Academy has often been criticized because its curriculum is more technical than the other academies'. Its officials properly sense injustice in the criticism. They feel that their problems are different. They conclude that their solutions must be different. The heart of their position is that unlike things should not be treated alike. But this is exactly what they try to do themselves! Though their needs are more complex they try to meet them in the same four year period, thereby forcing different things into a common mold. One cannot have it both ways. If the concept of the versatile line officer is to be retained, and if a well-balanced education is to be given, we see no alternative but to lengthen slightly the period of preparatory training. It would still be shorter than the preparatory training necessary to enter many other professions.

[6] This testimony was given in House of Representatives, 83rd Congress, 2d Session, Committee on Armed Services, *Hearings on H.R. 5337*, January 13, 1954.

[7] In past years Naval officers sometimes were required to take a longer preparatory program. From 1845 to 1850, midshipmen spent a first year at Annapolis, three years at sea, and a fifth year at Annapolis. Between 1873 and 1912 the program was six years long; the last two years were served at sea.

When technical studies are abbreviated at any academy, we do not think *all* the time thus saved should automatically be used for additional formal courses in liberal arts. Some of it should be spread among existing courses to reduce the tempo of classroom work. The students, especially in their earlier years, are under considerable pressure throughout the day. This has its good points. They learn to weigh competing demands on their time and to live at high levels of tension. They acquire an exposure to a wide range of factual information. But the need to shift focus rapidly from one topic to another tends to lessen the impact of each. It also tends to dull the sense of discrimination, to lower standards of excellence, and to generate techniques for "getting by" or "beating the system." If the tempo of class work were reduced, we suspect that there would be a less ready acceptance of the final "word" authoritatively spoken, less need for frequent reviewing and coaching, and less memorizing beyond that essential in a given subject. As it is, the student is sometimes too busy, too harried and hurried, for his own good.

This brings us to the central question of method. The instructional methods of the service academies have substantial virtues. Less time is wasted because there is a definite mission and a definite plan for each hour of work. There are fewer teachers of a type sometimes found at civilian colleges: men who know their subject but cannot make students understand it. On the other hand certain aspects of the instructional system may inhibit critical or independent thinking. The "study and recite" method, where used, rewards diligence and accuracy rather than insight. As one of our most perceptive informants put it, academy students should be both meticulous and imaginative, but whenever both ends are pursued there is danger that only the first will be attained because it is easier to teach and to test. In some cases because of a shortage of funds, in some cases as a matter of convenience, cadets and midshipmen rely heavily on textbooks rather than on original sources, special studies, or collateral reading that might be pursued in the library; this is especially true at the two older academies. Rare is the textbook that inspires a student to creative thought or that quickens the curiosity necessary to sustain the habit of self-study in later life. We have also noted the effect on the teaching of all subjects of methods that have been developed primarily for engineering and science. In introductory engineering and science courses the student must be able to reason his way to the correct solution, but he knows that a correct solution exists and that his instructor has it. He does not often deal with imponderables. In the Tactical and Executive Departments the answers are often supplied by doctrine, custom, or authority. Some ways are sanctioned, others not, and the student had better know which is which. The first task of commandants and their company officers is to develop responsibility and loyalty, not intellect. Inevitably they must stress obedience and discipline. As one superintendent put it to his Board of Visitors, the company officer takes care to point out that there is neither time nor opportunity in a military organization to develop the background and reason for every command. The same theme appears in a few of the half-mock, half-serious rituals that accomplish the housebreaking of the plebe. One catechism starts, "What happens when a plebe thinks?" He is supposed to reply that when he thinks he gets tied up in knots—in other words, that he is not supposed to think. Small wonder that one academy psychiatrist described the student to us as more dependent than the average college man. Not only his course of study but many of his values, tastes, and habits are prescribed.

What is needed is a little more opportunity for cadets and midshipmen to sail on uncharted seas, to wander out of the safe waters of established fact, "school solutions," and conventional practice.[8] Even their extracurricular activities are sometimes subject to special restraints. At one academy where we had opportunity to examine the regulations it was stipulated that no student organization could be created without the permission of the commandant, and the content of radio programs "must be devoid of opinion, editorializing, or other comment." Controversial guest lecturers do not address cadets and midshipmen very often. At one institution a student lecture series program was abolished when, without prior notification of the authorities, the sponsoring organization invited one or two speakers not congenial to the

---

[8] It is a pity, for example, that the excellent term paper project at Annapolis cannot be done before the senior year. The paper is a necessary and valuable exercise in research. Midshipmen are warned against expression of opinion and urged to try to establish some segment of truth, however small. If such research ability could be developed earlier, it might be possible to require a later project that gave the midshipman an opportunity to state and defend as length his view on some large unsettled question.

academy at large. Both West Point and Annapolis have refused to permit students to enter into intercollegiate debates over the recognition of Red China.

This does not mean that controversial questions are avoided. Cadets and midshipmen can get into heated argument over labor-management relations, the welfare state, or the recognition of China. It means that there are constraining circumstances not usually present at other colleges.[9] The students are members of the armed forces subject to military law. Their superiors are commissioned officers who cannot be so quick as civilian faculty members to express publicly their opinions on highly sensitive issues. Their example is not lost on the students. The schools themselves are public institutions with a national audience. They cannot afford "incidents" that might cause but slight embarrassment to a private college. They are also *military* institutions. A capacity for open controversy is rarely valued by a military organization because it jeopardizes the teamwork required amid the chaos of battle. The close confines of shipboard life generate an understandable rule against discussing politics in the wardroom. An acidly critical intellect may win its possessor a reputation for being a troublemaker. "Sea lawyer" and "guardhouse lawyer" are ancient epithets. Those to whom such epithets are applied may be suspected of lacking something in the way of loyalty, good manners, a sense of duty, or even honor. No one would wish to disparage those virtues. An ideal that includes them is nobler for the inclusion. But an ideal limited to them can be profoundly conservative.

The cumulative effect of the methods and attitudes recounted above is a greater tendency than we think desirable toward conformity, rejection of the unorthodox, and acceptance of the *status quo*. This is probably the most formidable obstacle the academies will have to fight as they continue their search for an education valuable to both the combat leader of the next decade and the military executive of the next generation. Many civilian colleges take a system that rests on critical speculation and attempt to build into it a concern for character development. The academies take a system that rests on character development and attempt to

---

[9] By no means, however, do we wish to imply that civilian colleges are immune from all the practices noted above.

build into it a concern for critical speculation. Every undergraduate institution in America faces one or another of these two tasks and none solves it to its complete satisfaction.[10] In the case of the academies we believe the quest for an answer calls for constant experimentation with more liberal teaching techniques in the classroom. Outside of the classroom it calls for a greater readiness on the part of officials to encourage intellectual initiative and intellectual self-reliance on the part of cadets and midshipmen.

Curricula and teaching methods better adapted to the long run needs of the student will have to be administered by a faculty of high quality. Here the problem is simply one of encouraging trends already in existence. It may be that the great research scholar or brilliant platform lecturer will never fit comfortably into the scheme of military instruction. We were told this many times. But the academies can be expected to move, as they are now moving, away from amateurs and drillmasters and toward trained, imaginative teachers. We despair of finding an answer to the eternal question of whether these teachers should be officers or civilians. We suspect that both can do a fine or an abominable job. In either case their purely administrative duties should be reduced drastically and they should have room in which to work. Some of the office conditions we saw were terrible.

To the extent that civilian instructors are used, the problems are to conduct an aggressive search for talent, to give tenure to only the more successful, to minimize any signs, however subtle or infrequent, of disparity of status between military and civilian staff, and to provide men opportunity to develop their fields of special interest. To the extent that military instructors are used, the problems are to secure a reasonable priority in the selection of abler officers, to establish and maintain the principle that adequate postgraduate training must precede the teaching assignment, to retain all instructors a minimum of three years and some for a longer period, and to insure that their professional careers are not jeopardized by their teaching assignment. We also recommend that some military instructors, later in their careers, be assigned to appropriate staff groups and advanced schools, perhaps on an exchange basis. These men receive expensive postgrad-

[10] See John Sloan Dickey, "Conscience and the Undergraduate," *Atlantic Monthly*, April 1955.

uate training at outstanding institutions. They acquire invaluable teaching experience. It seems to be only good sense to make greater use of their training and experience. The academies in return might acquire useful information about their own programs. They might, for example, learn that they are trying to give their graduates specific details that can best be imparted at other levels of education.

The growing concern of the armed forces with political, economic, and scientific elements of defense policy also calls for cadets and midshipmen of increasing intellectual distinction. Schools can only refine the necessary ability; they cannot create it. There is no substitute for an input of qualified men at the start of the pipeline. Here the academies need help from higher levels of government. We shall put the matter as bluntly as possible. The noncompetitive elements in the system of nominations thrust upon West Point and Annapolis are absurd for schools that rest entirely on a national scholarship plan. For the sake of almost trivial political advantage members of Congress have long denied the nation talent it can ill afford to lose. High school students and their parents must be given reason to abandon the belief that political "pull" is necessary to secure an appointment. It matters not whether this belief is true, partly true, or false. The point is that it exists and that it discourages many applications. The competition for qualified applicants has become more intense as national foundations, business corporations, and individual donors increase the scholarship opportunities at leading colleges and universities. To the academies fewer applicants mean lower quality. Fewer applicants also force them into a variety of public relations activities. One such activity is big time football. Winning teams are an advertisement that reaches a certain audience effectively, but the pressure to get them creates a need for extraordinary vigilance in defense of academic and other standards.

State quotas can be retained. It may also be necessary, though we hope not always, to permit a member of Congress to put his seal of approval on most candidates. But we strongly recommend legislation that will require congressmen to nominate a much larger number of men for each vacancy *without designating principal and alternates*. Ten would be a good number; twenty would be better; there should be no upper limit. The academies would then select from this pool of nominees much as the Air Force Academy was authorized to do when it was founded. If some such plan were adopted it would also be possible for Congress to lower the age limit. Qualified applicants are now accepted by all academies if they have not reached their twenty-second birthday by July first of the year in which they enter. An age limit of 19 appears to us to be preferable except for those applicants who are or have been enlisted men on active duty.[11] We have encountered some sentiment that younger men make better midshipmen and cadets, and that applicants should not feel impelled to take a year or two of college before entry. A higher age limit may attract more candidates and give a second or third chance to the interested and able young man who fails to secure an appointment on his first try. But we would prefer to see the volume of applicants sustained by a widespread public conviction that nominations are not in the category of political patronage.

The foregoing recommendations should make it possible to reduce the rate of attrition during the four year course, to stiffen entrance requirements, and to save some of the time now devoted to a review of high school fundamentals in the first year. Responsibility for such changes rests squarely on Congress, especially on its Armed Services Committees. The Department of Defense has an obligation to tell Congress that the present system is intolerable. This task will not require elaborate research. It will require political courage.

As we review this critique we cannot fail to realize how little of it is new and how often some of its specific proposals have been rejected for reasons satisfactory to prevailing authorities at the academies. The programs of these institutions have been studied so frequently that the process of critique and response tends to resemble standard openings in a chess game, with time-honored gambits meeting time-honored defenses. The academies are willing to adapt to the new environment in which their graduates work, but in their own way and at their own pace. The question is whether this pace can be rapid enough to keep them within reasonably close distance of the more rapidly changing environment. Put in this form the question directs attention to the agents

[11] The Pye board recommended an upper age limit of 19 for the Naval Academy.

of change and their limitations. The principal agents of change are the superintendents, the department heads who constitute the Academic Boards, and the members of the Boards of Visitors.

Some superintendents have made important contributions. At this writing the academies have perhaps as able a group of superintendents as they have had in recent history. But it has been noted earlier that the effectiveness of even the most forward-looking superintendent is limited. Unlike a college president he cannot outwait his opposition. He can never be certain that his reforms will be retained after his brief tour of duty expires. We do not contend that superintendents should be given permanent tenure, but we see no reason why tours of duty should in every case be as short as they are. If a particular superintendent proves unusually effective, and if he desires a more prolonged tour, it would seem to make sense to lengthen it. Sylvanus Thayer did not build West Point in three years.

The Academic Board at West Point is better designed to insure stability than progress. Except in periods of major crisis or upheaval its individual members do not readily accept curtailment of the offerings of their departments. At Annapolis the members are not assigned to the institution long enough to exercise sustained leadership either on the board or in their departments. The Naval Academy defends its system of transient department heads on the ground that it permits continuous refreshment of teaching programs by officers newly arrived from the fleet. This may well be true in the teaching of a subject like ordnance and gunnery. It is more difficult to see how it applies to the teaching of Chaucer, national income theory, or the Constitution. On the whole the system of permanent department heads appears preferable in departments that do not deal with naval science. But it creates a need to guard against the man who may simply be looking for a soft berth, or who may "go to seed" after a few years, or who has secured his appointment through "pull" rather than his own abilities. Greater thought should be given to the procedures under which permanent appointments are made at West Point and the Air Force Academy. It is helpful to canvass widely and to seek the opinion of officers in the service when vacancies occur. In some cases, however, mistakes or irregularities might be avoided by a requirement of prior discussion with nonmilitary specialists, perhaps in committee with one or more specially qualified retired officers and academy authorities. Analogous procedures are sometimes used in the case of major appointments at civilian schools.

Boards of Visitors have been helpful but within definite limits. In the nineteenth century they sometimes made extended trips to West Point and Annapolis, examining students and making detailed inquiry into conditions at the schools. Some of their reports were widely read and discussed. In this century the boards on the whole have been less active. It is true that they have supported consistently, and sometimes with great vigor, higher academic standards and a more liberal program.[12] They have urged the academies to teach basic science rather than, in the words of one board, "a minute familiarity with existing gadgetry." They have counseled greater attention to such major developments as aviation and atomic energy. They have defended stoutly the need for more work in the social sciences and the humanities. They have sought better libraries, a less crowded curriculum, better-qualified instructors, a less mechanical approach to classroom instruction, and greater opportunity for students to do advanced or specialized work. But the boards, for reasons that will be discussed in chapter twenty, work under handicaps that seem to grow more serious with each passing decade.

It is our conclusion that responsible officials concerned with the academies will need additional support if they are to continue their efforts to adapt their programs to the growing responsibilities of career officers. The major burden, of course, will continue to rest on them. But given the difficulties under which superintendents, Academic Boards, and Boards of Visitors work, and given the strength of the obstacles to rapid evolution that were noted earlier in this chapter, some part of the initiative must come from outside the academies, indeed from outside the military services themselves. We shall comment further on this matter in the final chapter.

---

[12] At Annapolis the report of the 1923 board was so outspoken that, contrary to custom, it was not released. Later reports—for example, in 1933 and 1940—have contained pungent dissents.

CHAPTER TWELVE

ROTC AND OTHER UNDERGRADUATE

EDUCATION

THE three service academies are important to this study because most of their graduates devote their careers to the military service and because they produce a large proportion of the officers in the highest ranks. They also are important because they define the professional standards that the ROTC, OCS, and other programs seek to attain. But by no means do all officers receive their undergraduate education at the academies. The services commission officers from other sources, and among these the Reserve Officer Training Corps program conducted in civilian colleges and universities is the largest. The services also utilize these civilian institutions for other forms of officer education at the undergraduate level.

The primary function of the ROTC program is not preparation for a military career. In the period since world war II, however, it has assumed a new significance in each service. Present military requirements demand more active duty officers than the service academies can produce. Although most ROTC graduates serve on active duty no longer than required, official policy now regards the ROTC as a source of *long term career* and *regular* officers. For this reason, and also because the separate ROTC programs reveal a number of things about the approaches of the different services to officer education, a few observations concerning ROTC instruction are relevant to the central theme of this book.

The Naval ROTC

We have seen in chapter six that provision for procurement of regular Naval officers from the nation's colleges and universities was a prominent feature of the Navy's Holloway Plan, developed in 1946. High school graduates are selected for the "regular" NROTC program on a competitive basis upon completion of an aptitude test and other requirements. They receive full tuition and certain allowances for four years. Upon graduation they are commissioned and are obligated to serve three years of active duty in the Navy or Marine Corps. During the third year they may apply for permanent commissions in the regular Navy. Otherwise they transfer to the Naval Reserve. "Contract" students also may be admitted to the NROTC program by the professor of naval science at each of the participating institutions. These men are called to active duty in the Navy or Marine Corps only as needed —for two years at the present time. Students who elect flight training following commissioning are obligated to serve a minimum of three years. Regular and contract students constitute total annual enrollments of approximately 6,200 and 8,000 respectively, in 52 participating schools. The maximum legal strength of the two programs is 15,400.[1]

The Army ROTC

As indicated in earlier chapters, the Army ROTC program has had a long history and its graduates have made an extremely important contribution in both of the world wars. Throughout this history it has been oriented toward the Army's *reserve* requirements. Following the outbreak of the Korean conflict in 1950 the program was expanded quickly and the number of units increased. By the 1953–1954 academic year, for example, more than 147,000 students received Army ROTC training at the college level, and 12,000 graduates were commissioned as reserve officers. There were at this time units in 246 civilian colleges and universities and 9 military colleges.[2] Under the terms of the reserve forces act of 1955, graduates may be ordered to active duty for either two years or six months, depending upon the planned requirements of the

[1] The NROTC regulars graduating in 1950 numbered 800, and in 1951, 1,400. Of these men 80 were accepted in 1954 and 205 in 1955, respectively, for retention as permanent regular officers. A total of 161 were selected for permanent commissions in 1956.

[2] In addition to the college level units, there also are units at 262 high schools and 37 military preparatory schools. The complete training in these is equivalent to one year at the college level. There also are units in a few military junior colleges.

Army. Those drawn for the shorter period must remain in the ready reserve for seven and a half years and maintain periodically a certain minimum of training. With the recent expansion of the program there also has developed an increasing interest in ROTC as a source of *career* officers. In 1956, for example, the Army offered regular commissions to more ROTC graduates than to graduates of West Point.

Traditionally the Army ROTC units were branch-affiliated, that is, they prepared candidates for reserve commissions in one of the separate branches of the Army. Frequently the branch was related to the special interests of the host institution. The schools of technology, for example, had Engineer, Ordnance, or Signal Corps units.

Following the expansion of Army ROTC during the Korean conflict, however, the "branch material" program produced a number of serious difficulties. It did not make for the orderly procurement of junior officers. The output of reserve officers by branches was determined not by the Army's requirements but by the random establishment of branch units in colleges and universities across the country. Secondly, there were relatively few combat arms units (Infantry, Armor, Artillery) and it was in these branches that more officers were needed. The combat arms, recognizing the contribution of ROTC officers in world war II, were anxious to get a larger slice of ROTC graduates. Some flexibility was introduced by redistribution of graduates among the branches according to need, but this was not satisfactory. Apart from administrative difficulties and uncertainties, it placed a heavy burden upon the basic training programs of the branches because officers were assigned to them with varying degrees of preparation.

Accordingly pressures built up for the introduction of a general military science, or "branch immaterial," program. This was introduced on an experimental basis in several institutions in 1952–1953. This program did not prepare the student for a specific branch of the Army, and graduates were subject to assignment to any branch, in which they secured further training in the branch course. The experimental program was judged to be a success and all host institutions were invited to consider the change to GMS. By the academic year 1955–1956, 181 out of a total of 235 had made the conversion and others were expected to follow. Some institutions, particularly those with technical or engineering schools, have been reluctant to make the shift because of their traditional association with a branch. But others, including some liberal arts colleges, have regarded it with favor because of the generalized approach.

The Air Force ROTC

The greatest changes of an educational character have come in the Air Force program. These developments directly reflect the Air Force's determination to raise the educational level of its regular officer corps, providing well-qualified leaders for an expanding service. It hopes to secure about 80 percent of all active duty officers and about 50 percent of all regulars from the ROTC, even after the full operation of the Air Force Academy. In the light of Navy experience, it is unlikely that it will achieve the latter goal, but it continues to seek the objective. The Air Force, moreover, has made a very serious effort to strengthen the educational value of its instruction, with emphasis upon its long term contribution both to the student and to the service.

Prior to 1935 the old Army Air Corps had supported seven ROTC units within the Army ROTC program. In 1946 the Air Force ROTC was reinstituted, before the creation of a separate Air Force. Air officers were assigned to the Army units on a number of campuses to offer appropriate instruction, and students in these units were eligible for commissions in the Air Force Reserve. In 1949 the Army and Air Force ROTC units were separated at the institutional level. Prior to the Korean conflict graduates who were commissioned came on active duty on a voluntary basis. Members of the class of 1951 were the first who were ordered to active duty. At this time also the number of units, which began with 78 in 1946, was increased until it reached a total of 209, at 188 separate colleges and universities, with an enrollment of up to 145,000 cadets.[3] The program at this time was still oriented toward reserve training. Administratively it was supervised by the Continental Air Command, through its four numbered air forces, which are concerned with reserve activities. The course of study

[3] In 1956 the Air Force announced that the number of participating institutions would be reduced to 180.

was limited to military subjects. It offered a variety of specialized options, such as armament, communications, aircraft maintenance engineering, air installations, comptrollership, administration, and logistics. The purpose of this specialized approach was to qualify the officer candidate in the speciality he would pursue in the service. It also permitted him to elect an option closely allied to the subject matter of his regular college program.

During this period an attempt was made to accomplish two objectives, that is, to prepare a young man for duty as an officer in the Air Force, and at the same time to qualify him in his military speciality. Actually neither purpose was being accomplished properly in the short amount of time available for instruction. The program was failing to provide the attributes and motivation of an officer. The assumption that it was producing reserve officers qualified for duty immediately upon mobilization was not valid. Thus in each respect it was not meeting the Air Force's requirements. This was particularly so after the programing of an Air Force of 137 combat wings, following the Korean crisis. This action produced a rising demand for rated officers, young men who could meet the rigid physical and aptitude qualifications for flight training and responsibilities. The complexities and high speed of jet aircraft are such that officers, in order to maintain flying proficiency, must be retained on active duty rather than in a reserve pool where their skills soon become "rusty." It would have been possible to secure pilots and observers through the aviation cadet program, drawing in young men with little or no college education, as was done during world war II. But the Air Force wished to avoid this. Looking ahead, moreover, it realized that it must prepare young officers not only for a relatively few years devoted largely to flying and related activities, but for a longer period of service at the higher command and staff levels. Thus the Air Force redefined the objectives of its ROTC program. In the summer of 1953 the emphasis was shifted to procuring rated officers (pilots and observers) and fewer numbers of engineers and technical specialists. Moreover, the role of the ROTC as a primary source of the active duty officers required by the expanding Air Force stimulated concern for the long range educational value of the program.

At the administrative level these objectives resulted in transfer of command responsibility for the Air Force ROTC from the Continental Air Command to the Air University. The new AFROTC headquarters, commanded by Brigadier (now Major) General Matthew Deichelmann, soon initiated the preparation of a new generalized curriculum, designed "to produce well-rounded junior grade officers who possess high growth potential, just as a liberal arts education should produce a well-rounded graduate who has a clear picture of how individuals and nations fit into a world society." [4] This was a large undertaking. It involved the establishment of a headquarters staff composed of over 200 individuals, both military and civilian, many of whom were experienced in the field of education. It involved also the utilization of a host of civilian educational consultants, first in designing the over-all curriculum, and then in preparing special texts and teaching materials. The new generalized curriculum was placed in operation in 1953–1954.

The ROTC Curricula

These developments of recent years have increased the importance and potential value of the three Reserve Officers Training Corps programs. They are a good deal more than mere reserve training activities. They are geared to the procurement of large numbers of junior active duty officers and a smaller but significant number of career officers. Although enrollments are not as great as they were during the Korean conflict, they still exceed 200,000 annually, and there are almost 500 separate ROTC units distributed among approximately 350 different colleges and universities. In about half of these schools, including almost all of the land grant colleges, ROTC instruction is required of all freshmen and sophomores.[5] Both the Army and Air Force divide their programs into basic and advanced courses, each requiring two years. Only about a quarter of all students enter advanced ROTC. To be accepted the student must pass physical and aptitude tests and sign an agreement with the government to accept a commission, if offered, upon graduation. Since 1953 the Air Force

---

[4] Air University, AFROTC, *Introduction to AFROTC,* June 1953, p. 26.

[5] In recent years there has been a tendency to abandon the compulsory feature of basic ROTC instruction.

also has required most advanced students to agree to take flight training. They must, of course, qualify for this training.

Utilization of the ROTC programs as a source of career officers means that their mission in many respects has approached that of the service academies, particularly with respect to the motivation of young men toward professional military careers. In chapter ten we noted that the academies are designed to provide instruction in four principal areas. The first is leadership and character formation and motivation toward a professional military career. The second is military studies and practice, the third basic engineering, and the last liberal arts and sciences. In a sense the services in their ROTC programs are now attempting to do something in each of these areas. But whereas the academies have almost complete control of the cadets and midshipmen for four years of their lives, the ROTC units have the college undergraduates only a few hours each week and for relatively short summer training periods. Moreover they operate in an atmosphere that provides none of the supporting features that are the very essence of the academies.

LEADERSHIP AND MOTIVATION

Career motivation is perhaps the most difficult task of the ROTC units today, and is one that gives the services a real sense of frustration. Young men do not come to college to enter upon a military career. Very few of the NROTC regulars accept the financial aid of the government for a four year college education with the thought of a career in the Navy. As we have seen, motivation is a serious problem even at the academies. If this is so, can it be expected that the average undergraduate in a civilian school will resist all of the other claims upon his interest and loyalty that are presented by a prosperous American culture and accept the sacrifices involved in a military career? [6] Is it possible to persuade

[6] The whole problem of career motivation has received a great deal of attention from the services. See, for example, the testimony of Lieutenant General Emmet O'Donnell, deputy chief of staff, personnel, USAF, in Senate, 84th Congress, 2nd Session, Subcommittee on the Air Force of the Committee on Armed Services, *Hearing on Study of Airpower*, May 1956, pp. 321–367. On the question of the intentions of young officers, for example, see George W. Baker, *Attitudes and Judgments of Some Lieutenants Related to Present Active Duty Intentions*, and Fred R. Crawford and Frederick H. Esch, *Situational Factors and Attitudes Expressed toward Duty with ARDC*, Technical Research Reports No. 14 and 19, Air Research and Development Command, Human Resources Research Institute (now Officer Education Research Laboratory), Maxwell Air Force Base, 1953.

him to accept with enthusiasm even two or three years of active duty? The ROTC programs attempt to meet this challenge by stimulating interest in the service at every opportunity. In the Army and Navy programs the principal course in the freshman year is devoted to military history. The 30 hour Army course dwells almost exclusively upon the operations of the Army in combat, from the revolutionary war to the present. According to the directive for the course, it is designed "to provide the ROTC student with a sound foundation in the principles of the art of warfare as they are exemplified in American military history, and through this knowledge, to aid in *motivating* the student toward an understanding and acceptance of his future role as an officer of the United States Army."[7] The NROTC program devotes twice as much time during the freshman year to a course in American naval history. This now employs a text prepared by several members of the faculty of the Naval Academy for use at that institution.[8] The purpose in scheduling the course in the first college year, according to official explanation, is to stimulate interest in the Navy and understanding of the role of sea power in human affairs, just as the Army's military history course is expected to develop support for the Army.

The Air Force has taken a somewhat different approach to this problem in its new curriculum. During the freshman year it offers two short courses designed to stimulate interest in air power. The first is a 10 hour unit on the fundamentals of global geography. It considers the use of maps, weather, climate, geographical elements of national power, population, minerals, and a comparison of the geography and resources of the United States and the Soviet Union. The second course, entitled international tensions and security structures, provides a 15 hour summary treatment of such topics as political, military, and moral factors in world power, imperialism, nationalism, the military strength of the Soviet and anti-Soviet blocs, the League of Nations, the United Nations, NATO, and other regional security arrangements. It concludes with emphasis upon the world leadership of the United States. The avowed purpose of these two introductory courses, as well as a

---

[7] Headquarters, Continental Army Command, Subject Schedule NR401, June 1955.

[8] E. B. Potter, ed., *The United States and World Sea Power*, Englewood Cliffs, N.J., 1955.

separate introductory course in aviation, is to excite the young student, to stimulate his interest in aviation and the Air Force. As one officer at AFROTC headquarters declared to us, the philosophy of this program is based on the recognition that the Air Force has an opportunity to educate a large share of the male population of the country in understanding the air age. It is hoped that many students will elect to go on to the advanced program and to a commission and active duty service. But even among those who are exposed only to the basic course it is hoped to instill an understanding of the Air Force that will stimulate continuing support among the citizenry.

As at the academies, instruction in leadership and character formation is accomplished as much by intangible means as by formal training. But the opportunity for accomplishment is much less than at West Point, Annapolis, or the Air Force Academy. Not only is little time available, but the seemingly casual pattern of behavior of the college campus militates against acceptance of the precepts of the military unit. We believe that the significance of this difference is more apparent than real, as demonstrated by the excellent war records of some of the most casual or "unmilitaristic" of the men who were undergraduates during the 1930's.[9] Nevertheless the situation presents difficulties for the unsophisticated officer assigned to ROTC duty.

Instruction in military leadership is accomplished in classroom courses, weekly "laboratory" and drill periods, and summer camps and cruises. The central purpose here, of course, is to enable the newly commissioned shavetail or ensign to act like an officer when he assumes his first duties. He must know how to handle himself with superiors, equals, and subordinates, and must be able to assume responsibility within a disciplined military organization. All three ROTC programs include formal classroom instruction in leadership. The Army provides 10 hours in the junior year, emphasizing leadership problems in military units. An attempt is made to introduce the student to psychological concepts of leadership, including personality structures, personal adjustment, and leadership principles and techniques. This is followed by a 20 hour unit on military teaching methods, to equip the officer

[9] See, for example, General Omar Bradley's tribute to one of these young officers in his *A Soldier's Story*, New York, 1951, p. 47.

candidate with the ability to instruct others. The NROTC program devotes a considerable portion of the final course in the senior year to the duties and responsibilities to be expected by the newly commissioned officer. Emphasis is placed upon the situations faced by the watch officer and the regulations and procedures that he must follow. The new Air Force curriculum also devotes a great deal of attention to the development of the skills and characteristics of leadership, as we shall point out below.

The summer training periods afford a better opportunity to provide instruction in military leadership and to motivate the student toward a military career. Regular NROTC students are required to complete two summer cruises and one shore-based summer training program in aviation or amphibious warfare. Contract students take only one summer cruise. The Army and Air Force programs require attendance once at a summer camp. During the weekly drills emphasis is placed upon such matters as military courtesy and customs, wearing the uniform, handling weapons, and the exercise of leadership. Students are organized into cadet corps or battalions of midshipmen under the leadership of student officers. Advanced students are given considerable responsibility in the training of freshmen and sophomores. A variety of devices, including honor societies, crack drill and rifle teams, visits to military installations, and special ceremonial occasions, are used to stimulate *esprit de corps*. The success of these enterprises and of the entire effort to develop officerlike qualities in the young undergraduates depends largely upon the leadership demonstrated by the professional officers instructing in the units.

MILITARY STUDIES AND PRACTICE

A second purpose of the ROTC programs as well as the service academies is to provide instruction in military subjects. This instruction makes up the greater proportion of the ROTC curriculum in the Army and Naval programs and extends through the four years in all three programs. It also is accomplished during the summer training periods. In the Army program, for example, the first year of the general military science curriculum includes a short introduction to the organization of the Army and ROTC and 25 hours of instruction on the handling of individual weapons and marksmanship. The second year includes map and aerial photography reading (20 hours) and crew-served weapons and gunnery (40 hours). During the junior year the advanced student receives 30 hours of instruction in the organization, functions, and missions of the arms and services, and 60 hours in small unit tactics and communication. In the senior year he studies operations (55 hours), logistics (20 hours), military administration and personnel management (25 hours), and service orientation (20 hours).

Likewise naval subjects occupy most of the classroom and laboratory time of the NROTC student. In first year orientation 30 hours are devoted to naval courtesy and customs, discipline, naval organization, and the functions and component units of naval ships and aircraft. The second year course on naval weapons covers ballistics, ordnance, fire control equipment, and the operations of the gunnery department of a ship. Classroom work is amplified by laboratory exercises and demonstrations, using gunnery equipment, models, and training aids. The third year consists of courses in naval machinery and navigation, both supported by laboratory work. In the fourth year the first semester course on naval operations covers tactical communications, rules of the road, maneuvering and screening instructions, and weather. The course on naval administration covers such matters as shipboard organization, correspondence, naval justice, command, and leadership. Students in the NROTC program who are candidates for commissions in the Marine Corps take a separate sequence of courses in the junior and senior years. The first of these covers the historical development of warfare from classical times to the present. This is followed by study of basic strategy and tactics and of amphibious warfare.

The Air Force curriculum devotes considerably less time to military subjects. It provides study of the Air Force and its mission, functions, organization, weapons, and operations. This commences in the first year with a general introduction to aviation, and progresses through the elements of aerial warfare (targets, weapons, aircraft, bases, operations) in the sophomore year and applied air science (aerodynamics, propulsion, navigation, weather) in the junior year, to military aviation and the evolution of warfare in the senior year. These courses are reinforced by the six weeks of camp during the summer following the junior year, required of all advanced students.

These approaches of the three services to military subjects in the ROTC programs reflect practices at their academies. We have noted that West Point and the new Air Force Academy do not attempt to prepare the graduate fully for his first duty. This is true also of the Army and Air Force ROTC programs, particularly since the introduction of the new curricula. Following commissioning, the new Army second lieutenant, whether a graduate of the Military Academy or an ROTC unit, attends a branch school; his Air Force counterpart receives flight training or some other special training. This intensive military training is the responsibility of the Army branch schools and the major training commands of the Air Force. Graduates entering the Marine Corps also undergo intensive military training before assuming their first troop assignments. In both the Naval Academy and the NROTC units, on the other hand, emphasis is placed upon preparing the new ensign for his first deck watch. This means, of course, that the Navy is obliged to crowd the undergraduate program, whether at the Academy or in the NROTC, with more detailed information concerning military functions and operations and to provide more specific training experiences.

BASIC ENGINEERING

In the field of basic engineering the ROTC units provide little or no instruction themselves, although many students take regular course work in this field offered by the host institution. In some instances, as at schools of engineering and technology, this may exceed the instruction provided at the service academies. In the Army "branch material" units it may be elected with particular reference to the functions of the branch. For example, a student in a Signal Corps unit may elect advanced work in electronics. The Navy requires its regular NROTC students to complete mathematics through trigonometry either in high school or in college, and requires one year of college physics. It is suggested, but not required, that they take a sequence in mathematics extending through calculus and including spherical trigonometry, and a second year of a physical science. Some consideration is given to naval engineering in the NROTC course in machinery.

LIBERAL ARTS AND SCIENCES

We come finally to instruction in the liberal arts and sciences. This is primarily the province of the host institution, and whether the student receives a broad liberal education or a more specialized technical preparation depends upon the requirements and character of that institution. Even so, the services are giving more attention to this matter, now that they have turned to the ROTC as a source of active duty and regular officers. The Navy, characteristically, is most interested in those courses supporting its military training. The Air Force and to some extent the Army are tending toward a broader, less specialized preparation of ROTC officers.

In the case of the Air Force, this development has resulted in the inclusion within the AFROTC requirements of a number of courses in subject areas normally found in the usual college curriculum. In total classroom hours these courses amount to almost three quarters of the time allocated to AFROTC subjects. They have been included in order to provide what the Air Force believes to be the minimum background for "well-rounded junior grade officers who possess high growth potential." As finally worked out, they represent the expenditure of a very considerable amount of thought, talent, and energy by AFROTC headquarters personnel and their professional consultants. We already have mentioned the freshman courses on global geography and international tensions. In the senior year the AFROTC program includes a separate course entitled "military aspects of world political geography." "The underlying philosophy of this course," according to one of our informants at AFROTC headquarters, "is simply this: Our students need to know as much as possible about the world in which we live. The world's geographical and political relationships as they respond to the impact of air and atomic power is our special concern." As a result of all of the instruction in the AFROTC program culminating in this course, the student "will have a fund of information and a framework of reference with which he, as an officer and as a citizen, will be able to evaluate and continue to reevaluate the world situation at any specific time." To accomplish this purpose, AFROTC headquarters prepared a two volume, 950 page textbook of readings for this course, with the assistance of advisory committees of the Association of American Geographers and the American Political Science Association. Part I deals with the impact of air power upon global geography, expanding on the theme of the first year course. The rest of the course, in broad outline, bears a close resemblance to many regular college international relations courses. The readings for Part II (the framework of international politics) and Part III (factors influencing the power of states), for example, are drawn largely from standard college texts. Part IV is a country-by-country study of world powers and strategic areas.

In its instruction on leadership, the AFROTC program also gets into an area handled by regular civilian courses. In the advanced program considerable attention is devoted to the development of the skills and characteristics of leadership in group situations. Here the emphasis is upon the development of growth potentialities. The junior year commences with a brief course on the Air Force commander and his staff, followed by longer study of problem-solving techniques and oral and written communication. As we shall note in the following chapter, these are subjects for which the Air Force has shown a great deal of concern in recent years. In the problem-solving course an attempt has been made to break away from the cut-and-dried formalistic approach that has characterized much of the military instruction in the past and to emphasize some of the newer concepts of "group dynamics." The AFROTC manual on problem-solving techniques is supplemented by Alex Osborn's *Imaginative Thinking*. Osborn, a New York advertising man, wrote this book for business executives.[10] The communications manual introduces the student to such factors as the role of symbols, social and psychological barriers to communication, and the problems of being a good listener and reader, as well as to the formalities of Air Force correspondence. Junior year also includes a seven hour unit on instructing in the Air Force.

In the senior year these areas of instruction are carried forward in a 38 hour seminar on the principles of leadership and management. The focus here is upon the primary professional responsibility of the officer in his handling of men. According to the text,

[10] Alex F. Osborn, *Applied Imagination, Principles and Procedures of Creative Thinking,* New York, 1953.

the course applies "new knowledge of human nature and group behavior to the military setting." It defines leadership as "the process through which the leader inspires effective individual effort in a group effort to achieve an assigned mission." The student is told that he must have "new knowledge in the social sciences [that] is now available to help you." Thus the emphasis in the leadership and management seminar is "upon the nature of American adult behavior—the basis for it, the social influences that help mold it, and its effect on other people." The greater part of the text is concerned with human motivation, including the biology of behavior, personality development, the nature of intense motivation, American attitudes and values, and the individual and the group. In the seminar the students are introduced to practical exercises and group problem-solving situations.[11]

The Army's interest in a broader, less specialized type of preparation for its officers is reflected in the introduction of the general military science curriculum. Except in a few cases in the remaining branch material units, the Army imposes few limitations upon the student's choice of courses outside its own requirements. Unlike the Air Force, it does not include within its curriculum instruction that normally is provided in civilian courses. The only exception to this practice is a course of 10 hours in the senior year on "the role of the United States in world affairs and the present world situation." The declared purpose of this instruction is "to orient the student on world geographic and economic factors and their influence on the division of peoples into nations and the causes of war." The directive for the unit suggests that the instructor present to the class an analysis of the geographic and economic resources of the United States and that the students do the same in individual reports on selected countries abroad.[12]

Even before the formulation of the generalized Air Force ROTC curriculum, the Navy pioneered instruction in international affairs. During world war II Secretary of the Navy Forrestal was among those who felt the need for broadly educated officers.

[11] Air University, AFROTC, *Principles of Leadership and Management,* June 1954. See also *Student Handbook for Principles of Leadership and Management,* 1955. This is a series of recent journal and periodical articles on various aspects of business and military leadership.

[12] Headquarters, Continental Army Command, Subject Schedule NR 463, August 1954.

He personally was responsible for the introduction in the V-12 and NROTC programs of a new course on foundations of national power. As conducted experimentally at Princeton by Professor Harold Sprout and subsequently at a number of other institutions, this course emphasized the role of power in international affairs. It was initially planned to include the course as a requirement in the postwar NROTC curriculum, with instruction provided by the civilian faculty. Now the course or its equivalent is suggested only as an elective, if it is available. Although the course was not carried forward by the Navy, it exerted considerable influence upon the teaching of international relations in the immediate postwar years in both civilian and military institutions.[13]

The Navy now permits contract students to select any course of study leading to the baccalaureate degree but excludes regulars from medical, dental, veterinary, pharmacology, and theological study. Nor may a regular NROTC student major in music or art. Otherwise he is free to study as he wishes beyond the Navy requirements. He must complete the college requirements in written and oral expression. It is suggested that he take a one year course in personnel management and administration, two years of a foreign language, and a course in public speaking.

CONCLUSIONS

Because of the context of this book and the present limits of the ROTC as a source of *career* officers, a full survey and evaluation of these programs is not possible here. In actuality that part of the four year experience that lies outside of the military training requirements—and this is upwards of 80 percent of the total curriculum—has the most direct bearing upon the educational preparation of the individual and upon his subsequent career interests and accomplishments. Obviously an infinite variety of course arrangements, major programs, and degree requirements are possible within the more than 300 separate institutions having ROTC units, and these differ widely as to content and quality. We have undertaken no systematic examination of this aspect of ROTC education, but we do have a few general observations.

[13] See the book of text and readings that resulted from this course: Harold and Margaret Sprout, eds., *Foundations of National Power*, Princeton, 1945, and New York, 1951.

We believe that ROTC training coupled with a college or university experience now provides a suitable and in many cases a highly satisfactory undergraduate preparation for military service. We have been told many times by experienced officers that junior officers procured from this source generally perform as well as their contemporaries from the service academies. This does not mean that the ROTC programs do not require continuing review. Following world war II, as during the interwar period, there was considerable criticism of the ROTC programs on college and university campuses, and much of this remains. The courses have been regarded as superficial and many of the instructors as poorly prepared for classroom responsibilities.[14] Within more recent years the services have expended much time, talent, and money to provide a more meaningful curriculum and adequate texts and teaching materials. A sustained effort has been made to secure officers better qualified to serve as instructors. Unfortunately the services have had to work against a tradition that an ROTC assignment was not in the best interest of the individual officer who sought career advancement and promotion.

When the ROTC programs were relatively small and the services were satisfied with conventional military training, these were not serious problems. But more recently, as efforts have been made to enrich the content and to introduce instruction in such fields as international relations, geography, psychology, and group dynamics, inadequacies have become apparent. Much has been done to overcome the weaknesses of the initial courses and to prepare officers for teaching duties. So far, however, the orientation of instructors has been concerned more with instruction techniques than with the substantive content of the courses to be taught.[15] At a few institutions local arrangements have been worked out whereby resident civilian instructors assist in the presentation of certain courses in the newer fields, or even assume full responsibility for a course. We feel that it would be to the advantage of both the services and the host institutions to do more of this sort

[14] See, for example, Harold W. Dodds, "Your Boy and the ROTC," *Atlantic Monthly*, March 1953, pp. 25–29; *The Impact of an ROTC Program on a Liberal Arts College, A Case Study at Colgate University*, March 1953.

[15] In the summer of 1956 the Ohio State University introduced a pilot course for AFROTC instructors dealing with the *substantive content* of certain nonmilitary courses and a special course for Army instructors in military history.

of thing, experimenting with different programs on different campuses and ultimately introducing more variety and flexibility into undergraduate precommissioned education.[16]

Finally we come to the particular theme of this study, the preparation of officers for participation in the formulation of national policies. We believe that a strong case can be made for greater utilization of the ROTC programs and the nation's colleges and universities as a source of *career* officers. This would help to meet the increasing demand for officers with interests and educational background in ever-widening areas of knowledge. It would provide proportionately more regular officers with the kind of broader educational experience that we recommended in the last chapter in our comments on the service academies. In this connection it must be admitted, however, that the graduates of some technical schools are more narrowly educated in a specialized sense than are the graduates of the academies.

Actually, as we have seen, the services would prefer to have many more ROTC graduates seek regular commissions. The trouble is that relatively few young reserve officers are attracted to a military career. This raises again the fundamental issue of career motivation. The armed forces cannot expect to attract more regular officers from among college and university graduates until a military career is made more attractive in a highly competitive and prosperous economy and until American society places a higher value upon the military profession. Yet the demands made upon career officers call for more college-trained men.[17]

A number of steps might be taken to meet the present situation. In the first place, the feature of the Navy's ROTC program providing generous financial assistance to all "regular" students might be extended to the Army and the Air Force. At the same time the military obligation of individuals who accept such assistance might

[16] We have in mind, for example, the modified general military science program introduced at Harvard University in 1956. This includes regular academic courses in the history of civil-military relations and on government and defense, taught by members of the civilian faculty.

[17] The services probably could secure more career officers from among non-college-graduates were they willing to do so. For example, while only 10 percent of the AFROTC officers graduating in 1953 and 1954 and 8.4 percent in 1956 expressed a definite intention of staying in the service beyond a three year tour, about 55 percent of OCS graduates of recent years would stay in. *Air Force Times,* April 14, 1956, p. 8.

be made the same as the obligation of service academy graduates. At the present time an NROTC regular, at the end of three years' active duty, may either go off active duty or request transfer to permanent status. He is given permanent status only if such transfer is in the national interest. An Annapolis graduate, on the other hand, is permitted to retire from the service only if the national interest permits. The same standard should apply to NROTC regulars and to the graduates of similarly subsidized Army and Air Force programs. Secondly, every effort should be made by the services to provide equal treatment to ROTC and academy graduates. Much has already been done, but we observe that the former need full assurance that the career opportunities available to them will be no less favorable than those awaiting their academy contemporaries.[18]

Lastly, we believe that the colleges and universities of the country should do much more than they have done in the past to acquaint their students with the importance and rewards of a military career. This requires greater attention to the military aspects of our national life in established courses in history, economics, and political science, as well as some specialized courses in problems of national security and defense planning.[19]

A number of unresolved issues relating to the ROTC programs, while beyond the terms of this study, should be mentioned because they might conceivably lead to fundamental organizational changes in the future. These issues stem from the impact of ROTC requirements upon the curriculum as a whole. It must be remembered that these requirements take a bite of up to 20 percent of the courses that a student may take, limiting his choice of electives, particularly where he must satisfy other requirements set by the host institution. In many professional programs this may present serious problems. Some civilian educators believe that the quality of the total educational product is threatened by this situation. While accepting the necessity of military training, they

[18] For example, the commissions of "distinguished military graduates" of the Army ROTC program who accept offers of regular commissions are automatically dated one day after those of Military Academy graduates.

[19] See, for example, Harvard University, Graduate School of Public Administration, *Report to the Ford Foundation on Grant for the Harvard Defense Studies Program Academic Year 1955–56,* Cambridge, July 1956.

suggest that it be accomplished in some manner less disruptive to higher education. A related issue arises from the plans of institutions of higher education to adjust to expanding enrollments. It is likely that as these enrollments continue to increase the conventional four year pattern will not survive, at least in its present form, because existing and even expanded facilities will be put to maximum use throughout the year. This raises the question whether the present ROTC programs will be compatible with a reorganized calendar. While not attempting here to suggest solutions to these issues, we would express only the conviction that such changes as may be made be designed, among other things, to increase rather than diminish the proportion of college and university graduates among career officers.

Other Undergraduate Programs

There is one additional aspect of education at the undergraduate level that deserves attention. This relates to the efforts of the services to raise the educational level of younger officers already on duty through the use of civilian institutions, extension programs, and correspondence courses.

The Air Force has done the most along this line. The reason for this is that the Air Force has been deeply concerned over the educational deficiencies of its active duty officer corps. This situation is a direct consequence of world war II. During the war the AAF experienced phenomenal growth, expanding from an officer contingent of 2,636 in 1939 to a peak of about 388,000 in the spring of 1945. Educational requirements were lowered periodically in the haste to secure personnel. Consequently the bulk of the officers who were integrated into the regular service following the war were young combat veterans whose formal education had been interrupted. The problem in the Air Force was more acute than in the other services, which had turned to their ROTC-trained reserves for college-educated officers. By July 1948 only 41 percent of the regular Air Force officers possessed the baccalaureate degree, in contrast to 75 percent in the regular Navy and 72 percent in the regular Army. The vast majority of Air Force officers without degrees at this time were between the ages of 29 and 34.[20] By 1955 the figure had risen to about 47 percent, for all active duty officers below the rank of general. The percentage with degrees was considerably higher for general officers, however. As of February 1954, for example, 75 percent of all brigadier generals on active duty in the Air Force held the B.S. or B.A. degree or higher. Forty-five percent were graduates of West Point.[21]

To meet this situation the Air Force took advantage of a civilian institutions program authorized by Congress in 1946. In each of the next two years approximately 1,000 Air Force officers were enrolled in full time undergraduate studies. Subsequent budget cuts and limitations imposed by Congress have reduced this program materially.

After the war the Navy faced a similar situation, although of less serious proportions. During the emergency the Navy also commissioned a large number of officers who had not completed a college education, either in the reserve or by temporary transfer of enlisted men to officer status. Those who were accepted for regular commissions following the war were assured that they would be given opportunity equal to their Naval Academy contemporaries. Accordingly provision was made to fill out their educational experience. The so-called "five term college program" was devised for these officers who transferred to the regular Navy, permitting those with no more than two years of college education to obtain up to two and a half years of additional experience at any college in which there is an NROTC unit or at George Washington University.[22] In addition, former Naval Reserve and temporary officers received military and technical instruction at the General Line School to make up for their lack of formal instruction in professional naval subjects. The Navy has regarded the provision of these opportunities as the fulfillment of a pledge to these officers when they were encouraged to enter the regular service.

[20] T. J. Barrett, *Mobilization for Education,* unpublished M.A. thesis, Ohio State University, 1949.

[21] Officer Education Research Laboratory, *Graduate Academic Degrees of Brigadier Generals of the United States Air Force,* Maxwell Air Force Base, 21 April 1954.

[22] The program initially was limited to officers transferring to the regular Navy prior to January 1, 1949. By June 1956 the requirements of these officers were taken care of and the program was opened to reserve and temporary officers transferring after that date.

All three services also have encouraged officers, as well as enlisted personnel, to enroll in off-duty courses at nearby colleges and universities. Frequently an officer assigned to a civilian institution as an ROTC instructor will complete work for an undergraduate or advanced degree at that institution while performing his regular duties. In the early years following world war II the Air Force placed great emphasis upon its Operation Bootstrap, an off-duty program. In the year 1948–1949 about 5,000 Air Force officers and enlisted personnel were taking off-duty courses at the college level. Initially much of this instruction could be secured by officers of all three services at government expense, but under existing law the program is largely limited to enlisted personnel. Those officers who are enrolled in undergraduate courses are taking work directly related to prospective assignments in special fields. Officers also may enroll in the Armed Forces Institute, which offers over 300 correspondence and self-teaching courses, a considerable proportion of them on the college level. Officers and enlisted personnel also may enroll in the off-campus and overseas programs conducted by the University of Maryland and several other civilian institutions. The student pays one fourth of the cost of this education.[23]

Insofar as all these programs provide future military leaders with a broad basic education, they lay a foundation on which advanced military schools can build, and they equip officers with some of the knowledge and skills required in policy level positions.

[23] The Maryland program was established in 1947. In 1955–1956 the overseas program alone enrolled 17,450 students in 168 centers in 12 countries and maintained a roving faculty of over 300 members. Since 1954 the director of the overseas program has been Dr. Herman Beukema (Brigadier General, USA, Ret.), former head of the Department of Social Sciences at the United States Military Academy.

PART FOUR

INTERMEDIATE MILITARY EDUCATION

CHAPTER THIRTEEN

PREPARING FOR MILITARY ASSIGNMENTS

THE first 10 to 15 years of an officer's commissioned service, like similar periods in other professions, determine in large measure the direction and level of performance of his career. At this time he gains the experience that qualifies him for increased responsibility and advancement. In chapter two we stressed the central importance of professional military competence. It is during this critical early period in an officer's career that this competence is established. Much time is devoted to training activities. Most of it is spent in the field with troops, at sea in ships of the fleet, or with operating air and support units. Generally this experience is developed within a defined area of specialization, such as one of the branches in the Army, Naval aviation or submarine warfare in the Navy, or with fighters or bombers in the Air Force. The area of specialization may become even more narrowly defined, e.g. communications, meteorology, finance, and so forth. During these years the young officer develops work habits and attitudes that characterize him throughout his career. His contributions to the service and his prospects for advancement and higher responsibility are critically measured and his reputation established.

Assignment to military schools constitutes a regular feature of this 10 to 15 year period. These include the branch schools of the Army, the General Line School and other divisions of the Naval Postgraduate School, and the Squadron Officer School of the Air Force, as well as specialist programs of all sorts. A limited number of selected officers, including many of those with the best chances of advancement to the higher ranks, also attend the Command and Staff Schools or the Armed Forces Staff College. These outstanding officers are likely to be selected for these schools soon after becoming eligible. Thus they attend the professional military schools well before the completion of 15 years of service.

The schools that we are discussing here are concerned with the development of professional military competence. In terms of the substantive content of their courses they would *not* appear to contribute to the cultivation of those other areas of knowledge and personal skill that seem to be called for among officers assigned to policy levels. This is not their purpose. Rather they are designed to provide the armed forces with effective leaders for combat operations. From among the best of the graduates will be selected during the succeeding 10 to 15 years the men who will maintain the armed forces of the nation in combat readiness and lead them into action if necessity dictates. The graduates of the Command and Staff Courses will serve as the commanding officers of divisions and corps, major naval vessels, squadrons and task forces, and air wings and divisions, and the principal staff officers at these and higher levels. Thus these schools are concerned with the organization and employment of armed forces in combat and related support activities.

Yet to dismiss these schools lightly would be to lose sight of their real significance. They are important because they help to create and to reinforce the image that the armed forces have of themselves. One of their functions is the development of "doctrine," the formulation of standard procedures and ways of doing things. These schools are important also because of the emphasis upon those techniques that so impress civilians when they first come into contact with the military in a responsible way and which have a real impact on officers who may be assigned to policy level positions. This is particularly characteristic of the Command and Staff Schools. Here officers with different backgrounds, experience, and specialties are indoctrinated in the ways and outlook of the entire service.

Within the frame of reference of this book, we have not attempted to judge these schools with respect to their primary function, the development of military skill and competence. The experience of the armed forces of the United States in the second world war and the testimony of many observers suggests that they have performed this function well. There are certain characteristics that appear to be relevant to our purpose, however. In the first place, the orientation toward combat operations naturally limits the time and effort that can be devoted to other matters. Thus the programs are more in the nature of training than education. Certain of the characteristics ascribed in chapter three to military training activities also are evident in these schools, particularly the emphasis upon uniformity and upon the "distributive" quality of the training function. They must deal with large numbers of individuals, usually for relatively short periods of time. The focus is upon weapons and their tactical employment, upon organization, and upon staff procedure. Nevertheless the courses of study also reflect the wide scope of military responsibilities and the concern of the armed services to prepare their officers for all types of problems now facing them. This concern takes two forms, on the one hand in the programs of the schools that serve the broad purpose of career development (e.g. the branch schools and Command and Staff Schools), and on the other in the addition of a variety of new specialist schools and educational opportunities. In the former, while instruction remains centered upon combat operations, there has been a marked shift in emphasis throughout the decade since world war II toward inclusion of instruction on other matters of increasing significance to military personnel. Some of these matters bear upon the newer roles and responsibilities that pose the central problem of this book.

Basic Schools

THE AIR FORCE SCHOOLS

The Air Force schools have gone further than those of the other services in this direction. An article in the *Air University Quarterly Review* describing the Squadron Officer Course suggests what the Air Force hopes to accomplish by this trend. The article characterizes a hypothetical officer upon enrollment in the course in the following manner: "Although Joe was a top-notch pilot, he ran into trouble in performance of duties other than flying. The problems which bothered him were those requiring judgment and perspective. When, for example, he served as adjutant, supply officer, and later as acting squadron commander, he made several hasty, impractical decisions on squadron administration and policy. What Joe needed was training in the skills of logical, organized thinking and problem solving. There were other ways in which Joe felt uncomfortable and unsure of himself. In writing readable staff reports, in speaking articulately and convincingly, and in cooperative staff work demanding organization and direction of a group effort, Joe's deficiency and uncertainty was reflected in the caliber of his work. But then Joe was a pilot. His training for a specialty, like that of thousands of other young Air Force officers, had never developed the wide range of skills needed by commanders and staff officers. What Joe and most squadron-grade officers of today need is basic professional training for greater over-all versatility, regardless of job assignment or [specialty classification]." [1]

Accordingly, the theme of the Squadron Officer Course is "Think, Communicate, and Cooperate." It places heavy emphasis upon the skills of oral and written communication and upon the development of leadership qualities. More than 60 hours of instruction are devoted to communications, including principles of logic, effective speaking and writing, problem solving, conference techniques, and negotiation procedures and skills. Although 700 officers are enrolled in the course, a great deal of the instruction is accomplished in small groups composed of about 12 students and one instructor, in order to maximize the opportunity for self-expression and "learning by doing." The course also devotes about nine hours to the study of human behavior, in which the art of working with people is stressed. For this area, among others, a civilian psychologist has been appointed to the faculty. The concern of the Air Force for community relations also is reflected in the curriculum. Considerable attention is given to such matters as the problems of a base commander in dealing with the neighboring community.

With all of this attention to the development of a polished, diplomatic negotiator, the course does not, however, neglect the aggressive qualities of a combat officer. Basically it is designed "for the fighting officers of the Air Force, to show how vigorous individual and team efforts prepare the officer for the arduous

[1] "The Squadron Officer Course," *Air University Quarterly Review,* Fall 1953, p. 96.

physical and mental demands of combat." [2] The course includes a rigorous physical conditioning program. It employs the slogan "Every Man a Tiger," using the tiger as a symbol of the fighting qualities associated with military leadership. The "Tiger Trek," for example, is an all-night field problem involving escape and evasion behind "enemy" lines. But even in this part of the program, the importance of team cooperation as well as individual leadership is demonstrated.

Public and international affairs also receive attention in the Squadron Officer Course. Twenty-four or more hours of instruction are devoted to lectures, panel discussions, and group conferences on such topics as factors of national power, instruments of national policy, the United Nations, world trouble spots, the theory and practice of communism in the Soviet Union and elsewhere, United States foreign policies, and United States organization for national defense.

THE ARMY SCHOOLS

The Army also shows a trend toward a broader educational program in its schools that are concerned primarily with the development of professional military competence. Thus, for example, the common subjects taught in all Army branch basic courses include several hours each on such topics as character guidance, company administration, intelligence, methods of instruction, public information and community relations, and troop information and education. These topics are taken up again in the later branch courses. The advanced course also includes short periods of instruction on military government, civil disturbances, Congressional relations, general management, and the foreign military aid program. Beyond these common subjects, separate schools have added other topics. The advanced course at the Armored School, to cite but one example, now provides considerable instruction in public speaking and conference and committee techniques. It also includes a six hour study of the theory and practice of communism. The Department of the Army also has encouraged the Army schools to invite representative military, civilian, and government figures to participate as guest speakers.

[2] Air Command and Staff School, Squadron Officer Course Curriculum, Class of 1954-B, p. vi.

THE NAVY SCHOOLS

The schools maintained by the Navy for its younger officers are principally for technical and engineering studies. The courses conducted by the Naval Postgraduate School likewise are in these fields. Yet in the Navy an effort also is being made to provide a broader educational experience, although to a considerably smaller degree than in the other services. The new one year curriculum of the General Line School, introduced in 1955–1956, now devotes some attention to principles of administration and management, public relations, communication skills, and international affairs. The latter item, for example, covers briefly the present role of the United States in world affairs, the organization and functions of the Department of State and Department of Defense, and the military and economic aid programs. During the last third of the program increased emphasis is placed upon problem-solving situations and individual reading and study.

The Command and Staff Colleges

The Army, Navy, and Air Force schools so far described are usually attended by officers of the respective services in the normal course of career advancement. The Command and Staff Colleges, on the other hand, are attended only by selected officers, presumably those who show promise of greater responsibility. This makes these colleges of particular importance to this study, since many of their graduates will go on to assignments at the policy level.

THE ARMY COMMAND AND GENERAL STAFF COLLEGE

In terms of the primary job of the Army to fight and short of that to be prepared to fight, the regular course at the Command and General Staff College at Leavenworth is the most important single educational experience open to the career Army officer. The branch schools may give him more detailed information about his field of special competence, and the Army War College, National War College, or Industrial College may provide better preparation for assignments at the highest levels, but only Leavenworth equips him for the principal command and staff responsibilities with large combat units. It is the senior Army tactical school and the only school of *combined arms and services,* that is, it is the only school concerned with the employment of all of the branches of the Army as an integrated fighting team. As such it is the common training ground of officers from all the different sources utilized by the Army—West Point, the colleges and universities, the ranks, and civilian life—and from all branches, combat and technical and administrative. Here the common Leavenworth stamp is placed upon a George Marshall of VMI and a Dwight Eisenhower of West Point. For most officers, moreover, it is the last educational opportunity. In the event of large scale mobilization, these officers will constitute the professional nucleus of the expanded Army.[3]

The Department of the Army defines the instructional mission of the Command and General Staff College as follows:

"1. To prepare officers—

"a. For duty as commanders of divisions, corps, armies, and comparable commands in the communications zone.

"b. For duty on the general staff of divisions, corps, armies, and comparable commands in the communications zone.

"2. To provide instruction in the light of modern developments and war lessons to ensure—

"a. Effective development and employment of all field forces within the framework of the field army and the communications zone.

"b. Efficient personnel, intelligence, and logistical support of the fighting forces."

As already indicated, attendance is on a selective basis. The eligibility requirements are 8 to 15 years of commissioned service, age less than 41 years, and credit for completion of an advanced branch school course. Potentiality for assignment to high command and staff positions as indicated by actual performance of duties is also considered. Officers of all branches of the Army attend, in a ratio of about four combat arms officers for one from the supporting area. About 50 percent of all eligible officers are selected to attend the regular course, usually while in the grade of major or lieutenant colonel. In 1955–1956, 529 United States

[3] The entire issue of *Military Review* for May 1956 is devoted to the Command and General Staff College.

officers, including 9 Naval and 9 Air Force officers, and 78 allied officers, representing 40 nations, were enrolled in the nine month course.

This regular course consists of seven principal parts. The first three provide a common background for officers of all branches, and are largely descriptive. The following four, involving application of principles to particular types and levels of operations, are more analytical. The instructional hours given below are for the 1954–1955 academic year.

1. *Orientation and General Subjects* (158 hours). This part introduces the officer to command and staff principles, fundamentals of combat operations, and atomic weapons. It also covers the organization of the government for national security and the Army's role in this organization, and the principal organizational features of the United States Navy and Air Force and the British and French services.

2. *General Staff Functions and Techniques* (67 hours). This provides information on the functions and basic staff techniques of the four "G's"—G-1 (Personnel), G-2 (Intelligence), G-3 (Operations and Training), and G-4 (Logistics). G-5 (Civil Affairs) was added in 1955–1956. Throughout this part emphasis is placed upon the relationship of these functions to the commander.

3. *Division Operations* (378 hours). This is the largest part of the course, consuming more than one quarter of the total time. It is concerned with the employment of infantry, armored, and air-borne divisions, including action in arctic, mountain, and amphibious warfare.

4. *Corps Operations* (156 hours). The title is self-explanatory. The instruction covers air-borne corps operations and the tactical use of atomic weapons.

5. *Army Operations* (86 hours). The title is self-explanatory. All three of the "operations" courses provide instruction in defensive, offensive, and retrograde action.

6. *Administrative Support of Large Forces* (105 hours). This is concerned with the communications zone, including the duties of the commanders and general staff officers of the major components of this zone organized in support of a field army and large scale airborne and amphibious operations. This part, as well as

the instruction dealing with operations in the three previous parts, makes use of historical examples.

7. *Joint Operations* (35 hours). This final part includes an exercise requiring the preparation of plans for a large scale joint operation involving an amphibious-airborne assault on a hostile nation, including the zone of interior replacement and overseas support systems.

The Command and Staff College employs a range of instructional methods, in common with other military schools. In addition to the usual lectures, and conferences, the college makes extensive use of exercises of various sorts, including map and terrain exercises, map maneuvers, operational plans, and individual staff plans. These are subjected to close review by the faculty and frequently are followed by a critique, in which a preferred solution is presented. The case method of instruction, involving several operations in world war II, also is employed. The manuals, directives, faculty lesson plans, and other study materials used at the Command and General Staff College are prepared with meticulous care.

Leavenworth is famous—some might be tempted to say infamous—for the demands it makes upon its students. Stories of nervous breakdowns and even suicides among students are legendary. Likewise, outstanding success in the course is a mark of great distinction in an officer's career. Dwight Eisenhower, for example, graduated first in the class of 1926. Unlike the senior service colleges, which, as we shall see, cultivate an informal atmosphere and eschew formal grading of students, Leavenworth subjects its students to frequent and exhaustive examination and to detailed evaluation.

Although the course at Leavenworth is focused upon command and staff duties in combat operations, it does include instruction that is relevant to the theme of this book, the preparation of officers for positions involving participation in the formulation and implementation of national policy. The amount of such instruction is proportionately small and its principal effect is indirect. Yet there is a growing interest in subjects of this nature at the college.

Many topics that are essentially military spill over into matters that point up the intimate relationship of military and nonmilitary factors. This is true, for example, of the brief study of strategic intelligence, in which political, economic, and sociological considerations are evaluated. It applies also to the intelligence function in the communications zone, the rules of land warfare, the treatment of prisoners of war, the civil affairs function in occupied areas, psychological warfare, troop information and education, and problems of military leadership.

The curriculum also reflects the interest of all three military services in the field of management. At Leavenworth about six hours are devoted specifically to management problems, including the operations of the Army's Management Improvement Program and its programing, budgeting, and auditing systems. The purpose here is not only to cover the techniques of management of a large headquarters but also to demonstrate the close relationship of war plans to requirements, and these in turn to the national budget and to the long lead time involved in securing military hardware and personnel.

On the other hand Leavenworth has not ventured far into the areas of national and international affairs that have become a principal concern of the senior joint and service colleges. A total of about 10 instructional hours is devoted to United States national policy. While the precise subjects vary from year to year, the 1954–1955 program is representative. One lecture covered national interests and objectives and the organization of the government for policy formulation. Another outlined the objectives and operations of the foreign aid program. The relationship of the Army to the Congress was developed in lectures by a member of Congress and the Army's principal Congressional liaison officer. Additional lectures were given on the public information function, on communism in the United States, and on maritime transportation. Problems of economic mobilization were handled in a four hour presentation by a visiting team from the Industrial College.

Another block of about 10 hours was devoted to foreign areas and related matters. Separate lectures were scheduled on the British Commonwealth and the French Union, and on another occasion a representative panel of student officers from Commonwealth nations responded to questions on military and nonmilitary affairs in their countries. The Soviet Union, with particular reference to the Red Army, was considered in a four hour conference-discussion.[4] Still other lectures covered the significant geographic features of Europe, the Middle East, and Asia. In this connection it also should be noted that some of the operations exercises involve considerable geographic, political, and economic information on the foreign areas selected for the hypothetical problems. Informal social association with their classmates from allied nations also provides the American officers with opportunity to become better acquainted with the attitudes and customs of foreign nations.

Recent changes in the curriculum of the regular course at Leavenworth initiated by Major General Garrison H. Davidson, commandant from 1954 to 1956, have been designed to increase the "educational" as contrasted with the "training" aspects of the program. General Davidson emphasized the critical importance of developing more creative military thinking to keep pace with technological changes and the expanding responsibilities of the Army. He proposed that students be given a broader experience designed to encourage more independent thought and analysis. Consequently an effort is being made to substitute more analytical, problem-solving type of work by the students for the traditional descriptive instruction-examination routine. He also reduced the number of examinations and tried to decrease the traditional emphasis upon memory work. Because of the pressure to cover a multitude of topics that are considered essential to the mission of the college, this approach is being applied only in the last third of the course, but it is hoped that it can be introduced eventually throughout the curriculum. A change in the visiting lecturers program will reduce the number of talks on subjects covered in the regular program of study, permitting more of a broader nature to provide a change of pace and a broader perspective. During the 1955–1956 year these lectures by guests thus were divided into three categories. Those in the first category dealt with current operations of the primary staff sections at the Department of the Army level, particularly those concerned with national and international affairs. Those in the second were devoted to material developments and their significance for the future; and in the third

---

[4] Time devoted to the Soviet Union was increased to 13 hours in 1955–1956.

to foreign countries and peoples, and to economic and international matters. Of a total of 51 hours, 23 were devoted to the third category.

In 1955 General Davidson proposed to the Department of the Army that Leavenworth return to a two year course of study, following the practice of 1927–1936. This recommendation stems from a growing dissatisfaction of the faculty with the present crowded program and the inescapable pressure to add even more subjects. The reasoning is that while command and staff duties in combat are his primary function, the average officer spends only 5 to 6 percent of his career time in the study and practice of combat operations. Yet the complexities of modern warfare make it increasingly difficult for him to master all of the ramifications of his job. An adequate understanding of these ramifications cannot be acquired in a "cram course," but requires instead sufficient time for careful study and reflection in an atmosphere conducive to intellectual stimulation and development. It is planned to use the second year to slow down the pace, to give more attention to topics outside of the present focus upon tactical operations, including national and international affairs, and to introduce greater use of small seminar type instruction and problem-solving techniques. General Davidson's plan provided for an enrollment of approximately 500 officers of whom about one half would remain for the two year course. The odds are probably against approval of the proposal in the near future. In any event its implementation must await the construction of a new academic building. Congress appropriated funds in 1955 for the preparation of detailed building plans.

An outside survey commission appointed by General Davidson came up with a different answer to this situation in 1956. It concluded that it was a mistake to try to prepare officers for responsibilities at a level that they would not reach for another 10 to 15 years and recommended accordingly that instruction extend only to the duties of the division commander and general staff officers of divisions, corps, and armies, and comparable levels in the communications zone. Preparation for tactical responsibilities at higher levels would then be provided by Leavenworth in an advanced tactical course for carefully selected colonels at a time nearer to their advancement to general officer rank, and when presumably the course would be more relevant to their more immediate needs.[5]

In addition to the regular course, the Command and Staff College also conducts abbreviated associate courses of 17 weeks for reserve and National Guard officers, and several shorter special weapons and refresher courses. Students from allied nations assigned to the regular course are enrolled first in an eight week preparatory program. The college also is responsible for the preparation and supervision of a variety of extension courses and special short self-taught courses for reserve units.

The instructional function, moreover, is only part of the assigned mission of the college. Leavenworth has long been a principal center for the formulation of Army "doctrine"—that is, standard concepts and procedures—and the incorporation of these in training literature and instruction. This responsibility includes the review of doctrine formulated by other agencies of the Army. The college also publishes *Military Review*. This monthly journal contains 6 to 10 articles, brief notes on foreign and domestic military news, digests of articles in foreign military journals, and book reviews. Each issue totals more than 100 pages. A considerable number of the articles are written by instructors at the college and at other Army schools. Occasional articles are prepared by students at the college or other schools.[6] The contents of the *Review* run mainly to matters of professional military interest, including strategy, tactics, command problems, military leadership, weapons and weapon systems, and Army organization. A few articles from time to time deal with issues more directly related to the newer areas of military responsibility with which this book is concerned, such as the organization of the Department of Defense, the relationship of military strategy to foreign policy, and political developments abroad. *Military Review* is distributed to Army units and to paid subscribers. It also is published in Spanish and Portuguese editions, which are distributed at government expense to military authorities in the American republics to the south.

[5] *Report of the Educational Survey Commission, Command and General Staff College*, Fort Leavenworth, 1 June 1956.

[6] Of a total of 91 articles in Volume XXXIV (April 1954 to March 1955) 14 were contributed by instructors at the Command and General Staff College. Frequently these are assigned as a part of the job. Six articles were contributed by instructors at other Army military schools and two by members of the West Point faculty. There were two articles by students at Army schools.

THE AIR COMMAND AND STAFF SCHOOL

The Command and Staff School of the Air Command and Staff College at Maxwell Field is still a relatively new institution, having been established as one of the constituent units of the Air University in 1946. The events of the last decade disrupted the orderly development of the school as originally planned, and it has only been since 1954–1955 that its operations have been stabilized. Because of this situation, as well as its recent origin, its graduates have not yet made an impact upon the Air Force comparable to the long influence of Leavenworth upon the Army. The Air Command and Staff School is now open on a selective basis to career officers holding the rank of lieutenant colonel or major and who have had at least 10 and no more than 15 years of service. The Air Force goal of attendance by about 60 percent of all eligible officers will not be attained for some time. Only about 25 percent are now able to attend. For most of them this is the last educational opportunity.

Initially, in 1946, the Air University established a single nine month course at the field grade level, known as the regular command and staff course. But the creation of the Air Force as an independent service the following year, coupled with the deterioration of the international situation, presented unanticipated demands for officer personnel. Consequently the command and staff course was reduced to 22 weeks, and subsequently, for several years after the outbreak of war in Korea, lasted only 15 weeks. In 1946 the Air University also had organized a Special Staff School, with separate courses in communications and electronics, logistics, intelligence, and comptrollership, to provide staff officer specialists in these fields. Because of other demands on personnel, an officer could not be spared to attend one of these courses and the command and staff course as well. Accordingly in 1952 it was determined that the specialist courses should be equated with the command and staff course for purposes of crediting an officer with school attendance. Also all of these courses were extended in length from 15 to 22 weeks to permit inclusion of a common core of instruction in the command and staff area. In the meantime, the Special Staff School had been closed as a separate institution and the specialist courses transferred to the Command and Staff

288

School. Thus by 1954 this school offered five 22 week courses "at the same level," the regular course and four specialist courses, each of which theoretically provided majors and lieutenant colonels with equivalent preparation for command and staff responsibilities. This situation was not satisfactory to responsible individuals at the Air University, who clearly were convinced that the preparation of officers for performance as members of an integrated staff called for a common educational experience, in which officers of varying backgrounds and specialities studied together. Consequently plans were initiated to merge the regular and specialist courses into a single nine month program, to be known as the Command and Staff School within a newly designated Air Command and Staff College.[7] The first full year course was offered in 1954–1955, and the following year the school commenced a move into new buildings at Maxwell constructed for its use. These facilities made possible a planned enrollment of 1,000 per class.[8] The official definition of the mission of the school is "to increase the professional qualifications of selected USAF majors and lieutenant colonels and to improve their abilities to execute the command and staff tasks required to implement air strategy and missions of the Air Force and to contribute to the development of air doctrine, strategy, and tactics." The specific objectives of the school are listed as follows:

"a. To increase the student's ability as an individual and as a member of a group to analyze, appraise, and develop sound solutions to problems.

"b. To increase his knowledge of effective and integrated command and staff action.

"c. To increase his knowledge of the capabilities and limitations of current and future weapons systems and their relationship to sound employment doctrine.

"d. To consider the special significance of moral and ethical responsibilities of military officers."

To accomplish its mission, the Command and Staff School must (according to a statement in its curriculum directive) increase

---

[7] The Squadron Officer School is the other principal unit within the Air Command and Staff College.

[8] For the 1956–1957 year, enrollment was cut back to approximately 800 because of a shortage of officers in the Air Force.

the individual's ability to contribute to the effective employment of air power. It should:

"1. Improve his ability to think clearly and objectively.

"2. Increase his desire to keep himself abreast of dynamic changes in the world.

"3. Teach him the techniques of planning for subsequent application in the field.

"4. Increase his ability to command and to fill staff positions throughout future assignments."

Some of the reasoning behind the present program of the school is suggested in a report prepared in 1953 in connection with plans for a nine month course:

"The problem of schooling officers for advanced command and staff positions in the Air Force, while similar in many respects to comparable schooling tasks in the Army, Navy, or in civilian industrial, business, and banking organizations, has certain unique aspects. One of these is the highly technical and costly nature of Air Force weapons and equipment. Another is the mission requirement to maintain H-hour readiness in a large segment of its total force. In order that those who command do not find themselves forced blindly to rely on technologists for their employment as well as managerial decisions it is necessary to have in an Air Force commander a more thorough understanding of technical requirements and limitations than is usually necessary in top executives. The requirement to maintain a large force in H-hour readiness denies to the Air Force the opportunity which might otherwise be available for broadening the scope of many of its officers by job rotation.

"It would seem, therefore, that advanced officer education in the Air Force must include coverage of all principal areas of command interest in terms of substantive acquaintance, as well as solid grounding in the techniques of leadership, command, management, and the skills necessary to these functions." [9]

The Command and Staff School curriculum is divided into two phases of 15 and 24 weeks' duration. These in turn are divided into units of instruction. The school utilizes many instructional

[9] Headquarters, Air Command and Staff School, *Memorandum for Commander, Air University,* "The AC&SS Program of Courses at the Field Grade Officer Level," 13 November 1953.

methods, including lectures, panel discussions, conferences, seminars, and exercises of various sorts. In keeping with the practice of all Air Force schools, it places particular emphasis upon small group situations.[10]

Phase 1

Unit 1. *Introduction* (2 weeks). The principal feature of this unit is instruction in the so-called "communication skills," that is, in oral and written expression, conference techniques, and problem solving.

Unit 2. *Elements of Power* (2 weeks). Much of this unit resembles, in outline, a standard college course in international relations. It deals with communism, fascism, and democracy, the nature of conflict, the factors of national power, and international organization. It also includes consideration of scientific and psychological aspects of the atomic revolution.

Unit 3. *Basic Doctrine* (1 week). After a brief review of the classical military doctrines of Clausewitz and others, this unit presents basic United States Army, Navy, and Air Force doctrines.

Unit 4. *Command* (2 weeks). This is designed to improve the student's capacity for effective command responsibility. It examines principles of command, including the commander's responsibilities and obligations, and identifies the tactics, techniques, and devices available to him for effective leadership. It also considers the significance of morals and ethics and the role of the Air Force commander in community relations.

Unit 5. *Air Staffs* (5 weeks). The purpose of this unit is to provide the officer with an understanding of staff functioning at all levels of command. It is concerned with staff organizational patterns, staff functions and responsibilities, and the command process of planning. It concludes with the preparation of a training program for an air wing, as an exercise in staff planning.

Unit 6. *Air Operations Exercises* (3 weeks). This final unit in the first phase provides opportunity for application of the basic doctrines studied in the previous unit and for the handling of the

[10] Because of the frequent changes to which the school has been subjected throughout its history, its program has undergone frequent experimentation and revision. The outline that follows is based upon plans for 1955–1956.

details required in "laying on" a series of combat missions. It covers such matters as the employment of combat air forces in offensive and defensive reconnaissance and other tactical actions, and includes study of the latest weapons developments.

Phase 2

Unit 7. *The Enemy* (3 weeks). This unit is concerned with the political, economic, social, and military structures and operations of the Soviet Union, its European satellites, and communist China.

Unit 8. *The Free World* (3 weeks). This is a study of the non-communist nations, with particular emphasis upon the relationships of the United States to its allies. It includes study of allied military alliances, the military vulnerability of the Western Hemisphere, and the military significance of the uncommitted nations.

Unit 9. *The United States* (2 weeks). This unit of instruction is concerned with the formulation of policy at the highest national level. It examines the organization of the government for national security, research and development, and over-all strategic guidance. It also goes into the mechanisms of joint military planning.

Unit 10. *Air Force Plans and Programs* (3 weeks). The next unit moves on to the level of Headquarters, USAF. It includes study of the philosophy of Air Force planning, war planning and programing procedures, and the integrated functioning of the Air Staff in support of Air Force plans and programs. As a part of this unit, representatives of the principal agencies of the Air Staff present briefings on their current programs.

Unit 11. *Command Planning* (5 weeks). This unit centers around the three major combat commands of the Air Force—the Air Defense Command, the Strategic Air Command, and the Tactical Air Command—and provides an understanding of the planning process and current plans at this level. It makes extensive use of command employment exercises, including one for NATO air forces.

Unit 12. *Evaluation of Basic Doctrine* (2 weeks). In this unit the students, organized in seminars, review and evaluate the basic Air Force doctrinal manuals.

Unit 13. *Application* (3 weeks). This last unit consists of specific problems in the application of air power in support of national objectives, in situations ranging from cold war to total war. Some relate to use of specific weapons, others to actions in designated parts of the globe. Long range trends and their impact upon the future Air Force are discussed. Together with students of the Canadian Air Force Staff College, who visit Maxwell at this time, the class develops a long range plan for the security of the Western Hemisphere. The year concludes with a number of summary presentations. These cover matters that will be of immediate concern to the officer in his next assignment, in the budget, weapons, personnel, and support fields.

Like its counterparts at Leavenworth and Newport, the Air Command and Staff School is designed to prepare officers for the command and staff responsibilities to which they will be assigned as majors, lieutenant colonels, and colonels. Its purpose is not to prepare them for the sort of high level positions involving participation in the formulation of national policy that are of central concern in this book. Yet it does attempt to provide an understanding of these policies, on the assumption that its graduates will thus be better equipped to carry them out. Moreover, many of these graduates will advance to high responsibility without further educational opportunity. The school, as it makes a place for itself with growth and maturity, will have increasing influence upon the cultivation of the characteristic attitudes and behavior of Air Force officers, comparable to the role of the Air Force Tactical School in the interwar years. This influence should be particularly forceful with respect to the development and application of Air Force doctrine.

For this study, perhaps the most significant development at the Air Command and Staff School is the emphasis upon matters which not so long ago would have been considered beyond the scope of a military school. This reflects the very deep concern, almost preoccupation, of the Air Force with the successful promotion of its concepts of the national interest and of its role in protecting that interest. Thus the school devotes a great deal of attention to the refinement of individual skill in the communication of ideas and the negotiation of a position. The observer gets the impression sometimes that the Air Force, perhaps still sensitive to the relative youthfulness of its officers, is most concerned with successful negotiating with the Army, Navy, or other agencies of the government. The course also helps to prepare the officer to handle community relations—an area of increasing headaches for a commander, for example, whose jet aircraft operations arouse the angry protests of neighboring housewives.

In an earlier chapter we traced the trends in the programs of the senior service colleges that have brought about increased emphasis upon instruction in national and international affairs, subjects that initially were to be left largely to the National War College. The recent changes at the Air Command and Staff School made possible by the reinstitution of a nine month course show that this trend is now reaching down to this level, insofar as the Air Force is concerned. Here again, this reflects the growing concern of the Air Force for responsibilities that are global in scope and effect. Comparison of the present curricula of the Command and Staff School and Air War College indicates striking similarities. The time devoted by the former to national and international affairs is approaching that of the latter, although the manner of treatment appears to be less detailed. Noteworthy also at the Command and Staff School is the sharp distinction made between "the enemy" and "the free world." This is a typical example of a general tendency of military schools to incorporate into the structure of their curricula the axioms of current military policy.

In addition to the regular course, the Command and Staff School has a number of other responsibilities. Like Leavenworth, it enrolls a considerable number of allied officers, although they attend only during phase 1 of the curriculum. A special six week preparatory program, including intensive language study, is provided for these officers prior to the opening of the course. While the preparation of Air Force doctrinal literature is centered in the Evaluation Staff of the Air War College, Command and Staff School faculty members and student personnel sometimes participate in this function. Certain members of the faculty also have instructional duties in the Squadron Officer School, the academic instructors course, the short air weapons course, and the reserve officer orientation course, all of which are enterprises of the Air Command and Staff College.

Although organizationally not a part of the Command and

Staff School, reference should be made here to the *Air University Quarterly Review,* published by an editorial staff at Maxwell Air Force Base. This journal is the Air Force's counterpart of Leavenworth's *Military Review.* It is published to stimulate professional thought concerning air strategy, tactics, and related techniques. Each issue consists of 136 pages, including about six feature articles, generally on matters of direct professional interest to Air Force officers, several shorter articles prepared by the staff on special Air Force problems or developments, and book reviews. The *Quarterly Review* publishes occasional articles by members of the faculties of Air University schools and of its headquarters staff. In recent years an effort has been made to develop the *Quarterly Review* as an authoritative source of information on Air Force doctrine. This has resulted in an increase in material produced by its own staff, so that this now constitutes 40 to 50 percent of each issue. The magazine is distributed to faculty and students at the Air War College and the Command and Staff School, to Air Force units, and to paid subscribers. Spanish and Portuguese editions are distributed in the American republics. In 1952 the *Quarterly Review* was declared a Department of the Air Force publication.

THE COMMAND AND STAFF COURSE, NAVAL WAR COLLEGE

The Navy has not placed the same emphasis upon officer education at the command and staff level as have the Army and the Air Force, at least in quantitative terms, in spite of various suggestions along this line going back to 1919. The Pye board in 1944 recommended that 50 percent of all lieutenant commanders attend a command and staff course, and estimated that this would mean an annual enrollment of about 1,000. It was not until 1950 that the junior course at the Naval War College was renamed the Command and Staff Course. Most of the program is conducted in a building separate from but near the main Naval War College buildings at Newport. Although present facilities would permit an enrollment of between 200 and 300, classes have increased from 33 in 1951 to 125 in 1956, including in the latter case a total of 12 Army and Air Force officers.

The stated purpose of the Command and Staff Course is "to

provide lieutenant commanders, junior commanders and equivalent ranks with an opportunity to further their understanding of the fundamentals of warfare with emphasis upon the operational functions of command, and the organization, functions, and procedures of operational staffs, including participation in joint and combined committee work."

The course catalog defines the academic objectives of the Command and Staff Course as follows:

"a. Development of the powers of logical thought.

"b. Improvement of the working knowledge essential to the exercise of command at the level of an operational commander responsible for fleet operations in a theater of war. This includes:

"1. Understanding of the weapons and weapon systems, both current and future, and the tactics for their employment.

"2. Appreciation of the fundamentals of interservice operations.

"3. Understanding of basic logistics, including the agencies responsible and the forces involved in providing logistic support of the Fleet, and the operational techniques involved.

"4. Knowledge of the organization and procedures of military staffs, including joint and combined, and those civilian agencies responsible for the security of the nation.

"c. Appreciation of the fundamentals of strategy with emphasis on the role of the Navy.

"d. Familiarization with certain important strategic areas.

"e. Understanding of international relations, including international law, international politics, and international organizations.

"f. Cultivation of ability in both written and oral expression.

"g. Preparation for higher education."

The Command and Staff Course is divided into so-called curriculum items of varying length. Some of these are further divided into smaller segments and offered concurrently with other items. The course utilizes lectures, seminars, committee work, and individual assignments.

First Term—Basic Elements of Warfare

Operational Planning and Command Decision (10 days). This item is designed to familiarize the student with the techniques of solving military problems by the use of the military planning process. This process, as taught in the Command and Staff Course, employs a three step method of analysis, involving the estimate of the situation, the development of the plan, and the preparation of the directive. Concurrent instruction is given in the techniques of oral and written presentation and small group discussions.

Weapons Study (16 days). This is designed to provide an understanding of the capabilities, limitations, and support requirements of certain weapons and weapon systems, including mines and mine countermeasures, submarines, guided missiles, surface forces, amphibious assault forces, and aircraft.

Organization Study (12 days). This item is concerned with organizational arrangements for the formulation and execution of national security policy. It commences with study of the United States government at the highest levels, then devotes a week to the operations of military staffs. It concludes with joint and combined command organizations, including the NATO combined commands.

Operations Problems (nine in number through the year, involving 100 days). These are the backbone of the instructional program. Acting in some instances as individual commanders or staff officers, in other cases as members of the staff at various levels, the students work out plans for increasingly complex operations. Usually an appropriate operations problem is scheduled at the conclusion of a block of instruction in the naval operations study. The first is a plan for a task force commander who is assigned responsibility for protecting allied sea lines of communication in a strategic area at the outbreak of war. Others involve logistics planning, carrier operations, surface actions, amphibious operations, and so forth. The final problem is a two-sided affair involving joint and combined forces engaged in an amphibious assault upon a designated objective in enemy territory.

Nuclear Weapons (4 days). This is an orientation briefing on recent nuclear weapons developments.

International Law (5 days). The study of international law has long been a fixture at Newport. Consideration is given to the principal characteristics of international law, and to the problems of jurisprudence, laws of war, and positions of individuals in international law.

Army and Air Force Operations: Army, Naval, and Air War College Presentations (8 days). The first of these items is a survey, by Army and Air Force teams, of the essential characteristics, organization, employment, and support of the major combatant components of these two services, in a theater of operations. The War College presentations are devoted to concepts of future warfare, under varying conditions.

International Organizations (2 days). This short study is concerned with the United Nations and the mutual defense alliances of the allied nations.

Command Psychology and Leadership (4 days). This is a consideration of certain problems faced by a commanding officer, such as morale problems, officer–enlisted–civil service relations, and command leadership and administration.

Short Paper Program. During the academic year each student conducts individual research and prepares several short papers, usually on a topic of professional naval interest. Some of these are presented orally to groups of students.

Global Strategy Discussions (5 days). At the conclusion of the year, all students of the Naval War College, including the Command and Staff Course, joined by more than 100 reserve officers and invited civilian guests, participate in a series of lectures and discussions directed toward the formulation of an over-all global strategy for the United States.

About 20 percent of the Command and Staff Course is conducted in conjunction with the naval warfare 1 course of the senior college. This includes parts of the weapons and naval operations studies, one operations problem, the short curriculum items on nuclear weapons, international law, and Army and Air Force operations, and the Army, Naval, and Air War College presentations.

Although the focus of the Command and Staff Course at Newport is upon professional naval subjects in preparation for operational duties with the fleet, it has been the aim to broaden the experience and outlook of the officer. The introductory work in group dynamics and communication skills and the short paper program were designed for this purpose. Of even more significance is the inclusion of instruction in international law and organization, and participation in the Global Strategy Discussion. Students in the Command and Staff Course also attend about 25 to 30 lectures on national and international affairs scheduled for the senior courses. Among the topics included in this part of the program are a number dealing with the history, resources, and ideology of the Soviet Union, others on problems of American foreign policy, and several on economic mobilization and related issues. The speakers are most frequently representatives of the Department of State or university professors. In 1955 a prominent official of the CIO lectured to Naval War College students, including Command and Staff. In addition to these lectures, the Department of State advisor on the college staff conducts regular foreign affairs briefings for students of the Command and Staff Course, providing background information on current developments. He also gives most of the briefings on political and economic characteristics of the foreign countries and areas involved in the naval operations problems, and the students themselves are required to take these characteristics into account in preparing their solutions. Altogether these various features of the Command and Staff Course add up to considerable attention to matters beyond conventional professional naval subjects. The Air Command and Staff School actually devotes more time to these matters, but the students at Newport have the advantage of participation in some of the activities of the senior courses of the Naval War College.

In 1956 the Naval War College instituted a Command and Staff Course for foreign naval officers. Rather than accommodate these officers in the regular course, as is done at Leavenworth and Maxwell, a separate program was set up, including some topics presented in the more advanced courses at the college.

The three Command and Staff Schools play a very important part in preparing selected officers for leadership in combat operations. Because of its longer history and availability to a larger proportion of career officers, this is particularly true of the Army

Command and General Staff College. Within the Army its prestige is extremely high. While we have encountered Army officers who are skeptical of the value of the senior joint and service colleges, we have found none who have questioned the Command and General Staff College. To the Army, Leavenworth is more than a school; it is the source and fount of doctrines and procedures as well. The first of these is the doctrine of the estimate of the situation—the orderly, if sometimes mechanical, way of sizing up a problem with particular emphasis upon the precision and clarity of statement and analysis. The second is the doctrine of completed staff work, which gives the subordinate a large role in policy determination. The third is the principle that the headquarters must know the needs of its customers, that is, the troops in the field. This leads to the practice of frequent rotation of assignments, so that the officer in headquarters comes to the job with a direct understanding gained from experience of the needs of the forces in the field. Rotation, in turn, amplifies the essentiality of standardized procedures. And lastly there is the American doctrine that commanders in the field ought to be given considerable latitude once their mission has been defined.

While the term doctrine is not used, the Command and Staff Course at the Naval War College likewise places great emphasis upon orderly procedures. The course commences with instruction in a formalized technique of solving military problems, a process that is applied subsequently throughout the year in developing the solutions of the operations problems. The Air Command and Staff School also stresses doctrine, although because of the relative newness of the Air Force and the revolutionary technological developments to which it is exposed, much uncertainty concerning the status and value of doctrine remains, and its place in the program is questioned by some.

In summary, then, the Command and Staff Schools are centers where basic values, techniques, and procedures of the military services are nurtured, cultivated, and propagated. The officers who pass through these centers, already picked out from among their peers, are indoctrinated in these "doctrines." The military academies inculcate in the mind of the officer-to-be an image of his role as a professional soldier, sailor, or airman. The Command and Staff Schools give that officer, now entering upon responsibilities as combat leader or staff officer, an understanding of his service as a total fighting force and the standardized tools and techniques of its operation. By 1955 this function was assuming even greater significance than in the decade following world war II, because the officers moving into the zone of eligibility for attendance had not had actual combat experience in war at this level. Even most of the veterans of the Korean conflict had advanced beyond the zone.

Yet, in spite of the focus on combat and related support operations, the Command and Staff Courses reflect the same concern that is observed in other military educational activities for the broader problems facing responsible officers. Here there are differences among the three schools, but the same basic trend is evident at all of them. It is shown in interest in the principles and practices of administrative management. One sees it also in the attention given to the development of the skills of oral and written presentation and to what is now identified as group dynamics. This is particularly true of the Air Force and Navy schools at Maxwell and Newport. Both of these institutions accentuate the importance of preparing their graduates for situations in which they will be representing their services in negotiations with officers of other services or of foreign nations. They also stress the problems of community and public relations and how to meet them. All are anxious to broaden the officer's understanding of national and international affairs. Here the Air Command and Staff School has gone the furthest, the substantive content of its programs approaching that of the programs at the senior school level. This is characteristic of the desire of the Air Force to broaden the educational experience of its officer corps.

Finally, it should be noted that all three services are attempting to "upgrade" the command and staff level of instruction. Although the number still is small, enrollment at Newport is rising. Leavenworth has given thought to a two year program, and the Air Command and Staff School has recently extended its course to nine months. In large part these changes are motivated by recognition that for most Command and Staff graduates this is the last educational opportunity. But they also will permit a rise in the instructional level of the senior schools, with considerably less attention to what the military call "nuts and bolts" and correspondingly more to matters of broader strategic significance, of importance to officers assigned to policy level responsibilities. When graduates of the Command and Staff Schools become available for the senior schools, this advance will be possible. In the case of the Navy, the opening of the General Line School course for regular officers in 1955 should be reflected in a number of years in changes at the Command and Staff Courses. In turn these changes subsequently should make possible the termination of the first year senior course at the Naval War College and attendance by all officers selected for this level in the present second year course.

In spite of this commendable progress, we have concluded that certain features of the Command and Staff Schools require further change. These schools still exhibit many of the characteristics of lower schools that are devoted almost exclusively to military training. While we have more information on the situation at the Army Command and General Staff College, we suspect that similar conditions prevail at Newport and Maxwell. Leavenworth has been noted for its emphasis upon the rigid lesson plan, the daily recitation, frequent examinations, and the listing of class standings. We are encouraged by the efforts of a recent commandant to reduce this emphasis, but we suggest that there is more to accomplish. The commission that surveyed the college in 1956 concluded that the curriculum was overcrowded, that it was excessive in terms of the amount of subject matter covered, number of classroom hours, and instructor work load. It recommended that the program should be planned for the learning and application of principles in problem situations rather than for the mastering of information and skills for their own sake. It declared that this could be done through greater attention to independent thinking by students, originality, resourcefulness, initiative, imagination, judgment, evaluation, and so forth rather than to information, skills, and solutions as such. The commission urged abandonment of rigid adherence to meticulously prepared lesson plans and "school solutions" to problems. It urged adoption of more flexibility, particularly in means of evaluating student performance. The commission concluded that these features of Leavenworth with which it took exception bear adversely upon the preparation of officers for combat command. We conclude that they also inhibit the most effective performance of officers in policy level assignments.[11]

Specialist Schools and Civilian Universities Programs

The developments that we have been discussing so far in this chapter are taking place in the general schools, those that are attended by officers regardless of specialty. In addition, as already noted, the new demands upon military personnel are reflected in extension of existing specialist schools and training programs and establishment of new ones. Many officers, in addition to exposure to instruction on a variety of topics touching upon the wide range of military responsibilities, also have opportunity to secure intensive educational preparation within one or more specialized fields. Reference has been made to the Army's Language, Information, Psychological Warfare, and Intelligence Schools, and to the Navy's Intelligence School. Examination of these programs is beyond the scope of this book, except to note that the preparation of officers in these fields does bear upon the performance of the armed services at the policy level. Such preparation broadens the collective outlook of the officer corps of each service, as well as providing individual officers who are better qualified to deal with specific nonmilitary problems.

Of special importance along this line is the extensive use made by the armed forces of civilian universities for the graduate education of their officers. Historically this practice commenced with the assignment of Army medical officers to medical schools for advanced preparation. Before world war II both the Army and Navy regularly sent selected officers to civilian schools of engineering for advanced degrees. A small number of officers also attended law schools and institutes of business administration. Also before the war students at West Point and Annapolis were permitted to compete for Rhodes scholarships.

Since 1946 civilian graduate education for officers of all three services has been expanded under statutory authorization, both as to numbers of officers concerned and fields of study covered,

---

[11] *Report of the Educational Survey Commission.* The members of this commission were Dr. Jacob S. Orleans (chairman), Dr. Harl R. Douglass, Lieutenant General M. S. Eddy, USA (Ret.), Dr. H. F. Harding, Lieutenant General Geoffrey Keyes, USA (Ret.), and Lieutenant General Troy H. Middleton, USA (Ret.).

reflecting the new demands being made upon military personnel.[12] A considerable number of officers are now enrolled as regular students for one academic year or more in the principal American and a few foreign universities. They must be under 35 years of age and agree to serve a minimum of four years after completion of graduate studies. While the largest number of officers pursue studies in engineering and scientific fields, both the Army and the Air Force have opened up opportunities in a variety of other fields, including foreign areas and languages, international relations, political science, economics, business administration, comptrollership, and industrial management. The Navy likewise has assigned officers in fields other than engineering and science, but did not authorize advanced study in the social sciences until 1956. At that time two commanders were enrolled in international relations at the Fletcher School of Law and Diplomacy, and it was anticipated that a total of five officers would be enrolled in several schools the following year.

In the ten year period 1946 to 1956, about 3,100 Army officers studied as full time graduate students in civilian institutions. For fiscal year 1955 the number was about 430. More than half were in engineering and scientific fields, 63 in business administration, 28 in comptrollership courses, 29 in foreign area programs, including 10 in the Russian area, 20 in international relations, 17 in industrial management, 9 in law, and small numbers in a variety of fields, such as personnel administration, political science, psychology, and accounting. The corresponding number for the Air Force was about 360, including 138 in management fields, 106 in meteorology, 72 in engineering fields, 17 in the biological and physical sciences, and 28 scattered in international law and relations, economics, political science, and psychology. During this same year 305 Naval officers were taking postgraduate work at civilian institutions, most of them in engineering and scientific subjects, but 59 in business administration, 19 in comptrollership, 6 in advanced management, 5 each in personnel administration, law, and religion, and 2 in public information.

Under the law all graduate education must be justified in terms of specific requirements for trained personnel. Although officers may apply for graduate study, they are accepted only insofar as

[12] Public Law 670, 80th Congress.

the need for their subsequent services can be demonstrated. The Army and Air Force, for example, assign some officers to graduate study before they report to the academies as instructors. The program operates on the principle that its purpose is to meet the personnel needs of the armed forces rather than to advance the educational level of the individual officer. Regulations require that officers be utilized in accordance with their training experience. It is possible for an officer to go on to the doctor's degree, if a specific recommendation is made by the university in which he is doing his work, but approval depends upon the need of his service for an officer with this additional educational experience. In the Army more than 140 officers now hold the Ph.D. degree, most of them having completed their work since the war under the expanded civilian institutions program. One of the first Army officers to receive a doctor's degree in international relations after the war, Colonel Andrew J. Goodpaster, was appointed by President Eisenhower in 1954 as White House staff secretary. All of the officers who have completed graduate work on this program and whom we have interviewed have been extremely enthusiastic about the experience and have been convinced that their value to the service has been greatly increased.

Not the least important result of the assignment of officers to civilian universities for graduate study, particularly in the social sciences, has been the contribution that they have made to these institutions. We have talked with a considerable number of professors about these men and with very few exceptions they have testified that the officers have made excellent students and have added much to the conduct of seminars and other activities. Moreover the association of professor and officer has served to increase the mutual understanding between the two professions that was stimulated during world war II.

In addition to full time graduate work, the services also turn to a number of civilian institutions for special shorter training programs, some of them especially designed for military needs. All three services, for example, send officers to the Advanced Management Program of the Harvard Business School, a 13 week course offered twice each year to approximately 150 corporation executives. Other officers attend a course in Management Problems for Executives at the University of Pittsburgh. George Washington University conducts a special management course for the Air Force. The 1946 law, mentioned previously, also authorized the assignment of officers of all three services to industry for training purposes.

In conclusion it can be emphasized again that the Army, Navy, and Air Force provide a considerable range of educational opportunities to their officers as they advance through the first 10 to 15 years of their careers. These opportunities, with the exception of the civilian institutions and a few other programs, are concerned with the development of professional military competence. As stated early in this chapter, their purpose is to graduate officers prepared for leadership in combat operations. The emphasis is upon weapons and weapon systems, tactical operations, command leadership and organization, and staff procedures.

Yet these professional military schools have a direct bearing upon the performance of their graduates at the policy level. As we have suggested above, this influence is felt through the cultivation of characteristic behavior patterns, including attention to the doctrine of the estimate of the situation and to completed staff work. In the past the schools probably contributed to a somewhat narrow, inflexible approach to policy issues, although recent trends have mitigated this danger. For our purposes the significant element here has been the marked increase at all of these schools in study of matters outside their primary professional military focus. The programs are now related to the broader responsibilities facing military personnel, including those at the policy level. Although the instruction in many instances is brief and superficial, attention is given to such substantive matters as administrative management, international relations, and the organization of the government for policy formulation. The opportunities for graduate study in civilian universities, moreover, provide the services with specialists in such fields. Even more time and energy are devoted in the military schools to cultivation of skills in communication, presentation, and negotiation. Particularly in the Air Force schools, officers are given practice in problem solving in small group situations. If these trends continue, it is likely that the "training" features of these schools will diminish and even disappear.

CHAPTER FOURTEEN

THE ARMED FORCES STAFF COLLEGE

THE Armed Forces Staff College in some respects is similar to the Command and Staff Schools. But it possesses one very important distinguishing feature: it is a *joint* institution. The college is a product of the world war II experience of the services in working closely together in joint undertakings. Actually it is a continuation of the Army-Navy Staff College, established in 1943 at the suggestion of General Henry H. Arnold to prepare Army ground and air officers and Naval officers for joint operations. The present school, established in 1946, is under the policy direction of the Joint Chiefs of Staff. The positions of commandant and two of the deputies rotate among the three services. A third deputy, who serves as executive officer, is of the same service as the commandant. The college is located in Norfolk, adjacent to the present headquarters of the Supreme Allied Commander, Atlantic (SACLANT), an international NATO command organization. The Navy is the host service, responsible for the "housekeeping" aspects of the college's operation and maintenance.[1]

The official statement of the mission of the college is "To educate selected officers of the Armed Forces in joint operations, including the planning thereof, and to provide background for an appreciation of combined operations."

The Joint Chiefs of Staff have approved the following outline of the scope of the course of study at the college:

"a. Characteristics, organization, and employment of land, sea,

---

[1] The college occupies temporary structures erected for a wartime Naval receiving station. Plans for permanent quarters have never materialized.

and air forces and the relation of those forces to each other, with adequate exposition of their capabilities and limitations.

"b. Principles involved in the organization of joint and combined commands and staffs and their responsibilities and procedures.

"c. Organization, composition, and functions of unified commands (both joint and combined) and joint task forces, with respect to the following: strategical, tactical, and logistical responsibilities of the commanders thereof, with emphasis upon war conditions, and the organization and composition of current major combined commands in which the United States participates.

"d. Aspects of joint operations, including command relationships, organization, and planning.

"e. Trends of new weapons and scientific developments and their effects upon joint operations.

"f. Military, political, geographic, historical, economic, psychological, ideological, and other factors affecting the capabilities and limitations of our actual and potential allies and enemies."

Each class of about 185 students is composed of Army, Navy, Marine Corps, and Air Force officers, almost all of whom are regular officers. In 1955 the Department of State, which had been represented in the Army-Navy Staff College during the war, finally responded to the annual request of the commandant to assign a Foreign Service officer as a student at the college. There is one civilian representative of the Central Intelligence Agency. The class also includes a few British, Canadian, and French officers. All but about 30 of the faculty and students live on the station, with their families, facilitating the development of interservice understanding.

Early plans for the college suggested that it would be maintained at a level, measured in terms of the rank and experience of its students, somewhat above the Command and Staff Schools. The selection policy of the Army has, in fact, followed this principle. The selection zone for Army officers ranges from 10 to 21 years, in contrast to 8 to 15 for the Command and General Staff College. Many Army officers selected for attendance at the Armed

Forces Staff College are graduates of Leavenworth. The majority are in the grade of lieutenant colonel; the balance are colonels and a few are majors. The Navy, on the other hand, not having as extensive a school system as the other services, has for practical purposes equated the college with its own Command and Staff Course at Newport. Officers are chosen to attend the two programs from the same selection zone, 10 to 16 years of service. The Navy group, accordingly, has been of lower average rank and experience, and has included a few lieutenants. Air Force practice formerly was similar to that of the Navy. It also assigned a larger proportion of reserve officers than the other services. But recently the Air Force, recognizing that the prestige of the service was at stake, has made an effort to raise the level of its students. Selection is now made from officers in the grade of lieutenant colonel, with 11 to 16 years of service.

These differences in selection policies have presented some difficulties for the college faculty. Because of the lower experience and educational achievements of Navy and Air Force personnel they have felt obliged to pitch some of the instruction at a level that has seemed elementary to Army officers. The faculty feel, moreover, that the Navy and Air Force students are unable to contribute as much as they should to the program, the success of which depends in large measure upon the give and take among representatives of the three services in committee and other group situations. These officers are much less well informed about staff techniques than are the graduates of the Army schools. The Navy, on the other hand, has argued that the earlier in his career an officer gets this experience in a joint school the longer is the contribution that he can make to his service.

The program of the Armed Forces Staff College, as its mission suggests, is focused upon joint operations, and particularly upon the joint headquarters overseas. The greatest emphasis is upon staff procedures and operations. In recent years increased attention has been given to combined operations as well. Because the time is short and the problems complex, the college does not expect to produce officers who are skilled in the techniques of all of the positions on the staff of a unified command, or other major joint force. It is concerned rather with the application of sound principles and reasoned judgment. For purposes of planning, the curriculum is divided into three principal parts, portions of which overlap each other.[2]

Part One. Orientation and Background Instruction

Slightly less than one third of the total instructional time is devoted to the functions, organization, capabilities, and limitations of the three services. Approximately one week is spent on each service. In addition to lectures by faculty and guests, instruction is conducted in small committees of joint composition by the student members of the service under review. The Army block, for example, covers organization, functions, and characteristics; ground combat; Army logistics; new weapons developments; and the organization, mission, and problems of the United States forces in Europe. The Navy block covers comparable topics, including air, submarine, antisubmarine, and mine operations; and nuclear energy propulsion. Instruction on the Air Force goes into such matters as matériel functions, global air transportation, target selection, theater air operations, air defense, and strategic air operations. During this part of the course the students participate in practical demonstrations away from the college, including an overnight trip on an aircraft carrier and a six day trip to Eglin Air Force Base and Fort Benning to observe the techniques and procedures in the use of aerial firepower, and trends and developments in infantry operations, respectively. They also observe a three day demonstration of amphibious techniques, and make a one day trip on a submarine, as well as shorter visits to installations in the Norfolk area. Also, during the first period, instruction is provided in the preparation of staff studies, emphasizing the formal technique and mechanics of preparing these staff papers.

Part one also includes intermittent lectures on a variety of topics not related directly to the course. Several lectures, for example, are concerned with the organization and problems of the intelligence function. Another is devoted to the operations of the Department of Defense; still others deal with selected military problems, such as "Preventive Psychiatry in the Combat Zone," a recent lecture.

[2] As at the other military schools, the details of the curriculum change from time to time. The following outline is based upon a recent typical year.

Part Two. Joint and Combined Planning and Operations

More than half of the instructional time is devoted to this part of the course. It is designed to prepare the officer to perform detailed joint planning, and to give him an appreciation of combined planning. This is introduced by a series of lectures on joint operations, in which the complexities and magnitude of detail of joint planning are stressed. Then follows description of the planning cycle. The faculty has devised a large chart, affectionately known as "The Thing," which diagrammatically shows the interrelationship of the parts of the planning process, such as identification of national interests and implementation of these through military strategic decisions and through subsequent action at combined and joint theater and task force levels. It shows the organs and agencies of government and of the military forces involved in the process. Encircled and crisscrossed by flow and feedback lines, "The Thing" looks most like a Rube Goldberg invention.

Instruction in joint and combined planning is broken down further into five component parts, as follows:

"1. Organization of an area of military responsibility.

"2. Responsibilities of a joint, combined, unified, and specified force commander.

"3. Various types of staff structure for joint and combined commands.

"4. Form, content, and scope of plans for: personnel, intelligence, operations, logistics, communications-electronics, and civil affairs, military government, and a procedure for planning.

"5. Instruction in planning amphibious and airborne operations."

In this connection, lectures are scheduled on the organization and problems of the principal NATO commands and on the military assistance program, to which a considerable number of graduates are likely to be assigned. Additional lectures are devoted to the Soviet Union and to the principal allied nations.

The primary preoccupation of the students during the second part of the course is with six exercises or problems, designed to illustrate the entire planning process. Some of the elements are provided by the faculty; students prepare all of the others. The titles and content of these six problems are:

Problem 1. *Form, Content, and Scope of Joint Operational Planning Documents and Demonstration of the Planning Process* (7 hours). This problem consists of three phases of instruction: (1) the campaign plan and annexes, (2) estimates, concepts, and the operation study, and (3) operation plans and annexes.

Problem 2. *Organization and Command Relationships* (32½ hours). This covers basic factors and considerations that influence organization of a United States unified command in an overseas area, such as mission, policies of the commander, role of the united command, and relations with allied forces and friendly foreign powers.

Problem 3. *Initial Planning in a Unified Command* (35 hours). This is designed to familiarize the student with the initial planning that takes place in a unified command prior to the commencement of hostilities. Each student section constitutes an initial planning group of a combined headquarters, eventually to be formed in the Middle East, which will exercise operational control over forces allocated by various allied nations. Each section must produce an oral intelligence estimate, a commander's written estimate of the situation, and a written emergency war plan. The mission involves a delaying action, followed by a planned build-up of forces and a counteroffensive.

Problem 4. *Amphibious Operations* (40 hours). This includes instruction in the interrelationship between the various planning documents, between operational and logistical planning, and between planning required at area command and joint force levels for a major operation. It also covers the techniques and procedures peculiar to amphibious operations, and the employment of a joint logistic command in support of a unified command. The problem commences with the issuance of a campaign plan and embraces the intelligence estimate, operations study, logistic estimate, commander's estimate, base development study and base development planning directive, base development plan, and logistic plan.

Problem 5. *Air-Borne Operations* (24½ hours). This covers methods and techniques connected with establishing and maintaining a major airhead in enemy-held territory wherein significant Army and Air Force units are employed to seize and hold the airhead for an extended period of time pending a linkup with a major land force. The enemy is accorded the capacity to employ atomic and chemical, bacteriological, and radiological weapons.

These five problems familiarize the student with all of the basic elements in the planning process. The final problem pulls together all of this experience in a single large scale command and staff planning exercise.

Problem 6. *Campaign Planning* (100 hours). Acting in the role of commanders and their staffs, students work out plans for a major campaign in the European area by unified and combined military forces. They examine United States problems involved in planning for and conducting such a campaign, and consider the employment of atomic weapons. The strategic problem covers plans for a campaign to halt enemy advances, regain lost territory, and effect a limited penetration into the enemy homeland.

Part Three. Trends of War

Most of the Armed Forces Staff College program is concerned with the preparation of military plans according to formalized procedures. This final section, constituting less than one sixth of the instructional time, provides an opportunity for study of unresolved issues and future prospects, including those produced by new politico-military arrangements as well as by new weapons. For the most part this section is scheduled at intervals throughout the 22 weeks of the course.

A number of lectures and question periods, for example, are devoted to the Soviet Union, including military geography, population, armed forces, and the nature of communism. Others deal with the peoples of Europe, Asia, and Southeast Asia, and with the Western European allies and the British Commonwealth. Early in the program a lecture is given on the law and conduct of international relations; toward the end one is scheduled on war and the conduct of international relations.

During the final two weeks of the course the students are exposed to a taste of the sort of thing studied at the senior joint and service colleges, that is, national strategy at the highest level.

Guest lecturers are invited to speak on the following subjects: basic factors underlying national strategy, Europe as a factor in world strategy, Asia as a factor in world strategy, ideological warfare, the role of diplomacy in the East-West struggle, the place of war in international relations, and the impact of atomic weapons on national policy. Finally, a 15 hour summary discussion is held, in which the interdependence of political and military factors are emphasized. Students are directed to consider the national interests and objectives of the United States, and its policies and commitments. They review the responsibilities of the executive branch of the government for the formulation and implementation of national strategy, and the war aims of the United States in the event of global conflict. The period concludes with examination of three problems currently facing the United States that illustrate political, economic, and psychological aspects of national strategy.

The Armed Forces Staff College makes use of a number of different instructional devices, as do all military schools. Lectures, usually by individual guests, are a regular feature. About three quarters of the speakers are from the military services and these frequently include officers holding the highest positions in the three service departments and the commanders or principal staff officers of the major joint and combined headquarters overseas. Civilian speakers include representatives of executive agencies in Washington and a few academic figures. Relatively little formal lecturing is done by the resident faculty. These individuals participate in panel presentations, lead group discussions, and direct group studies. Much of the work of the students, including the preparation of solutions to the six problems, is accomplished in committees of about 14 members each. Some of the solutions are presented orally to larger groups of students; a few are presented to the entire class. These are followed by somewhat abbreviated faculty critiques based upon a document maintained for each problem. After completion of each problem, students receive a faculty solution. It is pointed out to them, however, that this does not represent the only possible solution, and that, although it embodies approved techniques and doctrines and the best efforts of the faculty, it is not the only solution or necessarily even the best one. Throughout the course, required and supplementary collateral readings are assigned.

The greatest contribution of the Armed Forces Staff College is derived from its joint character. For most students this is the first opportunity to learn of the principal characteristics and problems of the other services. Of even more consequence is the experience of living, working, and playing with officers of these services. Graduates have indicated to us that this is the most important thing that they get out of the college. A former deputy commandant declared to us that this was of greater significance than the formal instruction.

It is not the mission of the College to prepare officers for positions involving the formulation of national policy. It is concerned rather with responsibilities at those somewhat lower levels where decisions involving high strategy are implemented. As we have seen, the emphasis is upon the procedures and problems of the joint staff overseas, and to a lesser degree of the combined staff; a particular focal point is the technique of drafting staff papers. Yet the experience appears to have a broadening effect. Whereas the members of a large joint staff frequently serve as specialists with respect to a specific area of responsibility, the approach at the college is upon the general, over-all problems of the staff, particularly the relationships of the various parts to the whole. The circumstances of recent years, moreover, have caused the college to pay increasing attention to combined operations, that is, those involving not only the armed forces of the United States but those of its allies as well. Analysis is made of how a combined headquarters is organized and functions, and of such questions as how much responsibility should be retained by the United States and how much and what kind assigned to allied nations. The problems of negotiating with allied powers and the effect of such negotiations upon the status of forces are discussed. The political complications of overseas base development is another example of the sort of issues that are considered at the college. The British, Canadian, and French officers in each class enliven discussion of these issues.

The military assistance program also receives a good deal of attention. It has been the practice to show how this operates at various levels. Officials from Washington tell about the program at the national level, including such matters as its relationship to the budget. Then officers recently returned from military advisory groups overseas will discuss operations at the other end of the line, in recipient countries.

Thus, while the Armed Forces Staff College does not attempt to get into any detailed study of the strategic problems and related matters that have become a principal concern of the service War Colleges as well as the National War College, its program does show the same effort to broaden the educational experience of the professional officer that now characterizes almost all military education. Study of the joint staff remains the primary job, but within the narrow confines of the 22 week course the college now also includes consideration of political developments in the Soviet Union, Western Europe, the British Commonwealth, and the Far East. It provides some instruction in the organization and operation of the government at the policy level, and it concludes the course with a two day seminar on national strategy. This feature was planned as a means of whetting the appetite of the student, stimulating his interest in these matters and his desire to keep himself informed and alert. It also demonstrates to the student the relationship of his task to the total responsibilities of the nation. Perhaps the most significant contribution of the college is in cultivating among its students an appreciation of the problems of the other services and an understanding of the requirement for a joint approach to security planning as well as operations.[3]

[3] For a further appraisal see Lieutenant Colonel Harry D. Easton, Jr., "The Armed Forces Staff College," *Military Review*, September 1956, pp. 23–27.

PART FIVE

SENIOR MILITARY EDUCATION

CHAPTER FIFTEEN

ORGANIZATION AND METHODS OF THE

WAR COLLEGES

THE National War College, the Industrial College, and the three service War Colleges stand at the summit of professional military education. Many of the officers who are selected to attend are destined to occupy positions of high rank and authority. These senior colleges are unlike other conventional institutions of higher learning. They are designed for a specific function. They are, to paraphrase the words of one observer, well-organized instrumentalities for conducting a large scale, complex, year long seminar on problems of national security and national defense, for selected officers. This is accomplished by group listening, group discussion, group analysis, and group findings relative to these problems. Organization and methods are tailored to support this central purpose. These colleges, then, are at the very center of the focus of this study of military education.

Apart from specificity of purpose, a number of other features distinguish these institutions. The students, unlike those in other professional graduate schools, are mature men who already have had heavy responsibilities and rich and varied experiences. The faculties, unlike those in other schools, are not instructors in the usual sense. They are rather planners and administrators of a program in which opportunity is maximized for the students to learn from visiting speakers and from each other.

Part five is a detailed description of these senior colleges. Since they possess many common features, much of this account is arranged topically rather than individually by schools. A separate chapter is devoted to the Industrial College because of its somewhat specialized mission.

The National War College

The alert traveler flying into Washington from the northeast catches sight of a domed structure on a point of land near the confluence of the Potomac and Anacostia Rivers as his plane settles for the approach to National Airport. This is the building planned by Elihu Root and designed by Stanford White for the Army War College and occupied since 1946 by the National War College. To one side, somewhat hidden by trees, stands a gray, shingled building. This is the Industrial College. Even to many people in Washington, these two institutions remain rather mysterious, since their affairs are conducted "off the record."

As a joint institution the National War College is under the jurisdiction of the Joint Chiefs of Staff. The command responsibility is shared by the three services, in rotation. The commandant, a lieutenant general or vice admiral, serves for three years. Each of the other services not represented by the commandant provides an officer of two star rank as deputy commandant, serving for two overlapping years. The Department of State is represented by a deputy for foreign affairs, who has no command responsibility. The position most frequently has been held by a Foreign Service officer in the grade of career minister or class one, serving one or two years.[1]

The instructional faculty of the college consists of approximately 16 officers, usually of the rank of colonel (Army, Air Force, and Marine Corps) and captain (Navy), and four or five civilians. The majority of the officers are graduates of the college. The average age is about 45 years. Usually several have had previous experience particularly relevant to the purpose of the college. The majority have had command experience. They serve from one to three years. For working purposes they are organized into divisions or groups, each with joint service representation. The civilian faculty was originally composed of university professors on leave from their regular duties. In recent years the group has been divided between professors and government officials. The latter, however,

---

[1] The National War College commandants have been Vice Admiral Harry Hill, USN, Lieutenant General Harold Bull, USA, Lieutenant General Harry Craig, USAF, and Vice Admiral Edmund Woolridge, USN. George Kennan was the first deputy for foreign affairs.

have been individuals with advanced academic education and teaching experience. It has been the practice for at least one civilian to return for a second year. Until 1954–1955 the civilians served only for the first semester.[2]

The student body, because of its joint military and civilian composition, is perhaps the outstanding feature of the National War College. Initially enrollment was limited to 100 and the class was composed of 30 officers each from the Army, Navy, and Air Force and 10 Foreign Service officers. Subsequently the number was raised to 120, to include departmental representatives from State and other civilians from the Foreign Operations Administration (now International Cooperation Administration), Central Intelligence Agency, United States Information Agency, Departments of Commerce, Defense, and the Treasury, and Bureau of the Budget. In 1954 the enrollment was increased again to 131, and the class was composed of 35 Army, 27 Navy, 7 Marine, 1 Coast Guard, and 33 Air Force officers, and 18 representatives of the Department of State (12 of whom were Foreign Service officers), 4 of the USIA, 3 of the Central Intelligence Agency, and 1 each of the Foreign Operations Administration, Department of Commerce, and National Security Agency. The military officers have been in the grade of colonel-captain, and the civilians of comparable rank. Average ages in the class of 1955 were 42 for the Air Force, 44 for the Marines, 45 for the Army, and 47 for the Navy.

The selection of the students remains the prerogative of each participating service or agency, since the Joint Chiefs of Staff have no command responsibilities in this respect. The Joint Chiefs plan for postwar education initially proposed a requirement of 25 years of commissioned service, but this was lowered early in the discussions, and in practice the services required a minimum of about 18 years. Until the last few years, while attendance at the college was neither a prerequisite for, nor a guarantee of, promotion to general or flag rank, it was presumed that the service personnel attending the college would be officers of distinction who would

[2] Civilian faculty members who have returned for a second year have included Thomas A. Bailey, Royden Dangerfield, Harold C. Deutsch, Mose Harvey, Jere King, Ralph L. Powell, Albert C. F. Westphal, and Rudolph A. Winnacker. Karl Anderson and Warren Walsh served for a period of three years.

be called upon for heavier responsibilities and thus would achieve higher rank. The promotion record of graduates bears out this presumption.[3] Recently the services have altered their practices so that officers are now selected for the National War College and the service War Colleges on the same basis with respect to age, years of service (15), and experience. This has produced a slight lowering of the age and rank levels of the students. The class now includes several lieutenant colonels and commanders. The reasons for this change were explained in chapter eight. Some of their implications are discussed in chapter twenty-one. Although a quota arrangement is employed within each service to secure representation of all or most branches, the class is weighted toward the combat arms in the Army, the line in the Navy, and rated pilots in the Air Force.

The National War College is well housed. The only serious limiting condition is a shortage of space to which individual officers, wishing to read or write in solitude, can retreat. Fort McNair offers extremely attractive surroundings for a relaxed approach to the college's purpose. Along one side flows the Washington boat channel. With its handsome elms, wide lawns, and Georgian colonial quarters, the place provides a sense of isolation from the hurly-burly of Washington. An officers club on the post is a center for student and faculty social life. A small golf course, tennis courts, squash courts, and other recreational facilities also are available. The commandant, the two military deputies, the State Department deputy, and the executive officer live on the post, but there are no residential facilities for students. From time to time there has been talk of constructing a student residential area on contiguous land outside Fort McNair.

The operation of the National War College is a sizable undertaking. Since the college is located on an Army post, the Army provides administrative support. An Army colonel serves as executive officer. Backing up the 150-odd faculty and students are approximately 25 military personnel and 90 civilians. These in-

---

[3] A study of the graduates of the first eight classes revealed that 50.2 percent of the Army officers, 41.7 percent of the Air Force officers, 32.1 percent of the Naval officers, and 28.6 percent of the Marine Corps officers had achieved general or flag rank. The percentages for the first three classes ranged close to 75 percent. *Memorandum for the Commandant,* 8 October 1954. Seventeen of the 39 captains selected for rear admiral in August 1955 were graduates of the college.

clude librarians, secretaries, stenographers, verbatim reporters, the staff of the visual aids section, janitors, and guards. The direct cost of operation provided in the annual budget amounted to approximately $448,000 in fiscal year 1955. If such costs as maintenance and pay and allowances of the military faculty and staff are added, the annual total cost amounts to between $800,000 and $900,000, or a cost per student in the neighborhood of $6,500. If the salaries and allowances of the students themselves are added in, the over-all cost comes to between $2,000,000 and $2,500,000, a cost per student of about $17,000. The figure would be higher if the college were charged for its share of the cost of maintaining Fort McNair.[4]

The Army War College

Once the decision was made to reopen the Army War College, the Army moved quickly to rebuild a strong institution. After one temporary year at Fort Leavenworth the college was moved to its new permanent home at Carlisle Barracks, Pennsylvania, in the Cumberland Valley about 18 miles west of Harrisburg. It now occupies the entire post. In some respects the college has the appearance of a civilian campus, as it is the only one of the War Colleges with residential quarters for students as well as faculty and staff. The academic program is conducted in two well-equipped buildings. Here, as at Fort McNair, the only notable shortcoming is the lack of space for secluded individual study.

The college is headed by a commandant, who has over-all supervisory responsibility, including command of the post. Since 1950 the position has been held by two lieutenant generals and three major generals.[5] The nominal tour of duty is two years, although in practice it has varied considerably. The deputy commandant, a brigadier general, also serves for two years. This officer is in direct charge of the academic program. The authorized instructional faculty numbers 34 officers, most in the grade of colonel. There are

---

[4] House of Representatives, 83rd Congress, 1st Session, Subcommittee of the Committee on Appropriations, *Hearings on Department of Army Appropriations*, 1953, pp. 1097–1100.

[5] Lieutenant General Joseph Swing, Lieutenant General Edward Almond, Major General James Moore, Major General Clyde Eddelman, and Major General Max Johnson.

usually two or three vacancies. The average age in 1956 was about 43, contrasted with 50 in 1937–1938, and the average years of service 19, contrasted with 26 at that time. The tour of duty is three years, although frequently officers are reassigned sooner. Most of these officers are graduates of the college, the National War College, or one of the other service War Colleges. Almost all of the faculty have attended the Command and General Staff College or received equivalent credit. The Navy, Air Force, and Department of State are represented on the faculty by a captain, colonel, and Foreign Service officer, class one. They participate in the general planning work of the faculty, advise on instruction relating to their respective services, watch over the welfare of officers of their services among the students, and make themselves generally available to all students. The college is authorized to employ about 70 civilians, including librarians, secretaries, the staff of the printing shop, and the like. The budget for these personal services and other direct support activities comes to about $325,000.

The annual class at the Army War College has remained at 200 for several years. It usually consists of about 180 Army officers, 4 Air Force officers, 4 Marines, 2 Naval officers, and 1 each from the Department of State and CIA. Neither the Air Force nor the Navy have regularly filled their quota of 8 each. State was unrepresented between 1953 and 1955 but has resumed the practice of assigning one Foreign Service officer, of class two or three. The enrollment was initially fixed at 100 and then raised to 150. There has been thought in the Department of the Army of going to 300, a figure recommended by the Eddy board as an ultimate target, but this is resisted at the college as a threat to the quality of instruction. Army officers selected to attend the college must have credit for the Command and General Staff regular course or the general staff officer course (a shorter version offered during the war), have a minimum of 15 years and not more than 21 years of commissioned service, and be under 46 years of age. Although in earlier years most of the students were colonels, about one third of the class of 1956 consisted of lieutenant colonels, and the average age was just over 42 years. The average length of service was just over 16 years. The recent change in the service requirement from 13 to 15 years is now being reflected in a rise in the average age of the class. But even so, officers are younger than before world war II. A comparison with prewar figures suggests the change in the composition of the officer corps in the last two decades. The average age of the class of 1938 was just under 45, the average length of service was 20.5 years. These officers ranged in grade from captain to lieutenant colonel. Forty-four percent of the Army officers in the class of 1956 were graduates of West Point, a drop of 11 percent in three years, reflecting the increase within the selection zone in the proportion of officers who were integrated following the war. The class includes officers from all of the combat arms and technical services of the Army, but 80 percent of all spaces are allocated to the former. In the past there have been two or three National Guard officers or members of the organized reserve called up for active duty.

The Naval War College

The Naval War College still occupies the site on Coaster's Island overlooking Newport Harbor selected when the institution was founded by Stephen Luce. The senior courses are conducted in several large interconnected buildings. The Command and Staff Course occupies a separate, detached building. Command and Staff students come up "the hill" to participate in lectures and other activities of the senior students. The physical facilities are ample.

The presidency of the Naval War College is an honored and cherished billet. In the period since the war it usually has been occupied shortly before retirement by senior officers who have had distinguished careers in the service, normally for a two year tour.[6] The president, in addition to supervising matters of policy and performing ceremonial functions as the head of the institution, devotes considerable attention to the relations of the college with the rest of the Navy, particularly the chief of Naval operations and the chief of the Bureau of Personnel. As a senior officer he is personally acquainted with these individuals, and he usually visits Washington three or four times a year. Likewise, these officers frequently visit the college, as lecturers and participants

---

[6] Vice Admiral Raymond Spruance, Vice Admiral Richard Conolly, Vice Admiral Lynde McCormick. Following the death of Admiral McCormick in 1956, the college's chief of staff, Rear Admiral Thomas Robbins, was named president.

in the program. Associations such as these, which are usually duplicated at the working levels of the college, the Navy Department, and major components of the fleet, are of importance in gearing the program to the ideas of the "consumers" of its products, and also securing support for the college. Similar relationships are maintained by the commandants and deputies of the Army and Air War Colleges, but none are as senior and as intimately acquainted among the very top officers of their services as the president of the Naval War College.

Internally the activities of the college are supervised and coordinated by the chief of staff, a rear admiral. The total faculty and staff group numbers about 100. It is considerably larger than those of the other War Colleges because the staff of the Command and Staff Course and a smaller section that handles correspondence courses also are included. The faculty group directly associated with the two senior courses numbers about 45 officers, a somewhat larger group than its counterparts at Carlisle Barracks and Maxwell. The group includes a few more commanders than captains. The majority of those concerned with instruction are graduates of the Naval Academy and the college. A few have attended the National War College, the Industrial College, or the Army or Air War College. The regular tour of duty is two years, although actually many officers are reassigned before this time and the average tour is less than two years. The Department of State is represented on the staff by a Foreign Service officer, usually class one, who serves a two year tour as adviser. The Army and Air Force also are represented by advisers, in the grade of colonel, and a number of other officers assigned to the faculty. The Marine Corps is also represented on the faculty. The faculty now includes a small civilian group. As already indicated, the work in international law was for many years directed by George Grafton Wilson and Judge Manley Hudson. This position is now filled on an annual basis by a civilian professor of international law. In 1952, in connection with an advanced study and research group, two chairs in maritime history and social and political philosophy were established, filled annually by civilians on leave from regular teaching positions. These now are designated the Ernest J. King and Chester W. Nimitz chairs, and a third regular professorship, in the physical sciences, has been added.[7] With the introduction of the second year course in naval warfare in 1954 the college received authorization to employ a number of additional civilian instructors in the social sciences for the period from August to December, to be appointed annually.

The total enrollment in the two senior courses is about 130, equally divided between naval warfare I and II. In the classes of 1955 the first year group was composed of 56 Naval officers, four Marines, four Army officers, and one Coast Guard officer. One of the Naval officers had previously attended the Air War College and six Naval officers had attended the Armed Forces Staff College. The Navy group in the naval warfare I class consisted of 12 captains and 44 commanders. All of the captains, with the exception of one Naval dentist, were graduates of the Naval Academy. Their average age was about 42, and average length of service about 19 years. About a dozen of the commanders were integrated officers, having entered the service during the war. All but one or two of these were graduates of civilian colleges or universities. The average age of the commanders was about 38 years.

The second year group was composed of 43 Naval officers, 7 Marines, 7 Air Force officers, 6 Army officers, and 1 representative of the CIA. Beginning in 1955 the Department of State again assigned a Foreign Service officer to the college. Among the Naval officers in the advanced class all but one were captains, a larger proportion than anticipated by Admiral Conolly when he initially proposed the two year program. The average age was 44 years and average years of service about 21. All of these officers were graduates of the Naval Academy. Twenty-one Naval officers in naval warfare I were held over for the naval warfare II course in 1955–1956. All but two of these were captains. Because more command, planning, and policy-making positions, and particularly the most important of these, are filled by unrestricted line officers, the quota for line officers at the college (as well as at the joint

[7] Incumbents of the King and Nimitz chairs have been Ollinger Crenshaw, James Field, Keener Fraser, John Kemble, Douglas Haring, William Jones, William Mc-Govern, William Reitzel, and Hiram Stout. Recent professors of international law have included Leo Gross and Bronson MacChesney. Walter Albertson holds the chair of physical science.

schools) is larger than for other categories. All but 14 of the Naval officers in the first year course were line officers (including unrestricted line, aviators, and submariners), and all but one of the officers in naval warfare II were. The faculty also consists very largely of line officers.

The Air War College

As a constituent part of the Air University the Air War College is located at Maxwell Air Force Base, at Montgomery, Alabama. It enrolled its first class in 1946. In the summer of 1950, following the Korean crisis and the resulting shortage of Air Force officers, the course at the Air War College was canceled on short notice. The faculty was held together, however, and in the following January the college was reopened for a short, five and a half month course. There have been no other interruptions in the program. The school is commanded by a major general, who is assisted by a vice commandant, usually a brigadier general, and a faculty and staff of about 33 officers.[8] The deputy supervises the academic program and usually serves for two years. The Department of State is represented by an adviser, a Foreign Service officer in class one or two, who usually serves for two years. The Army, Navy, and Royal Air Force are also represented by liaison officers.

The academic faculty, charged with the conduct of the regular course of instruction, numbers about 25 officers in the grade of colonel. The regular tour of duty is three years. The average age, 39 years, is below that of the other War Colleges. Almost all of the faculty officers are rated pilots, and almost all have college degrees. Most of the group are graduates of the Air War College. The faculty includes two civilians and at least one officer from another service.

The size of the college has increased over the years, as the requirement for graduates has grown. Following the practice developed by the Army and Naval War Colleges in the interwar period, the Air War College class includes officers from the sister services and usually single representatives of the Department of State and the Central Intelligence Agency. Unlike the other War

[8] The commandants have been Major General Orvil Anderson, Major General Roscoe Wilson, Major General Delmar Spivey, and Major General Robert Tate.

Colleges, the Air War College enrolls British and Canadian officers. The class of 1955 consisted of 160 officers, including 10 Army, 10 Navy and Marines, 4 RAF, and 1 RCAF, of whom 151 were in the grade of colonel (or the equivalent). The Department of State, because of budget cuts, had no student in the classes of 1954 and 1955, but it is represented in the class of 1956.

The Air Force selects younger officers to attend the Air War College than do the Army and Navy for their schools at Carlisle and Newport. The rank level, on the other hand, is higher, reflecting the characteristic rank pattern of the postwar Air Force. The average age of the class of 1955 was 39. Less than one sixth were graduates of West Point, but about one half were graduates of civilian colleges. About four fifths were rated pilots. For the class entering in 1956 two appointments were made available to reserve colonels not on active duty, this for the first time.

The Air War College buildings are less pretentious than the structures at Fort McNair, Carlisle, and Newport, but are adequate and well equipped. The only serious handicap appears to be the smallness of the seminar rooms and, as at the other schools, space for private, individual study. The college is encompassed by a large and busy organization at Maxwell. In addition to serving the Air University, Maxwell is an operating base for a wing of Strategic Air Command tankers and for an air rescue squadron. Many aircraft are assigned to the Air University itself for proficiency flying and for transport purposes. The Air War College does not experience the relative isolation of the National and Industrial Colleges at McNair, the Army War College at Carlisle Barracks, and the Naval War College at Newport. It manages nevertheless to maintain a certain detachment and distinctiveness.

Methods of Instruction

The war colleges are characterized by considerably less formality than other military schools. Rank is minimized and students and faculty alike are generally known by first names. At the National War College, the Industrial College, and the Naval War College students wear civilian clothes. Special effort is made to avoid a classroom atmosphere and a conventional teacher-student relationship. Instead, learning from each other is one of the most important, if not the most important, instructional method. The task of each of the colleges is to broaden the outlook of men who have been essentially specialists prior to this time and to facilitate their transformation into generalists. The exchange of information and ideas among themselves contributes much to this end. Accordingly, special measures are taken to maximize personal contact among the men. Office, committee, and seminar assignments are rotated regularly so that each officer serves with every one of his classmates, and each has the responsibility of a chairmanship. Students are responsible to no commander above them; nor do they have any subordinates. All are equals, even to the point of typing up their own papers when the stenographic pool becomes overloaded. For the officer who recently has commanded a ship, base, or post, with a sizable staff at his call, this may be quite a change. Throughout the day, and sometimes into the night, in car pools to and from work, in committee and discussion rooms, during numerous coffee breaks, the talk proceeds. Out of this talk emerge not only new friendships but a widened appreciation and understanding of the varied and complex responsibilities facing the professional military officer.

By and large all of these institutions employ similar instructional methods although the emphasis upon each varies among them. Most of these devices were in use at the Naval and Army War Colleges in the interwar period, although they have been refined to meet changing demands. In spite of stress upon the importance of individual initiative, none appear willing to let the student alone for long periods of time to study as he wishes. On the contrary, all are characterized by a standard course of study utilizing a compact, carefully calculated schedule, and featuring group rather than individual activity. Every Monday morning the student knows where he is expected to be and what he is expected to do each part of the day for the rest of the week. Even so, the program is less rigid and crowded than at lower military schools.

THE LECTURE AND QUESTION PERIOD

The lecture remains the method of presentation most relied upon. A lecture is given almost every day throughout the academic year, sometimes twice and occasionally three times a day, generally by an outside speaker. The students are exposed to an imposing array of talent, consisting of holders of some of the highest elective and appointive positions in the government, the highest-ranking officers of the services, specialists from the Department of State, the Department of Defense, and the intelligence agencies, academic scholars, a few journalists, and occasional business executives, labor leaders, and clergymen. The usual practice is to follow the formal lecture with a question period. Because of a firmly observed rule that all remarks are off the record and not to be attributed, these affairs sometimes become quite frank and open. Both speakers and students are urged to express themselves with utmost candor.

With the introduction of its second year program in naval warfare in 1954, the Naval War College has made use of a variation of the lecture method. Some of the lectures in this course, which are presented to groups of about 60 officers, are informal in nature. The speaker remains seated, and questions and discussion are invited during the course of his remarks.

Usually the speaker is invited to remain after the question period for an informal conference with a smaller number of students. The National War College developed the practice of having him sit with one of the regular discussion groups for further discussion of the topic of the day. The other schools frequently organize a special conference on a rotation basis for this purpose. In the former situation the attempt was made to have the speaker participate in a group discussion. In the latter he merely responds to direct questions by the students. Whenever possible a number of students, again on a rotation basis, have an opportunity to meet with the guest at luncheon. Thus the usual day for most students at the colleges includes about two hours listening to a speaker's presentation and his response to questions. For a smaller group it may involve as much as half a day with him.

There is a common agreement at the colleges that this arrangement is not ideal. At least some of the lecturers should remain for several days, or even longer, to meet with small groups and to explore in depth some issues raised in the formal presentations. Usually a speaker is at the college only part of a day and his time is well filled before he is whisked off after a pleasant meal to plane or train. Frequently the students feel that they have done no more than scratch the surface of his special knowledge. But to hold an individual for more than a single day is more easily said than done. Most academic people cannot be away from their own classrooms for more than a day at a time, and government personnel likewise are tied to their desks. The National War College for a time, as described below, employed a small group of economists for a full week, each one lecturing once but all remaining for the week's program. The Air War College holds a few of its academic specialists over for several days. The Army War College has tried to meet the need by providing consultants, as distinguished from lecturers, who remain in residence for a week or two. The Naval War College employed a similar arrangement during the first round of naval warfare II.

THE DISCUSSION GROUP

All of the colleges employ the discussion group or seminar in one form or another. At the National War College these groups are composed of Army, Navy, and Air Force officers and civilians, and at the other colleges mixed service representation is provided insofar as possible. The composition of the group is changed every two or three weeks. Usually the group is moderated by a member of the faculty during the first term, and by a student thereafter, although practices vary. The purpose is to discuss the topic of the day, as covered by the lecturers and in assigned readings. At the National War College the only restraint on the nature and direction of the discussion is imposed by the moderator or group itself. At the other schools there is more likely to be a given question or series of questions for consideration. The Air War College, for example, uses the discussion group for reports by students on books that have been assigned. The Naval War College, in naval warfare II, has the individual students read short papers on selected topics as a means of getting discussion started. Other devices of this sort have been used from time to time at each of the schools.

THE COMMITTEE PAPER

The committee paper has been used in the advanced military schools for many years and remains one of the most important devices. For this purpose the members of the class are divided into committees of about 8 to 12 men each, with one man assigned as chairman. The committee has its own room, with a desk for each member. At the National War College, as in the discussion groups, all services and the Department of State are represented in each committee. Usually each committee is assigned a problem in connection with each course or curriculum item, with several committees working on each of 6 to 10 problems. The National War College has made the greatest use of the policy problem. In the language of the college's catalog, the problem has the following characteristics: "(1) It utilizes the subject matter of the course as a whole, (2) it is of a policy type, calling for definite conclusions and recommendations, (3) it is current and practical, in that it might be under actual consideration within the government, (4) it is susceptible to effective committee—rather than individual—action; and the solution is susceptible to effective presentation from the platform." Each committee prepares a written solution to the problem. Then several solutions are chosen by the faculty for formal presentation by the committee chairman or designated members to seminar groups or to the entire college. Frequently, the procedure ends with a critique. At the Army and Air War Colleges the policy orientation is not employed, and the latter generally places less emphasis on the committee. At the Naval War College the committee device is employed in connection with operational problems, a characteristic feature of this institution that is described in a later chapter. At all of the colleges the committee is the unit used for preparation of strategic estimates and war plans.

COLLATERAL READING

Students are expected to complete regular reading assignments. For this purpose they are provided with a directive or study guide for each course or principal unit of the curriculum. These are elaborate and carefully prepared documents. The National and Air War Colleges indicate required readings, as well as bibliographies in support of the topics. Others simply list bibliographies. In these cases the usual practice is for the committee chairman to divide up the list and to assign titles to individual members so that coverage is secured. The Air War College designates regular hours during the week when the readings are to be completed.

Generally the reading lists consist of chapters or excerpts from books, journal and magazine articles, reprints of lectures delivered at the college, and classified materials. The colleges make it as easy as possible for the students to use the materials. Generally these are reproduced and distributed to the students' mail boxes. In one year at the National War College this amounts to some 5,000 pages of text. The Air War College is the only one to make a serious attempt to have the students read selected books in their entirety and to report on these to their classmates, although all encourage their students to read on their own. The National War College, for example, issues a reading list to each student shortly before he reports in August. Here and at the other schools the library and faculty prepare a biweekly book and periodical bulletin. The libraries display new books and accept purchase orders from the students.

FIELD TRIPS

The National, Army, and Naval War Colleges conduct field trips as a regular part of their educational programs. The trips of the joint institution have been the most extensive. Each spring the class is divided into three or four separate groups and trips of three weeks' duration are made by Military Air Transport planes to northern Europe, southern Europe, the Middle East, Central and South America, or the Far East. There are usually from 7 to 10 major stops on each trip, where the group is briefed by American and local officials. In 1955 the northern European group, for example, stopped at London, Paris, Madrid, Vienna, Heidelberg, Wiesbaden, Bonn, Berlin, and Oslo, and visited the major NATO as well as American commands in these cities. The Middle East group traveled as far as Teheran, the Far East group as far as Bangkok. The National War College also schedules a short trip to United Nations headquarters in New York, and arranges for visits by small groups to Congress.

The Army War College offers two field trips. The first, lasting two days, is to United Nations headquarters. The Army students, like those from the National War College, attend sessions of the General Assembly and committees, and are addressed by members of the Secretariat, the United States Mission, and several foreign missions, including in the past those of Yugoslavia and India. The second trip includes visits to the Army proving ground at Aberdeen, Maryland; the Norfolk Naval Base, headquarters of the Supreme Allied Command, Atlantic, a NATO command; Nike antiaircraft sites; and Langley Air Force Base; and a cruise of two nights and a day on an aircraft carrier. With the introduction of the two year program, the Naval War College instituted a summer field trip for officers held over for the second year. In 1955 the group visited military installations in the United States; in 1956 one group went to Europe, a second to the Pacific and Far East.

THE INDIVIDUAL STUDY OR THESIS

These methods all feature group activity and responsibility. The colleges also require each student to undertake an individual project, in the form of a thesis. Usually the student selects an area in which he would prefer to work, and indicates his order of choice from among specific topics listed by the college. He usually gets at least his second choice. Students are also permitted to propose their own topics. The criteria here (using the requirements of the Army War College as an example) are that the topics must: "(1) Be of high level importance, and of current interest to the Army. (2) Require research and original thought rather than merely a synthesis of the writings of others. (3) Allow wide flexibility in the student's thinking. (4) Not be so broad as to be unmanageable. (5) Be within the present capacity of the Army War College Library to support." Students are encouraged to pursue subjects in which they are peculiarly well qualified because of experience or training, enabling them frequently to commit to paper ideas and conclusions that they have been turning over in their minds for some time.[9]

Except at the Naval War College, where one paper is required each term, topics are assigned in the early autumn and submitted in the spring. They usually run between 5,000 and 10,000 words, and must follow a prescribed form, with footnote references and bibliography. Each student is assigned to a faculty supervisor, who

[9] Representative thesis titles, selected at random at several colleges, include: "Propaganda and the Cold War"; "Petroleum and World Strategy"; "Western European Integration"; "NATO—Strength, Weakness, and Future"; "Limited and Unlimited Wars"; "Air Power as an Instrument of National Policy"; "Collective Security in an Air-Atomic Age"; "Impact of Missiles on Military Structure."

advises on the organization of the paper and selection of bibliography, and may review a preliminary draft. At the National War College students are able to interview military and civilian officials of the government in connection with their research. Officers at the Army War College may also do this during the Christmas recess or during other breaks in the schedule. With the regular flight of planes to Washington from Maxwell, this can also be accomplished by some students of the Air War College. At this college a total of 110 hours is set aside and identified on the schedule during regular work days for the completion of the thesis. At the others it is expected that the work will be crowded in between assignments and after hours. At Carlisle Barracks, where everyone lives close by, this means that the library is well occupied on Saturday mornings and in the evenings.

The National War College and the Army War College in the past have required each student to give an oral presentation of 20 to 30 minutes to part of the class, summarizing his paper or developing some aspect of it. At the former institution for some years these presentations were scheduled one after another within a period of two weeks, before the entire class. Inevitably everyone suffered from a severe case of logorrhea. The solution was to spread the presentations throughout the year and to schedule them appropriately in association with the rest of the program. Also the size of the audience was reduced to about one half of the class. In 1955, as an experiment, only a few oral presentations were scheduled. At the Army War College these presentations are made to seminar groups, and only a few are selected for plenary sessions.

The thesis is primarily an exercise in an educational program, but it offers potential value of greater consequence. Accordingly each of the institutions has developed the practice of circulating within the government a list of topics and authors and making copies available upon request. Some papers also are listed in subsequent years as suggested reading in connection with appropriate courses or studies. The Air War College has the most elaborate distribution system for its student papers. Outstanding theses of general interest are published each year in the *Air War College Studies* series, and circulated throughout the Air Force. Others are reproduced in lesser quantity and forwarded to agencies of primary concern. The Army and Air War Colleges also encourage students to submit papers for journal publication, whenever security regulations permit. At the latter institution the *Air University Quarterly Review* is available for this purpose.

PUBLICATIONS

From time to time the question is raised whether the senior joint and service colleges should engage in the publication of a journal similar to *Military Review* and the *Air University Quarterly Review*. Acting upon the recommendations of their boards of consultants, the commandants of the National War College and Industrial College have made frequent attempts to secure authority to produce their own publications. These requests have been denied by the Department of the Army, upon which the colleges depend for fiscal support. At one time the Joint Chiefs proposed a single publication. This was firmly rejected by the National War College as—to use the words of a former deputy— "making no more sense than combining *Foreign Affairs* and *Business Week*." The Army War College also has sought authority for a publication. The plan was endorsed by a civilian advisory board, which pointed out that such a publication might help the college "assume a continuing interest in the intellectual welfare of [its] graduates." [10] This proposal likewise has not been approved by higher authority, presumably because of the expectation that added personnel would sooner or later be required. The Naval War College issues a modest monthly, the *Naval War College Review,* consisting of reprints of two or three lectures delivered at the college. Except for several pages of annotated book notes prepared by the library staff, it contains no original material. It is given limited distribution to Naval units and reserve officers.

STRATEGY SEMINARS

In 1949 the Naval War College instituted the practice of inviting a large number of civilian and military guests to Newport to participate in a five day study of international affairs, with particular emphasis upon a global strategy for the United States, including political and economic as well as military policies. This undertaking, called the Global Strategy Discussions, has since become an annual event, and is now scheduled just before gradua-

[10] *Report of the Civilian Advisory Group,* Army War College, January 1954.

tion in June. In 1955 there were 150 civilian guests, including prominent businessmen, bankers, and journalists, and a few clergymen and educators. Officers of the three services from the Pentagon and elsewhere and representatives of the National War College and the other service War Colleges also attended. Usually an aircraft carrier and a smaller vessel are berthed in the harbor for the week, and those civilians who wish may live aboard. The senior officers of these ships participate in the discussions. Also in attendance are more than 100 Naval Reserve officers, in the grade of captain and commander, on two weeks' active duty. These officers spend a week being briefed on developments in the Navy, before joining the Global Strategy Discussions.

This affair consists of a series of lectures, question periods, and round tables. The latter are composed of about 15 to 20 members, including students in the Command and Staff Course as well as the naval warfare I and II courses, Naval Reserve officers, visiting Army and Air Force officers, and civilian guests, and are chaired by students. In 1955, for example, lectures were delivered by the president of the college, Admiral McCormick, on the current world situation, by Admiral Robert Carney, chief of Naval operations, on the principles of sea power, by President Henry Wriston of Brown University on political limitations of strategy, and by General William Donovan on the United States in the cold war. The round tables examine military, economic, and political considerations affecting the formulation of strategy in separate meetings, then develop a global strategy concept and supporting measures, for presentation to a final plenary session.

The Air War College in 1954 inaugurated a similar program, calling it a National Security Forum. In this case, however, the guest list is limited to about 25, and includes representatives of business and industry and a few journalists, scientists, and others. These individuals participate for one week in the regular lecture and discussion group meetings of the college. The event is scheduled in April, when the class studies formulation of a strategy for the United States in a continuing cold war situation. In 1955, for example, none of the formal speeches were given by representatives of the Air Force, but the guests were given special briefings on Air Force developments by members of the faculty.

Not to be left out, the Army War College in 1955 started its

National Strategy Seminar, a three day conference in March. About 50 guests participated; they were principally civilians, but some high-ranking officers from the General Staff and other Army headquarters and a few senior Navy and Air Force officers were included. The plan is similar to that at Maxwell. The guests joined with the students in the lectures and discussion groups during the regular course on strategy. The Army War College program did not include special briefings on Army developments, but two of the four speakers were Army officers, one of them the chief of staff. In 1956 the time of the seminar was changed to June.

The National War College has not attempted anything of this kind, possibly because the three services in their collective capacity do not have the same interest in cultivating civilian guests and also because conducting such an affair in Washington would be more difficult than at one of the service colleges. Several years ago a strategy seminar was arranged for the students only, but this was dropped after the single try.

LIBRARY FACILITIES

All of the colleges maintain substantial libraries. These are fully adequate for the requirements, as a description of the library of the National War College will indicate. This library is a legacy from the prewar Army War College, and is one of the richest military libraries in the country. Since 1946 an effort has been made to build up the accessions in politics, economics, and international affairs. The collection now numbers about 300,000 books, pamphlets, bound journals, and public documents, and some 65,000 cataloged classified documents in a separate section. The library subscribes to about 400 journals, of which roughly 50 percent are in the broadly military category. Sixty-eight periodicals are in international affairs, 50 in business and economics, 34 in political science, 27 in bibliography, and 14 in science and technology. Special collections include the United Nations Documents series. An experienced university librarian, after a recent visit to the National War College, observed that "here was an unusually fine library facility, so fine and so unusual, in fact, that to view its services and resources constitutes a distinctive, new experience. To state, after a short visit of three days, that the arrangement, organization, and administration of a library appear perfectly adapted to the academic program it is designed to serve is . . . unusual; and yet, this statement is accurate with respect to the National War College library." [11] Very few libraries indeed are prepared to offer the sort of services rendered by the staff of this one. Numbering 25, for a total student and faculty community of about 150 people, this staff does most of the hard searching for and evaluating of material that is usually done by the individual student or instructor elsewhere, thus freeing a tremendous amount of student time and effort. For example, every one of the 400 periodicals coming into the library is scanned by a member of the staff; articles of special interest are marked and indexed and many are abstracted. Each student is provided with elaborate bibliographies for the individual papers and committee problems. As the librarian quoted above has remarked, "A student need only express an interest in some portion of a subject field and within a short time he is the recipient of a generous quantity of bibliographical materials. . . . In many universities this degree of service would be described as luxurious. . . ."

The library facilities of the other institutions, while possessing smaller book collections, appear to be just as complete with respect to current materials and areas of special interest. The services rendered to faculty and students are of the same general order. The bibliographical services of the new Army War College library and also of the Air University library are even more extensive.[12] The Mahan Library of the Naval War College, which contains over 100,000 bound volumes, is a highly specialized technical library, but in recent years an effort has been made to strengthen its resources in international affairs, economics, and related fields. Appropriations for book, periodical, and document purchases have been stepped up from a few thousand dollars a few years ago to $13,000 in 1955. The Naval War College also maintains a highly specialized logistics library. The Air University Library is now housed in a spacious new building which was completed in 1956. It has been named appropriately the Fairchild Library in memory of the founder of the Air University. It contains some 100,000 bound volumes and over 500,000 documents, and receives over

[11] *Memorandum Submitted to the Commandant,* March 1955.
[12] See Jerrould Orne, "An Experiment in Integrated Library Service," *College and Research Libraries,* October 1955, pp. 353–359.

1,600 journals and periodicals. Its annual budget is approximately $500,000. The Air University Library is the official depository of Air Force records concerning the air phase of world war II and contains considerable material on air power. Because the *Reader's Guide* and other indices do not index most military periodicals, the Air University Library in 1949 inaugurated its own *Air University Periodical Index,* which now indexes 60 titles. A separate branch of the Air University Library, consisting of a working reference collection of about 1,350 bound volumes, 97 periodicals, and 15 newspapers and supervised by a professional librarian, is maintained at the Air War College.[13]

VISUAL AIDS

The War Colleges should be the delight of those modern educators with a penchant for the latest audio-visual devices. The National War College, for example, has a visual aids branch that prepares maps and charts of all sizes and descriptions. It has complete facilities for photographic, photo-offset, mimeograph, and ozalid reproduction. The principal auditorium of the college is equipped with public address, recording, motion pictures, television, radio, and other facilities. Students, even more than guest speakers, make extensive use of this equipment.

There are precious few educational institutions that are able to support their programs with services and facilities as complete as those of the War Colleges. While none of the latter are by any means extravagant or luxurious, they certainly are ample. The only exception here is the relative lack of secluded space for the individual student, but, with the emphasis that all of the colleges place upon group activity, this probably appears to those responsible to be less of a problem than it does to the outside observer.

[13] It is interesting to note that professional military librarians have formed military libraries sections in both the American Library Association and the Special Libraries Association.

CHAPTER SIXTEEN

THE CURRICULA OF THE

WAR COLLEGES

FOR each of the senior colleges there is an official statement of mission and objectives. This is the official image of the institution, spelling out what it is expected to accomplish. Frequently the statement has been prepared, at least in the first instance, at the college itself. In any event, it is issued by the highest authority—the Joint Chiefs for the National War College, the chiefs of staff for the service schools—after circulation through appropriate channels. In response to these official statements of purpose, each of the colleges has developed a distinctive curriculum. The purpose of this chapter is to provide a brief summary of each of these curricula and a comparative analysis of their content and substance.[1]

The National War College

The Joint Chiefs have defined the mission of the National War College as follows:

"1. To prepare selected personnel of the armed forces and other governmental departments for the exercise of joint high level policy, command, and staff functions, and for the performance of strategic planning duties in their respective departments.

"2. To promote the development of understanding of those agencies of government and those factors of power potential which are an essential part of a national war effort."

[1] These curricula undergo frequent change. The following analysis is based upon our observations of the colleges during four academic years. The course outlines are based upon the last of these, 1955–1956.

342

They have stated that the scope will include:

"1. Analysis of the nature and interdependence of the several factors of national power of the United States and other nations.

"2. Study of the integration of military and foreign policy.

"3. Study of the role of the United Nations and other means designed to avoid armed conflict between nations.

"4. Determination of the influence of the possession or deficiency of economic, scientific, political, and social resources upon the capability of waging war.

"5. Study of the interests and objectives of significant nations in their international relations, areas of disagreements, and measures short of war.

"6. Study of:

"a. The military force necessary to implement national policy in peace and war.

"b. Strategy and war planning.

"c. Impact of science and technology upon the armed forces.

"d. Departmental and interdepartmental problems which concern the national security.

"e. Employment of joint forces on the joint expeditionary force and higher levels."

The difficult task of translating an idea for a joint military-civilian institution into a ten month curriculum has been a continuous, never-ending process. Only one thing has remained constant, the practice that the college offer a single course of study, in which all students participate as a group regardless of individual differences of prior education or experience. By and large the basic pattern of subjects has remained the same, although the emphasis on different substantive areas has shifted from time to time and the organizational structure of the curriculum has undergone almost annual change. For the first seven years the program was divided into two more or less distinct parts. The first, extending from the opening of the college in August to the Christmas recess, was devoted to political, economic, and social affairs; the second, from January to June, was devoted to military affairs. While this division was maintained, the small civilian faculty group carried primary responsibility for the administration of the nonmilitary studies, and terminated their residency when these were completed. Since the academic year 1954–1955, the civilian group has been employed for the full year, and the two parts of the curriculum have been merged into a single program.

Since the academic year 1954–1955, the curriculum of the National War College has been presented in the form of a "staff problem," consisting of three principal parts: "the statement of the problem," "the facts bearing on the problem," and "conclusions." This is a form with which all military personnel are familiar. It is as if the students were the staff of the National Security Council and were directed to prepare a basic security strategy for the United States, with relevant supporting policies. The following outline will suggest the manner in which this is accomplished.

Part One. Statement of the Problem

Course 1. *The World Today* (1½ weeks). An introductory description and analysis of the present world situation, including the principal conditions facing the United States.

Part Two. The Facts Bearing on the Problem

Course 2. *Tensions and Conflict* (1 week). An examination of concepts concerning the causes and nature of tension, conflict, and war.

Course 3. *The Elements of National Power* (4 weeks). The component elements of national power, including political, economic, sociological, military, scientific, and geographic factors which together comprise a nation's power.

Course 4. *The Employment of National Power* (3 weeks). The principal means employed by states to implement their objectives, including persuasion (diplomacy, international organizations, economic policies, military aid, and information and propaganda), coercion (political warfare, covert operations, and economic sanctions), and military action (land, sea, and air forces).

Course 5. *Free World Allies and Associates* (6 weeks). Area studies of the United Kingdom and Commonwealth, Western Europe, Latin America, and Asian allies. Examination of the problem of unity in the free world.

Course 6. *The Communist Bloc* (4 weeks).[2] The political, economic, military, and social characteristics of the Soviet Union, Communist China, and satellites.

Course 7. *The Uncommitted Areas* (3 weeks). Study of Southeast Asia, India, Africa, and the Arab world.

Course 8. *Formulating National Security Policy and Military Strategy* (3 weeks).[3] Organizations, processes, and factors involved in the formulation of security policies in the United States.

Part Three. Conclusions

Course 9. *A National Estimate of the Situation* (3 weeks). A summary and reexamination of previous studies. Organized as separate committees, the students prepare their own estimates of the world situation, focusing attention on the relative strengths and weaknesses of the two great power blocs. One half of the committees prepare an estimate from the United States point of view, and one half from the point of view of the Soviet Union.

Course 10. *The Development of National Security Policy and Subsidiary Policies* (5 weeks). Separate committees prepare national security policies, with supporting subsidiary policies in the military, political, and economic fields, again for the United States and the Soviet Union.

Course 11. *Field Trips* (3 weeks).

Course 12. *Cross Briefings and Reexamination of Policy and Strategy* (2 weeks). A final summary and review.

The Army War College

The curriculum of the Army War College is derived from the statement of the mission of the institution set forth in the basic Army regulation issued by the chief of staff. As most recently revised, this declares the mission to be:

"a. To prepare selected Army officers for the highest command and general staff positions in the Army, and for such high level positions within the Department of Defense or other governmental agencies as the Army might be called upon to fill.

---

[2] The order of courses 5 and 6 was reversed in 1956–1957.
[3] This course was placed after course 3 in 1956–1957.

"b. To further interservice and interdepartmental understanding, with emphasis on Army doctrine and operations through the attendance, in limited numbers, of officers of the other United States Armed Forces and selected members of other United States departments and agencies.

"c. To study concepts of Army forces to assure the most effective development and employment of land power in future warfare."

To fulfill these responsibilities the college has devised a three part curriculum. Part one deals with the Army's missions and the way it is equipped to handle them. Part two deals with national and international affairs. Part three of the curriculum is concerned with strategy and war planning. The following outline lists the separate course units.

Part One. The Army

Course 1. *World Scene and the Army* (3 weeks). An introductory course, dealing with the current world situation and the role, mission, and capability of the Army to meet its responsibilities.

Course 2. *Operations and Intelligence* (5 weeks). Consideration of weapons, weapon systems, organization, training, types of operations, intelligence systems, and command relationships.

Course 3. *Logistics and Manpower* (6 weeks). Army command and staff responsibilities in the fields of personnel, logistics, and matériel.

Part Two. International Relations [4]

Course 4. *The Communist Bloc* (3½ weeks). The ideological, geographic, political, economic, social, and military characteristics of the Soviet Union, Communist China, and satellites.

Course 5. *National Security Policy Formulation* (3 weeks). An examination of the decision-making process in the United States, including the organization of governmental machinery.

Course 6. *United States Foreign Relations* (5 weeks). The significance of selected areas of the free world to the national security,

[4] Until 1955–1956 the part on international relations preceded the part on the Army.

346

prestige, and power position of the United States; the effectiveness of United States policy with respect to these areas; and alternative courses of action for the cold war period.

Part Three. Strategy and War Planning

Course 7. *Military Strategy* (2 weeks). A review of fundamental concepts of national and military strategy, the relationship of military strategy to the attainment of national objectives, and the application of strategic concepts to future warfare.

Course 8. *Joint and Army War Planning* (4 weeks). The objectives and methods of war planning at the level of the Joint Chiefs of Staff and the Department of the Army. Current major war planning problems, with emphasis upon the role of the Army.

Course 9. *Theater War Planning* (7 weeks). Factors and procedures in the preparation of theater war plans; identification of actual and projected conditions and problems inherent in military operations in selected areas of strategic importance; plans for military operations in such areas under varied assumptions.

The Naval War College

According to its officially published mission, the purpose of the Naval War College is "To further an understanding of the fundamentals of warfare, international relations, and interservice operations with emphasis on their application to future naval warfare, in order to prepare officers for higher command." The college catalog lists three objectives that are derived from this mission:

"The increase of each officer's knowledge of the fundamentals of Naval warfare, and of other related subjects which contribute to an understanding of warfare.

"The improvement of each officer's mental power and ability to relate this knowledge to the solution of military problems.

"The provision of intellectual leadership in the field of sea power and maritime strategy for the armed services and for the United States."

The catalog goes on to declare that the college seeks to further an understanding of the fundamentals of modern warfare. Pointing out that modern warfare is an art as well as a science, involving "an extremely complex web of political, economic, social, and military factors," the college rejects the notion that it might advocate a "fixed set of rules by which wars may be conducted or battles won." The catalog declares that "It is essential for a naval officer in high command to have a thorough understanding, not only of his own service, but also of the interrelations of the political, economic, social, and military factors of national, military, and naval strategy. The end in view is that the graduate may assume duties in high command with a full appreciation of the national objectives and of the material and spiritual resources of the United States."

The Naval War College, as explained in chapter eight, accomplishes its mission through programs at three separate levels.[5] The Command and Staff Course is described elsewhere. Here we are concerned with the two naval warfare courses. Naval warfare I, it will be recalled, is a combination of the former strategy and tactics and strategy and logistics courses. It is concerned primarily with "basic professional level" education, to use the college's term, and is presented from the command point of view. The focus remains largely *within* the field of naval operations, although considerable effort is made to relate these operations to other military operations and to broader problems of strategy. The subjects considered in the first year course fall into three broad categories, all closely related. These are *strategy,* including the political, social, economic, and military factors of national strategy, *tactics,* and *logistics.* In this course, emphasis is placed on the integrated employment of all elements of naval power in the accomplishment of the Navy's task and responsibilities.

Unlike the curricula at the sister institutions, the naval warfare I program is not presented as a series of courses or studies, one following after the other in a logical and clearly developed sequence. Rather it is composed of units of instruction, identified as "curriculum items," that frequently are offered concurrently and often are broken into several detached segments. The justification of this arrangement is that it permits concurrent consideration of a number of related themes, which can be pulled together at regular intervals by means of a number of devices, particularly the

---

[5] In 1956–1957 the Naval War College added a command and staff course for foreign naval officers, making four separate courses at Newport in all.

operations problems, which are a distinctive feature of Naval War College instruction.

Naval warfare II, the second year course, deals with the "strategic level." Although it repeats almost one third of naval warfare I, it aims to accomplish much the same purpose as that of the other War Colleges, including the National War College. Here the emphasis is on the strategic employment of sea power in furtherance of national objectives. It also is presented from the command point of view. It is the second year course that more positively manifests the Navy's interest in the preparation of its officers for policy level assignments.

The following outline will suggest the nature and scope of the two programs.

Common to Naval Warfare I and II

Introduction to Naval Warfare (5 days). Opening week introduction to present world situation.

Strategy Studies (11 days). A review of the nature and elements of national strategies, including concepts of land, air, and maritime strategy.

Introduction to Sound Military Decision (3 days). The elements and processes of decision making.

Nuclear Weapons Study (4 days). Briefings covering recent developments and applications.

International Law Study (5 days). Basic principles of international law, as they affect the military establishment.

Army and Air Force Operations (4 days). Survey of essential characteristics, organization, employment, and support of the major combatant components of the Army and Air Force.

War Planning Systems Study (15 days). Study of the various offices and agencies of the United States government responsible for national security planning; NATO; principles, doctrines, and procedures of joint and combined commands.

Army, Navy, Air War College Presentations (4 days). Team presentations of concepts for joint operations under conditions short of global war and for global war.

Global Strategy Discussions (5 days). A final summary review of United States objectives and supporting strategy.

Naval Warfare I Only

Planning Study (14 days). A systematic study of military planning, including the estimate of the situation, logistic planning, development of the plan, preparation of the directive, and logistic annex.

Naval Operations Studies (41 days). A comprehensive survey of naval operations, including logistic support agencies, weapons and weapon systems, communications systems, and operations to control the seas.

Operations Problems (total of 88 days). The operations problem remains one of the most distinctive features of the Naval War College. Essentially it is a highly developed case study. Naval warfare I students participate in problems involving fleet logistic support, amphibious operations, and task force fleet and joint theater operations. They participate with students in naval warfare II in a strategic war game.

Naval Warfare II Only

Basic Strategic Studies (14 weeks).[6] A comprehensive study of the current strategic world situation from the point of view of a United States military planner. The content is roughly similar to that of the international relations phases of the Army and Air War College programs. This study concludes with the preparation of a working paper on guide lines for the formulation of United States national strategy, similar to a National Security Council paper.

Strategic Planning Study (12 weeks). Using the working paper as a basic directive, naval warfare II students prepare operations plans at the Joint Chiefs, theater, and Department of the Navy levels. The period concludes with a strategic war game, playing out all of these plans, testing feasibility under varying conditions short of global war and of global war.

The Air War College

The Air War College, like its sister institutions, employs a standard curriculum, providing the same course of instruction for

6 This part was identified as National Security Studies in 1956–1957.

all students. Initially the curriculum was concerned with preparation for command and staff functions with large air units and supporting forces, and with the strategic employment of air power. This remains the principal mission, but over the years increasing attention has been devoted to politico-military affairs, reflecting the Air Force's concept of the college as its highest educational institution, on a par with, if not superior to, the National War College.

The official mission of the Air War College is to:

"a. Provide instruction to prepare senior officers for high command and staff duty with large Air Force units.

"b. Promote sound concepts on the broad aspect of air power to assure the most effective development and employment of air power."

This statement also declares that the scope of the course of instruction will include:

"a. The fundamental nature of international relations and an understanding of the current world conflict.

"b. The organization, characteristics, and strategic and tactical employment of air forces and larger air units.

"c. Air Force logistics and their coordination with surface requirements.

"d. Education of all students in those intelligence requirements necessary to support sound plans for the employment of air power.

"e. Effects of the application of atomic energy and other technological developments of air warfare.

"f. Strategic considerations concerning defense against air attack with particular emphasis upon possibilities inherent in new developments.

"g. General organization, characteristics, and employment of surface forces and supporting services; and their coordination in combined operations with air.

"h. Critical analysis and evaluation of military history in terms of cause and effect to determine fundamental relationships and principles that are applicable to future warfare.

"i. Critical examination of current equipment, techniques, and accepted standards; and trends in development, with the direction of thought toward improvement.

"j. War planning considerations for current and future strategic concepts.

"k. Responsibility of air commanders and staffs on air force and higher levels with respect to leadership, administration, military management, public information, discipline, security, and civil affairs.

"l. Seminar study of such Air Force problems as may be assigned."

The Air War College curriculum is now organized into three phases, roughly parallel to the three parts at the Army War College. The first of these is designed to give the student a broad understanding of international affairs. The second phase deals primarily with military affairs, and particularly with air power, and the third is an evaluation of national strategy in the light of the year's work.

Phase One. Orientation and International Relations

Study 1. *Fundamentals* (1 week). A review of principles and techniques of learning, problem solving, and communications.

Study 2. *Elements of Power* (6 weeks). An examination of the development and structure of the modern nation-state, traditional policies of the United States, United Kingdom, and Soviet Union, the communist threat, and case studies demonstrating the means employed by selected states in the quest for security.

Study 3. *Current World Conflict* (6 weeks). A review of international developments in the period since 1945. Analysis of the commitments and capabilities of the two power blocs. Study of the organization and procedures for formulation of security policies in the United States.

Phase Two. Military Strategies: Concept and Employment of the National Weapon System

Study 4. *Military Tasks and Management of Resources* (5½ weeks). Analysis of the relationship of the tasks assigned to the armed forces and the programs developed by them to carry out these tasks.

Study 5. *Home Defense* (4 weeks). A study of the defense of the United States, including the national weapon system, the vulnerability of the home base to attack, and the agencies and forces responsible for its defense.

Study 6. *The National Weapon System in the Attack* (4 weeks). A comprehensive examination of the offensive employment of armed forces in war of unrestricted character on a global scale, including a survey of enemy strength and vulnerability, the strategic concepts of the various services, and assessment of Air Force offensive capabilities and techniques; and problems of command and control.

Study 7. *The Weapon System in Defense* (4 weeks). The capacity of the national weapon system to protect the security of the attacking force, including air-surface relations, tactical air operations, control problems in selected areas, and defense of bases, supplies, and personnel.

Phase Three. Evaluation of National Strategy

Study 8. *The Continuing Conflict* (4 weeks). A reexamination of the strategy of the United States, under conditions short of unrestricted global war, in the light of recent weapons developments. This includes an evaluation of the capabilities of the free world and the communist bloc, and the concepts of the Army, Navy, and Air Force for limited military operations.

Study 9. *Concepts of Future War* (4 weeks). The long term requirements for national and allied security.

Analysis of the Content of the Curricula

From this review of the programs one thing stands out clearly. The War Colleges now define the responsibilities of the senior professional officer in a broad context of political, economic, and social relationships. While the missions of the schools are still identified in traditional terms of preparation for command and staff duties, the programs offered suggest a very broad interpretation of these duties. Military plans and operations are considered not as separate operations, but only as part of the employment of *all* of the resources of the nation, under conditions short of war as well as in wartime. National strategy is defined in terms of four substrategies: political, economic, social (or, as they like to call it, "psycho-social"), and military strategy. The last of these, the responsibility of the professional soldier, sailor, and airman, is considered in relation to the others. In terms of policy levels, all of the schools, in varying degrees, now study military affairs at the level of the National Security Council. All examine the relationship of political ends to military means, and consider the political, economic, and social implications of military actions. All, moreover, devote increasing attention to these external relationships, both domestic and foreign. While uncertainty remains as to how they can best accomplish this purpose—and indeed debate should continue as long as the schools retain a healthy vitality—certain definite patterns of response have developed.

GRAND STRATEGY

As might be expected from its history and mission, the National War College places the greatest emphasis upon a broad interservice approach. It was designed for this very purpose. The whole curriculum, as outlined above, is presented as a "staff problem" at the National Security Council level. Actually, the college devotes considerably less attention to military matters than to other topics. Only one quarter of the lectures are by military officers, for example. Approximately half of the speakers are scholars or representatives of civilian agencies of government. About two thirds of the curriculum is devoted to nonmilitary affairs. The faculty of the National War College has designed the curriculum with great care in order to integrate consideration of all factors throughout the entire program. The Army and Air War Colleges, and the Naval War College in its new second year course, do not give as much separate attention to nonmilitary aspects of national strategy as does the National War College, but they have gone a long way toward approaching it. They now devote about 12 weeks to study of national and international affairs. Throughout the rest of the year, while the focus is upon military plans and operations, these are examined within the broad context of strategy employed by all of the schools.

The program at the Army War College illustrates this situation. Fourteen weeks are devoted to the part on the Army. This part of the curriculum is the closest to being "purely military" in content. But even so the Army's procedures and problems in the fields of manpower, logistics, operations, and intelligence are studied as part of a larger undertaking in behalf of national security. Part three, strategy and war planning, requiring 15 weeks, is likewise a course of instruction in military affairs, but here even more than in part one the approach is broad. The strategy course examines the nature of war, classical concepts of strategy, the national objectives of the United States, the roles of sea and air as well as land power, and the influence of alliances upon strategy. The war planning courses examine the nonmilitary implications of military plans and operations. Developments at the Air War College are similar.

Until the second year course was established in 1954, the Naval War College devoted more attention to military operations than its sister institutions, with correspondingly less attention to political, economic, and social affairs. The reasons for this situation were explained in chapter eight. Nonmilitary affairs, moreover, were presented in more or less supplementary form rather than as identifiable courses, as at the National War College and the Army and Air War Colleges. With the establishment of the second year, the Naval War College now offers a program very similar in content and distribution to the others. Thus a large part of the August-December period is devoted to the study of national and international political, economic, and social affairs. The rest of the program, while it is concerned with plans for military (largely naval) operations at the levels of the Joint Chiefs and joint and combined theater headquarters, handles these in the broad strategic context that now characterizes the other senior service schools.

The naval warfare 1 program is still geared to study of professional naval subjects. The courses on naval operations, naval logistics, Army and Air Force operations, and the six operations problems consume more than three quarters of the total time. Nevertheless even here an attempt is made, within these time limitations, to expose the first year students to national and international affairs through an introductory week on the current world situation, lectures on American foreign policy, a strategy course which is offered in short segments throughout the first term, lectures and a term paper on the Soviet Union, a four day course on international law, and the final Global Strategy Discussions.

The service War Colleges devote a great deal more attention to military operating functions than does the National War College. It is the principal business of each of them to provide instruction on the operations of its own parent service. The National War College, on the other hand, is not designed for this purpose. It could not possibly devote the detailed attention to the functions and operations of the Army that the Army War College does and also do as thorough a job for the Navy and the Air Force, and at the same time accomplish its own joint politico-military mission. Military operations constitute but a fraction of the curriculum. No more than summary treatment is given to matters that are handled at considerable length at the appropriate service War College. Only one day each is allocated to military topics that received prolonged attention at the latter.

LOGISTICS

The handling of instruction in logistics, because this subject opens up significant questions of the relationship of military plans and operations to nonmilitary considerations, is of particular interest. At the National War College there is no separate study of logistics as such. Until recently, a separate two week course on joint logistical planning was given in cooperation with the Industrial College. Following this course, student teams from the two schools worked out the logistic implications of a war plan that had been developed at the National War College. The purpose was to determine whether the proposed strategic plan was at all feasible. But this cooperative venture was dropped.[7] Now the logistics factor is taken up in connection with other matters, in the broadest context. In the course on the elements of national power, for example, the students consider manpower and industry. In the course on policy formulation they go into financial issues, and the impact of industry, labor, and national resources on national security. In this course they also devote a day to the logistic implications of the strategic concept. During the latter part of the program, when they prepare national estimates and actual strategic plans and sup-

[7] This and certain other issues involved in the relationship of the National War College and the Industrial College are discussed in chapter twenty-one.

porting policies, they must give due consideration to economic and logistic factors.

The Army War College devotes about four weeks to logistics. This starts out with lectures on the commander's appreciation of logistics and the Army's logistics system, then takes up such topics as mobilization requirements, petroleum, transportation, procurement, industrial mobilization, and so forth. Throughout the course the logistics factor is related not only to other military operations, but to questions of resource capability and to civilian and interallied requirements. The special experience of the Naval War College with instruction in logistics was discussed above in chapter eight. It was described how a separate logistics course, introduced initially to prepare trained naval logisticians, was gradually merged into the strategy and tactics course and how the two finally were combined in the present naval warfare I. Although emphasis in this first year course now is upon the relationship of logistics to command, the approach is more closely geared to military operations than at the Army War College. About seven days are devoted to study of the functions of the Navy's logistic support system, and eight days to the integrated logistic support of the fleet. Some of the daily topics covered are: logistics problems of the chief of Naval operations, the Navy supply system, the Military Sea Transport Service, continental United States base support of overseas operations, mobile logistic support requirements, and advanced base development. In naval warfare II the attention to logistics is somewhat similar to that at the National War College. It is not examined as a separate subject, but is considered as an important element of strategic planning. Before leaving this brief account of instruction in logistics at the Naval War College, it should be noted also that the faculty here is organized along functional lines. There is a separate strategy and logistics department composed of officers who make it their business to see that study of logistics is not slighted.

The approaches to the study of logistics at the Army War College and in the first year course at the Naval War College are direct reflections of the actual practices in this field that characterize these two services. Army officers for generations have been engaged not only in the distribution of supplies to the field forces, but also in the extensive contacts with domestic industry and commerce that are associated with their actual production and procurement. Many of the top positions in this field of producer logistics were filled by line officers rather than specialists or civilians. In the Navy, on the other hand, direct fleet support came under the control of line officers in the Office of the Chief of Naval Operations, but the relationship with industry tended more to be controlled by the civilian assistant secretaries. At the operations level, moreover, these contacts with industry were handled by technicians who for the most part were not line officers. Thus the Naval War College does not exhibit the interest in producer logistics that is essential at the Army War College.

At the Air War College the curriculum does not provide study of logistics as a separate subject. Although initially there was a two week course on logistics, and a Logistics Department within the faculty, consideration of support problems now is given in connection with other matters. The approach appears to be somewhere between those of the other two service schools. On the one hand some attention is given to the relationship of resource capabilities to policy at the highest level. There are lectures on such topics as the resources of the United States for meeting its commitments, the world distribution of resources, world-wide transportation systems, mobilization in the atomic age, the world petroleum situation, and the economics of maintaining an adequate military force in the decade ahead. On the other hand other topics deal with "consumer logistics." These include lectures on support measures in selected military operations in world war II, the Air Force base program and its defense, and the problems of world-wide aerial and surface resupply. As at the other colleges, the students take into account the logistic factor in the development and testing of strategic plans.

INTERNATIONAL AFFAIRS

In their treatment of nonmilitary topics, no two of the schools are alike. The National War College, because it devotes about three quarters of its time to these topics, provides widest coverage. The others are somewhat more selective. A note of warning should be entered at this point, however. An analysis of the curriculum in terms of hours for this, number of lectures for that, and so forth, while it does suggest the approach employed, does not give a complete picture of the consideration of nonmilitary topics. We have observed at these institutions that the students do not permit the schedule to tie them down. They feel no restraint to limit their discussion to the assignment of the day. They range widely over all sorts of nonmilitary topics, both in connection with their work on military problems and in less formal settings.

In general, when these institutions depart from military topics, as they do increasingly, they show the greatest interest in international affairs. Initially the nonmilitary studies were handled more or less separately from the rest of the program. But very soon this detachment began to disappear, so that now, in spite of precise course labels, attention is directed to international affairs almost continuously. Moreover a conscious effort has been made, particularly at the Air and National War Colleges, to integrate this dimension throughout the entire program. Characteristically the colleges show more concern for foreign affairs and foreign policy problems than for political and economic developments within the United States. The National War College, the Army War College, and the Naval War College, in both naval warfare I and II, devote the entire first week to a summary review of the current international situation, attempting to identify the principal forces that are operating on the international scene, and the implications of these for the United States. At all of the colleges there is a major preoccupation with the Soviet Union. The dominant theme is the Soviet threat and the Western response thereto, and the study of international politics is cast in terms of a power conflict, or "struggle." Considerable time is devoted to the study of communism, the Soviet Union, and the satellites. At the National War College and the Army War College the formal Soviet courses run for about three weeks. The Air War College and the second year course at the Naval War College devote almost this much time to the Soviet Union. No other nation receives this much attention. All of the colleges consider the major allies in the Western alliance to some extent. The National War College does the most in this respect, devoting 25 days to the free world. The first year course at the Naval War College does the least, providing occasional lectures and readings. The Army War College takes up these countries in the context of United States policies.

For the most part, the emphasis in these area studies is upon the current situation, and it is more descriptive than analytical. In the Soviet course the focus is upon Soviet political and economic organization and military capabilities. There appears to be relatively little systematic probing of Soviet intentions. The National and Air War Colleges have scheduled lectures on Marxist theory. The Army War College course on the USSR includes a committee study on communist ideology in which the students are expected to inquire into Marxist and Leninist theory and the historical foundations of communism; at the other service colleges there is some consideration of contemporary communist ideology, but it does not appear to be given much historical depth. In the naval warfare I course, in addition to attending a number of lectures on Soviet affairs, each student prepares a term paper comparing the Soviet Union and the United States, with respect to foreign policy objectives and war capabilities.

A notable exception to the usual emphasis upon contemporary affairs is the approach employed at the Air War College in connection with the foreign area studies. Here an attempt is made to give the student a sense of historical perspective in his understanding of selected countries. This is accomplished through a number of devices. In the first place, lectures are presented on the United Kingdom, the United States, the Soviet Union, and Japan which emphasize the traditional objectives and heritages that underlie the international behavior of these states. Then follows a lecture on the objectives and policies of the major powers at the peace conferences following the first world war, and another on the principal problems faced by these powers during the interwar years and the policies developed by them at that time in response to these problems. These lectures are supported by the reading program and committee discussions.

Preoccupation with the Soviet Union and with the Western alliance has left less time for the Middle East, South Asia, and Africa. In the past relatively little time was allocated to these areas, but in recent years they have received more attention. In 1955–1956 the National War College lengthened the course on the "uncommitted areas" from two to three weeks. The other colleges give considerably less time to these areas.

The National War College curriculum devotes the most attention to international politics as a separate analytical study in itself. Although subject to frequent change, in general structure and outline the treatment has been similar to the pattern of undergraduate college courses in this field in recent years. Consideration has been given to the geographic, demographic, and economic factors of national power, and to the instruments of statecraft employed by states to achieve their objectives in international affairs. Altogether about seven weeks are devoted to this investigation of international politics. All of the colleges give some attention to international law and organization. The National War College accomplishes this in a course on the "Employment of National Power," considering the United Nations and regional organizations as instruments of "persuasion," along with diplomacy and economic aid. National War College students visit the United Nations headquarters on a voluntary basis. In keeping with a long tradition at Newport and with the special interest of the Navy in international law, the Naval War College devotes four days to a separate curriculum item on international law, attended by students in both naval warfare I and II. Three lectures are devoted to legal issues (jurisdiction, the laws of war, and the position of individuals in international law) and one to the United Nations and regional organizations. The Army War College presents one lecture on international law and organization, and arranges a two day visit by the entire class to the UN headquarters.

AMERICAN GOVERNMENT AND POLITICS

In recent years all of the War Colleges have given increasing attention to the organization and procedures of the United States government for the formulation of national policies. The National War College, as one would expect from its background and purpose, has had a separate course in this area from the beginning. As presently constituted this is a two week presentation with lectures and readings on the Presidency, the Department of State, the National Security Council, Congress, and so forth. This same course also examines certain selected domestic factors that influence policy formulation, such as public opinion, resources, industrial capacity, and the labor force. The Army War College has a similar program, initially almost a duplicate of the National War

College course, and now slightly longer and more systematically organized. Both of these courses are more descriptive than analytical. The Naval and Air War Colleges incorporate their consideration of the organizational aspects of policy formulation into study of war planning systems. Accordingly they focus more upon military planning mechanisms than upon civilian agencies of government. At all of the colleges the civilian dimension is represented by the presence of representatives of civilian agencies, on the lecture platform, and on the staff and among the students. Lectures in this area frequently are presented by the practitioners themselves, sometimes by members of the Cabinet or other high officials.

The result of this instruction is that the students, particularly at the National and Army War Colleges, have opportunity to learn of the mechanisms and operating procedures of the government for the formulation of national policy, and to gain insights into the workings of the policy process. In recent years there has been a rising interest in the role of the military in policy formulation. Professional military officers reiterate their faith in the principle of civilian control of the armed forces in the United States. But honest differences of opinion exist among military men, as among others, as to the meaning of civilian control and the precise definition of the responsibilities and functions of the officer, particularly in high level policy positions. At the War Colleges consideration of this matter finds its way into the program in many connections. In the courses on the organization of the government it is most likely to receive formal study.

At the National War College, for example, lectures are presented on the Department of Defense and the National Security Council. Students investigate the problem of integrating military and civilian considerations in the making of policy. The Army War College goes beyond this. A separate lecture usually is scheduled on the role of the military in national policy formulation. A number of years ago this lecture was given by a professor of history who was extremely critical of what he claimed to be the incapacity of the "military mind" for present responsibilities. Significantly, this lecture was reproduced and has been listed in the bibliography for the course. Moreover one of the problems, on which three separate committees work, concerns the influence of military factors in the formulation of national policy, and several other committee problems consider questions of military participation in policy formulation. The bibliography for this problem is comprehensive, including items representing a variety of views, many of them by specialists.[8] When this course is completed, the students at the Army War College have engaged in considerable discussion of such issues as the relationship of the Joint Chiefs to the secretary of defense, the National Security Council, the Congress, and the President, the extent to which the officer, in his official capacity, should make known his views when they run against those of his civilian superior, and so forth. The greater interest of the Army War College in this subject is not surprising in the light of the Army's greater involvement in politico-military relations. Committees at the Army War College already were working on such topics in the 1930's. It should be emphasized that no attempt is made to define a proper role for the military. Rather this is a matter of continuous discussion and debate at these colleges, as in fact it is within American society at large.

ECONOMICS

The experience of two of the colleges with instruction in economics is of interest. Early in its history the National War College instituted a separate one week course on economics, in the belief that an understanding of the fundamental principles of economics and the tools of analysis employed in economic concepts would be of considerable value to the officer in handling national security problems. Professor Klaus Knorr, then of Yale, prepared a special text for this course, describing fundamental principles and analytical devices. Knorr spent the week at the college supervising the course, and he was joined by three or four other professional economists, who lectured to the class and conducted seminar discussions. After a number of years it was decided that the treatment of economics should be integrated with the rest of the program. The economic factor was then given

[8] The sources used in this connection include Sapin and Snyder's *The Role of the Military in American Foreign Policy,* Jerome Kerwin's *Civil-Military Relationships in American Life,* Louis Smith's *American Democracy and Military Power,* Edward Corwin's *Total War and the Constitution,* and Elias Huzar's *The Purse and the Sword.*

more consideration in connection with particular issues and problems, but as a consequence the systematic study of economic fundamentals and tools very largely disappeared.

In its new naval warfare II course the Naval War College has attempted something along the same lines. Here again, a professional economist was brought in to organize and supervise the work. As initially presented in 1955, three days early in the first term were devoted to informal lectures and readings on economic principles and the use of economic indices and other measurement devices. Subsequently five days were spent on the relationship of economics to strategic planning, with particular emphasis upon economic mobilization. The approach employed was quite theoretical, involving such questions as the limitations on economic capabilities in the short run and the long run, growth and full utilization of the economy, and the application of input-output analysis. Changes made the following year suggest that the theoretical approach will be modified and perhaps even dropped, as at the National War College. The other War Colleges have not attempted anything of this sort, although at the Army War College an effort was made in 1954 to employ a professional economist as a resident member of the faculty for the first term. Failing in this, an economist has been brought in as a consultant for two weeks, meeting informally with the committees during the course in connection with the preparation of their papers on the influence of economic factors in the formulation of national policy.

DECISION MAKING

The Naval War College for almost a half century has been concerned with what has come to be known as "sound military decision." For many years this involved instruction in a highly formalized procedure for the solution of military problems, using a text prepared for the purpose by Admiral E. C. Kalbfus, onetime president of the college.[9] In recent years this instruction and particularly the text were criticized by faculty and students, who found this method too rigid and artificial, tending to reduce all

---

[9] U.S. Naval War College, *Sound Military Decision,* Newport, first published in 1936 and revised at intervals thereafter. The 1936 publication was based upon a text first prepared as early as 1910.

factors to absolutes and to present problems as all black or white. In the senior courses an attempt has been made to develop a more realistic approach to decision making, utilizing the latest work of social scientists in this fast-moving area of study, including the theory of games, and minimizing the traditional formalized procedures. Those responsible for the Command and Staff Course, on the other hand, have preferred to retain a formal approach, although they too have been preparing a new text. This situation has produced some disagreement among the two staffs. The other War Colleges have not set aside a separate part of the curriculum for decision making, although the process is given some consideration in connection with various planning studies and examination of the formulation of national policies by the United States government. The Air War College, as indicated below, includes study of problem solving in its introductory course.

PRESENTATION TECHNIQUES

Generally throughout the military services one encounters a very heavy emphasis upon the importance of "presentation," that is, upon the ability to speak and write well, to present ideas and plans, and to participate in conference and group discussions. No group in American society has developed the art of briefing as fully as the military. It has become almost as stylized as ecclesiastical ritual. John Marquand caught the spirit of this in the passage in *Melville Goodwin, USA* in which the hero is introduced to the reader. It is not surprising, therefore, that the War Colleges give considerable attention to the development of "communication" skills. Their preoccupation with this area is not as deep as it once was, but it is still one of the most characteristic features of these institutions.[10]

The Air War College at one time devoted the most time and energy to this sort of thing. During the first several years the program commenced with about four weeks of study of semantics, group discussion and problem-solving techniques, and oral and written expression. Following the war senior AAF officers were convinced that air officers were deficient in negotiating skills. As a young service they felt that they had been denied the oppor-

[10] See Lieutenant Carl M. Guelzo, "The Conduct of Briefings," *Military Review,* June 1954, pp. 31–34.

tunities to demonstrate the full value of air power because they had been "outnegotiated" by the Army and Naval officers. During the war they were very favorably influenced by what they believed to be the superior skill in speaking and writing of their associates in the Royal Air Force. Moreover they were acutely conscious of the fact that the level of educational experience of air officers was lower than in the other services. Thus they looked to their new educational institutions to rectify the situation.

With the passage of time this part of the program at the Air War College has been reduced to a few days during the opening week. The college brings in several professional teachers of speech who instruct the officers in fundamentals of communication, discussion and conference techniques, and methods of problem analysis. The work in semantics has been eliminated. One officer, who experienced one week's worth of this several years ago, declared that the result of the instruction in semantics was to get the officers so confused in the use of words that for some weeks thereafter they were afraid to say anything, for fear of being misunderstood!

Some of the colleges provide opportunity for instruction in public speaking. The procedures have varied from institution to institution, and from time to time, but the most common practice is for a course of several weeks' duration to be organized under the direction of an outside professional teacher. Participation is nominally voluntary and at the student's personal expense, but the great majority of students, and frequently members of the faculty as well, join in. In the early days the National War College set up a required course in rapid reading, but it was abandoned after about three years. One member of the faculty remarked, "We increased our reading rate all right, but we found that we didn't understand what we had read!" At the Army War College equipment for self-instruction in rapid reading is available on a voluntary basis.

As already indicated, at the colleges the students are required in varying degrees to make presentations to their fellow officers. At the National and Army War Colleges each student gives a formal talk to at least part of the class on some aspect of his individual research project. At both of these institutions, and at the Naval and Air War Colleges, reports and solutions of the committees are selected for presentation either to seminars composed of several committees or to plenary sessions.

The observer at any one of these military colleges is impressed by the breadth of the curriculum. They are unique in this respect. At no other place can an individual secure instruction on the full range of factors, considerations, and circumstances that bear upon the security of the United States today and during the foreseeable future. Within this range the National War College emphasizes the formulation of security policy at the highest level. The service colleges, while devoting as much as a third of the time to this, place their emphasis upon the employment of their respective forces within the national military establishment. In the following chapter we essay the difficult task of determining how good a job they all do.

CHAPTER SEVENTEEN

AN APPRAISAL OF INSTRUCTION

IN THE WAR COLLEGES

EVALUATION of the joint and service War Colleges is a difficult task. Fortunately there is no question about the need for these institutions. Indeed the extraordinary significance of this need is the underlying theme of this entire book. All of these colleges are now geared to meet requirements for senior officers created by the varied responsibilities that have been assumed by the armed forces in recent decades. A reading of the official statements of mission in the preceding chapter indicates that all of the schools (with the exception of the first year course at the Naval War College) are charged with the preparation of officers for the highest command and staff responsibilities, including strategic planning at the highest levels. The National War College is the only one of the four that devotes its entire curriculum to the specific objective of preparing officers for assignments to positions involving the formulation of policy on the national and international levels, but the other three now concern themselves increasingly with this area.

Thus the need for these schools is not at issue. Probably their mere existence in itself constitutes a considerable contribution to the security of the United States. If they did not exist, they would have to be created. But the question remains, how well do they accomplish this purpose?

The scope of this study does not require a judgment of the quality of instruction in military subjects, such as the organization and operation of a strategic air force or amphibious task force, or the tactical employment of nuclear weapons. Our task here, rather, is to appraise the contributions that these schools are making to the preparation of their graduates for assignments in which they participate in the formulation of national security policies at the highest level, taking into account nonmilitary factors and dealing with civilian agencies and personnel. This task is not an easy one. The term "evaluation" suggests a norm, a given set of standards, by which an institution may be judged. But the War Colleges are unique. As educational institutions they form a classification by themselves, unlike conventional institutions of higher learning. They must be judged in terms of their stated objectives and of the demands made upon the officer personnel of the three armed services. The nature of these demands we have discussed in part one of this book. Here we shall attempt to judge the senior colleges in terms of the requirements that were set forth there.

The observer is tempted to compare these colleges to conventional educational institutions, particularly the professional graduate schools. The administrators of the military schools themselves frequently make this comparison. But there is a real difference. The senior military schools are designed to meet the peculiar requirements of the government, and particularly of the armed services, of which they are parts. They enroll mature men in their late thirties and early forties who already have had heavy responsibilities and wide and rich experiences, and provide them with unique opportunities to learn from each other and from visiting experts. The conventional graduate schools, on the other hand, are charged with a different purpose. Their students usually are younger and much less experienced. They are required to devote much of their attention to fundamental concepts and to the acquisition of tools requisite to the mastery of their profession or field of knowledge. The military colleges and the conventional graduate schools must be judged by different criteria. The first are designed to maximize the opportunity for the exchange of ideas and experiences and for self-education among selected groups of mature men. The latter are conducted to provide instruction in the fundamentals and techniques of different areas of knowledge and to evaluate the student's mastery of them.

Although these military schools are not widely known to the general public, we have found that almost all individuals who have come in contact with them, in connection with their official duties in the government or as lecturers or visitors, have a favorable opinion of their achievements. We have heard very little criticism and much praise. Former Secretary of Defense Robert Lovett, in an interview, characterized the National War College as a "fine institution." Likewise we have heard similar favorable testimony from the chiefs of agencies in the Pentagon that are staffed, in part at least, with graduates of these schools. Almost without exception they have told us that they favor the assignment of graduates to their staffs, although they point out that school attendance in itself is not a mark of distinction and therefore is to be considered along with other criteria. Generally the chiefs of Department of Defense and joint agencies have indicated a preference for graduates of the joint college while those in the service departments either show no preference or favor graduates of the service's own War College. Likewise we find that the prestige of the schools among officers who have not attended any of them is high.

By and large the testimony of graduates runs along the same lines. Although we have heard criticism of specific details of the programs, we find that graduates give the schools a very good rating. An Army officer, graduated from the National War College and serving as lieutenant governor of the Panama Canal Zone government, for example, writes: "The National War College was a perfect background of training for the political-sociological-economic job that I inherited down here. Such things as labor relations, employee relations, public relations, property appraisals, corporate accounting, diplomatic protocol, maritime law, the whole field of public education—these are the subjects that give us the greatest headaches. While the National War College is not a specific for any one of these, the broad background of the . . . curriculum enables one to start digging from a firm foundation." This officer suggests the value of subject matter content. A Naval officer graduate, on the other hand, points to the less tangible but equally significant interservice and interpersonal relationships developed at the college. He writes: "My new job . . . with SHAPE has led into some strange and interesting alleys, . . . [including] my association with the NATO council and international staff in connection with the . . . NATO Annual Review. I can truthfully say that my two years at the National War College, first as a student and then on the staff, were priceless in preparing me for the duties I have had over here. I was in attendance in Paris during the meeting of the ministers . . . and attended most of the sessions. Even more interesting were the sessions of the ministerial working group on Infrastructure. If you . . . think that a National War College Committee can be hairy, you should sit in on one of the ministerial working groups. Nothing at the College entirely prepared me for such an experience but without the War College background I would have indeed been a lost soul. . . . Certainly from my own experience the College experience has been extremely valuable."

Although we have substantial testimony of this sort from the graduates of all of the colleges, we felt the need for more systematic evidence of the performance of the senior joint and service colleges than could be obtained from random interviews and correspondence. Accordingly we administered a questionnaire to officers holding jobs for which the schools are designed to provide preparation in selected organizations in the Department of Defense, the Joint Staff, and in the headquarters of the three services. The questionnaire was given to all officers, whether they had attended one or more of the senior schools or not. Generally speaking, analysis of the responses to the questionnaire confirmed our judgment that the schools are regarded with satisfaction and respect by graduates and nongraduates alike.[1]

Thus the testimony of individuals who are acquainted with the colleges and their graduates, as well as of the graduates themselves, indicates that they are indeed serving an indispensable function and that they are achieving their challenging objectives to a substantial degree. Although attendance is not necessarily followed immediately by planning and policy level assignments, graduates are more and more in demand for this type of duty and an increasing number are serving in key positions in the Pentagon, on high level joint and combined staffs, and in a variety of other positions closely related to the formulation of national security policy. Experience indicates that the colleges do increase the effectiveness with which the graduates perform these subsequent duties. They have been exposed to a wealth of factual informa-

[1] Copies of the questionnaire and reports analyzing the responses are on deposit in the libraries of Dartmouth College, the Air University, the National War College, the Army War College, and the Naval War College.

tion concerning the operations and problems of their own services, of other services, and of civilian agencies of government. Of more importance, they have had an opportunity to gain a new appreciation of the complexities of the problems with which they deal. Many of the students enter the colleges as specialists with outstanding records, but with relatively little experience in broader areas of planning. They gain an appreciation of the wide range of domestic and external factors that must be considered in the process of formulating policy, and of the relationship between one policy problem and another. With this sort of understanding, hasty and narrowly based decisions should give way to more sober and reflective judgment.

In many respects the joint and service War Colleges operate at a level of performance far above the usual civilian college or university. The students are mature and experienced individuals; they gain much from association with each other. Moreover these institutions command rich resources. The services provided by administrative and library staffs appear luxurious to a college professor used to much improvisation. The facilities leave little to be desired. The substantive courses of instruction include a number of outstanding features. The curricula are designed with great care and attention to the needs of the military services. The organization and content of the programs are subjected to constant scrutiny by students, staff, and outside parties and are revised annually to satisfy changing demands. Particular effort has been made to integrate the different topics into a logical and meaningful whole. Instructional directives, reading lists, and memoranda are prepared in meticulous detail. Much more time and effort is expended on planning and administering the program than is possible at a civilian institution. The colleges, moreover, turn constantly to outside consultants. The Air War College has developed the practice of sending several members of its faculty for short visits to the University of Chicago, Columbia University, and other civilian institutions to meet with instructors and to discuss international relations study programs. Probably no other educational institutions seek as much outside help and advice. In part this arises from the rotation of the military faculties and their relative inexperience in educational matters. But it also results from a genuine desire to improve performance by obtaining competent guidance and judgment. The colleges generally take the recommendations of these visitors seriously.

In other respects these military colleges offer features that are not matched elsewhere. The lecture programs, particularly at the National War College, are unequaled anywhere. Probably no other institutions can command the services of so many of the individuals who appear regularly on the platforms of these colleges. The field trips of several of the colleges, again particularly the overseas trips of the National War College, provide unusual opportunities.

An Appraisal of the Curricula

Thus the military services have provided amply for the conduct of these joint and service colleges. But what about the actual substance of the academic programs? In the pages that follow we comment on certain aspects of the curricula. We realize the temerity of this, understanding full well that the colleges continually are subjected to pressure to *add* to their programs, with scarcely a suggestion that anything be dropped. But the comments that follow call not for the addition of new topics, but rather a shift of the emphasis upon, or a different interpretation of, existing topics.

STRATEGIC CONCEPTS

In the last chapter we noted that the National War College and the service War Colleges all approach the study of military operations in a broad context involving political, economic, scientific, social, and other considerations. There remains the task of evaluating the strategic doctrines and concepts presented at the colleges. Our observations, supported by testimony of many others, including students and graduates, indicates that there is a striking difference in the concepts developed at each of these institutions. This is not surprising in the light of the essentially different character of each. The service War Colleges emphasize by design the doctrines of their own services. This is to be expected. Each one concentrates on the preparation of its officers in the operations of his own service, including those with which he has had no previous experience, so that in future assignments, including those of a joint character, he will be well grounded in its capabilities and limitations. For if *he* is not prepared, as the authorities at these colleges point out, who will be? The emphasis upon the single service, however, carries beyond operations to fundamental doctrines and concepts, and here is where the differences become significant.

The characteristic differences in the presentation of strategic concepts are closely related to the responses of the colleges to the impact of technological developments and particularly to nuclear warfare. From the standpoint of this study, it is significant that these responses were not the result of new ideas generated at the colleges themselves, but rather of the impingement upon them of issues pointed up by debate within the responsible planning and operating agencies of the armed forces and the government at large. Concepts such as "deterrent force," "graduated deterrence," "limited war," and "peripheral war" have become a part of the strategic planner's lexicon. The colleges did not anticipate this debate, as might be expected of institutions of higher learning. Characteristically the concepts encountered at each of them are those which are identified with the parent service.

Thus the Army War College, as one would expect, has gone the furthest in accepting the strategic concept of limited war. As one member of the faculty put it, "Everyone here knows that a global war no longer has the promise of the political profit it has held in the past, so we ought to think more in terms of the limited variety." The Air War College, on the other hand, while investigating the possibilities of limited war, devotes most attention to the offensive employment of strategic air power and to operations of global dimensions. The Naval War College, recognizing the development of a strategic bombing capability of its own, appears to be closer in doctrine to the Air Force than to the Army, although it recognizes the validity of concepts involving limited use of force. After all, the Navy has been involved in this sort of action—although for different reasons—at intervals since its birth during the undeclared war with France in the 1790's.[2]

We agree that each of the service War Colleges should be concerned with the responsibilities, operations, and doctrines of its parent service. Yet we conclude that the heavy emphasis upon

---

[2] We wish to emphasize that none of the colleges presents an official "school solution" with respect to strategic doctrine. Our conclusions are based upon our impressions of the sum total of instruction.

the strategic concepts of that service has been carried too far and that the differences exhibited at the colleges in this respect may contribute to serious interservice rivalries. The reports of competent observers make it clear that in spite of progress toward integration of the armed forces since enactment of the national security act of 1946, these rivalries remain. They are not mere disputes over allocation of budget dollars or the capabilities of particular weapons; they stem from fundamental conflict over basic strategic concepts, including the appropriate employment of force and the very nature of modern warfare. If continued, they may threaten the national security of the United States.[3]

We feel that the War Colleges should serve to diminish rather than to exacerbate this situation. Their graduates, rather than being indoctrinated in the latest strategic concept of the service, should be exposed to the widest possible appreciation of the concepts of all services so that they may participate in the formulation of appropriate *national* rather than merely service policies.

The situation at the National War College is different. It is a joint institution, with additional civilian participation. Because of the composition of its faculty and student body it is virtually impossible for it to present a narrow, unbalanced strategic concept, "slanted" toward any one service. The college contributes much to the cultivation of an appreciation of the other services by each of its students. Unfortunately, however, the evidence suggests that the college does not accomplish as much as one might hope for toward the development of independent strategic concepts. In a special study of the National War College, the Human Resources Research Office of the George Washington University concluded that in discussion of problems of an interservice nature students avoided a frank and candid consideration of basic differences rather than provoke disagreeable arguments.[4]

NATIONAL AND INTERNATIONAL AFFAIRS

We turn next to the area of national and international affairs. We already have seen that each of the colleges, with the exception

[3] See, for example, the articles in the *New York Times* by Anthony Leviero, May 19, 20, 21, 1956, and by James Reston, May 23, 1956.
[4] Human Resources Research Office, George Washington University, Technical Report No. 10, "Committee Problem-Solving Techniques at the National War College," Washington, September 1954.

of the naval warfare I course at the Naval War College, devotes a considerable portion of the curriculum to the specific study of these matters. What is the nature and quality of this instruction? The individual with academic teaching experience looking over the curriculum of one of these institutions is impressed by the tremendous range of topics covered and the relatively short time devoted to each. His reaction usually is that the program must be superficial, that it can hardly be otherwise. He feels that no topic is really covered adequately and the "take away" value of the experience must be limited. Many students have complained about the programs along these lines. These officers had looked upon the year at a senior college as an opportunity to do certain things they long had been eager to do, to reflect on past experiences, to explore new areas, and to formulate ideas on the problems facing the services and the country. They anticipated a minimum of routine. Instead they found that the programs were crowded, with tight schedules. They salvaged relatively little opportunity for the relaxed study that they had looked forward to.

These comments pose a dilemma familiar to any professional educator. What is the approach? How can the student best be educated: by extending the range of his knowledge, or by developing to a greater degree his understanding of certain selected areas? Those who speak for the colleges do not deny that their coverage is indeed very extensive and that the schedules are tight. They agree that they give a "broad brush" treatment to most topics, and that they skip lightly over many complex problems. This is a charge with which they are familiar, and they almost uniformly meet it in the same way. They point out that the colleges are not designed to produce accomplished experts in any one field, military as well as nonmilitary. Such is not their responsibility. Rather they emphasize the nature of the situation faced by the officer as he moves into positions of greater responsibility bearing upon the formulation of national policy. He must have a knowledge of the full range of factors involved in a decision. The military strategist at the level of the Joint Staff, for example, must have an appreciation of foreign and domestic politics, financial implications, technological developments, problems of mobilization, and supply. He must comprehend what is feasible as well as what is desirable. In particular he must understand the relation of each of these factors to the military planning process viewed as a unity, as a single seamless web. In other words he must think in terms of large relationships and endless complex ramifications.

The purpose of the senior college, the authorities at these institutions declare, is to stimulate an attitude rather than to load the individual with facts on a few problems. It is to show the officer the realities of the policy-making process, to give him an awareness of all relevant factors, a concern for their implications, and an appreciation of the responsibilities of other individuals and agencies. An officer grows up faced with the task of completing specific assignments according to specific directives. His directives are firm, his objective fixed. Success is measured in tangible qualities. The military schools that he attends as a younger officer, including the Command and Staff Schools, train him to perform these tasks effectively, but emphasize standard doctrine and procedures. But when he comes to one of the senior schools he is being prepared for a different set of requirements. Directives tend to become ill defined and even vague. Objectives are sometimes blurred. And there is no immediate and tangible measure of success.

The problem then, according to this explanation, is to expose the student to the full range of these factors. The purpose is not to give him a thorough knowledge of any one of them, but enough of an understanding to make him aware of their existence and their general nature and implications. The authorities suggest that the officer is not being prepared for a job in the Department of State. Moreover they reveal a latent fear that too much sensitivity to nonmilitary factors may not be desirable, that it may damage the main purpose of the officer's career, the cultivation of his qualities as a trained fighting man, upon whom the nation must depend for its ultimate survival when all the chips are down. Consequently, they load the curriculum with heavy doses of military subjects that they insist the officers must know. The net effect is to widen even further the broad coverage of the curriculum.

In this context the charge of superficiality takes on a different light. Clearly the task of the colleges is not to prepare experts, but to facilitate the growth of specialists into generalists. "A little of everything" is precisely what is wanted by the colleges because the problem is to sensitize the individual to the wide range of considerations relevant to his future responsibilities. The testimony of others and our own observations indicate that students do develop a meaningful awareness of the range of factors involved in making decisions about national security. It is possible to watch this happen to individual students. Frequently an officer, during the early weeks, will become frustrated by the program. He is troubled when lecturers fail to give clear, precise solutions, and by the discovery that there are no easy answers to the problems posed in committees. He wonders why the Department of State cannot spell out in detail just what it will do if certain events take place. But slowly he comes to realize that he is dealing with a vast complex of variables, that there are situations where precise operational plans would be worse than useless, and that there is sometimes virtue in living with problems rather than trying to solve them. He even comes to understand that military decisions frequently are just as complex. As one Naval officer at the National War College jokingly exclaimed following his graduation ceremony, "What we need now is to be reindoctrinated in absolutes!"

Some might raise the question whether the colleges are producing a situation where a little knowledge is worse than no knowledge at all. Is it not possible, they might ask, that some graduates, having been exposed to information on a variety of subjects new to them, will jump to the conclusion that they have become experts on all of them? Certainly this is always a risk, but we believe that it is one that must be taken. Moreover we have no evidence that it is so. Perhaps there are officers who act as though they are experts on foreign affairs, for example. But we have no reason to conclude that one of the senior military schools made them this way. On the contrary, our evidence suggests that the experience at one of these schools is more likely to give the officer an insight into his own limitations than to make him feel that he has all the answers.

If the purpose of the colleges is to give the officer a sense of "awareness" of the broad range of considerations involved in the formulation of national policy, then it may be said that they achieve their goal. The development of this critical awareness in itself is a significant contribution to the preparation of officers for policy level assignments. We have concluded, however, that the colleges should make a greater effort to go beyond this achievement, placing more emphasis upon intellectual rigor and discipline. We shall discuss this matter later on in this chapter. Before doing so, however, we shall comment on a number of specific areas of study in the curricula of the colleges.

In the last chapter we observed that all of the colleges devote major attention to the Soviet threat, within the context of a global power struggle. While recognizing the central importance of the conflict with the Soviet Union in the formulation of security policies for the United States, we feel that the colleges overemphasize this conflict. It is our conviction that even without the Soviet Union the United States still would be faced with serious situations arising in other parts of the world. The impact of modern technology and of large scale population growth upon economically underdeveloped areas, the breakup of the old colonial system, and the conflict of ideas around the globe present a series of unresolved problems that, although aggravated by Soviet policies and actions, exist independently of the Soviet Union. In an era of cold war or coexistence, moreover, the relationship of the United States to the Soviet Union may be affected as much by the direction of developments outside of the Soviet Union, particularly within China and the underdeveloped areas, as by developments within that country.

The colleges might well devote more attention to this dimension in international affairs. The 1955 Board of Consultants of the National War College, for example, expressed the hope that the college would "lessen the stress on the bi-polar nature of the world and upon the sense of the inevitability of conflict," and would examine why some nations remain uncommitted and the part that these uncommitted nations play on the world scene. We do not suggest that the colleges should spend more time on the study of particular countries or regions. We do suggest that consideration be given to analysis of underlying factors affecting the relationship of the underdeveloped to the developed parts of the world, and to basic trends and attitudes in these respective areas, particularly in China, India, and other parts of Asia.

Likewise the colleges might give more attention to the relationship of the attitudes and policies of other peoples to the formulation and execution of American policies. In spite of the time devoted to foreign area studies, there appears to be a tendency to view policy problems unilaterally. At the National War College, for example, the Board of Consultants in 1953, reiterating a point made previously in 1950, suggested that more systematic effort be made to view the world from the vantage point of other countries. More recently a special survey board on the National War and Industrial Colleges proposed that more attention be given to the "combined," i.e. international, aspects of strategic planning. We feel, moreover, that the colleges do not give sufficient study to international organization and to the peaceful resolution of international conflict. At none of the colleges, including the National War College, has serious thought been given to the problems of the regulation of armaments. Only the National War College and the Army War College plan field trips to the United Nations headquarters or give more than minor notice to the UN in the curriculum.[5]

We wonder whether, in their preoccupation with the Soviet threat and the means of dealing with it, the colleges concern themselves sufficiently with an understanding of the ideals and practices underlying American society. Earlier we noted that all of the colleges study the organization and mechanics of policy formulation. They fail, however, to give the same attention to the basic nature and characteristics of American democracy, to its historical, ethical, spiritual, philosophical, or psychological roots. We find no curriculum topics covering such fundamental issues as the relationship of individual rights to the authority of the state in the context of American ideals and experience, or the maintenance of laws and institutions to safeguard these rights, or the peculiar problems for a democratic society raised by a high level of military mobilization in peacetime. We have failed to observe frank and penetrating discussion of the tension points in American society.

There is one aspect of democratic practice for which the colleges do express considerable concern. This is the relationship of public opinion to foreign and security policies. The National War College and Army War College have scheduled one or more lectures on this topic and have selected prominent journalists or well-

[5] The Naval War College is planning a UN trip for the foreign officers course but not for its regular students.

380

known public opinion analysts to deliver these lectures. Discussion groups that we have observed have suggested that the students are deeply interested in the problems of formulating and executing national policy in a democratic society. But it has been our experience that this concern arises primarily from a feeling that special interests or pressure groups frequently stand in the way of proper action by the government, or a feeling that the public at large is apathetic, failing to approve programs of obvious necessity. This reflects a sense of frustration in dealing with the public on policy issues. It does not appear to extend to a questioning of democratic ideals and practices. Yet we feel that the colleges might examine more thoroughly these ideals and practices in the context of today's issues, if officers are going to furnish the sort of creative service that we suggest in chapter two.

None of the colleges, with the exception of the Air War College, attempt to provide the student with a sense of historical perspective. In the last chapter we noted that they concentrate largely upon the current scene. There appears to be relatively little interest in probing into background developments. Rather the faculty and the students alike persistently demand the latest "top secret" information in the seeming belief that it is more important to have the latest detailed report than a firm understanding of historical and other conditioning factors in a situation. They are most interested in the operational aspects of policy issues, the problems facing the fellow with the responsibility of getting the job done. A majority of the lecturers brought to the colleges, for example, are actual operators, fresh from their desks, talking about their latest problems, if not in their formal lectures, certainly in the after-lecture conferences that are commonly scheduled. This approach is reinforced by pressures from outside of the colleges, i.e. from their respective services, to include instruction on current developments.

The consequence of this is an absence of concern for the historical and theoretical aspects of security problems. It might be said that the "level of abstraction" is not high. There appear to be few attempts to investigate or formulate theoretical propositions about the nature of the international community and the underlying factors motivating national political behavior. This approach seems to be avoided for fear that the programs will become too "academic." This situation was particularly apparent a few years ago at the National War College when a definite effort was made to make the curriculum more "practical" by getting away from the courses on international politics and economics that had been designed initially by the civilian faculty, and substituting the National Security Council "staff paper" approach that is now employed.

This shying away from a theoretical grounding presents a special problem in the study of economics. All of the War Colleges devote considerable attention to problems of an economic nature, in recognition of the interdependence of economic, military, and political issues. But the emphasis is largely upon planning and use of resources, without attention, except in the new naval warfare II course at Newport, to systematic presentation of the principal concepts and methods of inquiry of economics. Security policies cannot be properly formulated without constant evaluation of their economic components and consequences. Moreover an understanding of domestic economic problems is frequently essential to a full comprehension of international political and military problems. Some understanding of the tools of measurement and methods of analysis of economics can facilitate assimilation of the economic factors. The instruction in the elements of economics and the economics of national security at West Point gives the cadet this understanding. But the present generation of officers at the War Colleges, including the graduates of the Military Academy, have not had the advantage of these courses, and even if they had, fresh study and consideration of recent developments would be appropriate. Accordingly we suggest that all of the War Colleges might employ the pattern for study of economics recently developed at the Naval War College in the new second year course.[6]

One observer once remarked that these military schools were preoccupied with a "stockpile" approach to the study of international affairs. He meant that they thought in terms of "counting, piling, and storing." We feel that this comment is exaggerated, but

[6] For further suggestions along this line see the stimulating article by Klaus Knorr, "Economics and International Relations: A Problem in Teaching," *Political Science Quarterly*, December 1947, p. 552.

it does properly suggest the emphasis that is placed upon geography, natural resources, industrial development, manpower, and political administrative organizations, things which are more or less measurable in determining national "capabilities." Considerably less attention is given to the intangible topics that relate to "intentions" and to the implications of cultural interactions. This is reflected in the selection of speakers. The greatest use is made of government officials who are qualified by their positions to discuss current political and economic developments. Among academic speakers, political scientists and economists appear most frequently. Only an occasional psychologist, sociologist, or anthropologist is used.

We do not wish to suggest that the War Colleges employ only a materialistic approach in their studies of international affairs. They do make some attempt to investigate the motivations of national behavior. But in terms of time, special qualification of speakers, and readings, this aspect of international affairs receives relatively slight attention.

SCIENTIFIC RESEARCH AND DEVELOPMENT

This discussion indicates that the joint and service colleges give clear recognition to the necessity of examining critically all doctrine, organization, and practice in the light of technological change. The question remains, however, to what extent they give the students a full appreciation of what might be called the "scientific dimension." In chapter two we suggested that the general line officer assigned to policy levels needed insight into the relationship of scientific research and development to strategic planning. Since the joint and service colleges prepare officers for assignment to strategic planning and related activities it is pertinent to examine their instructional programs in this area. Before doing so, we should point out again that it is not the function of these institutions to provide scientific specialist training for professional officers. This is accomplished largely through the assignment of officers to civilian institutions for graduate study and through special programs operated by the armed services themselves, such as those of the Air Force Institute of Technology at Wright-Patterson Field. We are not interested here in the training of specialists, but rather in the preparation of officers at policy levels for handling the scientific or technological factor in the course of their responsibilities.

The initial plans for the curriculum at the National War College appear to have been based upon a conviction that high level planners should be prepared to deal with problems of a scientific nature, such as the impact of new weapons. These plans were prepared during the first year after the atomic bombs were dropped on Hiroshima and Nagasaki and shortly after the tests at Bikini. The situation was explained by Admiral Hill, the first commandant, in testimony before a House committee several months before the opening of the institution. He said that the program would commence with lectures by scientists regarding the meaning of the new scientific age, and on how we must orient our thinking on industrial, political, and military matters. He explained that the college would not try to make mathematicians or scientists out of the students, "but we want to inform them in the development of scientific progress and inform them of what may be expected in the next four or five years." [7] Subsequently the definition of the scope of the program, as approved by the Joint Chiefs of Staff, indicated that it would include study of "the influence of the possession or deficiency of economic, *scientific,* political, and social resources upon the capability of waging war, and of the *impact of science and technology upon the armed forces.*" [8]

For the first three years the National War College program opened with a one week course on the atomic age. The next year this was moved to the second week. As designed in that year the course consisted of lectures on the atomic age, the impact of the atomic bomb on warfare, the magnitude of atomic bomb development, international control of atomic energy, and the United States Atomic Energy Commission. The following year this was dropped as a separate course. The purpose in scheduling the course early in the year had been to dramatize the impact of atomic developments on human affairs. After four years it was felt that this emphasis no longer was required, since the implications of the

[7] House of Representatives, 79th Congress, 2d Session, Subcommittee of Committee on Appropriations, *Hearings on Military Establishment Appropriation Bill,* May 28, 1946, p. 823.

[8] Italics added.

atomic age were fully recognized by mature officers. During this period attention also was devoted to technological developments in connection with discussion of other new weapons.

More recently at the National War College direct attention to science and technology has been associated with consideration of the latest developments in weapon systems. Separate lectures are given on nuclear energy and classic doctrine, nuclear politics (political blackmail and bribes), nuclear electronics, science and technology, uses and effects of nuclear energy, and weapon systems. It appears, however, that these topics are largely descriptive and relate to the technical employment of weapons, rather than to the sort of analytical approach that Admiral Hill had in mind in 1946.

The Army War College curriculum places heavy emphasis on technology as it relates to the functions and operations of the Army, and also to the Army's research and development programs. The part that deals with the Army opens with an orientation course in which about a third of the lectures deal with the impact of technological developments. The lectures treat such topics as the effect of current and projected nuclear and conventional weapons on Army strategic, tactical, and logistic concepts, the role of military power in the era of mass destruction, the Army's research and development program, and combat developments and operations research. The course concludes with a panel discussion of the effect of nuclear warfare upon ground forces.

In subsequent courses the impact of new developments is considered. In the course on logistics, for example, there are lectures on the vulnerability of theater logistic operations in atomic warfare, and on the impact of atomic warfare on medical services. One of the committee problems deals with the impact of atomic and chemical warfare upon theater logistic operations. The first week of the course on Army operations is devoted to special instruction in technical developments affecting the conduct of future warfare, presented by teams from the Armed Forces Special Weapons Program and other special projects, and from the Office of the Chief Chemical Officer, and by an engineer from a leading aircraft manufacturing company. The course includes several lectures dealing with weapons developments, and a committee study on the impact of new weapons on land warfare. The war planning courses also get into this field, particularly in the presentations by teams from the Naval and Air War Colleges on concepts of future warfare.

Although technological developments are scarcely ever absent from discussion of plans for the employment of armed forces, the Naval and Air War Colleges do not single out this field for such extensive treatment as does the Army War College. At Newport students in naval warfare i and ii take a four day orientation course on nuclear weapons, covering the capabilities and limitations of available and projected weapons, employment techniques, and passive defense measures. Naval warfare i considers the latest weapons developments in the Army and Air Force as well as the Navy. Naval warfare ii includes no other separate treatment of the scientific factor in strategic planning. The Air War College devotes considerably less attention to scientific research and development as such than one might expect of a service in which this field is of primary significance. During the first years at the college there was a separate course on technology as applied to military operations. This is no longer given, and its subject matter is integrated into other courses.

This brief review indicates that the students at all of the senior colleges are exposed to a great deal of information on technological developments in the weapons field. They are given considerable information that would be of great value to the strategic planner as well as the commander in the field employing these new weapons. They consider the impact of such developments upon tactical and strategic concepts and doctrines. At each of the colleges the faculty is responsible for obtaining current information on research and development projects in the services. At the Naval War College a small section of the staff is designated for this specific purpose. It should also be pointed out that at all of the colleges, and particularly the Air War College, many of the students have had specific training and assignments in the development field. But except for the Army War College, the colleges do not study the specific role of research and development, or the broader implications of technological change as they bear upon strategic planning.

Vannevar Bush, more than any other individual, has been concerned about the relationship of the scientist and the soldier. At one time he recommended that the idea of the National War

College should be extended to include "an advanced military college devoted to the evolution of weapons and its relation to strategy." [9] We do not agree with the notion of a separate school. But we do suggest that a somewhat different approach to consideration of science and technology at the existing schools might be made. We feel that some sacrifice could be made in the detailed study of weapons developments in order to give greater attention to broader aspects of the relationship of research and development to national security problems and plans. Particularly we see need for examination of the delicate question of the relationship of the professional military officer to the scientist and to theoretical research. While officers should have more knowledge of scientific principles and developments, they must recognize their own limitations and the expert role of the civilian scientist. The objective here is a relationship wherein the officer, as the expert on military applications, can communicate his needs to the scientist and in return can adjust with flexibility to new scientific developments. We question whether sufficient attention is given to this relationship at the colleges. We note, for example, that the special board established by the Joint Chiefs in 1954 to survey the National War College and the Industrial College concluded that more emphasis at these schools should be placed upon scientific and technological factors.[10]

STRATEGIC INTELLIGENCE

Strategic planning can be no better than the intelligence upon which it is based.[11] During and since world war II it has been recognized generally that the intelligence services of the armed forces have suffered because many officers have frowned upon intelligence assignments as harmful to career advancement. During this period much has been done to improve the situation. At the tactical level, operational methods and training techniques and

---

9 House of Representatives, 78th Congress, 2d Session, Select Committee on Postwar Military Policy, 26 January 1945, p. 237.

10 *Report to the Joint Chiefs of Staff of the National War College and the Industrial College of the Armed Forces Survey Board*, Washington, 1955, p. 9.

11 The *Dictionary of United States Military Terms for Joint Usage* defines intelligence as "The product resulting from the collection, evaluation, analysis, integration, and interpretation of all available information which concerns one or more aspects of foreign nations or of areas of operations, and which is immediately or potentially significant to planning."

facilities have been extended and perfected. At the strategic level, among other advances, there has been the establishment of the Central Intelligence Agency, a central fact-finding and coordinating body composed of civilians and military personnel. It will be recalled that the Army's Gerow Plan for postwar military education called for a joint Intelligence College as one of the five constituent units of the proposed National Security University, "to insure effective overall organization and operation of intelligence and counterintelligence." [12] This college was never established, however. The Army does now operate in Washington an intelligence training program in which the Air Force participates, but this is concerned with preparing military attachés and officers assigned to other intelligence functions. The Navy has a similar training program.

All of the senior colleges give some attention to strategic intelligence. The National War College usually has devoted a full day to intelligence as an element of national power. The 1954–1955 topic, for example, included a lecture by the director of the Joint Intelligence Group of the Joint Staff. Some of the questions suggested for investigation in the course outline were: How can we insure against a recurrence of a disaster similar to that of Pearl Harbor? Do we make adequate use of the potential advantages of intelligence? Is the United States maintaining too many intelligence organizations? The Army War College concerns itself more directly with the intelligence responsibilities of the Army. The course on operations and intelligence includes lectures by the chief of Army intelligence and his deputy on the G-2's problems and on theater intelligence problems. One of the committee problems in this course is on theater intelligence. The Army War College schedules a lecture on the organization of the intelligence community at the strategic level in its course on national policy formulation. At the Air War College a similar lecture is given in connection with the study of military tasks and resources management. Other lectures deal with intelligence in connection with military operations, such as one on the problems of obtaining information on enemy capabilities and intentions within the Euro-

---

[12] *Report of War Department Military Education Board on Educational System for Officers of the Army,* Washington, April 1946.

pean theater. At the Naval War College interest in intelligence problems is also at the operational level.

It appears that study of the full relationship of intelligence to security planning is neglected at the War Colleges. The students are exposed to descriptions of current organization and problems and methods of operation, but this is about as far as they go. There appears to be no attempt to get into the much more complex and difficult matter of evaluating intelligence evidence, developing rigorous, logical methods of analytical interpretation of sources and of data, and thinking systematically about intelligence matters. There is no study of classic historical examples of erroneous intelligence estimates, or investigation of the kinds of reasons why faulty estimates are made, such as the preconceptions and stereotype concepts in the mind of every human that distort the image of reality. We hasten to add, however, that this problem is not unique to the joint and service colleges, nor is it confined to this country. We found, for example, similar criticism of British practices in a paper by a scientist who served with the Intelligence Branch of the Air Ministry. He declares that while intelligence was of great significance in the war, it was rarely discussed and understood. ". . . As a result, while much thought has been given to the principles of strategy and while penetrating treatises have been written on the subject, a coherent philosophy or doctrine of intelligence has so far failed to develop." [13]

In the evaluation of the substance of instruction at the senior colleges one matter remains. The commandants and faculties recognize that while the principal function of the colleges is to prepare senior officers for high command and staff assignments, they also should participate in the development of new ideas and doctrines. As mature and experienced officers, with high potentialities for advancement and greater responsibility, the students ought to be free to challenge existing assumptions and raise basic questions, and they ought to let their minds range freely over all problems of security policy. Thus the colleges place great em-

[13] Dr. R. V. Jones (presently professor of physics, Aberdeen University), *Journal of the Royal United Services Institute*, August 1947, pp. 352–369. We are indebted to Mr. Saville Davis of the *Christian Science Monitor* for calling our attention to this article.

phasis upon freedom of thought and upon lack of any sort of school solution or party line.

Although we hesitate to judge the extent to which the colleges are fulfilling this goal, we feel that we can make some comments. We find, for example, that the authorities of the colleges go out of their way to reiterate to their students and to visitors that absolute freedom of thought and expression prevails. The rule that all remarks are completely off the record is observed scrupulously to facilitate this freedom. Students are asked repeatedly to challenge assumptions and existing doctrines, and visiting speakers are told to expect stiff questioning. There is no doubt that the colleges genuinely strive to cultivate the greatest possible freedom of thought among their students. Yet we conclude that while absolute freedom exists in a technical sense, certain circumstances tend to limit its actual exercise and to impose upon these institutions a pattern of conformity. There is an underlying and largely unexpressed conflict between the genuine desire for unlimited freedom of inquiry and expression and these circumstances.

In the first place the senior military colleges are publicly supported institutions. In a sense they have the same problems as state universities. But while they are spared the glaring publicity and the fishbowl quality of the state institutions, they are under closer scrutiny from their "regents" or "trustees," the command and staff agencies of the military services, which have a more direct professional knowledge of and interest in what they do. Moreover they are closely knit socially. The commandants are the peers, perhaps even classmates, of the chiefs of staff or office directors who are responsible for supervision of the colleges. By their own choice the colleges tend to remain intellectually close to prevailing thought in the services. They depend very largely upon the operators in the Pentagon and Department of State for lectures on military and foreign policy problems. They make almost a fetish of getting the very latest, most highly classified data on current problems and policies. And the colleges are administratively close to their parent services, because the future careers of students and faculty alike are directly controlled by the Pentagon. Under these circumstances we doubt that any War College in the years since the formulation of the Truman Doctrine and the Marshall Plan could have organized the curriculum on any premise other than the "cold war," or that the Industrial College, following the Korean conflict, could have organized its curriculum on any premise other than the "mobilization base." And if these premises should change at the Pentagon, is it not inevitable that they should change at the colleges?

The tendency to conform to a prevailing pattern of thought is manifested in a number of ways. The list of visiting speakers, while bringing a great deal of talent representative of various opinions in and out of official circles, seems to avoid individuals who might involve the colleges in public controversy. Very few representatives of organized labor appear. Certain attitudes of the students, moreover, tend to diminish controversy. In their committees and discussion groups, we are told, an officer looks upon the others as his peers, with recognition that he will probably be serving with these men in the future, and that some may be in important command positions. There develops among some students an unconscious reluctance to press for a position or view that runs contrary to the prevailing consensus. Positions are put forth rather cautiously; if too far out of line they are withdrawn or modified. Some officers, of course, persist in expressing a particular view. But frequently classmates become politely critical of the student who presses his opinions regularly. The sensitive officer, when he becomes aware of this feeling, tends to keep his views to himself. This tendency extends to the faculty. In the next assignment, as suggested above, the situation may be reversed and the officer now a student may have command over a present member of the faculty. Even the faculty members conform and avoid standing out. These tendencies are not peculiar to these military colleges. Unfortunately they are operative in higher education generally. Yet the cultivation of bold, independent, and imaginative thinking at these colleges is of the greatest importance if the security of the nation is to be advanced.

CHAPTER EIGHTEEN

THE INDUSTRIAL COLLEGE OF THE

ARMED FORCES

THE Industrial College of the Armed Forces, like the National War College, is a joint institution on the highest level in the educational system of the armed forces. It is located at Fort Mc-Nair in Washington adjacent to the National War College and in the past has utilized its neighbor's auditorium for its own program.[1] Although the Industrial College is similar to the National War College and the service War Colleges in many respects, its mission and curriculum are distinctive and deserve separate description and analysis.

Organization

In 1946 the Army Industrial College was reestablished as a joint institution, and subsequently was placed under the jurisdiction of the Joint Chiefs of Staff. It is headed by a commandant, normally a major general or rear admiral.[2] There are two deputy commandants, normally brigadier generals or rear admirals. These positions are rotated among the three services in such a manner that each is always represented. There is no position, such as exists at the National War College, for a civilian deputy. One military deputy is in charge of the Education Division, which administers the ten month resident course. The other is head of the Extension

---

[1] In 1956 Congress authorized a long-sought new building for the Industrial College.
[2] The commandants since the college was reconstituted as a joint institution have been Brigadier General Donald Armstrong, USA, Brigadier General Edward B. McKinley, USA, Major General Arthur W. Vanaman, USAF, Rear Admiral Wesley M. Hague, USN, and Major General Robert F. Hollis, USA.

Division, which administers both the national resources conferences and the correspondence course.[3]

The professional staff consists of about 56 persons. We are concerned, however, only with the professional staff of the Education Division. Its deputy commandant is assisted by a vice deputy and a civilian director of instruction. The remainder of the division consists of six branches, each responsible for a portion of the resident course. From 35 to 40 faculty members are assigned to these branches. About 11 are civilians. Each branch normally contains officers of all three services and one or two civilians. The ranking officer in the branch is frequently appointed branch chief. This is not usually done when he is a new member of the faculty. No civilian has served as branch chief since 1949. The branch chiefs, the director of instruction, and the vice deputy constitute a faculty board that advises the deputy for education on curricular matters.

Nearly all officers on the faculty hold the grade of colonel or its equivalent. About one half have devoted their careers to supply, technical, or administrative fields. The others have had line or command careers. The average age is 46. A majority are graduates of the college. Most of those who are not have attended a War College. About one third have master's degrees. The average turnover rate in the division is 40 to 50 percent each year. Tours range from a few months to as long as four years.[4] Continuity is preserved only by overlapping tours and by the presence of a nucleus of permanent civilians. Most of the civilians came to the college from government agencies in the 1940's and initially were

[3] A desire to educate more personnel than a resident course could reach was expressed as early as 1923. But the national resources conferences did not start until 1947. These are held annually in about 16 major cities for reserve and National Guard officers, industrialists, and prominent citizens. Local military commands and civic organizations provide joint sponsorship. Instruction is given by teams of six officers supplied by the Industrial College. Each conference is attended by a maximum of 170 officers and roughly the same number of civilians. Thus several thousand individuals are reached each year. From a public relations standpoint the conferences serve somewhat the same purpose as the strategy seminars of the War Colleges. The correspondence course is available to selected regular, reserve, and National Guard officers, on both active and inactive duty, and to selected civilian officials and private citizens. It is based on 22 texts, each of about 100 pages, prepared by the college staff. Several thousand officers have taken the course.

[4] One year the Education Division began its work with a new deputy commandant and new chiefs in each branch. The turnover rate among Naval officers has averaged from 50 to 100 percent a year.

employed to participate in its research division. When this division was abolished they were transferred to the faculty. In a typical recent year, of the 11 civilians in the teaching branches, 6 had had earlier experience in industry, 4 in university teaching, 1 in the Foreign Service. Three had made substantial contributions to scholarship in addition to their work on college publications. Four had doctor's and three had master's degrees. Their civil service grades ranged from GS 12 to GS 15. The average age was 56.

The class at the Industrial College consists of about 145 students, with the following quotas: 40 Army, 40 Air Force, 35 Navy, 6 Marine Corps, 24 civilians. Age, rank, and years of service criteria are the same as for the National War College. About three out of four hold the grade of colonel or its equivalent. The others are lieutenant colonels or commanders. The Navy sends a larger proportion of the more junior officers.[5] The Air Force sends only full colonels. Most students are in the early forties, a trifle younger as a group than National War College students. In the case of Army students, high-ranking officials concerned with supply, such as the assistant or under secretary of the Army, frequently have maintained an interest in selections for the college. The proportion of graduates achieving flag or general officer rank, while not negligible, is only about one seventh as great as at the National War College.[6] One reason for the difference is that officers of the combat arms, line officers, and rated pilots, who tend to fare best in promotions, rarely constitute more than half of the college's student body. The Navy, Air Force, and Marine Corps, however, send a much higher proportion of such personnel than the Army, which reserves from 80 to 85 percent of its quota for the technical and administrative services.[7] In a typical recent year nearly a third of all officer students held advanced civilian degrees. These included 23 master's degrees, 3 Ph.D.'s, 2 LL.B.'s, 2 M.D.'s. There

[5] From 1949 to 1954 the Navy sent 64 commanders to the Industrial College, none to the National War College.

[6] A study of the classes between 1947 and 1954 revealed that 60 officers, or about 6 percent of all military students, had achieved flag or general officer rank by the autumn of 1954. The promotion rate was highest in the case of Army students, lowest in the case of Naval students.

[7] In 1948 the Bureau of Naval Personnel wanted to send *only* staff corps officers but it was overruled by the under secretary. The Navy does, however, tend to send line officers who fall into a semitechnical category, that is, they have done advanced work in ordnance or engineering without having become specialists.

are also one or two dozen officers in each class who have not completed an undergraduate education.

Civilian students have been admitted to the resident course since 1949. With some opposition from the services the college gradually increased the quota from 5 to 24. The size of the auditorium long placed an upper limit on the number of civilians that could be accommodated without decreasing military quotas. Whenever the civilian quota is not entirely filled, the vacancies may revert to the services. This has not occurred in recent years. Components of the Defense Department now supply the largest number of the civilian students. Others have come from State, the Atomic Energy Commission, the Office of Defense Mobilization, the Bureau of the Budget, Central Intelligence, the National Security Agency, Treasury, Commerce, Labor, Agriculture, and the General Services Administration. All are required to have status and experience comparable to that of the military students. The commandant is authorized to reject any nominee whose credentials are unsatisfactory, an authority he does not enjoy in the case of military students.

Civilian students ordinarily return to their parent agency after completing the course. About four fifths of the officers return to their parent service. The others are assigned to a joint or combined headquarters, to a civilian agency, or to the staff of the college. Of those who return to their parent service about one fifth are immediately assigned to duty at the General Staff level in Washington.

In the fiscal year 1955 the cost of operating the resident course, including pay and allowances of military faculty, was $745,000. The cost per student was $5,600. An additional $580,000 was required for the extension programs. In 1956 the college finally was authorized to request funds for a large, modern building that will face the National War College from across the golf course at Fort McNair. This will provide offices, classrooms, library space, and an auditorium with a capacity of 556. The library is designed primarily for reference rather than research. It contains about 50,000 books and documents, plus classified items, relating primarily to the economic capabilities of the United States and other nations. Students enjoy access to the vast resources of other government libraries through an efficient loan service.

Methods of Instruction

The college operates five days a week; each day consists of four class periods of 90 minutes each. A fifth period is set aside for lunch and athletics. Class periods are assigned by weekly published schedule to lectures, discussion groups, seminars, or study. About 40 percent of all periods are reserved for study. In addition students are expected to work from 8 to 10 hours a week at their homes.

As at other senior colleges, many students in an important sense are also instructors. This follows from their wide experience in responsible positions. Each student is assigned a faculty associate who is available for advice throughout the course. Faculty members also assist student committees and discussion groups. They conduct research and prepare teaching materials. But a great deal of their energy is poured into the extraordinary administrative work required by the meticulously planned and organized program. The faculty also has commitments outside the college. Because the college is the only institution that specializes in the economics of warfare at the highest level, its staff members often lecture at other service schools and sometimes to business or professional groups.

Well over 200 lectures a year constitute the major method of presentation. The number is unusually high because students attend roughly *two out of every three* National War College lectures in addition to their own.[8] To a limited degree this means that they are taking both courses simultaneously. National War College students, on the other hand, attend very few Industrial College lectures. The number of lectures given by the faculty has declined steadily since 1950. The civilian staff delivers about a half dozen a year on substantive topics. The military staff delivers orientation lectures at the start of each unit of the course. Nongovernmental civilians, especially businessmen and college professors, appear on the platform most often. Leading civilian officials are the next largest category. They are followed by leading military officials.

[8] This practice dates from the 1920's when Army Industrial College students attended Army War College lectures.

Great reliance is also placed on the exchanges that take place in small groups containing representatives of all three services and of civilian agencies. Faculty members are expected to play only a subordinate role in such meetings. Designated students lead the discussion. An important variation on the discussion group is the seminar. Its distinctive feature is the presence of two or three visiting specialists. This technique is used to give students close and informal contact with military and civilian officials most of whom are at the "indian" level in national security agencies but some of whom are distinguished authorities in the field in question. As many as seven seminars may be scheduled in the same period. Each student attends the one directly related to the particular research he is required to do. He receives a form containing suggestions about topics that might be discussed and biographical data about the guests of the day. Additional seminars may be arranged if students feel a need for them. Individual conferences or interviews with outside specialists are also encouraged.

Each branch prepares formidable bibliographies for the units of the course that it administers. Some reading is designated "essential" for all students, and some is for groups working at special tasks. Altogether about 800 titles are listed. Rarely, however, is a whole book assigned; it is usually a matter of a few pages here and there. Students do much of their reading in their offices. The library is unattended by staff in the evening. The students go home to their families.

Each student makes at least one oral presentation of 12 to 15 minutes in length before the entire college. Although these presentations are distributed throughout the year, they take up a lot of time. Near the end of the course a few students also make one hour oral presentations before the commandant and his principal assistants. The most effective of these are then selected to appear before the assembled bodies and staffs of the National War College and the Industrial College. Distinguished guests are invited to this occasion and the presentations subsequently are published. Each student also is expected to complete a substantial term paper during the year, usually on a topic of his own choice. Each branch submits from 10 to 30 topics to facilitate choice. In addition each student prepares two written reports of about 10 or 15 pages.

In a typical recent year one of these had to deal with the area of requirements and logistic systems, the other with the area of production or procurement. A number of the individual reports are essentially descriptions of organizational or procedural problems, either current or historical. Faculty members rarely reject reports as unsatisfactory or require them to be rewritten. Outstanding reports are reproduced for wider circulation. Finally, each student is required to contribute to committee reports in certain units of the course in which he does not write an individual report.

The use of committees to analyze policy problems dates from the founding of the Army Industrial College. Committees may contain from 10 to 17 members representing the three services and civilian agencies. To insure active participation by all, each member has a specific task on which he must report back to the committee. A specific example may be illuminating. In a recent year the class was divided into committees each of which had to compare the economic capacity of the free world and the Soviet bloc to support a general war. The committees spent two days organizing and orienting themselves. Individual members were then assigned to study the economic potential of a particular area of the free world or the Soviet bloc. To do this they joined forces with members of other committees assigned to the same area. Thus, for example, a Middle East research unit was created with representatives from each committee. The unit organized its work so that each member made a special study of one component of economic strength (industrial plant, manpower, and so forth) in the Middle East. Each such "specialist" reported his findings orally to the entire unit. In the end, therefore, all members of the Middle East unit had at least a minimum knowledge of all components of economic potential in that area. During this period the entire class received about 13 lectures on economic potential. It also heard testimony from experts in seminars. From two to four seminars were held for each research unit.

With this background each student then devoted seven afternoon periods to assimilating and organizing knowledge of his particular area in order to be able to make a specialist's contribution to his parent committee. The committee reconvened to hear and discuss reports on each area. It then spent one long afternoon drawing conclusions as to the relative strengths of the two major blocs of nations. The end product was a brief written committee report.

Field trips also were instituted by the prewar Army Industrial College. At the present time the class is divided into about 11 groups to visit steel mills, aircraft plants, oil refineries, assembly plants, and other industrial facilities in selected regions of the United States. A week is devoted to these trips in the spring. In addition several shorter visits are made to military research and development centers and to industrial plants in the Washington area.

Like the other senior institutions, the college does not "test" or grade students. Note is taken, however, of their aptitudes, attitudes, and performance. This is done both to appraise their potential as future instructors and to acquire a basis upon which efficiency, effectiveness, or fitness ratings can be submitted to their services. This is in relation to academic matters only. No student has ever been expelled, although a few cases have come up before the faculty board. The college operates on the principle that it is dealing with mature men who have a responsible concern for their future careers and for the country they serve.

Each year the college's staff prepares or revises monographs on mobilization and readiness problems. These are often designated as essential reading for the students. Other publications include a historical document series and a set of bibliographies on selected topics. In the mid-1940's the college engaged in research on a larger scale. About 40 persons, primarily civilians, were assigned to such work. The research division maintained relations with learned societies and with 20 industry advisory committees. Special seminars were held on appropriate historical questions. Altogether more than 100 research reports were initiated in this period, many of them dealing with specific commodities. But after the reactivation of the Munitions Board in 1946, questions arose as to the relationship between it and the college's research division. The industry advisory committees and a number of staff members were transferred to the Munitions Board, and the research division was abolished.

Mission and Curriculum

The mission of the college, as assigned by the charter issued by the Joint Chiefs of Staff, is "To further prepare selected military and civilian personnel for important policy making, command, and staff assignments within the national and international security structure."

Although this language makes no specific reference to economic affairs, the charter goes on to state that intensive courses of study will be conducted in:

"1. All phases of our national economy and in the interrelations of the economic factors with political, military, and psychological factors.

"2. Joint logistic planning and the relation of this planning to joint and combined strategic planning and to national policy planning.

"3. Peacetime and potential wartime governmental organizations and the most effective wartime controls."

The charter states that the *scope* will include:

"1. Orientation in the broad aspects of world political, economic, and power patterns.

"2. Study of the economic potential for war of the nations of the world and the blocs of nations which might have special significance in peace or war and analysis of the relationship of the economic potential to political, military, and psychological factors in our national strategy.

"3. Study and analysis of the organization and administration of the Department of Defense, Department of State, and other governmental agencies concerned with mobilization of the national economy for war and later reconversion to a peacetime basis.

"4. Study of methods of formulation and means of implementation of joint and combined logistic plans and the relation of these plans to joint strategic plans and to the economy of the nation.

"5. Study of the production aspects of mobilization of the national economy and analysis of those factors vitally affecting the production program during mobilization and reconversion.

"6. Study of the procurement and distribution aspects of mobilization for war and reconversion to a peacetime basis.

"7. Study and analysis of manpower problems in connection with mobilization of the economy and mobilization of the military forces.

"8. Study of the relationship between technological progress and the mobilization of the national economy.

"9. Study and analysis of any phase of economic mobilization of the United States or foreign countries which is considered significant to the defense of the nation."

In pursuit of these goals the college offers a course divided into nine units of instruction. During much of the year two units are presented concurrently, often alternating with each other from day to day. The following outline is typical of the manner in which the program is organized.

Unit 1. *Orientation* (69 periods).[9] Theory and history of economic mobilization; administrative problems and trends; elements of economics; executive development, including human relations.

Unit 2. *Manpower* (64 periods). World manpower resources; civilian and military manpower requirements, utilization and controls; social welfare problems; training; industrial relations.

Unit 3. *Economic Stabilization* (42 periods). Price and profit controls; allocations and priorities; rationing; wage stabilization and fiscal controls; federal budget processes.

Unit 4. *Natural Resources* (47 periods). Resources of the United States and other nations; technological progress in extractive industry; critical and strategic materials; stockpiling.

Unit 5. *Requirements and Logistic Systems* (87 periods). Origin of requirements; dependence of strategic plans on logistics; balancing total requirements with resources to support strategic plans; American and foreign logistic systems; service, joint, and combined logistic operations; role of transport and communication.

Unit 6. *Production* (81 periods). Critical industrial areas; conversion, expansion, and reconversion; impact of scientific advance; production controls and readiness measures.

---

[9] The only precise way to indicate the relative amount of time devoted to each unit is to state the number of 90 minute periods assigned to it, because any given unit may occupy only a portion of a day.

Unit 7. *Procurement* (50 periods). Military pricing; procurement planning; joint, single service, and international procurement.

Unit 8. *Economic Potential* (97 periods). Area studies of economic strengths and weaknesses; international economic relations; economic intelligence; foreign economic policy, including economic warfare.

Unit 9. *Mobilization* (97 periods). Critical evaluation of current plans for readiness and partial or total mobilization in the light of current political, technological, economic, social, and psychological conditions.

Analysis of the Course of Instruction

This brief outline suggests the breadth of the college's interests. It has traveled a great distance from the Army Industrial College of 1924, though we shall note later that progress has not been uninterrupted. Its original concern was with details of procurement and with the organization and powers of war agencies. The broad picture is one of evolution from this to industrial mobilization generally; then to economic mobilization, including manpower and economic stabilization as well as industrial mobilization; and finally to the emerging phase which can be described as the use of economic resources in support of national security policy, including but not limited to mobilization policy. In the process the program has been expanded to include consideration not only of economic resources but of foreign affairs, strategic plans, scientific developments, public opinion, and social and political institutions. As the college broadened its interests it also raised the level at which its program is conducted. The student no longer assumes the role of a subaltern in the Office of the Assistant Secretary of War for Procurement. In principle he operates at the governmental, that is, the Presidential, level. Indeed the directive in the final problem of the course requires him to evaluate current mobilization plans from the point of view of a member of a Presidential advisory commission.

Military affairs in the strict sense receive even less attention at the Industrial College than at the National War College. Only the unit on requirements and logistic systems deals exclusively

402

with this area. Other units, of course, touch upon it. The general lecture series includes a few addresses on roles, missions, and weapon systems. Students also attend about two dozen National War College lectures on the nature of modern war, the role of force, the elements of military power, and the employment of these elements. Here, as elsewhere, the inclusion of National War College lectures in the Industrial College's program helps give it a balance and completeness that perhaps no other senior college attains.

An impressive portion of the college's program is conducted in an international setting. In a typical recent year eight of the nine units of instruction touched on this area. The orientation unit included lectures on international trade and international economic institutions. The manpower unit discussed European labor resources, demographic characteristics of the NATO and Sino-Soviet blocs, and the use of indigenous manpower. A seminar was held on international economic mobilization. The natural resources unit provided lectures and oral reports on world food and raw material resources. The requirements unit devoted attention to military aid programs, foreign aid requirements, British, French, and Dutch logistic systems, and international logistics problems. The procurement unit dealt with the Foreign Operations Administration, international purchasing, and offshore procurement, including its political implications. In the mobilization unit a State Department team conducted a seminar on international aspects of economic mobilization. The greatest attention was paid to international affairs in the economic potential unit. This part of the curriculum was instituted in the early 1930's. The branch that sponsors it always is assigned some of the most effective officers on the staff. Its program includes not only the study of area potentials but also geography and national power, international relations, economic warfare, and economic intelligence. Finally, students attend about 50 National War College lectures on international affairs.

The very nature of its mission requires the college to spend more time than the War Colleges on American government, politics, and public policy. Its sensitivity to this area also stems from the Army Industrial College's experience in 1939–1941 when President Roosevelt felt impelled to set aside the mobilization plan on which it had worked so long. Since that time committee reports and oral presentations have contained countless references to public opinion and to the importance of business, labor, and Congressional support. The directive for the final problem expressly requests students to consider the political feasibility of any recommendations they may make. This does not mean that the students always get down to hard cases about the maneuvers of interest groups in economic mobilization. It means that they have been alerted to the importance of consent. Instruction on the executive branch is fairly detailed. In addition to the series of National War College lectures on the formulation of national security policy, students attend Industrial College lectures on the role of the ODM, the Budget Bureau, and the Departments of Commerce, Labor, and the Interior. Other lectures deal with problems and trends in federal administration and with reorganization in the executive branch. The role of Congress is examined in relation to military legislation, the budget, and military procurement. The course also touches on a very wide range of public policy issues. In a typical recent year these included public versus private power, small business, distressed areas, tax policy, including accelerated amortization, agricultural policy, price and wage policy, monetary and fiscal policy, public health, and labor relations policy. In the latter field attention is given to the rise of labor unions, the right to organize and to bargain, strikes, union problems during mobilization, the psychology of industrial relations, and the guaranteed annual wage. A deeply conservative tone runs through some of the student discussion of these topics. The college's roots have long been nourished by large industry, and a close tie is maintained with such organizations as the American Ordnance Association. Rarely have more than one or two representatives of organized labor appeared on the lecture platform in a given year. Some have refused invitations to speak. None has ever sat on the Board of Advisors.[10]

An intensive presentation of economic principles, concepts, and

---

[10] The Board of Advisors consists largely of leading business executives. It has also included the former director of the National Security Industrial Association and the executive vice president of the American Ordnance Association. In 1955 the latter organization published a handsome 31 page brochure about the college in celebration of the anniversary of its founding. The college's motto is *Industria et Defensio Inseparabiles*—"Industry and Defense are Inseparable."

methods is made at the start of the course. This consists of nine lectures, each followed by a lengthy discussion period. Topics covered include supply and demand, wages and prices, money and banking, economic indicators, national income data, and international economic problems. A separate discussion period is held on input-output statistics. Lectures are given by ranking university economists, and students are required to read an abbreviated text. Some economic theory also is presented in discussions of direct and indirect economic stabilization controls. Elements of labor economics and of price theory appear in the manpower and natural resources units respectively. In a larger sense all of the work in producer logistics deals with the field of economics. This includes a great amount of material in the units on productive facilities, manpower, resources, and procurement.

The subject of intelligence is treated very briefly. One lecture is given on economic intelligence. Students also attend a National War College lecture on intelligence as an element of military power. In the early postwar period the college provided a lecture on scientific intelligence but this has been discontinued.

Prior to 1954 a separate unit of instruction was devoted to research and development. It was first called the "research and development unit." Later the name was changed to "technological progress" on the theory that its scope should not be confined to weapons capabilities. Some of the material formerly covered in the technological progress unit is now taken up in other parts of the course. This includes studies of research and development in human resources and in industry. About six lectures are given on modern weaponry, science and national power, and related topics; some of these are delivered under the auspices of the National War College. A few students make oral reports on the influence of research and development on requirements.

The growing realism of the entire course is evident in the greater attention now being paid to partial mobilization and to mobilization under the conditions of nuclear attack on the United States. For many years the Industrial College's program was simply a reflection of the experience of modern nations in the two world wars. It rested on the assumption that the United States would move by stages from peace to a war of attrition in which its superior economic resources, adequately mobilized at last, would insure victory. Partial mobilization was given systematic consideration only after the start of the Korean war. Consideration of mobilization in the face of nuclear attack came still later. Despite Hiroshima and Nagasaki, only scattered references to this problem were made in the early postwar years. Even the 1949 announcement that the Soviet Union had tested an atomic bomb had no immediate effect, except that civil defense was given more emphasis. As late as the academic year 1952–1953 the final problem directive made no explicit reference to nuclear attack, nor did any of the lectures or seminars that accompanied the summary unit of the course.

The significance of nuclear warfare had been discussed within the staff for some time, however, and in oral presentations made in June 1953 a few student spokesmen insisted on the importance of estimating possible damage to the United States at the outset of another war.[11] In 1953 the Soviet Union exploded a thermonuclear device. In 1953–1954, committee reports on the final problem were devoted to mobilization of the national economy in the face of atomic attack. The lecture program for the final unit was devoted largely to this theme and to civil defense. On the other hand the student committees were directed to assume a relatively light attack: 50 kiloton bombs on 20 cities. It was explained that these hypothetical conditions were serious enough to require analysis of the problems of a badly disrupted economy, and that the assumption of a heavier attack would have made the problem unmanageable for the class in the time available. At this time also consideration of disaster planning was confined almost entirely to this final unit of the course.

In 1954–1955 the problems of mobilizing a severely stricken economy began to creep into occasional lectures, seminars, or oral or written reports in as many as six different units of the course. Some unit curriculum books directed students' attention to the impact of nuclear attack on problems studied in the unit. In 1955–1956 the final problem directive reflected still greater sophistication. It began with the statement that sound planning may not be based on any single premise; mobilization policy must be flexible

[11] See, for example, *Mobilization of the Economy for National Defense*, M53-346, Industrial College of the Armed Forces, Washington, 1953, p. 33.

enough to meet a range of possibilities, including peripheral wars, general war without massive nuclear attack, and unlimited global war. The first two alternatives were held to permit phased mobilization; the third was said to present a radically different situation. In the future it is probable that these fundamental points will be emphasized at the start and applied systematically in all units of the course. This might be facilitated if the staff included a specialist in technological developments whose principal duty it was to insure maximum realism in the program. The slow response of the college to the full implications of nuclear warfare was characteristic also of the War Colleges generally, as was suggested in the last chapter. These institutions have given systematic attention to the changing nature of warfare only after and not before these problems troubled planners in the services.

A second unit at the college in which continued experimentation is likely to prove fruitful is economic potential. Earlier this had been called the "foreign resources" unit. The present title is more suggestive of a policy orientation, but the course continues to emphasize a somewhat mechanical, almost arithmetic, analysis of the economic assets and liabilities of particular geographic areas. Relatively few lectures, seminars, and oral reports, fewer than in the early 1950's, deal with foreign economic policy. There is also a natural relationship that needs to be explored between this unit and parts of the procurement unit dealing with foreign aid and offshore purchasing. The economic potential unit might find it appropriate to alter the terms of reference of its committee report to require students, on the basis of their knowledge of economic potential, to evaluate foreign economic policies in the light of national security objectives. This would be comparable to the evaluation they now make of national mobilization policies in the final unit. We believe such a focus would lend added relevance and importance to the college's work in an era of "competitive coexistence."

A third promising area is the unit on requirements. This might gain strength from more systematic analysis of the impact on planners of changes in budget ceilings, strategy, and weaponry. At one time the old research and development unit was actually offered concurrently with the requirements unit. But the work consisted, and still consists, largely of a recital of important scientific innovations in weaponry and industry, and an account of the organization and procedures of research and development agencies. This is useful *background* material. It should, however, serve only to introduce the highly significant issues that a dynamic technology raises for military executives concerned with forecasting requirements. A series of case studies in this field could be an invaluable educational experience. The requirements unit might also profit from a far fuller treatment of the relationship between strategic plans, force levels, and logistic plans. Some of the most important top level policy issues that confront professional officers lie in this area. Here the Industrial College has suffered from the reluctance of the National War College to continue the experiment with a joint course on strategic-logistic planning. The divorce that occurred only perpetuates at the educational level something far too common in the actual conduct of American military planning: a tendency for the strategist to complete his work and turn it over to the logistician only to find out too late that his plan is impracticable. When variables are so closely related as strategy and logistics, policy making cannot consist of piling one completed action on another; it must be based on continuous interaction at all stages. Just as the National War College must study in detail the foreign policy that supplies many premises of strategic planning, and that cannot be allowed to run too far ahead of strategic capability, so the Industrial College must study in detail the strategic policy that supplies many of the premises of logistic planning, and that cannot be allowed to run too far ahead of logistic capability. The parallel is complete. If the National War College cannot supply the necessary guidance in this matter, it may become necessary for the Industrial College to import top level strategists in quantity.

Comparative and international mobilization and supply operations constitute a fourth area whose relative importance warrants greater emphasis at the expense of many other subjects. The adjective "combined" was added to the college's charter at the suggestion of the special board that reviewed the Industrial College and the National War College in 1955. The change was a recognition of problems peculiarly important for study at a school on the very highest level. Analysis of the experience of other nations not only supplies the indispensable basis for inquiry into combined resources planning but can stimulate critical thinking about our own mobilization and supply traditions. To facilitate such analysis the staff could occasionally take students overseas to observe foreign and international supply operations at first hand. Such field trips, comparable to the National War College's, might be alternated with the visits to industrial centers in this country.

To summarize, it is possible that the course might focus on a very few central themes. These would include examination of the relation of *economic resources* to: (1) mobilization planning in an atomic age; (2) joint staff planning, with emphasis on the interrelations of strategy, logistics, finance, and science; (3) foreign economic planning in support of national security objectives; (4) international defense planning. Emphasis on these areas need not destroy the genuinely educational character of the college's course or convert the institution into a training camp for specialists destined for particular military agencies, on both of which points it has properly been sensitive in the past. It would, however, mean less emphasis on procurement, consumer logistics, executive development, management principles, and organizational and procedural questions generally. (Many of these matters can profitably be examined in advanced service schools such as the Army's Supply Management School at Fort Lee, Virginia.) It would also mean a less complete and somewhat different treatment of the traditional areas of manpower, natural resources, and production. No one would argue that these are not basic subjects that must be studied. It is less clear that they provide the most meaningful categories around which the curriculum can be organized. To put it another way, it may prove desirable to consider them not as fundamental "factors" about which something should be known but as instruments of fundamental "policy."

An Evaluation of the College

Summary comments on all senior colleges will be made in the next three chapters. Here we are concerned only with problems peculiar to the Industrial College of the Armed Forces.

A gap exists, how wide is a matter of speculation, between the intrinsic merits of the college and the view of it taken sometimes by military men. Assignment to the college can be a highly valuable experience. The officer so selected is relieved of official operating duties and given the opportunity to work with men of other services in a stimulating atmosphere. Graduates and outside observers have testified that its program is worthwhile, indeed that its students work harder and cover more ground than students at some of the War Colleges. On the other hand the services have a clearer image of the mission of the War Colleges. The War Colleges seem to them to be a natural consequence of their concern for strategy and tactics. They rest naturally upon the lower echelons of the military school system. They were created and nurtured by military men. The Industrial College presents a more blurred picture. The unsophisticated junior officer may conclude it has something to do with post utilities, or that it deals solely with the "nuts and bolts" aspects of military procurement and distribution. The sophisticated officer appreciates its focus on the national economy. But this is a matter in which he feels less at home and on which he is more prepared to accept the views of civilian leaders. He is not sure he should be mixed up with it. He may realize that civilians played a major role in the creation of the college and that much of its support continues to come from private industry.

A small minority has even suggested that such an institution should not exist at the apex of the military educational system. Though we cannot accept this contention, we shall state as persuasively as we can the arguments of those who advance it. One line of reasoning is that many of the functions with which the college is concerned are coming to be performed by civilian personnel. When the Army Industrial College was founded, it is said, it made sense to train officers to plan the mobilization of the national economy and to outline in advance the necessary war organizations and procedures. In 1924 there did not exist an Office of Defense Mobilization, an assistant secretary of defense for supply and logistics, counterpart assistant secretaries in each service, all with large staffs, or a federal Bureau of the Budget responsible for administrative management. But supply and administrative planning are no longer mysteries to most and understood only by a few dedicated officers. In other words the market for the college's product is fast evaporating except at lower echelons where it can be satisfied by the output of less advanced military schools.

410

One weakness of this argument is that it assumes the college does or should train only specialists in the use of economic resources who are destined to devote their careers to supply. But this assumption is unwarranted. A second weakness is that highly important economic calculations will continue to be made by professional officers even though civilian personnel penetrate deeply into the military establishment. These calculations must rest on an understanding of the capabilities and limitations of the resources base.

A second line of argument is that the entire concept of mobilization is obsolete. It is said that the next major war will be over in a few weeks, that it is folly to suppose that our industrial potential will be decisive, that it will not even play a very important part because there will not be time enough to bring it into play. The only resources that will count will be those that exist in the form of finished weapons at the start. As for smaller wars, it is said they will not present serious mobilization problems anyhow, first because they will not require great masses of supplies, second because mobilization would start from a much higher plateau of readiness than in the past. We shall only have to climb halfway up the tree and we shall be starting from a point well above ground. One answer to this contention is that it contains too many assumptions to supply a firm basis for planning in such a serious matter. One might argue as well that the War Colleges are obsolete because technology has advanced to the point where the only strategic decision of importance is whether or not to engage in thermonuclear war, in other words that strategy becomes child's play in total war fought with modern weapons. Prudent men will not place all their eggs in either of these baskets. A second answer, and here we return to the Industrial College, is that its program should not be held to be concerned exclusively with mobilization planning. The sounder view is that it deals with the use of economic resources in support of a wide variety of national security policies.

A third line of argument is advanced by some who concede that career officers require an understanding of economic resources, and further that this should be imparted by a very high level school, but who believe it unfortunate that economic studies should be conducted apart from the studies of the National War

College. They observe that the programs of the two institutions have at no time been coordinated in any other than a superficial way. They believe the schools should be merged. This challenge has got to be taken more seriously than the others, but we shall postpone consideration of it to a subsequent chapter because it involves larger issues common to both colleges. The analysis that follows assumes that each school at Fort McNair will continue to maintain an independent existence. On this basis it explores measures to maximize the effectiveness of the Industrial College.

One area that deserves attention is the prestige of the institution. This has been referred to many times before. In some respects the fears of civilian officials that the college would be treated as a stepchild by the services have been realized. Although in principle it is on the same level as the National War College, there are signs that it has not been so regarded in fact. The fundamental difficulty is that supervisory authorities in the services, who are predominately "line" officers, identify it as a "service of supply" school. They regard it with some of the hauteur that knights of an earlier day displayed toward the husbandmen who served them. They have to be prodded into dipping into comparable pools to select officers for the War Colleges and the Industrial College. A few students are uneasy when they learn that they are going to the latter.[12] In canvassing prospects for its staff the college has had to guard against officers who would feel insecure or bored by the assignment, or who seek it only because they wish to stay in Washington for the sake of their families, or to pursue graduate work, or to await retirement.

Some measures, small in themselves but important in a symbolic sense, can be taken to deal with this problem. Certainly the commandants and the deputies of the two schools at Fort McNair should hold comparable rank. The new building will help. The name of the college, which is both awkward and misleading, might

[12] The questionnaire that we administered to about 550 officers in the Pentagon seems to lend support to this conclusion. Officers were asked whether, from the standpoint of career advancement, they would prefer to be assigned to the National War College, the Industrial College, or one of the service War Colleges in the event that they had to attend at least one. A heavy majority of the respondents indicated that the National War College was preferred to the Industrial College on this basis. The relationship held at all levels within the Defense Department, among all three services, and among men engaged in logistics as well as strategic planning.

be changed. Either War Resources College or Defense Resources College would be an improvement.

But lasting progress must depend on more substantial changes. Happily there are indications that some of these are under way. The curriculum of the college, as noted above, is being raised to the level of national policy. The creation of the Army's Supply Management School and other intermediate educational programs within the services will help reduce the burden on the Industrial College and free it to pursue lines of development appropriate to its high status. The supply function generally is gaining wider recognition as a result of the insistent hammering of the secretaries of the military departments, of Congress, of special bodies such as the Hoover Commissions, and of counterpart study groups within the military departments.[13] A significant step was taken when the newly created Office of the Deputy Chief of Staff for Logistics in the Army was directed to supervise and guard the careers of logisticians.

There is, however, one aspect of these trends that may be more favorable to the college in the short run than in the long. This is the desire of many civilian leaders to establish a kind of "two track" career pattern for military officers, some specializing in operations, others in support functions. Ultimately we think this would hurt the college. Unless drastic changes occur in the basic premises of professional officers, changes that we think unlikely, its prestige will depend upon a growing conviction that it is not concerned solely with the training of specialists. It is not easy to spread this conviction because in its first years the school *was* devoted primarily to the training of specialists. But any step that widens the gap between the strategist and the logistician simply makes it harder. We would therefore be wary of efforts to transfer jurisdiction over the college to the assistant secretary of defense for supply and logistics, or to subordinate the consideration of strategic affairs in its curriculum, or to rely too much on support from industry alone, or, most important, to select students largely from among staff corps officers, nonrated personnel, and the tech-

[13] See, for example, Commission on the Organization of the Executive Branch of the Government, *Business Organization of the Department of Defense,* Washington, June 1955.

nical and administrative services. In this regard we think it unfortunate that the Army allocates so little of its quota to officers of the combat arms. Our attitude on these points is based not only on a concern for the needs of the college but on a concern for the needs of the services and, ultimately, of the nation. There is ample historical evidence that it is precisely the line officer who needs to know much more about the economic bases of plans and operations.

Turning to the question of method, we feel that the college is distinguished, even among senior military institutions, by the heavy work load it places on its student body. There seems to be an implicit assumption that outside observers will grow suspicious unless students are constantly in motion or that Congress will snatch away unobligated time as it presumably snatches away unobligated funds. Since 1950 the college has made a commendably determined effort to curtail the number of lectures and other requirements. But we think there is still not enough time for independent study and reflection. A more leisurely pace is needed to induce a greater amount of critical thinking. It is not enough to make official statements encouraging a rigorous examination of prevailing doctrines and practices. Supporting conditions and devices must be provided. Of these the most important is time to think. Further stimulus might result from the admission of a larger proportion of civilian officials. A precautionary measure would be to review carefully monographs and other materials to delete any hortatory statements inconsistent with the idea that the college seeks to avoid imposing orthodox doctrine on its students.[14] A fourth possibility is to rely more heavily on the case method of instruction, which is ideally designed to stimulate critical thought. We have in mind particularly public policy cases comparable to those on economic mobilization produced under the auspices of the Inter-University Case Program.[15] The preparation of original case materials could well become a regular function of the civilian staff. We are, incidentally, persuaded that it is particularly desirable for the Industrial College to perform this

[14] Some literature that we examined contained phrases to the effect that certain mobilization policies or procedures were a "must," or were "necessary," or "will be required."

[15] See, for example, "The Reconversion Controversy," in Harold Stein, ed., *Public Administration and Policy Development,* New York, 1952.

or comparable research functions in order to maintain the vigor of its permanent personnel.

In order to ensure a continuation of the considerable progress that the Industrial College has made, the services will have to take the greatest care in the selection of commandants and deputy commandants. This point cannot be stated too strongly. The ability, the reputation, and above all the interest of the commandant is central to the success of the school. There have been too many occasions in the history of the Industrial College when its principal officers have lacked one or all of these qualifications. The college and the services would also benefit from a thorough review of the role of the Board of Advisors. In a typical recent year the board had 20 members. The majority were successful business executives; some were college administrators or lawyers formerly in the public service. All were appointed by the commandant. The members do not prepare periodic reports on the institution; indeed the board as a whole is rarely convened. Instead the commandant consults his advisors individually or in small groups. He may also keep them informed by newsletters. We believe the board should be smaller. It should also be less heavily weighted with businessmen; for this only strengthens the already conservative tendencies of the college and serves to identify it more completely with civilian industry. Finally, we suggest that the board visit the college at least once each year and prepare a written report of its findings for transmission through the commandant to supervisory authorities in the Department of Defense.

We believe the foregoing steps will strengthen an already fine institution. The present college and its predecessor have made a unique contribution to officer education for more than three decades. No other school, military or civilian, has a comparable mission. The increasing attention now being given to the college's program and needs suggests the conclusion that it will discharge its distinctive educational task more effectively in coming years.

CHAPTER NINETEEN

THE SENIOR COLLEGES EVALUATED

In the last analysis the real test of the senior military colleges is in the quality of the work of the individual officers assigned to them. Certainly the National War College, the Industrial College, and the service colleges offer their students a magnificent opportunity for study and reflection, scarcely equaled in any other profession. This can mean a great deal to an individual who takes full advantage of the rich resources available to him.

This leads to the question of the quality of the performance of the students. The colleges themselves stress the importance of quality of thought as distinguished from the mere acquisition of knowledge. A Naval War College catalog declares, for example, that "It is the educational policy of the Naval War College to devote principal emphasis to the promotion of the good judgment and intellectual leadership expected of a naval officer in high command." The basic philosophy of the National War College, as stated in its catalog, is "that the best preparation which can be given its students for their future work is an increased capacity to *think* broadly, objectively, and soundly along lines with which they will come in future contact—lines which have to do with national security in this exceedingly complex world in which we live. The emphasis, therefore, is on the *educational* process, as opposed to the *training* process." [1]

This, of course, is the cherished goal of every educational institution of higher learning. We know from our own experience that civilian colleges and universities fall short of this objective. How close to it do these senior military colleges come? As we have pointed out throughout this study, we are very much impressed by the accomplishments of the colleges. They make a direct con-

[1] Italics in original.

416

tribution to the security and welfare of the United States, their resources are of high order, and their accomplishments are substantial. The criticism that follows is not intended to detract from these virtues but rather to suggest areas where they can be strengthened.

Adequacy of Instruction

We turn first to the charge of superficiality, raised in preceding chapters. It is agreed at the colleges that many topics are covered in haste. But the faculties declare that in doing so they meet the requirement to give their students a critical awareness of the full range of problems facing the senior officer. We agree that the development of this sort of awareness is in itself a significant achievement, and that in sensitizing officers to the complexities of security problems the colleges are in fact stimulating intellectual growth. But we question whether this is enough for these high level educational institutions. Education is not just a distributive process in which information is passed out to all comers; it is a serious intellectual experience. In addition to developing sensitivity to a wide variety of problems the colleges should provide more opportunity for examination of a few problems in greater depth. In short they should display more concern for intellectual rigor and discipline, and for genuinely critical analysis of assumptions, examination of alternatives, and testing of conclusions. We agree that the major emphasis will have to remain upon fairly broad substantive coverage. With no substantial sacrifice in this respect, however, it should be possible to give more attention to the development of critical, analytical thought. As one officer put it to us, you have the choice of plowing the whole field or digging post holes. The best procedure is to plow the field, stopping every now and then to dig a few holes. This might be done in several ways. Fewer topics might be covered in a given year, and each taken up more thoroughly. Certain fundamental topics must be included every year. But others might be taken up on a selective basis.

Broad coverage by itself fails to indicate sufficiently the close relationship of all variables to each other and particularly to the military factor. A few lectures, a number of readings, and a committee study on a given subject, say a policy problem in the Middle East, cannot fully prepare an officer to deal with the relationship of high level command decisions to the political and economic conditions of that area. This is especially true when, as at present, most of the instruction is devoted to information on current developments which, though interesting and important at the time, is soon outdated and irrelevant. It is more valuable to stress basic principles and relationships than descriptive material and to develop habits of mind adequate to cope with complex security situations.

Practices at the Air War College suggest that a less crowded program is possible. More time is set aside there during duty hours for individual reading and study. Frequently, entire afternoons and even days are designated for this purpose. The Air War College, to do this, schedules fewer plenary and seminar sessions. It does not require oral presentations of individual theses, a time-consuming operation. The less formal pattern of the second year course at the Naval War College is a similar approach, although this is tending to become more highly organized.

When it is proposed that anything be left out of the curriculum, the faculty of a college promptly responds, "Well, show us what we can drop." This is a fair response. As already pointed out, the colleges are under continuous pressure to add to the program. The answer is to eliminate items that can be taught more effectively elsewhere, or that actually can be learned through experience on the job. The military services excel in providing extremely effective instruction in such things as the employment of a new weapon or the conduct of a military operation. This sort of thing should be related to the assignment of an officer to a particular job, and held to a minimum at the senior colleges. Rather these schools should concentrate their resources upon those areas of knowledge and skill that can best be handled in an educational institution and that relate to preparation for a variety of high level responsibilities. If our analysis in chapter two is correct, this means increased attention to the development of the skills of evaluating evidence, analyzing assumptions, organizing data, and developing carefully reasoned conclusions.

A change in the use of outside lecturers might contribute to this end, and also bring improvement in the lecture series itself.

The colleges could retrieve considerable time for more intensive and analytical study by placing less emphasis upon lectures. Good as the lectures are, the colleges rely on them excessively. Frequently the students can obtain more information in less time from assigned readings, especially when the lecturer has been selected to state an official position. Moreover, in spite of the effort made to prepare speakers ahead of time, duplication of material is inevitable. Although lecturers often comment on the high quality of analysis revealed in questions put to them, we conclude that all too frequently the premises and assumptions of a speaker are not examined critically. Ideally there should be fewer speakers, with some topics covered by readings. Some speakers should remain in residence for several days, or even a week, to give the students opportunity to explore ideas and special interests with them in some detail. This would very definitely raise the intellectual level of the colleges. The value obtained should warrant the effort to overcome the practical difficulties involved in obtaining speakers who can spare the extra time.[2]

Different use might also be made of reading assignments. The reading lists, as already suggested, are drawn up with considerable care by the faculties after initial preparation by the library staffs. The bibliographies are excellent and for the most part are broadly representative. Unfortunately the student finds himself reading a multitude of relatively short items. As presently organized, the reading lists are designed to provide wide subject matter coverage rather than to expose the student to a well-reasoned analysis of a particular problem or study area. As a consequence, assignments are not read critically enough. Only at the Air War College is the student asked to read an entire book and to assimilate the particular thesis or contribution of its author. This practice might well be extended to the other colleges. In this connection, moreover, it might be desirable to invite an author to spend several days at a college meeting informally with committees after they

---

[2] A technique employed by some civilian instructors, but most relevantly in this case by Professor Barton Leach of the Harvard Law School in his Defense Policies Seminar, and also by the Air War College, might be adopted by the other colleges. Prior to the appearance of a speaker, a panel of students prepares and circulates a memorandum outlining his special contribution to the subject matter under discussion. The panel also meets with the speaker to prepare an agenda for the question period.

419

had read and appraised his work. George Kennan, for example, might visit the college after the students had read his *Realities of American Foreign Policy*. Such an arrangement is not beyond the resources of these institutions.

The quality of the group discussions could be higher. We have observed that discussion frequently lacks direction and discipline. While we strongly endorse the practice at the senior schools of avoiding anything resembling a "school solution," we see the need for more thorough examination of students' assumptions and basic concepts. We have noted, for example, situations in committees where individual students have made errors of fact or judgment that went unchallenged. Moreover these discussions sometimes approach the superficial, drifting here and there without reference to central themes and without focus upon the search for significant conclusions. Too frequently decisions are reached by consensus rather than by hard thinking. At its worst, according to a faculty member at one of these schools, it becomes a case of "the blind leading the blind." This situation is due in part to the fact that faculty members do not give instruction or guidance in the conventional sense. Their status does not permit them to provide intensive intellectual leadership. Moreover it is now the usual practice at the colleges to turn over direction of the discussion groups to student chairmen on a rotating basis, at least during part of the year. At the Air War College a number of devices are employed to provide guidance to student chairmen, including seminar briefings by members of the faculty and the State Department advisor.

Our observations along this line appear to be confirmed by the special study of committee problem-solving techniques at the National War College conducted by the Human Resources Research Office (HumRRO) of the George Washington University, to which reference was made in chapter seventeen. As reported there, it was found that students felt that the college encourages an atmosphere of "agreeable conversation" in committees rather than the most vigorous argument possible. HumRRO declared that more candid discussion of interservice rivalries was needed and that both faculty and students should give more attention to problem-solving techniques. Specifically, the report suggested greater care in the definition of the problem by the committee, in use of working assumptions, in analysis of causation, and in use of words. The report concluded that while committee and conference procedures were generally satisfactory, they could be improved by placing greater emphasis upon analytical methods.[3] Similar conclusions about the limitations of seminar discussions at the Air War College were reached by a group of consultants in 1955.[4]

Likewise, the Board of Consultants to the National War College in 1951 suggested that the committees tended toward "over generalization" in framing policy recommendations. This is a tendency that we have observed at the other institutions. It results from the relatively short time available for the preparation of these recommendations and from insufficient tough-minded analysis. Moreover the critiques to which recommendations are subjected by faculty and other students in plenary or committee sessions usually do not probe deeply into underlying assumptions and reasoning.

It has been reported to us that a study of the Industrial College, made during its formative postwar years, indicated that students did learn and remember some descriptive material in the course of the academic year, but that their analytical capacities changed very little. A study of instruction in problem solving at the Air Command and Staff School conducted by the Human Resources Research Institute of the Air Force, while it did not deal with a War College, may have some bearing on this issue because the instructional methods used are similar. HRRI concluded that the school did improve the ability of committees of students to prepare written decisions and action plans. The gain was essentially in greater efficiency in communication with one another, reporting the actual decisions and actions, and accepting the goal for common action. "By contrast, however, the decisions written by individuals after instruction are not significantly different from those they had prepared as individuals in the opening days of

[3] George Washington University, Human Resources Research Office, *Committee Problem-Solving Techniques at the National War College,* Technical Report No. 10, September 1954.

[4] Ralph W. Tyler and others, *Analysis of the Purpose, Pattern, Scope, and Structure of the Officer Education Program of Air University,* Technical Memorandum OERL-TM-55-6, Officer Education Research Laboratory, Maxwell Air Force Base, May 1955, pp. 165, 167–168.

the course." The report speculated that the individuals as individuals were not given enough guidance in solving problems and that the quality of written reports could be improved by orienting the students to a schema for the analysis of problems and action plans.[5]

The intellectual level might also be raised by less emphasis upon presentation techniques. We do not question the value of oral presentations, particularly for officers who might find themselves testifying before a Congressional committee. Yet we have detected a tendency to give undue attention to the form of these presentations at the expense of substantive content. Because students appear before their peers, they place great significance upon a successful appearance on the platform. We have been told by students that they feel they are under heavy pressure to perform well. Consequently much time is devoted to polishing the text, preparing visual aids, and delivering several "dry runs" before small groups of associates. The Army War College and the Industrial College have equipped a special seminar room with miniature stage, lectern, screen, visual aid panels, and so forth for this purpose. For several years at the National War College members of the faculty found that students consulted with them on the substance of their oral presentations much less than they did with the public speaking instructor and the visual aid department on the form of presentation.

What we are suggesting is that students may be unduly preoccupied with formalities and refinements. We should like to see the same emphasis placed upon the quality of thought going into committee papers that is given to "dry runs," visual and audio aids, and other preparations for the formal presentations. The technique of the briefing, which has its place in the Pentagon, should not be substituted for education.

The individual research study or thesis is the specific feature of the program at each of the colleges that is designed to give the student an opportunity to dig more deeply into a subject, usually one of personal interest, and thereby develop skills of evaluation, analysis, and presentation. The quality of these studies varies

[5] Human Resources Research Institute, *Evaluation of Instruction in Staff Action and Decision,* Technical Research Report No. 16, Maxwell Air Force Base, December 1953.

tremendously. Some show evidence of extensive research and thought. A few of these each year constitute first rate achievements. We know of one that made a significant contribution to a major reorganization of a national security agency. Others are quite adequate to serve as reading materials at the colleges in subsequent years. But unfortunately many others are little better than the papers submitted in an undergraduate college course, and a few are below this standard.

A principal problem in the thesis program is that the students receive relatively little guidance from their faculty supervisors. The latter generally are responsible for as many as 20 or 25 students and frequently for subject areas in which they have had no special experience. Under these circumstances they are able to do little more than assist in the preparation of the bibliography and outline of the paper and comment on a preliminary draft. All of the colleges are aware of this situation and are attempting to strengthen the guidance supplied to their students. At the Air War College the most progress appears to have been made in this respect. One member of the faculty devotes his major attention to organizing and operating the thesis program. Other members of the faculty, under his direction, supervise the work of the students. Also, through the Air War College publication program, noted above, considerable emphasis is placed upon quality. Only at this institution are theses returned as unsatisfactory with the requirement that they be revised. All theses are evaluated more systematically and critically than at the other colleges.

Student Performance

Can mature men in their late thirties and early forties be taught to improve their analytical skills? The evidence of educational psychology indicates that they can. Certainly these senior military colleges can give them a deeper understanding of relationships not normally seen. Attention can be focused upon situations in new contexts. Education can teach an individual to look at an old problem in a variety of new ways and to appreciate that frequently there is more than one answer.

Alteration of the curricula and instructional methods might contribute to this goal, but its real achievement depends upon the quality of the resources of the institutions themselves, principally upon the quality of the students and instructional staffs. Although the students are selected with considerable care, their individual performances vary widely. Some officers devote a great deal of thought, time, and energy to the year of study. Others make little expenditure of these ingredients. Thus there is a marked difference in the quality of their contributions and accomplishments. While many students devote themselves to study with considerable diligence, others can and do get by without extending themselves. This situation is not readily apparent to the observer because carefully planned programs cover up inferior performances.

We shall discuss the selection of students in the next chapter. Here we limit comment to the issue of evaluating student performance. At lower level military schools, including the Command and Staff Schools, considerable emphasis is placed upon grading and a highly competitive spirit is maintained among the students. The Army Command and General Staff College in particular is well known for the heavy pressure placed upon its students. At the senior colleges, on the other hand, the commandants and staffs have taken pains to avoid this atmosphere and to cultivate the concept that each student is on his own and that none of his work is "graded." The usual fitness or effectiveness reports are filed for each officer, but they are not based upon any fixed norms of academic performance. The Air War College comes the nearest to a grading system. There the faculty members keep close watch on individual performance and counsel students regularly. About halfway through the year students whose work has been unsatisfactory are given written warning. Also each student rates every other student in the class on the basis of all-around characteristics. This system, of course, makes no attempt to evaluate intellectual achievement as such.

The absence of a formal grading system at the senior colleges undoubtedly contributes to the freedom of expression that prevails at these institutions, and the introduction of grading might well endanger their present accomplishments. Accordingly we agree wholeheartedly that students should not be graded. But even so, there appears to be a distinct need for more positive evaluation of individual achievements. This is needed not only to stimulate the work of individual officers, but to give the colleges some measure of their own success. They should concern themselves more with the degree to which students advance during the year. The units of the Air University have used the services of an Educational Advisory Office in the AU headquarters as well as outside civilian experts for this purpose from time to time. It would be appropriate for the other colleges to follow this lead, and to determine, for example, changes in levels of knowledge and attitudes over the ten month period of the course.

Without employing a formal grading system it should also be possible to set certain standards of performance. Definite standards could be fixed for the individual research papers, and papers failing to meet these requirements could be returned for revision. Committee reports and policy papers could be subjected to more rigorous scrutiny, and presentations could be followed by an effective critique, with greater attention to critical evaluation of issues, underlying assumptions, methods of analysis, and conclusions.[6]

The senior colleges, as already described, all employ a single curriculum. All students are required to follow the same prescribed course of study, regardless of past experience and education. This arrangement does not allow for individual differences in interest and capacity, and we conclude that it contributes to the wide variation in individual performance. The superior students, perhaps as many as the upper half of the class, are not pushed very hard. While these colleges certainly should never attempt anything approaching the elective system of civilian institutions of higher learning, arrangements might well be made to permit some students to pursue carefully selected investigations, either on their own or under faculty supervision. They might drop out of the regular course during a unit of instruction with which they already are familiar to do a separate research paper or to complete a field investigation of some significance. Or their talents might be employed for such periods in connection with the advanced research and study programs that most of the colleges are carrying on. These suggestions are rejected at the colleges. In the first place, they argue that detaching some students from the regular course, particularly from their committee assignments, presents administrative difficulties. Secondly, it is declared that this selection would appear to be unfair discrimination in favor of a

[6] Note, for example, the suggestions along this line in Tyler, *op.cit.*

few selected students. And lastly, they point out that the best officers contribute to the education of their fellows in committee discussions. We feel that the advantages of giving the very best students an opportunity to go beyond the limits of the prescribed course far outweigh these admitted obstacles.

Faculty Performance

If the achievements of the senior colleges are to be raised still higher, the principal task will fall upon the officers serving on the faculties. There are two separate but interrelated aspects of an evaluation of these groups. One concerns their roles and functions; the other relates to their level of performance. With respect to the first, we already have noted that these officers are not instructors in the usual sense. They are planners and administrators of programs in which the students learn from each other, from visiting speakers, and from personal reading and study. As discussion leaders they serve principally as moderators, and even in guiding individual research they do little or no real teaching. If they appear before the entire class as a lecturer at all, they usually do so no more than once during the year.

The colleges themselves are generally satisfied with the present role of the faculties. They do not expect them to be more than planners and administrators, and they emphasize the absence of a conventional teacher-student relationship. At the Naval War College the term "staff" is usually used rather than "faculty," and at the National War College several years ago one of the deputies proposed a similar designation.

We question this arrangement. If the colleges are going to engage in more rigorous intellectual examination of issues than is their present practice, leadership must come from the faculty. This will mean a somewhat different sort of faculty, involving redefinition of faculty responsibilities and different criteria of selection. At least some of the members should assume responsibility for instruction as well as administration of the curriculum. They should be required to participate directly by providing information, developing concepts, and demonstrating relationships. In group situations they should help guide discussion along logical channels, uncover incomplete reasoning, challenge false assumptions and facts, and question conclusions. They should participate more actively in the lecture program. At least a few should undertake independent investigation of research. This need not be the conventional research of the university. It might involve an occasional special assignment to investigate and report on some problem of current importance to the armed services.

These changes cannot be easily accomplished. Assignment to a faculty is not a lifetime career for a professional teacher but a relatively short tour of duty for a military officer in a field somewhat detached from more customary occupations. Moreover the informal atmosphere of the senior institutions, with its emphasis upon the absence of a grading system and upon quality of all members of the community, students and faculty alike, militates against a change in the status and functions of the faculty. Certainly this atmosphere should be maintained, but it makes the job even more difficult. The nondirected type of instruction, in which the leader remains in the background, actually calls for far more skill than the conventional classroom situation. Yet this aspect of the relationship does not appear to be clearly recognized. If faculty members are to become more than administrators, they must establish their leadership on the basis of respect for their intellectual qualities. Our suggestions imply, moreover, at least a degree of specialization, which raises problems of career management and of selection and assignment policies, questions that will be discussed below. But in spite of these difficulties we believe the attempt should be made.

The second aspect of faculty evaluation, namely the level of performance, also raises knotty problems. Only in a few instances are these officers distinguished from the students by reason of special educational or other qualifications. Rather they are officers of the same rank and experience levels and usually only slightly older in age. Except for the accidents of the assignment process, many faculty and student officers might find their roles reversed, since vacancies on the faculty usually are filled from the graduating class. The officer on the faculty is the one who happened to attend the college first.

This does not mean that the faculties are not composed of competent officers. On the contrary, our observations, supported by promotion and other records, indicate that they are a superior group. As with the students, they show wide variations. This problem is known in civilian institutions. Some are obviously unusually skilled officers with rich experiences and distinguished records behind them. Others appear to be totally unsuited for this kind of responsibility. We know of one officer on the faculty of a senior college who was the lowest man in his class at his academy.[7]

The quality of faculty performance at the senior colleges is determined not so much by individual capacities (which generally are now satisfactory) as it is by certain military personnel policies. Perhaps the most serious difficulty is the instability caused by a fairly high rate of turnover. This has been a perennial problem at all of the colleges, although at most of them improvements have been made in recent years. The commandants naturally demand the most highly qualified officers. But if such officers are sent to them, inevitably demands will be made for their services elsewhere. So the commandants must do running battle to hold their good people. Frequently they are unsuccessful. If another assignment includes promise of promotion to higher rank, they can hardly refuse to let an officer go.

The Army and Air Force have now set the tour of faculty duty at three years. At the Air War College it was briefly raised to four, but now has dropped back to three. The Navy tour is two years. This means that at least one third of the faculty at the Army and Air War Colleges and one half at the Naval War College is replaced each year. When premature reassignments are added in, the turnover becomes even greater. The Army and Air War Colleges, after initial difficulties, have suffered the least from this, the Industrial College and the National War College the most. The average tour of duty at the National War College during the first

---

[7] In our questionnaire we asked those officers who had attended a college whether the members of the military faculty were "outstanding officers." The replies show that the graduates rated them quite high. The figures for different colleges were as follows:

"Taken as a group, were members of the military staff
outstanding officers?"

	Yes	No
National War College	31	12
Industrial College	24	15
Army War College	16	3
Naval War College	18	9
Air War College	18	9

six years was about a year and a half. Moreover vacancies on the faculty here and elsewhere sometimes go unfilled for some months. Recently the commandant of one of the colleges chose not to fill several vacancies rather than to accept inferior officers. Also, he preferred to accept some outstanding officers with the knowledge that they would be withdrawn after a year instead of taking others of inferior quality.

Rapid turnover inevitably diminishes the effectiveness of the faculties. We have been told many times that it takes an officer one year to learn the job, and that during his last year he is thinking about his next assignment. If he serves a full three years, this gives him only one year at peak efficiency. The practice of rotation is defended, among other reasons, as a means of infusing "new blood" into the institution. But it does not appear to work out this way. As an officer at one of the colleges once remarked, "Lots of wonderful new ideas and suggestions are made every year. We all nod our heads in agreement. But before anybody can do anything about them, we are all gone. Next year, the new fellows, just as bright as we are, come up with the same ideas, but the situation is repeated all over again." Instead of bringing steady improvement, with faculty groups building on the accomplishments of their predecessors, this tends to perpetuate mediocrity, no matter how good the officers may be as individuals.

Another questionable arrangement is the practice of selecting most of the replacements on the faculty from the immediately graduating class. Inbreeding has the same ill effect upon the senior military colleges as it does upon civilian institutions.

There are additional factors that bear upon faculty effectiveness. Since these are military establishments, military practices prevail. Seniority rather than experience usually, although not always, determines assignment, and the senior officers present fill the positions on the principal policy board or committee. Also, balance is sought among representatives of different occupational specialities or branches of service. At the joint colleges committee and working group assignments must be made in such a way as to preserve equality of service representation.

These personnel policies tend to exaggerate even more the administrative functions of the faculty and to diminish their contributions to substantive content. One result, for example, is that an inordinate amount of time, at least by the standards of a civilian educational institution, is devoted to administrative details. Because the "institutional memory" is short, elaborate files must be maintained on each unit of instruction, on lecturers, and so forth, so that officers assuming responsibility fresh from other assignments can take over. This also leads to excessive tinkering with the curriculum. Obviously no two individuals will agree on how to organize such a vast array of disparate material as must go into the programs at the colleges. Each one develops a different organizing scheme or rationale. Certainly some plans are better than others, and changes must be made annually to keep up with shifting circumstances. But, on the other hand, just as in the production of a new aircraft, the design must be "frozen" at some point so that work can proceed.[8]

This situation is aggravated by the high rate of rotation of commandants and their deputies. The tour of the commandant at the National War College is three years. But the deputies at this institution and the commandants and deputies at the service War Colleges usually serve for only two years. Two of the commandants of the Industrial College served tours of four years; one served 21 months. Deputies have averaged a little less than two years. At the National War College on one occasion the commandant, the two military deputies, the Department of State deputy, and the senior civilian member of the faculty all were replaced within a period of a few months. At many of the colleges, moreover, vacancies have been allowed to occur between regular appointments. Such practices cannot help but create uncertainty and dislocation.

The impact of all these obstacles to effective instruction falls hardest on the areas of politics, economics, and international relations, the newer subjects into which the joint colleges and now the service War Colleges have moved with increasing emphasis in recent years. In these subjects the faculties are reluctant to carry instructional responsibilities themselves. Consequently they rely on the lecture programs and bring in academic and government

---

[8] During our visits to these colleges we have frequently been told by faculty members that they finally had worked out a curriculum that would require only minor changes in the future. These officers apparently did not realize that their predecessors had told us the same thing a year or two before. Civilian institutions (and also the service academies) suffer from the other extreme; with them curricular changes are frequently extremely difficult to make.

specialists to present the major blocks of information. But there still remains the problem of providing direction and intellectual leadership for this part of the program.

The use of at least some of the military faculty for this purpose is perhaps less of a problem than it is made out to be. Actually the faculty officers possess a great deal of knowledge and skill, although largely undeveloped, in the nonmilitary areas. The use of these officers for administrative duties wastes much of this potential talent. With some effort and care, duties could be rearranged so that at least some of these officers could have opportunity to develop special competence in one or more of the nonmilitary areas. Two or three years should allow for this if officers were permitted to serve in a curriculum area for the full tour of duty rather than be shifted from one area to another.

The experience of West Point and the Air Force Academy suggests some of the practices that would contribute to this end. It should be possible, for example, for selected faculty members to attend one or more summer sessions at civilian institutions, taking work directly related to their areas of responsibility. They might also be given opportunity to visit the leading experts in their special areas, and, when appropriate, to spend time observing the operations of relevant government agencies. In some instances summer travel abroad for study or observation would be in order. It might also be possible to take greater advantage of the civilian institutions programs, under which officers devote a year or more to graduate study before being assigned to positions utilizing the special educational experiences. All of these arrangements are used by West Point in preparing officers for instructional assignments. Similar effort in behalf of officers assigned to the faculties of the senior schools appears to be reasonable.

This approach to the employment of the military faculty has not been seriously considered by the senior colleges. Instead of developing the latent potentialities of their own military faculties, they have turned to the appointment of civilian personnel either on a permanent basis or, more frequently, on a term basis. The latter practice was initiated at the National War College when it was first established. The group of civilians assembled by Admiral Hill at that time exercised principal responsibility for the design and operation of the program during the first semester, which dealt with national and international affairs. As the years have passed and the administration of the curriculum has become more standardized, the independent influence of the civilians as a group has diminished. Until 1954 they remained in residence for the first semester only. In that year approval was finally granted for a group of four to serve throughout the year, and at the same time the distinctive separation of the program into nonmilitary and military phases was terminated. The National War College also developed the practice of inviting at least one of the civilians to return for a second assignment, to provide continuity in the civilian group. Recently the college inaugurated the practice of including officials of civilian agencies of the government in the civilian faculty. These have been individuals with prior academic training and experience.

Several years ago the National War College issued a statement describing the duties of these individuals. It pointed out that "Due to the character of the student body, and the mission of the College, the general educational methods differ considerably from the traditional type of a university or college. The basic theory is one of providing the students with intellectual stimuli by means of which they may instruct themselves. Accordingly, very little direct instruction is given. On the other hand, advice, guidance, and trained stimulation of thought are vitally important." [9] The col-

---

[9] The statement defined the principal duties of the members of the civilian faculty as follows:

"a) To mingle freely with members of the student body on the theory that both students and members of the faculty are members of the College; to establish with the students a rapport which will permit frank and easy discussion of all pertinent subject areas; to gain the confidence of the students and to enhance the prestige of the academic and intellectual approach.

"b) To assist in planning and administering the organized work as outlined by the curricula. (It should be noted that in its planning of the course of study, the College relies primarily on the collective group effort of the faculty as a whole, rather than delegation of complete responsibility for particular segments to individual members of the faculty.)

"c) To serve as moderators of organized discussion groups of approximately 12 members. . . . This function is looked upon as one of the most important involved.

"d) To give one or more formal lectures on a subject of mutual satisfaction.

"e) To hold several 'question and answer' periods for the student body within the specialized field of the individual.

"f) To render advice and guidance to the students on the preparation of their individual research papers.

"g) To render advice and guidance to student committees on the solution of their 'committee problems.'

"h) To serve as moderators of certain special activities, such as presentation of individual papers, presentation of committee solutions, and so on."

lege and university educators who have held these positions generally have been enthusiastic about the experience. Military personnel at the college likewise have been satisfied with the arrangement.[10] From time to time the appointment of a permanent or semipermanent senior civilian to the faculty of the National War College has been considered by the commandant and his deputies and by the Board of Consultants. It has been suggested by some that such an individual could provide intellectual leadership and administrative continuity. The idea has never been approved, however. Unless the position were defined to attract an outstanding educator or scholar, with status at least equal to the deputies, it is unlikely that it could be filled by an individual of the caliber of those who have been available on a short term basis.

The Industrial College has employed a civilian director of instruction for some years. Dr. Marlin S. Reichley, the professional social scientist who now holds this position, has been with the college since 1945. Prior to that time he was on the faculty of the School of Foreign Service at Georgetown University. He also served in the Army with the grade of lieutenant colonel. Dr. Reichley has had a major responsibility for planning and coordinating the academic program of the college. As noted in the preceding chapter, the college also employs about a dozen civilians on a permanent basis in the branches that administer its resident course. They assist in orienting newly assigned officer instructors, help plan and schedule the branch's program, and advise individual students, committees, and small discussion groups. A number of members perform research related to the college's program; a few give lectures. While some are clearly of high caliber, others seem to perform in a less satisfactory manner and student opinion of their contributions has not always been favorable. From time to time it is suggested that the college utilize public officials or academicians for periods of a semester or a year. But the prevailing view is that the public officials are likely to be too specialized, and that few academicians possess a systematic knowledge of economic mobilization.

The Air War College has employed a civilian educational ad-

---

10 In our questionnaire we asked graduates to rate the contribution of the civilian faculty. Thirty-two declared that their contributions were "extremely valuable"; 11 said "somewhat valuable"; none checked "not very valuable."

visor since 1949. Dr. Cyril F. Hager, who has held this position since that time, is broadly experienced in the social sciences and came to the college from 12 years of university teaching. He devotes most of his attention to planning the part of the program dealing with national and international affairs, to the reading assignments for this part, and to a faculty in-service training course. He also serves as chairman of a student seminar group during the international relations phase. Dr. Hager also makes a practice of visiting other military schools and civilian universities from time to time, and keeps in close touch with new developments in the teaching of international relations. His contributions in developing a framework or design for the curriculum and in the careful integration of its various parts manifest the considerable value of at least one permanent civilian. Recently Dr. Eugene M. Emme, who was formerly associated with the advanced study group (which is discussed below), has been transferred to the resident course, devoting most of his time to assisting students in the preparation of individual theses.

The civilians on the faculty of the Naval War College do more instructing in the conventional sense than those at the other War Colleges. Initially the civilian professors appointed to the King and Nimitz chairs worked almost exclusively with the officers in the advanced study group, as described below, but with the introduction of the two year program in 1954 they were at first drawn into planning for the new second year course, and then into its operations. Now they devote much of their time to this course. Also, in this connection, the college has added three civilian social scientists for the first semester only. These individuals have principal responsibility for the instructional program during this period. Not only do they play a major part in the preparation of the syllabus and reading lists, but they give numerous lectures and lead discussion groups. The Naval War College also employs on a permanent basis a civilian scientist as a member of its research and development group. He is responsible for keeping up to date on research activity in the Navy and making developments known to the faculty and students.

The Army War College also has felt the need of experienced assistance in connection with its instruction in nonmilitary subjects. In 1954–1955 it was planned to secure a resident economist and political scientist for the part of the curriculum dealing with national and international affairs. Approval came too late to make appointments for the year, however, so instead a number of professors were secured for a week or two at a time. Also several other individuals in academic or government positions holding reserve commissions were ordered to the college on active duty for similar periods. These specialists met with student committees and assisted in the preparation of papers and reports. The arrangement worked well and has since been repeated. The Air War College also has experimented with this arrangement. The Army War College, as already noted, uses another device that brings expert advice to its students. During presentation of certain topics, panels of specialists from appropriate military or civilian agencies spend several days at the college working closely with student committees. The Industrial College uses a variation of this same technique.

These arrangements at the joint and service colleges suggest that those responsible for these institutions turn to members of the teaching profession for assistance because of a felt need of experience in nonmilitary areas. By and large the civilians who have been associated with the colleges appear to have made substantial contributions. That they are being used at more of the colleges and on an expanding and continuous basis indicates that their services are well received. The colleges probably could make even more effective use of the civilian faculty members, however. Even at the National War College these individuals, in spite of their qualifications as teachers and scholars, are used primarily for planning and administrative duties. Only at the Naval War College do such civilians really have opportunity to teach in their respective areas of competence over a period of more than a few days.

Locating qualified civilians to serve at the colleges for a semester or a year has become a task of major dimensions. The colleges are anxious to secure individuals who not only have some standing in their professions but also possess the personal qualities that facilitate an informal relationship with students. The problem is not only one of finding suitable people; it is also one of finding those so qualified who can secure release from their regular duties.

One solution to this situation might be for the colleges to encourage the creation of a larger pool of qualified candidates. This might be accomplished by establishing a number of fellowships, along the lines of the National Science Foundation fellowships, whereby one or two young scholars in the social sciences with an interest in national security affairs would spend a year in residence, participating in appropriate portions of the program and engaging in research related both to their own interests and the needs of the military services. The fellows might be selected from among young men who have completed graduate training and about three years of teaching. They would be granted leave from their regular duties, and the fellowships should be so established as to give distinction to both the recipients and their own institutions. Presumably the fellows, after returning to their classrooms, would continue the lines of research initiated at the colleges and would maintain a consulting relationship. Such a scheme not only would advance the interest of American scholars in the relationship of military affairs to foreign and domestic policies, in military history, and in similar areas, but would enlarge the number of individuals upon whom the colleges could rely in the years to come for trained and experienced specialists as lecturers, consultants, and resident faculty members.

Advanced Study and Research

In concluding this analysis of the senior military colleges we return again to the issue discussed at the end of chapter seventeen. Do these colleges, as the institutions of higher learning that they claim to be, stand on the frontiers of knowledge? Do they challenge accepted interpretations of fact or accepted thought or doctrine? Do they probe beyond the bonds of convention, seeking out new ideas and new formulations of security policy?

The colleges acknowledge that while their principal function is to prepare senior officers for high command and staff assignments, they also should contribute to the generation of new ideas and doctrines. All of them have attempted by one device or another to conduct advanced study and research as a specialized function distinct from the regular course of study. For the most part this has proved to be a troublesome and disappointing endeavor. The scope and nature of the task have been defined, but adequate means to carry it out have not yet been found.

The underlying premise is that senior military colleges as institutions of higher learning should not only conduct a standard course for their regular students, but also should engage in research activities comparable to those of a civilian university. This activity should be closely related to problems of national security. In the minds of some advocates, what really is wanted is the production of a few twentieth century Mahans! Others, perhaps, would look to the senior colleges for research work of the kind now performed by the RAND Corporation, the Operations Research Office of the Johns Hopkins University, and other civilian contract research groups.

The Industrial College's ventures in research, which occupied as many as 40 individuals in the peak period between 1944 and 1947, were noted in the preceding chapter. At the National War College the Board of Consultants in the early years frequently proposed establishment of a separate research program. The case was argued eloquently, as indicated by the following passage from one of the board's reports: "The National War College . . . has demonstrated its great value as an educational institution. . . . But education in the broadest sense embraces more than instruction. It includes the constant and critical assessment of past experience and the 'inching out' of new thought based on analysis and reflection. All great educational institutions become the repositories and laboratories of ideas which in turn tend to stimulate and heighten the quality and range of instruction. It would seem to be in keeping with the mission of the National War College to become the national laboratory for the development of ideas governing strategy, just as our great universities have become laboratories for developing ideas in the natural and social sciences and the humanities. This implies a development in the National War College comparable to the development of graduate work in leading universities. As part of this enlarged function the National War College should provide the stimulus for creative and critical research of a long range character and as a means to this end, it should become the center for procuring and evaluating strategic studies from sources all over the world." [11]

As a start toward this difficult accomplishment, the commandant in 1950 established a Strategy and Research Committee, composed of an officer from each of the three services and a fourth member,

[11] Report of Board of Consultants, National War College, 1951.

437

a Foreign Service officer, representing the Department of State. Unfortunately this committee never got going. The members of the group were competent officers, demonstrated by their previous and subsequent service records, but they were not selected for special talents for or interest in research and writing. Much time and effort were devoted to attempting to determine what should be undertaken. After about three years the committee was dissolved as a separate research group and those members remaining were assigned to other duties related to regular instruction. In 1953 the Board of Consultants was less certain about the prospects for research at the college. Two members seriously questioned the feasibility of undertaking such a program at the present stage of development of the institution. The board as a whole concluded that ". . . the experience with the research and analysis committee has shown that distinguished research cannot be expected from a group in which the levels of training, interest, and intellectual curiosity are not uniformly high. Those of us who believe that the College can at present provide the center for a special research and writing program would urge that the program can succeed only if it is staffed with highly qualified and interested men." [12]

These board members proposed the inclusion of several distinguished civilian scholars in the research committee, and the holding of an experimental summer research seminar at the college for military and civilian research personnel. These recommendations were not acted upon and no further attempt has been made to reestablish a special research group.

The service War Colleges also have made serious attempts to undertake advanced study and research. At the Naval War College this came about as a consequence of the bitter public controversy with the Air Force in 1949 over the B-36 bomber and the roles and missions of the services. Certain influential Naval officers, concluding that the Navy had failed to make an adequate case for itself because of lack of a consistent strategic doctrine, were instrumental in establishing at the college in 1951 a group of about five officers to undertake advanced study. During its first year, under the leadership of an exceedingly imaginative officer, the members of this group undertook to ground themselves

[12] Report of Board of Consultants, National War College, 1953.

in the fundamentals of logic, philosophy, economics, and politics. They invited recognized scholars in these fields to be in residence for periods up to several weeks in length, directing individual study and conducting seminars. In the following year they undertook individual research, but continued to meet together in regular seminars. Most members of the original group were enthusiastic about the experience, although none had sought it. As a part of this program the college created the King and Nimitz professorships. The scholars who held these positions initially worked directly with the advanced study group and were encouraged to engage in their own research and writing. After the tours of the original officers in the group terminated, the Bureau of Naval Personnel failed to assign a full quota of officers to the group. Although somewhat more successful than the comparable experiment at the National War College, the Newport group experienced the same difficulties, and its status became uncertain.

The story of advanced research at the Air War College is similar. Here a graduate study group was established in 1952. It was anticipated that 8 to 10 officers would be assigned each year for a two year term. Actually the group never exceeded four members. These men were given the freedom and resources to investigate problems of their own selection, subject only to approval by the commandant of the college. A civilian scholar, an experienced military historian, also was employed to work with the military personnel. Some significant studies appear to have been produced, but in 1955 the group was abolished for lack of adequate support and the few remaining officers were transferred to the evaluation group of the Air University. This unit is not concerned with advanced thought and research but rather with the formulation of statements defining accepted Air Force practice and doctrine. The civilian member of the group was shifted to the regular faculty of the Air War College. In spite of these experiences at sister colleges, the Army War College in 1954 created an advanced study group. The four members were detailed from the existing faculty and were set to work on problems assigned to the college by the Department of the Army.

The senior colleges have not yet fulfilled the expectations of those who have looked to them for leadership in advanced study. The reasons for this situation are rather clear. While the value of research activity is recognized, uncertainty remains as to whether this should be accepted as a function of the colleges apart from their regular responsibilities. Another problem has been the tendency of the service headquarters to pass on to the limited research facilities of the colleges operational problems that they do not have time or staff to handle themselves. To prevent this practice the Joint Chiefs of Staff have prohibited the joint colleges to conduct any inquiry that would place them in a staff relationship to any government agency. Ideally research and advanced study at the senior colleges should be on long range problems instead of current applications. A more serious difficulty has been the operation of personnel policies. Rather than to assign to research activities those relatively few officers who have demonstrated an interest and capacity for this sort of thing, the services have attempted to fill the positions according to regular personnel practices, including rotation after a few years. Perhaps the fundamental cause of the disappointing record, however, is lack among individuals in positions of authority of an understanding of the nature and importance of an intellectual approach to problems of military and national strategy.

In considerable part the deficiencies suggested in this chapter can be corrected by the colleges themselves. But in larger measure they are limited by external factors, that is, by the kind of support that they receive from the parent services. In following chapters we examine the nature and the quality of this support.

PART SIX

HIGHER EDUCATION IN THE

ARMED FORCES

CHAPTER TWENTY

THE SCHOOLS AND THE SERVICES

UNLIKE civilian colleges and universities, military schools are not relatively autonomous institutions. They are part and parcel of the armed services, which have many responsibilities of which military eduction is only one, and not a primary one at that. The achievements of military education cannot be judged apart from this broader context. Its strengths and weaknesses are the products not only of what is done within the schools but of forces external to the schools within the services. The principal measures required to bring further improvement cannot be accomplished by the schools alone.

This dependence upon external factors takes several forms. It rests upon what the services call "support." The services provide buildings, equipment, and operating expenses. Likewise the selection of officers for faculty duty is a function of the personnel agencies of the services. The same holds for the selection of commandants, administrative personnel, and students. The selection process, moreover, cannot be considered apart from the over-all personnel resources and requirements of the services. What is true for the selection process applies to other features of military education as well.

In even larger measure the schools are an intimate part of the services. They remain close to the operators outside. This situation stems from the practice of relatively rapid rotation of commandants and faculty. Officers assigned to the schools bring from previous jobs positive ideas about what the schools should teach. They do not remain long enough to cultivate detached and independent thought. It is their responsibility to gear the instructional programs as closely to the immediate requirements of the services

443

as possible. Likewise the operators keep in touch with the schools. These arrangements certainly are as they should be.

Since the schools are so intimately a part of the services, the first issue of importance is the present attitude of the services toward education. In chapter four we noted that officer education prior to world war II had become a well-established function of the armed forces. Since that time, as this book has demonstrated, the services now attach even more importance to education, and have expanded their school facilities accordingly. To a greater degree than before, education is regarded as an essential part of the armed forces. Yet this emphasis upon formal educational opportunity has its doubters. One still encounters officers, particularly in the higher ranks, who declare that since they were too busy to attend the advanced schools themselves, they do not understand all the fuss about school attendance. A story told by one of the service chiefs of personnel is perhaps revealing. It concerns a priest who was particularly proud of the young boxers trained in the community center that he had founded. One of his protégés was seen by a journalist to cross himself as he stepped into the ring for the finals of a Golden Gloves tournament at Madison Square Garden. "Will that help him?" asked the newsman. "Yes, it will," responded the priest, *"if he is a good fighter!"*

Generally, however, most officers, and particularly younger officers, look upon school attendance favorably. Where a selective process is involved, as at the Command and Staff and War Colleges, they regard it as a mark of distinction. The immediate prospect of a good command is one of the very few reasons that would cause an Army or Air Force colonel or a Navy captain to avoid assignment to his service War College. Likewise the opportunities for graduate study in civilian universities have had a strong appeal.

Thus both the official and the generally prevailing attitudes are favorable to support of officer education. These attitudes, however, are qualified by a variety of interpretations and emphasis both among the three services and within each of them. These are by no means clearly and precisely defined. As we have noted, the services strive for the formulation of doctrine, the standardization of policies and procedures. Officer education is among those activities in which doctrine remains incomplete and variable. The uncertainties relate not only to the substantive content of education programs, but to such issues as organization of administrative supervision, quantity versus quality in education, selection of students and faculty, and assignment of graduates.

Administrative Supervision

The administrative pattern employed by each of the services in support of its education programs has a direct bearing upon the quality of that support. The military schools must compete with more dramatic and costly requirements of the armed forces for a fair share of available resources, personnel, and funds. Unless they have access to responsible leaders they face serious difficulty in holding their own in a highly competitive environment. Insofar as they maintain the interest and respect of these leaders, they may expect to prosper.

THE ARMY

Administrative direction of Army educational activities is scattered among several agencies at different levels.[1] General over-all supervision of all training activities is a responsibility of the General Staff. By delegation much of this is handled by the organization and training division in the Office of the Deputy Chief of Staff for Military Operations.[2] This division is concerned with such questions as whether a new school should be established, the definition of its mission and broad outlines of its curriculum, and whether and to what extent the Army should participate in joint and foreign schools. Personnel policies affecting the schools are the responsibility of the Office of the Deputy Chief of Staff for Personnel (formerly G-1). The actual selection of officers for school attendance, including graduate study in civilian institutions, is in the hands of the Career Management Division of the Adjutant General's Office for the combat arms and of the separate technical services for their officers. Other sections of the General Staff, such as Intelligence, Strategic Plans, Logistic Plans, and Research and Development, have opportunity to review the curricula of the

[1] One official report that we have seen indicated that there were 14 different agencies concerned with Army school policies.

[2] Prior to the Army reorganization of January 1, 1956, the division was located in the Office of the Assistant Chief of Staff, G-3 (Plans and Operations), which was eliminated on that date.

schools and to suggest modifications. They are particularly concerned with the doctrines that are taught in their areas of responsibility.

More detailed supervision of Army schools is exercised by the Continental Army Command, which replaced the former Army Field Forces in 1954. This command has primary responsibility for development of plans for and supervision of the training of individuals and combined units of the Army, including integration of the training activities of the staff sections of the General Staff and the technical services. It approves all training literature and doctrine. The branch schools and certain of the specialist schools of the Army are operated by their respective combat arms or technical services, but are now coordinated by the Continental Army Command. The six continental armies in the United States also have some responsibility for those schools that are situated within their geographic areas. For the most part these relate to supervision of military operations and approval of budget estimates, plans for new buildings, and other housekeeping matters. Actually, however, this authority may be so exercised as to have bearing upon educational plans and programs. Since 1954 the continental armies have been under the command of the Continental Army Command.

Supervision of the Military Academy, as was suggested in chapter nine, presents a special case. As one of the most solidly established and sacred institutions in the entire service, the academy is not subject to the sort of administrative control that the advanced schools experience. It has a great deal more autonomy with respect to its internal affairs than do even the Command and General Staff College and the Army War College. Those large policy issues that require outside direction are handled at the highest level, frequently on a personal basis, in the General Staff and the Department of the Army. Those matters which are delegated to staff sections are of a routine character. The ROTC program comes under the control of the Continental Army Command and the continental armies. At the General Staff level it is supervised by the Office of Reserve and ROTC Affairs in the Office of the Deputy Chief of Staff for Military Operations.

This brief summary indicates that professional military education in the Army not only is closely associated with training activities, which greatly overshadow education in terms of numbers of individuals and resources, but also is subject to diffused direction. There is no separate single organization that supervises and promotes the Army's education interests at a high level. In 1949 the Eddy board, which reviewed Army officer education, declared that the lack of central control and coordination was unsatisfactory. This board, which was composed of the commandants of five Army schools and representatives of the Army Field Forces and the Organization and Training Division of the General Staff, strongly recommended the establishment of a central agency or headquarters, under a director of the Army educational system, with "the rank, authority, and means commensurate with the task." This headquarters should function "both as a *command* (answerable directly to the chief of staff, United States Army), and as a *general staff supervisory agency.*" The Eddy board visualized that the director "would be the technical educational expert for all Army schools. As such he would plan, coordinate, and direct the educational activities of the various Army schools. These activities relate not to *what* is taught but to *how* it is taught. They would include educational methods and procedures, curriculum design, techniques of learning, and instructor training." [3] While this recommendation was not accepted, some of its objectives have been accomplished with the establishment of the Continental Army Command.

THE NAVY

In the Navy, officer education also is treated administratively as a part of the over-all training function. The Bureau of Naval Personnel is the organization most directly concerned. Several divisions within the bureau share responsibility for Naval education. The training division has general supervisory authority over educational matters, but for the most part it is preoccupied with its large scale training responsibilities. It directs training activities for enlisted personnel, including a variety of specialist training programs, correspondence courses, and an information and education program. It is responsible for the Naval ROTC officer candidate programs, and it conducts correspondence programs.

[3] *Report of the Department of the Army Board on Educational System for Officers,* 15 June 1949.

The training division also exercises administrative responsibility for the Naval Academy, the Naval Postgraduate School, and the Naval War College. In the cases of the academy and the college this is limited to handling fiscal affairs and logistic support.[4] The Postgraduate School, because of its recent reorganizations, has been a subject of more direct concern. Some questions concerning these institutions, such as whether a program is to be extended or curtailed, or whether age and length-of-service requirements for admission are changed, are the concern of the Personnel Plans Branch of the Bureau of Naval Personnel. The selection of line officers for duty as faculty or students is handled by the Officer Personnel Division of the bureau. This division also coordinates the selection of officers by the separate corps to fill their allotted quotas. The Navy's civilian institutions program is administered by the Postgraduate School.

Educational and policy issues relating to the Naval Academy, Postgraduate School, and Naval War College are the business of the Office of the Chief of Naval Operations, and sometimes of the chief of Naval operations himself. Likewise on substantive matters, such as instruction in a particular subject field, interested organizations in the Bureau of Naval Operations and other bureaus deal directly with the schools. All interested units are given opportunity to review the school curricula and to recommend changes.

THE AIR FORCE

With its establishment as a separate service, the Air Force had a rare opportunity to start from scratch in erecting an administrative structure for its officer education program. As early as 1945 the AAF turned away from the relatively decentralized control of the Army and the Navy and established a single, unified organization, which it called the Air University. This resulted very largely from the leadership of the late General Muir S. Fairchild, who served as its first commander. General Fairchild's success was not achieved without opposition, including the charge of empire building. It was facilitated by approval of General Eisenhower, then chief of staff of the Army, of which the AAF was still

---

[4] A director of the Training Division remarked to one of the authors that it was not likely that he, a captain, would suggest to the president of the Naval War College, a vice admiral, or to the superintendent of the Naval Academy, a rear admiral, how they might operate their institutions.

a part. The Air Force, moreover, in implementing plans for officer education, recognized a distinction between the education and training functions by placing them in separate organizations. The latter are the operational responsibility of the Air Training Command and the Continental Air Command.

As now constituted, the Air University is one of the major commands of the Air Force. The commanding officer reports to the chief of staff through the director of personnel procurement and training, in the Office of the Deputy Chief of Staff (Personnel).[5] The constituent units of the Air University are the Air War College, the Air Command and Staff College (which includes the Command and Staff School and the Squadron Officer School), the Air Force ROTC, the Institute of Technology, the School of Aviation Medicine, the Air Force Extension Course Institute, the Air University Library, and the Research Studies Institute. The Institute of Technology administers the Air Force's civilian institutions program as well as its own instruction in technical fields. The Research Studies Institute includes a Historical Division, which produces a wide variety of histories and special studies, including the seven volume *History of the Army Air Forces in World War II*, the Arctic-Desert-Tropic Information Center, which conducts research and prepares information on nontemperate zones relating particularly to survival in these zones, and a Documentary Research Division, which prepares monographs and other materials of interest to the constituent schools of the Air University and to the Air Force at large.

The Air University also includes the 3,894th School Group, consisting of all Air Force officers assigned as instructors to Army, Navy, and RAF schools. They are brought to Maxwell periodically for instruction in the latest Air Force doctrine. Transfer of command of the ROTC program from the Continental Air Command, which is concerned with reserve training, to the Air University signified the importance that the Air Force attached to the educational character of the program as well as to its potential as a principal source of active duty officer personnel. At Maxwell also is located the Officer Education Research Laboratory,

---

[5] The commander of the Air University normally has held the rank of lieutenant general. In 1955 the position fell vacant and was filled on an "acting" basis by the deputy commander, a major general. Finally, about a year later, this officer was designated commander; some months thereafter he was made a lieutenant general.

which is part of the Air Research and Development Command, but undertakes studies of interest to the various schools at the base. Air University headquarters includes a deputy commander for education (a general officer), an educational advisor (a civilian), and an Education and Research Division, staffed largely by civilians, which provides a variety of services including curriculum planning and evaluation to all of the schools of the university. The Academic Instructor Course of the Air Command and Staff College also serves the entire Air University, as does the Air University Library. Thus the Air University is an integrated educational system within a single organization, including research and service units as well as a number of schools at different levels.

The Air Force has not chosen to place its new Air Force Academy within the Air University system. As we have already described, the Air University was given the responsibility for formulating detailed plans for the academy, but direction of the project was elevated to a special staff section in Washington during the critical phase of securing enabling legislation for the establishment of the new institution. The secretary and the chief of staff have retained a personal concern for its progress. It can be expected that the academy will continue to be directed from the highest level, at least for some time to come.

Policy decisions concerning officer education, as with the Army and Navy, are made in Washington, principally by the agencies concerned with personnel matters in the Office of the Deputy Chief of Staff (Personnel). But here again the Air Force, unlike the other services, has separated education and training. The planning aspects of officer education are handled by a Professional Education Division; selection of faculty and students is the concern of the Schools Branch of the Officer Assignment Division.

The Air University system seems to offer positive advantages over the less centralized administrative pattern in the other services. Perhaps the greatest value comes from the standing and prestige that it affords to officer education within the Air Force. Education is separated from the training function. The Air University, moreover, is represented at regular meetings of the commanders of other major commands by its own commander. Here he may uphold the interests of Air Force schools against unplanned encroachments by the operational commands, while at the same time remaining sensitive to their needs. The headquarters organization of the Air University provides coordinated direction to all schools and related activities and furnishes useful supporting services. The location of the principal schools at Maxwell strengthens each of them in the same way that the separate units of a civilian institution are strengthened by membership in a university community.

Yet the advantages of the Air Force system should not be exaggerated, significant as they are. The Continental Army Command and the Bureau of Naval Personnel provide for their respective services coordinating and directing functions similar to, although less thorough than, those of Air University headquarters. In the Air Force, as in the Army and Navy, broad issues, such as the relationship of education programs to other activities, personnel assignment policies, and allocation of resources must be negotiated among numerous organizations within the Air Staff in Washington. We have concluded, however, that it would be of advantage to the Army and the Navy to follow the leadership of the Air Force in centralizing the command responsibility for officer education. This need not involve relocation of existing schools at a principal location, as the Air Force has done at Maxwell Field. But it should result in a clearer distinction between training and education activities and in greater prestige and influence for the latter within the services. In the last analysis, much depends upon the qualities of the officers selected to command the military schools, upon their capacities for leadership, and their abilities to represent education programs in dealing with responsible authorities.

CIVILIAN SUPERVISION

This brief account of supervisory arrangements and other evidence already cited suggest that the secretaries of the Army, Navy, and Air Force and their civilian associates in the three service departments do not ordinarily concern themselves with the professional education of career officers. This situation stems from a recognized division of labor among civilian and military authorities. The former are concerned with broad policy matters and with representation of the services to other executive agencies, to the Congress, and to the public. In the Navy, and to a less extent in the Army and Air Force, they also are principally responsible for certain "business" aspects of the services, such as procurement. Military authorities, on the other hand, are responsible for the functions of command, one of the most important of which is the training of personnel. Officer education, as we have indicated, is closely associated with training activities and thus falls within the traditional area of military responsibility. Insofar as civilian authorities do concern themselves with training, they do so in connection with consideration of the broad problems of procuring manpower and administering personnel.

A second cause for the relative lack of civilian interest in officer education is the fact that it rarely presents any serious problems, breaking a pattern of routine accomplishment. Rarely does officer education force itself upon the attention of the secretaries and assistant secretaries, who have plenty of controversial issues and recurring crises in other areas to preoccupy their time and energies. This does not mean to say that civilian secretaries and their associates neglect the schools. On the contrary, they frequently visit them and address the students. But they need do little more.

There are of course exceptions to this situation. It will be recalled from earlier in our history, that Secretary Bancroft established the Naval Academy by a departmental order. Secretary of War Root created the Army War College and inspired the development of the modern Command and General Staff School. During world war II Secretary Forrestal took a personal interest in certain aspects of Naval officer education, and he, Ferdinand Eberstadt, and other civilians followed the plans for postwar officer education with considerable interest. The Army Industrial College before the war and the Industrial College of the Armed Forces as recently as 1948 were under civilian supervision in the War and Army Departments. As was noted in chapter six, Secretary of Defense Louis Johnson unsuccessfully attempted to alter the structure of the military academies and to integrate the National War College and Industrial College. The academies and ROTC programs, because of interest of parents, friends, and Congressmen, do demand some attention. Final approval of the plan to establish an air force academy was facilitated by action by Secretaries Symington, Finletter, and Talbot. The latter continued to intervene in the affairs of the new academy, personally concerning himself with such matters as selection of the faculty, design of cadet uniforms, and prospects of the football team. But as a general rule, determination of the substantive content of education programs and supervision of military schools have been left up to military authorities. This situation is satisfactory to most military officers. They do not regard officer education as a fitting subject of civilian authority. While we are sympathetic with this position and do not wish to see the erection of needless administrative machinery within the service departments, we conclude that greater interest on the part of the secretaries and their civilian associates would be in the interest of officer education and of the services. Generally such interest, when it has been expressed, has stimulated progress toward the introduction of new areas and methods of study which have strengthened officer education. Unfortunately the turnover in the last decade of secretaries and assistant secretaries has been so rapid that few of these officials have had opportunity to become sufficiently well acquainted with the problems of military education. Reasonable stability of tenure is a prerequisite for any sort of civilian leadership in this as in other fields of responsibility.

Selection of Personnel

The quality of the military schools is not fixed finally by high level decisions about their missions. To a great extent it is determined by the decisions of the personnel agencies that select students, staff, and faculty. Their innumerable and detailed operating determinations may either support or undermine the lofty statements of intent that are drawn up at the start. It is therefore necessary to take a closer look at the mechanisms and policies of the three services in this area. Because of the special emphasis of this study, we shall limit our comments to the senior schools. We turn first to the selection of students.

STUDENTS

Approximately 700 vacancies are available each year at the National War College, the Industrial College, and three service War Colleges. Each service establishes its own eligibility criteria for attendance at its own schools and the joint schools. Criteria may include such factors as rank, years of service, promotion list standing, prior educational experience, and years of service remaining. Officers within the "eligibility zone" may volunteer for school assignment, but it is not necessary for them to do so because all those within the zone are automatically considered for selection. Boards of officers are convened annually to review the records of all eligible officers and to determine which ones should be selected for each school.[6] Alternates are also designated. The slate is then reviewed by higher authorities within the personnel departments of the services or by the chiefs of service or both.[7]

The pool of eligibles established by the formal criteria is not as large as one might expect. For practical purposes it includes only career officers. It is also limited by special administrative requirements. There are, for example, persuasive economic reasons why an Army officer who has just been transferred from Fort Sill to Korea should not be turned around to spend nine months at the Army War College in Pennsylvania, and then returned to Korea to complete his overseas assignment. Selections are more likely to be limited to those who are just completing such tours of duty, or who have one more year remaining in the United States before they are scheduled for overseas or shipboard stations. It is difficult to estimate the extent to which such factors limit the size of the pool of eligibles. But the ratio of actual "competitors" to vacancies probably does not average out much higher than four to one.

A somewhat different type of limitation follows from the tendency to give "line" officers a proportionately larger number of appointments. In the Air Force about 80 percent of those who are selected for the higher schools are rated (qualified for flight duty) officers. In the Navy the largest quotas are reserved for unrestricted

---

[6] A slightly different procedure has been used in selecting Army officers of the combat arms. Eligibles have been evaluated by means of a point system, and their scores have constituted a general guide to the Career Management Division of the Adjutant General's Office, which makes the selections. The weights assigned to different factors under the point system are varied from time to time, but the following weights, based on a scale of 100, are an example of how the system may work: efficiency reports (49), command experience (18), staff experience (13), combat experience (8), troop duty (8), rank (2), instructor duty (2).

[7] The selection of Army officers to attend the Industrial College has in the past been reviewed by an assistant secretary of the Army, but this is the only instance of review by civilian officials that we have been able to discover.

line officers. In the Army, combat arms personnel receive about two thirds of the appointments to the National War College. However, technical and administrative service officers receive about four fifths of the appointments to the Industrial College.

In selecting from the pool, the services make no special effort to determine which officers are most likely to do distinguished academic work. The question is which officers are most likely to excel in the service as a whole, not in school. This means that preference should be given to those whose past records disclose that they have great promise as professional officers and that they have not already been equipped with the knowledge and skill that the school seeks to develop. In practice some officers are selected simply as a reward for meritorious service. They may not even need the education. We know of a few men who were already so highly qualified in the relevant subject matters that they should have been sent to particular schools as instructors. Instead they attended as students.

In the past many schools have also had to battle a tendency of selection officials to choose officers simply because there were no other demands for their services—always an ominous sign! Admiral E. C. Kalbfus, who served two terms as president of the Naval War College, has said that right up to the early 1940's a number of officers were sent to Newport "who had no naval future," but who could be spared at the moment.[8] The Air Force invited a similar practice in the early postwar years when it permitted commanding generals in the field to "nominate" candidates for selection to schools. Happily this problem is somewhat less serious today.

But in the nature of things there must always be much pulling and hauling for the best men. They are few in number, widely known, and heavily in demand. The schools are only one of the many claimants. The case for giving them priority is similar to the case for diverting resources to capital formation rather than to current production in the hope that this will pay off in the long run. But regardless of what priorities are established, it becomes necessary to break the rules from time to time. Army officials have told us there are some officers whom they do not even

8 *The United States Naval War College,* a staff study, Newport, 1954, Appendix N, p. 13.

consider for selection at particular times because they know they could not get them released from "hot" assignments. The Strategic Air Command, which must stand in perpetual readiness for major crises, has often protested the draining off of highly qualified officers for school. Similar protests have been registered in the Navy. Not all these pleas, of course, are heeded; and often personnel officials can solve their problems with justice to all by waiting until an officer's current tour of duty is about to expire before plucking him out. Through such policies, and through a determined effort to resist demands for special considerations, selection officials have managed to hold the "slippage" rate to about 15 percent. That is, of the principals originally selected to attend the advanced schools, about 85 percent are actually on hand when classes start. The others are replaced by alternates, either because they have been selected for promotion to general or flag rank, or because of an irresistible demand for their services elsewhere, or because the officer himself does not wish to attend.

Selection officials have also been known to pass over a highly qualified officer because he cannot "afford" to go to school. His otherwise brilliant record may disclose that he has not yet had enough command experience in the field or at sea. If such an individual is selected for school at a time when this imbalance in his career could otherwise be corrected, his chances for eventual promotion may be jeopardized gravely. A Naval officer, for example, spends only about ten years in the grade of captain. During that time he must hold a major qualifying command if he is to go further in the service. Selection officials would consider it a real injustice to deny a promising captain such a command just to fill a school quota. The wise and ambitious officer knows these facts of life too, and he may refuse an assignment to school if he wishes to. There are also some "fireballs" who are much too restless to put up with this sort of an interlude in their careers. In one of the services we were shown a chart that indicated clearly that those officers who were regarded as the very best—perhaps the top 5 percent—rarely attended an advanced school. But the same chart indicated that a majority of the top 25 percent did attend, and that none of the bottom 25 percent attended. The conclusion we draw from all these facts is one that was actually voiced to us by an officer who has had a heavy responsibility for selections in his particular service. "We try to choose the best available," he said, "which is not exactly the same as choosing the best."

The greatest problem of all is beyond the control of selection officials. This is the question of whether the advanced schools are to be relatively small or large; in short, whether the emphasis is to be placed on *quality* or on *quantity*. The decision here has to come directly from the chiefs of the services. They cannot escape the issue; nor is there an obvious answer to it. Smaller student bodies probably make easier the maintenance of high standards of selection. But the growing complexity of military assignments continually generates fresh demands for high level education. In recent years the pressures for expansion have been stronger than the pressures for contraction. Some of these pressures are generated within the military establishment itself. For example, the promotion rate among school graduates is likely to be high whenever selection officials designate outstanding men for attendance. But many officers see only the correlation between attendance and promotion. They want to go to school. Personnel officers are then tempted to conclude that relatively large numbers must go in order to prevent spread of the idea that arbitrary competitive advantages have been conferred on a few. There is also a growing demand from field commanders who realize, shrewdly, that school graduates probably have to be better than average officers to get selected in the first place. This realization may be contagious, and the ultimate result may be a real clamor for "fair shares for all." Certainly in recent years assignment officers have had to ration the output of the schools quite closely. The Navy has acknowledged that the number of requests for graduates "greatly exceeds" the number of graduates available. The Air Force in 1954 received 1,700 requests for the 240 men it had available. In the Army, between 1951 and 1954, no requesting agency received more than 39 percent of the graduates that it sought. In most cases the figure was far lower. General Staff agencies, for example, got about 20 percent; overseas joint and combined agencies got from 5 to 10 percent.

FACULTY

The problem of securing qualified staff and faculty is still more difficult. One reason is that officers often feel—and with some justification—that their prospects for future advancement are poorer if they are sent to a school as members of the faculty than if they are sent as students. A second reason is that the services make less of an effort to get outstanding officers for such positions. For example, they do not use selection boards, point systems, or other competitive devices of the kind used in selecting students.[9] They may allow the schools to veto proposed assignments. They may even permit them to do a certain amount of informal negotiating to get particular officers by name. But on the whole the commandants do not have a great voice in the selection of their educational associates. They must fend for themselves in a competitive market in which they have relatively little to offer. If a field commander, for example, presses a request for a particular man who is also under consideration as a prospective *student,* personnel officials may deny the request on the ground that the school experience will increase the individual's long run value to the service. But if the man is under consideration as a prospective *faculty member,* this argument will not be used.

All this may explain why the advanced schools recruit so many of their staff members from each graduating class. At least they have had an opportunity to become acquainted with these officers; and they can count on some minimum amount of substantive knowledge as well as familiarity with school routines. Personnel officials are also likely to acquiesce since this system saves them a lot of trouble. As a general principle of recruitment it has little else to commend it. Despite the number of excellent officers who turn up in the process, the system does not really provide a faculty that is capable of exercising leadership in a serious intellectual enterprise. Many of the better men in each graduating class are requested by name for assignment outside. Others take the pains to negotiate their next assignment directly with personnel officials in their service headquarters. Some of those who volunteer to remain do so less because of their intrinsic interest in the school's

[9] This in itself decreases the prestige of the faculty relative to the students, who know they are "picked" men.

program than because they do not wish to subject their families to yet another move, or for other personal reasons.

The system of selecting civilian faculty members also leaves something to be desired. At a few of the institutions some of the civilians have semipermanent status. From an educational standpoint this makes sense only when a man has had to compete with other candidates for such status, and only when at least one of the candidates is a person of real intellectual distinction. These conditions are met at the better civilian universities. Unless they can be met at military schools, it would seem to be the part of wisdom to employ the majority of civilian instructors on a short term basis. This can be done with least hardship to individuals if the policy is applied to new staff members as they are employed rather to incumbents. It should decrease the danger of recruiting time-servers and increase the likelihood that men of the very first rank will be obtained. The latter objective, however, will not be attained unless there is also an aggressive search for talent and a readiness to make these appointments attractive in terms of salary, status, housing, and other amenities, and above all in terms of opportunity to participate constructively in the educational program. It is our impression that these conditions are not always met by all of those schools that employ civilians on a permanent basis.

Our concluding observation is that the selection of faculty is an area in which both the schools and the services could use a great deal more imagination than they do. Distinguished officers on active duty, for example, might be obtained if the schools were willing to take them for brief periods. Distinguished retired officers or retired public servants could be sought as instructors or regular visitors. There are many reserve officers who would be both interested in and qualified for such assignments. Some career officers have written widely in fields with which the schools are concerned or have serious research interests that they would like to pursue in an academic setting. Others, including many who have taught at the service academies, have had relevant and excellent postgraduate training at government expense, as well as assignments that have broadened their understanding of the problems considered at the senior schools. Greater efforts to secure such individuals could result in faculties of broader perspective or experience, greater readiness to insist on exacting standards of performance, and a higher capacity to generate a spirit of creative inquiry in what are, after all, the highest educational institutions in the armed forces. The services might also seriously consider establishment of a few permanent faculty positions at the senior colleges similar in status and distinction to the professorships at West Point.

ASSIGNMENT OF GRADUATES

One remaining personnel problem of great importance to all the senior colleges is the nature of the assignments received by their graduates. It should be noted at once that no effort is made to determine these assignments in advance. Rarely will an officer be sent to a particular school to prepare him for a specific subsequent position.[10] On the contrary, a conscious effort is made to avoid too close an identification between specific colleges and specific kinds of military duty. The theory is that the colleges should widen a man's horizons for the next step along the road. But this theory still leaves plenty of room for argument about whether assignments do or do not take into account an officer's special educational experience. Individual officers are heard to ask, "Why did they put me on this job after spending ten months preparing me for something else?" Officials at the schools are heard to debate whether their graduates should be assigned to operating forces in the field or primarily to high level staff and planning duties in Washington and in the major headquarters overseas.

In practice both types of assignments are quite common. The latter absorb from one third to one half of the graduates, the percentages varying from year to year, from school to school, and from service to service. In recent times slightly more than 50 percent of the Army graduates of advanced schools (usually colonels) have been assigned to what are termed the "administrative areas," although the agencies in these areas are relatively small and utilize only a fraction of all Army colonels. These agencies are at the General Staff or higher level. They include the Offices of the

---

[10] There are exceptions, e.g. officers who are sent to civilian universities to prepare for duty at a service academy, and those sent to the NATO Defense College prior to assignment to SHAPE and other NATO headquarters.

Secretary and Assistant Secretaries of the Army, the Joint Staff, and the Office of the Secretary of Defense. Less than 50 percent have been assigned to what are normally much larger customers for colonels, namely overseas commands, continental armies and installations, and technical and administrative services. This slicing of the pie clearly reveals a tendency to give priority to staff and planning functions. In the Navy, if a graduate gets a shore assignment, it is somewhat more likely to be the same kind of assignment he would have received if he had not attended an advanced school. The position of the Bureau of Naval Personnel is that "overall qualifications will have been enhanced, but not greatly altered," by attendance. In all services, of course, vulnerability for overseas (or sea) duty is a first consideration. In all services, also, consideration is sometimes given to the personal desires of the individual concerned. These are not, it should be remembered, junior officers.

To recount the actual practices of the services in this matter does not dispose of the issue of what those practices should be. On this point we have definite views. We are not sympathetic with those who wish to associate particular schools very closely with particular types of military duty. We see little merit in the contention that graduates of a service War College should almost invariably be assigned to a position in that service, while graduates of a joint college should almost invariably be assigned to a joint or combined headquarters. We wholly disagree with the argument that graduates of the National War College should almost invariably be assigned to strategic planning, while graduates of the Industrial College should almost invariably be assigned to logistics planning. Finally, we reject firmly the position that graduates of any of these schools should almost invariably be assigned to staff and planning agencies in Washington rather than to operating forces in the field.

We have several reasons for this. First, we agree with the contention made above that the senior colleges should be developers of men rather than training grounds for particular headquarters. Second, there are important practical reasons why high level staff and planning positions cannot always be filled by War College graduates. The position may have to be filled immediately; the graduate may not be available immediately. The position may

461

require a highly specific background. For example, a Naval attaché in Germany should be a very able officer, know the language and the country, and have some specialized knowledge of submarines. It may well happen that the only captain who meets all three qualifications is not a senior school graduate. Third, positions in high level staff and planning agencies in Washington are not always of the utmost importance. It is easy to be deceived in this matter by organization titles. There are relatively routine jobs in the upper reaches of the Pentagon just as there are very responsible ones in the fleets, the armies, and the air forces. Fourth, some of these assignments, even when they are of major consequence, promise less in the way of ultimate rewards to those who hold them. This unfortunately tends to be true of duty in such areas as public relations, comptrollership, intelligence, legislative liaison, procurement, research and development, foreign aid, and manpower supply. On the face of it these functions are tangential to the fighting missions. Officers engaged in them are often specialists who are destined to retire in the grade of colonel or captain. If not specialists, they are often "orphans" cut off from the service, or the component of service, in which they must make their reputations. Duty in these areas is often less highly regarded both by Congress and by promotion boards, which in this respect probably reflect the opinion of the professional officer corps.[11] Indeed the secretary of defense and some service secretaries have found it necessary to issue explicit instructions to promotion boards to give as much weight to assignments in these areas as to more conventional military duty.[12] Any senior school that is regarded as inseparably linked either to routine or to "dead end" positions will be avoided like the plague by the very officers it should seek to attract. Many times we have been told that such a policy would be the "kiss of death" to the college.

Our conclusion is that the criterion of a proper assignment is simply whether the position is in fact a responsible one, a more responsible one than the officer would have obtained had he not

[11] Congressional hearings on the number of senior officer billets in the services are revealing in this regard. Legislators tend to accept without question the need for such billets in the operating forces but to question sharply employment of admirals and generals in "desk" jobs.

[12] See, for example, letter from secretary of the Navy to president of selection board considering promotion of captains to temporary rank of rear admiral, 1 July 1955; text in *Army Navy Air Force Journal*, July 9, 1955, p. 1353.

been sent to an advanced school. Even this formula must be qualified. One thing wrong with it is that the present system of selection does not always result in sending the best qualified men to school. Some are sent who lack the talent to benefit from their special education or to undertake highly responsible work afterward.[13] Surely it is unreasonable that less capable officers should be assigned, say, to the Office of International Security Affairs in the Department of Defense simply because they have survived a senior military college. The other difficulty is that the formula itself is very vague—so vague that it lends itself both to misinterpretation and to deliberate abuse.

We believe that both difficulties become more serious as the number of officers selected for advanced education increases, and less serious as the number decreases. This brings us back to the issue of quantity versus quality. We believe this issue should be decided in favor of quality. The services must resist pressures to educate so many officers at the senior colleges that many who could not benefit are included, while others who could benefit fail to receive the attention they deserve from selection boards, assignment officers, or faculty members at the colleges. An attempt to put more and more officers through these schools can only lower their standards and their prestige.

Advisory Groups

An additional form of external support of officer education deserves consideration here. This is the use of Boards of Visitors, special advisory groups, and *ad hoc* review boards. These groups of varying authority, composition, and tenure provide an irregular but sometimes effective means not only of assisting the schools in strengthening their programs but also of bringing to the attention of appropriate officials the needs and problems of officer education.

Not all of the schools make provision for a Board of Visitors. At the military academies they are prescribed by law. By a 1948 act of Congress they now consist of 15 members: 6 private citizens, 4 senators, and 5 representatives, appointed by the President,

[13] One of our informants made the point bluntly: "If dogmeat is put into the grinder, dogmeat will come out."

the Vice President, and the speaker of the House, respectively. In practice the academies have a hand in the nomination of the Presidential appointees. They are authorized to inquire annually into the affairs of the academies and to report in writing thereon to the President. These "visitations," which date back to the time when West Point and Annapolis were founded, have often been very helpful. The boards have functioned both as *lobbyist* for the academies, supporting the requests they have made of higher governmental authorities, and as constructive *critics*. It also must be said that the boards have sometimes questioned their own effectiveness, and that their suggestions, although transmitted to the President and to the military departments, have rarely been regarded by academy officials as anything more than advisory opinions. A Board of Visitors, like a British monarch, can only advise, encourage and warn. It cannot, and should not, govern.

At the Air University General Muir Fairchild, the first commander, arranged for a Board of Visitors on a regular continuing basis. It is now authorized to "inquire into the organization, management, policies, curriculum, methods of instruction, physical equipment, and other matters relating to the Air University" and to "advise the commanding general . . . on matters of broad policy and assist him in the direction of [its] educational mission." It is composed of 12 members "who are outstanding authorities in the educational field," serving three year staggered terms.[14] While selected by the Air University, they serve at the personal invitation of the chief of staff of the Air Force. General Fairchild was instrumental in filling the first board with a distinguished group of university presidents, headed by the late Isaiah Bowman of Johns Hopkins. In recent years industrialists also have been appointed to the board. It has been a practice to include the United States commissioner of education. Usually the board meets for a period of four to five days each year, with about two thirds of the members present. It is briefed by the commander and members of his headquarters staff. Subcommittees spend several days in briefings and observations of the constituent schools, including those at some distance from Maxwell Field. A final report is approved by the entire board and forwarded to the chief of staff. The board also makes an informal oral report to the commander

14 Air Force Regulation 14–19, 15 December 1950.

of the Air University and his associates, discussing issues of special concern both to the board and to Air University personnel.

The Board of Visitors has proved to be a useful device to the Air University. The commander and his associates speak candidly of their problems and earnestly seek the help of the visitors. The annual reports indicate that while the visitors have little time for details they do examine large issues facing the Air University, including curriculum content, methods of instruction, and selection and tenure of instructional personnel. Frequently they commend to the favorable attention of Washington authorities the measures upon which the Air University seeks approval. At times the board takes the initiative in stressing conclusions reached by its own observations, such as the importance of an educational rather than a training approach to the mission of the Air University and the importance of providing a broad knowledge of the economic, political, and international setting of Air Force problems. One of the early boards looked into a situation involving apparent discrimination against an officer for speaking out in contradiction to Air Force policy. This caused the Air University authorities to reiterate their firm support of academic freedom. Another, in reporting on the Air War College, expressed some doubt as to the adequacy of preparation of officers "concerned with problems of policy and broad strategy, unhampered by allegiances to any particular service branch." [15]

The Army, lacking a unified command organization encompassing its educational activities, has not provided for a board similar to that of the Air University. But individual schools from time to time have employed advisory groups. At the Army War College, for example, such groups were convened in 1952 and 1954. In both cases board members already were familiar from previous experience with the special problems of officer education. Each group spent three days of intensive study at the college, listening to briefings, questioning the commandant and deputy, members of the faculty and class, and observing the program at first hand. The authorities indulged in frank and open discussion of their problems and the evidence indicates that the reports of the advisory boards were given careful study not only at the college but in the Department of the Army. Similar boards are used at Leaven-

[15] *Fourth Report of the Board of Visitors, Air University,* 1948.

worth and at the other Army schools. These schools also utilize the services of individual consultants for short periods. Except for the special case of the Naval Academy, the Navy schools under review in this book do not make the practice of using advisory groups, although they do turn to individual consultants from time to time.

Among the three joint colleges, both the National War College and the Industrial College have advisory groups. The Board of Consultants of the National War College usually consists of six or seven members, serving three year terms. The group usually has included one or more college or university presidents, and several others from the academic world, including one or two former members of the college faculty. In 1953 General Omar Bradley accepted an invitation to join the board, the first time a retired officer was included. The group meets at the college for two or three days in the spring, hearing briefings by the commandant and his associates and observing the program in action. Its reports, which upon occasion have constituted a comprehensive review of the college, are submitted to the commandant but are forwarded to the Joint Chiefs as a part of the annual report. At times, as in 1953 when the commandant was concerned about the large problem of the relationship of the college to the service War Colleges, the meetings of the board are preceded by thorough staff work by the college. The commandant at that time communicated with members of the board, acquainting them in some detail with the issues that he proposed to raise for their consideration. In recent years the Advisory Board of the Industrial College, which is composed for the most part of industrialists, has not convened regularly. It has been the practice of the commandant to seek the advice of the members informally and to communicate with them concerning special problems of the institution.

Advisory boards and similar devices appear to strengthen officer education. Where regularly scheduled annual meetings are held, the necessary preparation involved stimulates careful stock taking by those responsible for the operation of the schools. We have observed that these authorities are remarkably candid in discussing weaknesses as well as achievements. In this respect they appear to be more objective than many civilian educators. This sort of critical self-analysis is a healthy manifestation. Frequently the consultants can offer help in the solution of problems, providing a fresh, detached approach. An even more important contribution is the provision of outside support for officer education where it is sometimes needed most, among higher authorities. Such support at times may tip the scales. The intervention of the Air University Board of Visitors, for example, resulted in the reinstatement of provision for a new library in the building program after Air University protests had failed to halt its prior rejection. Congressional members of the academy boards may help to secure approval of appropriations or legislation sought by these schools. Lastly, the boards serve as a means of enlarging the area of public knowledge of and interest in military education. Broadly speaking, the boards have encouraged military authorities to extend instruction in nonmilitary fields, and to break away from a purely professional approach, stressing the value of a general as opposed to a narrow technical education.

On the other hand the effectiveness of this device is seriously limited, as numerous individuals who have served in this connection have reported to us. The boards meet for a period of only a few days and cannot possibly probe deeply into the many topics raised for consideration. This is particularly so of the academy boards, very few of whose members manage to remain for the full meeting.[16] A considerable number do not attend at all. Although they have complete freedom to investigate what they wish, the time of board meetings is short, the selection of issues for consideration perforce rests with the school authorities, and considerable time is devoted to briefings and social and ceremonial events. Moreover the boards have no means of following up on compliance with their recommendations, except in those cases where they meet annually and thus can ask at the next meeting what progress has been made. From the standpoint of the institu-

[16] The predicament of a board was never better stated than in the plaintive words used at Annapolis in 1933. "The Board of Vistors has discovered that fundamental questions are being raised about the aims, scope, methods, and teaching of the academy. . . . The Board of Visitors, confronted by far-reaching proposals of this character, finds itself in no position to make definite recommendations with regard to so complicated a program. A visit of a few days, with necessarily superficial and limited time for conference, cannot qualify members of a temporary board to reach authoritative decisions." The academy boards, by provision of the 1948 statute, are prohibited from visiting the academy more than once a year without the approval of the secretary of the service concerned.

tion under inspection a Board of Visitors imposes a burden of considerable dimensions. To arrange for appointment of members and conduct of meetings takes a good deal of staff time and effort and diverts attention from the main business, the regular program.

In spite of these limitations, more effective use can and should be made of visiting boards. In the first place the board should be placed on a regular basis with terms of at least three years so that members can become well acquainted with the problems upon which they are asked to give advice. It would be to the advantage of the schools to seek fewer prominent individuals as board members. Frequently such men are unable to attend meetings regularly and to give full time and attention to the task. Individuals of less prominence may in fact be better prepared through specialized experience to judge these educational programs. They may also be more inclined to prepare for meetings and to maintain an active interest in the institution throughout the year. Likewise we would favor the inclusion of fewer educational administrators and more active scholars. Ideally the relationship of the visitors to the institution should be similar to that of active trustees to a college or university. This sort of sustained interest and support could be of particular value to the military schools because of the rapid turnover of their own personnel.

It is easy to suggest the use of highly expert boards that will spend a longer time on the job. The difficulty with this answer is that it may undermine prerogatives that properly belong to the superintendent or commandant alone. In short the boards may become meddlesome and irresponsible. A more promising approach is to ask whether the boards have been forced to combine functions that may not be altogether compatible. In one sense they are inspectors, appointed by higher authority and reporting to higher authority. In a second sense they are lobbyists, pressing the needs of the schools on the attention of higher authority. In a third sense they are advisers to the superintendents and commandants on academic program and method. There is some evidence that they are not equally suited for all roles. From time to time their members have suggested that certain problems could better be explored by special commissions. West Point, for example, requested an *ad hoc* board of consultants to review its plans for adopting a three year program at the start of world war II, and for returning to a revised four year program after world war II. We suspect that more than one type of "visiting" body is needed, and that the function that particularly requires to be specialized is one of furnishing *confidential* advice on curriculum and method to the superintendent or commandant.

Congressional members of the academy boards have rarely shown great interest in this aspect of the work, seeming to prefer to busy themselves with the adequacy of physical plant and facilities. The academies might also consider appointing subordinate boards, possibly on an *ad hoc* basis, to give confidential advice to individual departments.

There is ample precedent for greater use of *ad hoc* review boards. This device has been used from time to time to examine and advise on educational matters. We already have reported in some detail on the work of the various groups that laid down plans for postwar military education, such as the Navy's Pye and Holloway boards, the Army's Gerow and Eddy boards, and the Air Force's Air Force Academy planning groups. The principal difference between these groups and the consultants discussed above is that they are concerned with specific problems, and that they usually have been composed of officers who are or have been closely associated with personnel and educational matters. The Eddy board, for example, included the commandants of five Army schools. Their reports have been geared closely to service needs and attitudes. They have not examined officer education with the degree of detachment that has characterized the Boards of Visitors, nor have they intended to do so. Thus they generally have been effective in advancing the interests of officer education, but have not constituted a means for critical impartial appraisal. The special cases of the Service Academy Board and the National War College–Industrial College Survey Board stand in marked contrast to these other *ad hoc* boards. These are the only groups in the postwar period whose establishment was initiated by outside civilian sources—the former by the secretary of defense and the latter largely through the recommendation of the Board of Consultants of the National War College. Their membership included prominent civilians as well as professional officers.

The Congress and Military Education

Lastly, it should be noted that the Congress has some influence upon officer education. For the most part its interests are limited and its effects spasmodic, indirect, and negative. Although members of Congress have the responsibility of nominating candidates for appointment to the three academies, and voting annual appropriations for these and all other military schools, the affairs of these institutions generally remain beyond their major concern. The military appropriation subcommittees have the greatest opportunity to examine military education. Each year they review the requests for funds to maintain the schools. After a very close scrutiny of the records of these subcommittees for the years from 1933 to 1950, Elias Huzar concluded that they "have not had much to do with the Army's educational system. . . ." [17] He found, as we would expect, that when they did turn to this area, the bulk of their attention was given to West Point. Our own less detailed examination of the period since 1950 and of attention to the other services leads to the same conclusion. Following the war some members of Congress were critical of the academies on the matter of service bias and appeared to favor some sort of unified academy. But by 1954 when legislation providing for the Air Force Academy was enacted, very little was heard of this complaint. Congressmen were much more interested in the permanent location of the new academy and in the style of architecture of its buildings. As we already have noted, however, the decision of the Air Force to include some flight training in the program was made in response to the attitude of Congressman Vinson, a member with very considerable influence on military matters. The cheating scandal at West Point in 1951 provoked a great deal of attention in the Congress, but none of this led to precise recommendations or demands for action.

Except for occasional questioning of costs and of numbers of officers assigned, members of Congress have given very little attention to advanced officer education. Frequently individual members accept invitations to speak at the schools. Generally the services have not been hard pressed to justify their requests for

[17] Elias Huzar, *The Purse and the Sword, Control of the Army by Congress through Military Appropriations, 1933–1950,* Ithaca, 1950, pp. 248–249.

funds. In 1953 a House subcommittee brought about the termination of the Armed Forces Information School largely because of the sentiment of some members that it was engaged in a needless function. The Army has continued the school for its own officers, however. The only other activity that has run into serious difficulty has been the civilian institutions program. Some members have been critical of the services for sending active duty officers to graduate school, particularly in law, when civilians already holding degrees might be commissioned. It has been this attitude that has caused the services to require that a definite need for graduate education must be identified before an officer is authorized to attend a civilian university.

We conclude that the net result of Congressional influence upon officer education is negative, that is, the direct interest and action taken by the national legislature are offset by the restraint which its presence places upon those responsible for conducting military schools. This has kept requests for funds and other resources within reasonable limits. Of more consequence, it appears to have inhibited activities that might arouse complaints from members of Congress. Although it would be difficult to prove, we believe that fear of Congressional retaliation sometimes has inclined those in charge of the schools to avoid controversy and behavior that might be misinterpreted.

In conclusion it might be noted that the general lack of Congressional concern for professional officer education reflects a much broader situation, that is, the absence of any significant public interest in this matter. For most functions of the armed forces there are highly organized and articulate groups able and willing to put pressure on the Department of Defense, White House, and Congress to ensure full and adequate support. Nothing comparable prevails with respect to officer education. The only exception that might be cited was the very real interest of the nation's colleges and universities during world war II in the establishment of training programs on their own campuses. But this concern was motivated by fear of extinction rather than interest in the nature and content of military education. The organized concern of the civilian institutions that are hosts to ROTC units is likewise of a specialized character, and does not extend, except in a few isolated cases, to an active interest in the substance of professional officer education. Groups like the American Council on Education are active with respect to specific problems such as selective service, ROTC programs, and the like as they bear upon civilian education. Many individual academicians, it is true, have contributed much to the instructional programs of military schools, particularly to the senior colleges. But with few exceptions, the relationship has not been of an intimate character. Military education is deserving of a wider and deeper understanding and appreciation by the academic profession. All too frequently one hears the expression of attitudes toward the academies and senior schools that have long since been outmoded.

All of this imposes a special responsibility upon the government itself, a responsibility to safeguard the welfare of professional officer education, since there is no group in the community at large to sustain it and since the community nonetheless has so much at stake in the maintenance of security and progress. This points up the fundamental burden which rests upon the Joint Chiefs of Staff and Department of Defense. In the case of the academies, for example, a unit located at the Joint Chiefs–Department of Defense level could recommend policy regarding entrance requirements, instruction in the liberal arts and sciences, and the selection and training of instructors. It could give close scrutiny to reports of visiting boards, which often fail to receive the attention they deserve. It might review the selection of superintendents to insure that the key positions are always held by fully qualified officers.

CHAPTER TWENTY-ONE

THE PREDICAMENT OF JOINT MILITARY

EDUCATION

FOLLOWING world war II, responsible military and civilian leaders placed heavy emphasis upon the need for a joint approach to the direction of military affairs. This resulted from a conviction born in conflict that the integrated employment of all of the armed forces and all of the nation's resources was essential for victory. From this conviction came the national security act of 1947 and subsequent organizational changes. That the goals expressed then have not yet been achieved has been demonstrated by open flare-up of interservice rivalry in 1949 and again in 1956.

In the postwar period many senior officers supported plans for joint military education as one means toward the achievement of a joint approach to military affairs. They declared, as was pointed out in chapter seven, that greater attention should be given to the preparation of officers for joint planning and operations assignments. They also proposed that arrangements be made for military officers and civilian officials, particularly from the Department of State, to study together at the highest level in the professional education system. Here again, the ideals expressed following the war have not yet been fully achieved.

In the last chapter we analyzed the principal external factors that limit the accomplishments of the separate education programs of the Army, Navy, and Air Force. These factors are operative also with respect to joint military education, but the problems that they create are of greater magnitude, compounded by the fact that joint education is dependent upon the support and good will not of a single service but of three services. Although the services actively participate in joint education activities, including the

473

three joint colleges, they do not devote the full effort and support to these endeavors that was anticipated in 1945–1946 when plans for postwar military education were formulated. This situation is a direct reflection of broader aspects of the present state of armed forces unification.

Interservice integration is most successful at the operational level, where individuals and units of the three services are thrown together with a job to do or a mission to perform. It presents the greatest difficulties at the highest levels, where questions of service roles and prestige are at stake, including such issues as the allocation of scarce resources and budget dollars, responsibility for research and development, control of new weapon systems, and even fundamental concepts of the nature of war. The same situation exists in the field of military education. In those training and education programs bearing upon combat operations, joint activities appear to present no serious problems. But in those at the top of the system, specifically at the joint and service colleges, where strategic doctrines and service pride and prestige are paramount, the same degree of success has not been maintained.

There are many complex reasons why the spirit of unification has lagged behind the expectations of many individuals at the end of world war II. The military leaders of that period were motivated by beliefs derived from wartime experience at both the interservice and international levels. These individuals, now retired from active duty, have been replaced by younger men whose wartime experience for the most part was at lower levels where the joint and combined aspects were not dominant, at least insofar as their personal responsibilities were concerned. In recent years, moreover, new causes for service rivalry have developed. Far-reaching technological advances and new weapon systems cut right across the traditional roles and structures of the three services. Externally imposed budget limitations sometimes cut into the heart of service doctrine.

It would be surprising if these issues were not reflected in educational activities. Yet this matter is of very great consequence to the effective formulation of national policy. Joint strategic planning has a direct bearing not only upon military plans and operations, but upon the total grand strategy of the nation. If joint plans are based upon unsatisfactory compromises covering fundamental disagreements between the three services, then the basic foreign and domestic policies of the nation and ultimately the very security of the nation are weakened.

Interservice Training

As we have suggested, integrated effort by the armed forces is most successful at the operational level. In the field of officer education the three services have made considerable progress toward this end in the decade since the war. The principal accomplishment has been achieved through continuation on a larger scale of the prewar practice of assigning officers of one service to the schools of another. The Army school system in the fiscal year 1955, for example, provided for an enrollment of several thousand Navy, Air Force, and Marine officers. The largest "invitational" quotas are in the branch schools. At the Command and Staff level the number of officers from outside of the parent service is relatively small. In 1955, for example, only four Army officers were assigned to the Command and Staff Course at the Naval War College and eight to the Air Command and Staff School.

Another device now regularly employed is inclusion of instruction relating to the sister services in the course of study of each service school. Below the Command and Staff level such instruction is relatively minor; at that level and above it is significant. In part the instruction on the other services is accomplished by the representatives of these services attached to the schools. In larger measure, particularly in the more advanced schools, it includes lectures and demonstrations by individual officers and teams from the other services. Occasionally students may observe field demonstrations of the operations of another service.

The value of these arrangements is clear. Through exchange of students and through interservice instruction, officers of each service now are given opportunity to become acquainted with the functions, organization, doctrine, problems, and characteristic attitudes of the other services. They also become acquainted with fellow officers of the other services through close association during the school experience. On each score they are better equipped to participate in joint planning and operations in the future. In terms of the total number of career officers in the three services, however, the effect is limited.

Undergraduate Joint Education

In spite of these substantial achievements, joint military education receives less than the full and enthusiastic support that is essential for continued progress and maximum effectiveness. This does not appear on the surface; it is more a matter of subtle emphasis and interpretation. Its effects are least significant in the intermediate military schools up to and including the Command and Staff level, which by design are concerned primarily with professional military matters within each of the services. They are more disturbing at the undergraduate level, and most serious at the senior colleges.

It was noted in chapter six that following world war II a number of distinguished individuals, among them General Eisenhower, emphatically favored some sort of arrangement to minimize the development of service rivalry at the academies. Before the decision finally was made to proceed with the establishment of a four year Air Force Academy, consideration was given to several alternatives, including a unified service academy. In retrospect we can see that these alternatives had little chance against the firmly established traditions of West Point and Annapolis. Yet the strong sentiment of the immediate postwar period for the cultivation of "jointness" was reflected at the two academies, and they began to experiment with a number of devices to promote a spirit of unification. One was CAMID. This was a two week joint maneuver conducted by the Commander Amphibious Forces Atlantic during the summer following second class (junior) year, in which cadets and midshipmen participated. Another was the exchange of "hospitality" visits during the spring of second class year. Each student spent a Friday and Saturday at the other institution, using the living accommodations, attending the classes, and following the full routine of his exchange. Officers of the Tactical (West Point) and Executive (Annapolis) Departments accompanied the students. Also several Army officers were assigned to the Naval Academy staff and several Naval officers to West Point, both in the academic and Tactical (Executive) departments. As a part of the arrangement whereby it commissioned graduates of the Military and Naval Academies, the Air Force supplied officers to fill regular staff and faculty positions at the two academies.

Fullest consideration of a joint approach at the academies was given at the time of the Service Academy Board, in 1949–1950. Again, the strongest support for this approach came from the older generation of war leaders, including General Eisenhower, and also from Secretary of Defense Johnson. The newer generation, already caught up in postwar service rivalries, played a hold-tight game; and they won. The Service Academy Board early made the crucial decision to retain the integrity of the existing academies and to establish a third. But having done so, the board members and their panels made an effort to secure modest innovations to promote jointness. The social science panel, for example, declared that hospitality visits and exchange professorships were not enough. It proposed a combined Academic Board to frame sets of problems that revealed uses and relationships of all services. These would be solved by teams composed of seniors from all three academies. The solutions would be preceded by lectures by officers of all three services.[1]

The Service Academy Board itself made a number of proposals, as follows:

"Basic indoctrination of all students in the concept of national defense as a single function of the entire military establishment.

"An integrated course in military history covering all arms.

"A minimum of six weeks in joint training or maneuvers.

"A consulting board in the Department of Defense composed of three civilian educators and the three superintendents to give attention to common problems of the academies.

"A study by the Joint Chiefs of the desirability of placing a new step in the education system between the academies and the first joint schools, because officers may need a joint experience within a few years after graduation."[2]

While the board was meeting a separate study was prepared for

---

[1] Service Academy Board, *Report of Social Science Panel.*

[2] *A Report and Recommendation to the Secretary of Defense by the Service Academy Board,* Washington, January 1950.

the Joint Chiefs by a special committee composed of general and flag officers. This group soon proposed an Academic Council made up of members of the Academic Boards of all three academies, to promote joint instruction, including indoctrination in concepts and roles of all components of the military establishment, an emphasis on an armed forces viewpoint, summer joint training and maneuvers, and exchange visits by students.[3]

These various recommendations had little or no effect. The hospitality visits and cross assignment of officers to the academy staffs have been retained in a very modest way, but CAMID was discontinued in 1954 because West Point declared that the cadets could not be spared for two weeks. In lieu of this joint maneuver the cadets now observe a number of Naval and Air Force installations during a summer field trip. While these briefings give opportunity to observe a wider variety of Navy and Air Force operations, they do not involve direct participation in an exercise with their contemporaries from the Naval Academy. A similar field trip is planned by the Air Force Academy for the summer of junior year. There is no common course on national defense, no consolidated military history course. The latter is unacceptable because the academies look upon military history as a means of indoctrinating the student in the traditions and achievements of his service. The services claim that they are too busy trying to make soldiers, sailors, or airmen, let alone all three. Moreover they reject the proposition that service rivalries are bred in the academies, declaring that disunity occurs only at upper echelons.[4]

On the other hand no one has been in a position to push the academies. The one major proposal of this period was that there should be some sort of administrative machinery above the service academy level to watch the problem and to "needle" the schools. Since this was not accepted, almost everything else has gone by the board.

A similar situation prevails with respect to the ROTC. Each service operates its own units and own programs. On campuses

[3] *ibid.*

[4] Those readers who may attach some importance to the effect of certain traditions of the academies upon interservice relations will be interested in noting that when asked, "What is your altitude, cadet?" plebes at the Air Force Academy are expected to reply, "Sir, my altitude is 5,240 feet and that is higher than either Annapolis or West Point." *Air Force Times,* July 23, 1955.

where units of more than one service are located, informal
service cooperation in social, ceremonial, and other functi
arranged, but the units and courses of study are completely independent of each other. The suggestion frequently advanced by
civilian educators for a basic two year program common to all
three services is met with disfavor. Military authorities point out
that the curricula must be tailored to the peculiar requirements
of each service. Likewise they firmly resist suggestions that certain
selected courses, such as those on military history, international
relations, and leadership, be offered on a common basis. At Princeton University, for example, the Department of History, with
the financial support of one of the large foundations, developed
a special course on the history of military affairs in Western society. The Army and Air Force accepted this in lieu of other
required courses. But the Navy agreed to go along only when
representations were made by the university at the highest level
in the Department of the Navy, and even then still required its
students to take the prescribed course in naval history. Subsequently this limited participation was terminated. As one officer
in the Bureau of Naval Personnel explained to us, "Princeton
doesn't understand our purpose. They are interested in teaching
history; we are interested in indoctrination."

Joint Education at the Senior Colleges

The slacking off of support for joint military education has had
its greatest effects in recent years at the level of the senior military
colleges. In chapter eight we described the changes that have taken
place at the service War Colleges, including broadening of the
courses of instruction, so that the services now equate their institutions with the National War College and the Industrial College.
The improvement of the service colleges is all to the good, but
we conclude that it has not advanced the cause of interservice
cooperation. In our discussion of the presentation of strategic concepts at the senior colleges in chapter seventeen, we indicated
that the separate service colleges served to intensify service differences. The National War College and Industrial College on
the other hand, while not accomplishing as much as they should,
nevertheless serve to diminish these differences.

In behalf of the service colleges, it should be made clear that they do expose their students to problems of the other services. At each War College the other services are represented on the staff, in the student body, and on the lecture platform. The curriculum devotes attention to the other services and to joint and combined planning and operations. Yet the interservice element, we believe, is subordinated to the dominant service approach. This is not the case at the joint institutions, and we believe that the graduates of the latter accordingly are better prepared for high level policy positions.

Before discussing this situation further, however, it is appropriate to describe present arrangements for the administrative supervision of joint military education, as well as various alternative schemes that have been proposed. The account will explain why the joint colleges do not find it easy to maintain their status as the highest educational institutions of the armed forces.

The story begins with the original Joint Chiefs plan for postwar joint military education, prepared in 1945 by the Army-Navy Staff College and the Joint Secretariat. This provided that the educational responsibilities of the Joint Chiefs would be exercised in their behalf by a director of military education. The director would also coordinate joint education with service education. While the actual selection of officers for attendance at joint schools would be a function of the services, the qualifications prerequisite to selection would be determined by the director.[5] The proposal for a director of military education was not acceptable to the chief of Naval operations, Admiral King, who apparently feared that the director might interfere with the training and education of Naval officers, which he regarded as a prerogative of Naval command. Subsequently Ferdinand Eberstadt prepared for Secretary of the Navy Forrestal a special report on unification in which he suggested the establishment of a military education and training board under the Joint Chiefs, composed of the chief of Naval personnel and appropriate representatives of the Army, Air Force, and Marine Corps. This board would occupy itself constantly with questions of military education, reviewing the systems of educa-

[5] Joint Chiefs of Staff, *General Plan for Postwar Joint Education of the Armed Forces*, 22 June 1945.

tion of the separate services as a whole and adjusting them into a balanced and integrated program.[6]

In the Senate the Thomas unification bill of 1946 (S. 2044) made specific provision for supervision and control of joint military education, but made them a responsibility of a civilian official rather than of the Joint Chiefs. The bill called for four assistant secretaries in the proposed Department of Defense, one of whom would have the following duties: "To supervise and coordinate education and training activities in the Department of Defense with a view toward the constant maintenance of our armed forces as a highly trained organization, the provision of adequate opportunities to all members of such forces to fit themselves for greater responsibilities, the joint education and training of members of the armed forces, and the responsibilities involving all of the components of the armed forces; and to coordinate the educational and training activities of the Department of Defense with those of other government agencies and of educational institutions." [7]

While the Thomas bill was still before the Senate Naval Affairs Committee the provision for four assistant secretaries was replaced by one for four civilian agencies, each headed by a director, including one for education and training. The Navy Department opposed both of these arrangements as well as other features of the Thomas bill. Mr. Eberstadt, appearing before the committee, declared that the Navy did not oppose the concept of coordination of military education, but felt that such responsibility should be a function of the Joint Chiefs rather than of a civilian officer or agency in the Department of Defense. He urged upon the committee acceptance of the provision for a board that he had recommended to Secretary Forrestal the previous year.[8]

The Thomas bill, for reasons beyond the scope of this story,

[6] Senate, 79th Congress, 1st Session, Committee on Naval Affairs, *Unification of the War and Navy Departments for National Security,* Report to the Honorable James Forrestal, Secretary of the Navy, Committee Print, October 22, 1945. Subsequently Mr. Forrestal proposed a council on military education, composed of representatives of each service, the executive departments of the government, and civilian educators, scientists, and industrialists. *Memorandum to Joint Chiefs of Staff from Secretary of the Navy,* November 29, 1945.

[7] Senate, 79th Congress, 2nd Session, Committee of Naval Affairs, *Hearings on S. 2044,* 1946, p. 3.

[8] *ibid.,* pp. 243–245.

481

provoked a deadlock. Subsequently the secretaries of war and the Navy, acting upon instructions from the President, outlined in a letter to him the areas of agreement and disagreement between the two services. Military education was among those issues on which there was agreement. The secretaries declared: "There should be an agency to review periodically the several systems of education and training of personnel of the military services to adjust them into an integrated program. If there should be a single department, this agency should be within the department." [9] This recommendation was endorsed by President Truman, who, as was explained in chapter five, favored increased emphasis upon joint education. But by the time the national security act became law all provisions for a separate director, agency, or board either in the Department of Defense or under the Joint Chiefs had been eliminated. The law simply charged the Joint Chiefs to formulate policies for joint training and to coordinate military education. In other words, it gave them authority to establish *policies* for joint training, but with respect to educational programs, joint or service, it limited them to coordination of the activities of the separate services. At the committee stage Mr. Eberstadt made a last plea for a stronger bill, but to no avail.[10]

The problem was considered again in 1948 by the first Hoover commission task force on national security organization, of which Mr. Eberstadt was chairman. In its preliminary report to the commission the task force declared: "The committee recommends the creation of a military education and training board or section, answerable to the Joint Chiefs of Staff, to be composed of a representative from each of the services—presumably the highest officers responsible for education and training in each service. An advisory board of distinguished civilians would complement and invigorate the work of the military board, and should be available to advise the Joint Chiefs of Staff and the Secretary of Defense. Members of such an advisory board should be men of large mind and varied experience. It would be their function to give continuing study to the major problems of education and training. They would be able, in a responsible way, to give stimulation and

9 *ibid.*, p. 204.
10 Senate, 80th Congress, 1st Session, Senate Armed Services Committee, *Hearings on S. 758*, 1947, pp. 674–675.

encouragement to the services in a continuing endeavor to improve the system. The relevance of education to the work of the committee needs no argument. The real and basic hope for true unification of the services lies in sound educational system and practice; real unification must come from within, not from without; it is a product of the heart and the mind and the spirit. The campaigns of a future war may well be determined in the imagination, intellectual initiative, and judgment that have been fostered by the system of military education and training." [11]

The proposal was not adopted, however, and the joint colleges have been supervised in practice by the regular administrative machinery of the Joint Staff. The national security act of 1947 provided that the Joint Chiefs are responsible for formulating policies for joint training and for coordinating the military education of members of the military forces. In other words they have authority to establish policies for joint training. With respect to service education programs their responsibility is limited to "coordination." Actually the Chiefs in their collective capacity devote relatively little attention to the joint schools. Their responsibilities are managed at the staff level on a *part time* basis by the Bronze Team, a unit of the Joint Strategic Plans Group of the Joint Staff, composed of an Army colonel, a Naval captain, and an Air Force colonel. These officers are the first to admit that they have limited authority and influence. They do not spend much time at the colleges and almost never confer with the Boards of Advisors or Consultants. Not until 1956 did the team include a graduate of the National War College, although several graduates of the Industrial College had served with it.[12] These officers make no decisions themselves, but merely prepare papers for approval by the Joint Strategic Plans Committee, on which the Army, Navy, and Air Force members sit in a representative capacity. Policy decisions on joint education are worked out by negotiation between the staff headquarters of the services and confirmed by the JSPC prior to formal agreement by the Joint Chiefs.

The National War College and the Industrial College, as al-

11 *Report to the Commission on Organization of the Executive Branch of the Government by the Committee on the National Security Organization*, Vol. III, November 15, 1948, p. 96.

12 One officer was sent as a student to the Industrial College a few years *after* he had completed a tour on the Bronze Team.

ready indicated, receive logistic support from the Army. Their annual budgets are included in the Army budget and are defended by Army representatives. The Armed Forces Staff College, on the other hand, is supported by the Navy. This situation, apart from its convenience, is necessitated by the statutory limitation prohibiting the Joint Chiefs from engaging in operations.

Real as contrasted with nominal responsibility for the joint colleges rests with the separate services. This is because the success of these institutions depends upon the quality of the personnel selected to serve as commandants, deputies, faculty, and students. These selections are made by the services, according to policies established by them. Although the commandants of the joint colleges nominally are appointed by the Chiefs, in practice each service makes its choice and the Chiefs merely confirm it.[13] Likewise criteria for faculty and student selection are formulated by each service for its own people. Moreover, despite the terms of the national security act, the Joint Chiefs appear to do little "coordinating" of the educational programs of the separate services. They prefer to allow each service to run its own schools without interference.[14]

It was indicated above that the secretaries of the Army, Navy, and Air Force and their civilian associates did not concern themselves much with officer education. This same situation prevails in the Office of the Secretary of Defense. The assistant secretary of defense for manpower and personnel is responsible for such matters as manpower requirements, utilization, and supply. The Military Personnel Division of his office "reviews, develops, and recommends personnel policies affecting military personnel . . . as individuals, including recruitment, induction, and placement; pay and allowances, career management, leave, and other benefits," and so forth. But neither the charter of the division nor that of

[13] We have seen a copy of a memorandum from one of the service chiefs to the Joint Chiefs declaring: "I propose to assign ———— as next commandant of the National War College and request that the Joint Chiefs note the above." As far as we have been able to determine, the Joint Chiefs have never vetoed a service nomination of a commandant of a joint college.

[14] The following experience illustrates the limited effectiveness of Joint Chiefs support. For many years the National War College had attempted to secure approval for publication of its own quarterly journal. Because the college is financed by the Army's budget, approval within the Army was required. Finally in 1953 after many delays the matter was carried to the Army chief of staff, who rejected the proposal. It was then returned to the college by the Joint Chiefs without action.

the office as a whole contains any explicit reference to officer education.[15]

At one time the Office of the Assistant Secretary for Manpower and Personnel examined the policies of the services for assignment of officers to military schools as a part of a much larger study of rotation of personnel. At another time, in response to a Congressional inquiry, it asked the services to justify the costs of military education. Former Assistant Secretary John Hannah, himself a professional educator, reviewed the plans for an Air Force Academy and testified before the House and Senate Armed Forces Committees in support of enabling legislation. But otherwise he and others who have occupied this office have refrained from involving themselves in military education policies and programs. If this office had been created before rather than after the joint colleges were set up, the situation might have been different. For then the assistant secretary might have been concerned with their establishment and retained an interest.

We now come back to the question of the decline in support by the separate services of joint military education. This development has threatened the prestige and integrity of the joint institutions. The three services have altered the criteria for the selection of students at the senior colleges. The change is illustrated by the case of the National War College. Initially the National War College was conceived to be at the top of officer education. While attendance at the college was by no means a prerequisite for advancement to general or flag rank, it was generally understood that most of its graduates would secure such promotion and responsibility. Age and years-of-service requirements for the service War Colleges were lower and it was anticipated that only outstanding officers would be selected for the joint institution. Not until 1950 did the Army reopen its own War College.

These selection criteria have now been equalized for the senior joint and service colleges, and for administrative purposes the schools are at the same level. The services now employ the word "apex" to describe the position of their own War Colleges.

[15] A technical exception is the assistant secretary's responsibility for policy supervision of the armed forces troop information and education program, which is actually administered by the Department of the Army.

Diagrams no longer show the National War College and Industrial College at the very top of the pyramid, but place them off to one side and at the same level as the service War Colleges. Army and Navy regulations have precluded attendance at either the National War College or Industrial College by graduates of their own War Colleges, and the Air Force has materially reduced the number of its own War College graduates who may attend the joint colleges.[16] In the actual administration of the selection process it now appears that the deliberate effort to assign only outstanding officers to the National War College is no longer practiced. Instead this school must share these individuals with the service colleges. If this practice is continued, it is likely that proportionately fewer of the National War College graduates will attain general or flag rank and correspondingly more of the service college graduates will achieve this honor, reversing the prevailing pattern in past years. These changes also have affected the selection of officers for faculty assignments. The National War College has experienced considerable difficulty in securing and holding well-qualified officers for its faculty, and the rate of turnover among its faculty has been disproportionately high. The changes are reflected as well in the policies governing the assignment of graduates. Here again, graduates of the National War College are equated with those of the service War Colleges.

Aside from the issue of adequate support of joint education, a second element of instability has troubled the National War College and the Industrial College. This is the issue of the relationship of the two schools to each other. In chapter eight we saw that Secretary Louis Johnson proposed that the two institutions be merged, and there have been numerous other external attempts to bring them into a closer relationship. Generally speaking, the National War College has resisted these attempts. For its part the Industrial College has cooperated by sending its own students to a considerable number of National War College lectures. But although the two institutions, by order of the Joint Chiefs, are at the same level, the Industrial College has felt that it has been overshadowed by its neighbor.

16 The Air Force, moreover, selects those who also attend the National War College at random rather than on the basis of prospect of advancement or aptitude for an additional educational experience.

A third element of instability in joint military education, and particularly in the National War College, lies in the participation of the Department of State. State has assigned about 18 officers to the National War College each year, in addition to the deputy for foreign affairs. It also has assigned one student to the Industrial College and one staff member and one student to each of the three service War Colleges. In 1953, following a reduction in force of its staff, State was unable to fill its student quotas. The decision was made to send a full complement to the National War College and to leave the quotas at the other schools unfilled, although assignments to the staff positions were continued. In 1955, with the personnel crisis largely behind it, State returned to the practice of enrolling single students in the Industrial College and the service War Colleges, and for the first time accepted a long-standing invitation to send a representative to the Armed Forces Staff College.

At the same time, however, following the report of the Wriston committee on State Department personnel in June 1954, the department began a concerted effort to restore its Foreign Service Institute to a strong position. In addition to a variety of new training opportunities for junior officers, the institute reinstated a mid-career program, roughly analogous to the military's Command and Staff level instruction. It also has considered plans for a course for senior officers.[17] If such a course is established, it will raise the issue whether the department should utilize its own facilities for these officers rather than assign them to the senior educational programs of the military services. An officer of the Foreign Service Institute pointed out to us, for example, that a three month course could produce 54 graduates annually in contrast to the 18 a year at the National War College. Also involved here is the matter of prestige. The Department of State, like the separate military services, is anxious to build up its own education program. While those State representatives who have attended the National War College generally have been enthusiastic about the experience and have testified to its value, we have detected some concern in De-

---

[17] House of Representatives, 84th Congress, 1st Session, House Committee on Foreign Affairs, *Checklist on Action Pursuant to the Wriston Committee's Report,* February 15, 1955. See also Department of State, *Catalog and General Information, The Foreign Service Institute,* Publication No. 5989, 1955.

partment of State circles over the ambivalent attitude of the military services toward joint military education. On an entirely different plane, there also has been a feeling among some that State's deputy for foreign affairs should be given more responsibility in the direction of the program and afforded higher rank. Thus for a combination of reasons State's participation in the National War College might be opened for review and reconsideration.

We firmly believe that the reduction or elimination of State's participation in the college would be tragic. No matter how well staffed and conducted, an advanced course at the Foreign Service Institute would not provide opportunity for the intimate association of State personnel with officers of the Army, Navy, and Air Force. Because of the close relationship of foreign policies to military plans and operations, this sort of association, now available at the National War College, should be continued. Just as military personnel need a better understanding of the responsibilities of civilian agencies of government, so do representatives of the Department of State need insight into military planning and operations. Of similar value is the contribution which State personnel make to the success of the college. The uniqueness of the college is derived in no small part from the presence of civilian students, particularly those from the Department of State. These individuals add a great deal to the educational experience of their military associates. Their absence would seriously limit the effectiveness of the opportunity and would remove what is perhaps its most significant dimension for military personnel. Likewise the presence of even a single representative of the Department of State at the Industrial College and the service War Colleges is of more importance than might at first appear.

By 1953 these factors had combined to cause deep concern among the commandants and other responsible officers of the National War College and the Industrial College about the status of their institutions in particular and of joint education in general. The National War College feared that it would not get a full share of the best-qualified students. It was concerned about the duplication of large segments of its curriculum by the service colleges. The Industrial College was even more sensitive to its failure to achieve the respect and prestige that it felt it deserved. The Armed Forces Staff College also was concerned about selection policies of the Navy and Air Force which resulted in the assignment of relatively junior and inexperienced officers.

The Board of Consultants of the National War College addressed itself to these matters in the spring of 1953 at the request of the commandant, Lieutenant General Harold Craig, USAF. The events that followed deserve to be related in detail because they illustrate how supervision by the Joint Chiefs of Staff works in practice. The Board of Consultants recognized the merit of the argument of the service War Colleges that there is need for a greater number of officers with broad political-strategic education than can be graduated each year in the National War College. But it stated that the duplication between the programs of the National War College and the service colleges tended "toward the dissipation of the unique mission" of the former. This uniqueness, the board declared, "lay in its essential 'jointness,'" and it added that there was "even greater need in 1953 [than when the college was founded, in 1946] for an institution at the highest level, where promising officers from all of the services and a select group of civilian officials can work together to obtain deeper insight into the complex requirements of national security." Accordingly the board recommended "a careful reexamination of the special functions which the National War College should perform." [18] Shortly thereafter General Craig recommended to the Joint Chiefs that such a review be made. He added that this review should include the service War Colleges and the Industrial College in order to relate and give direction to the entire system of higher military education.[19] General Craig was hopeful that this survey would be conducted by distinguished individuals from outside of the services and that it would result in restoring the National War College to a position of unquestioned preeminence in the system of officer education.

The first action taken on his recommendation was favorable. The Joint Staff drafted a paper authorizing the creation of a review board empowered to survey the missions of the War Colleges as well as the two joint colleges. But such a broad investigation was unacceptable to the services. Accordingly the paper was redrafted to permit study only of the joint colleges, their missions,

[18] Report of the Board of Consultants, National War College, 1953.
[19] Annual Report of the Commandant, National War College, 30 June 1953.

and their relationships to each other. The paper stated that the review board's study "will not include the service war colleges." [20]

After many delays this paper was finally approved by the Joint Chiefs in April 1954. A six member board was appointed consisting of James P. Baxter, president of Williams College and former member of the National War College's Board of Consultants; J. Carlton Ward, Jr., president of the Vitro Corporation and member of the Industrial College's Board of Advisors; and four officers of flag rank representing the Army, Navy, Air Force, and Marine Corps. All members had had experience relevant to their task.

The board met in Washington during the late autumn and early winter of 1954. It heard testimony from the principal personnel officers of the three services and the commandants and other representatives of the joint colleges. It filed its report to the Joint Chiefs on January 20, 1955. Final action on the report, such as it was, was taken by the Joint Chiefs on June 21, more than two years after the survey had been initiated by the National War College.

The report of the Baxter board was disappointing to the National War College, although it was reasonably satisfactory to the Industrial College. There was nothing in it to upset the service War Colleges. This was not surprising, for the terms of reference limited the board's freedom of action. Though it emphasized the importance of high level joint education and praised the accomplishments of these joint colleges, it made only modest suggestions to strengthen them. Its recommendations fell into several categories. One group dealt with the missions and operations of the joint institutions. The board declared that the existing statements failed to emphasize the combined as well as the joint aspects of strategy and failed to direct attention to the psychological and scientific as well as the military aspects of national security in peace and war; it recommended restatements to rectify this situation. It also recommended that participation of civilian agencies in the joint colleges should continue to be fostered, and that the tours of duty of commandant and faculty should be staggered to provide the essential degree of continuity. With respect to the relationships

[20] *Report to the Joint Chiefs of Staff of the National War College and Industrial College of the Armed Forces Survey Board,* Washington, 20 January 1955.

of the National War College and Industrial College, the board advised that they remain as separate entities but that they continue their efforts to integrate their work and, if practicable, to include some form of joint problem.

The board's strongest recommendations related to the selection of students. It declared that "in recent years there had been a deviation from the earlier ideas governing selection of students at the two colleges" and urged in effect that the services tighten up their selections. It recommended that more senior officers be sent to the joint colleges than to the service War Colleges, and that each class at the joint colleges include a proportion of graduates of each of the service War Colleges. Of particular interest to the Industrial College were the recommendations that an increased proportion of the student body be composed of line or combat officers who will be eligible for field command, that the positions of commandant and deputies be increased in rank to those of the corresponding officers of the National War College, and that a new building be constructed for it at Fort McNair.

The Baxter board also examined present arrangements for supervision of the joint schools by the Joint Chiefs of Staff. It concluded that these arrangements are not adequate. Its report declared "there was less assistance afforded the Joint Chiefs of Staff in guiding joint education than seemed desirable." Accordingly it recommended the establishment of two agencies to advise the Joint Chiefs. The first was a Joint Education Committee, composed of the commandants of the National War College, Industrial College, and Armed Forces Staff College. It suggested that this be established on a par with other Joint Chiefs of Staff committees, and that it give continuing study to the major problems of joint and combined education. The board members reasoned that in their collective capacity the three commandants might have more influence with the separate services and with the Joint Chiefs than in acting alone. The second agency was an Advisory Board, to include distinguished civilians, to be convened triennially or more often if deemed necessary to advise the Joint Chiefs on joint education matters. Here again, it was felt that such a group could speak out for the welfare of the joint institutions, dramatize their needs, and support their interests. It might serve as a conscience to needle the Chiefs into taking more seriously their responsibilities toward joint as contrasted with service officer education.[21]

The efforts of the Baxter board initially had no appreciable effect upon the status of the National War College and the Industrial College. The members of the board had hoped that their report would go directly to the Joint Chiefs. Instead it was first caught up in the machinery of the Joint Staff and joint committee structure. The Chiefs, acting upon the advice of the separate services, rejected the proposed Joint Education Committee and Advisory Board. They declared that no valid need for the committee was shown and that the present consultants to the joint colleges provide adequate advisory service. The comments prepared by the Joint Staff for the separate services merely transmitted the recommendations relative to the rank of the commandant and deputies at the Industrial College and to selection of students for the joint colleges, stating that these were matters for the services themselves to handle. A new building for the Industrial College was supported; provision of funds already was under consideration by the Department of the Army.

Several months after the Baxter board submitted its report, General Craig made his last report to the Joint Chiefs as commandant of the National War College. He took this opportunity strongly to urge again a return to the 1946 concept that the National War College should stand at the top of the pyramid of professional military education and should enroll only those officers holding high promise of promotion. When this recommendation went the rounds of the services in the Pentagon it was rejected and this rejection was supported by the Joint Chiefs. Had final action rested here, the story would have ended. But General Craig's successor as commandant, Vice Admiral Edmund Woolridge, was not satisfied, and he so indicated to the chairman of the Joint Chiefs of Staff, Admiral Arthur Radford. In September 1955 Admiral Radford asked the Chiefs to give further consideration to the selection and qualification of National War College students and faculty. He declared that the role of the college was of such importance and significance to military security that full consideration should be given to these matters and recommended that an

21 *ibid.*

appropriate agency of the Joint Chiefs be directed to study and report.

Four months later the Joint Chiefs responded, again negatively, stating that present personnel policies and directives with respect to the National War College were adequate. However, Admiral Radford persisted. After holding this reply for several months, he rejected its conclusions. He declared that the selection and qualification of students at the college were of increasing concern to him and that definite action had to be taken to preclude the possibility that the college be removed from the control of the Joint Chiefs or be discontinued. He urged that an *ad hoc* committee be established to submit comments and recommendations to the Joint Chiefs concerning ways and means for improving the caliber of the National War College. The Joint Chiefs agreed to this action, and a committee of four members, representing the Army, Navy, Air Force, and Department of State, was selected in May 1956.[22] The committee submitted its report in July, after reviewing the experience of the college since its founding and visiting the British Imperial Defence College, the NATO Defense College, and the Canadian Defence College. Its conclusions were substantially the same as those of the Baxter board, although its recommendations were more strongly stated. The committee declared that the Joint Chiefs, in permitting each service to establish selection criteria for its officers attending the college, had evaded their responsibility, and recommended that the Chiefs themselves establish specific criteria. The committee observed that in recent years the caliber of personnel assigned to the college had been somewhat below the desired standard that characterized the early years, and urged that the services assign only those officers having a high potential for promotion to general or flag rank. It rejected arguments against preselection of general or flag officers, declaring that preselection is a "fact of life," and a practice that is "basic to the American tradition of survival of the fittest." The committee also recommended that a substantial number of graduates of each of the service War Colleges attend the National War College. With respect to supervision of the college, it reiterated the Baxter board's

22 The members of the *ad hoc* committee were General Charles Bolte, USA (Ret.), Vice Admiral John Hall, USN (Ret.), Lieutenant General Idwal Edwards, USAF (Ret.), and Ambassador William Lacey, representing the Department of State. Admiral Hall and General Edwards had been members of the Baxter board.

proposal of a joint education committee, composed of the commandants of the three joint colleges. It suggested that the Chiefs should give greater attention to the affairs of these schools.[23] If approved and enforced, these recommendations will go a long way toward solving the problems of the National War College. As this book goes to press, the Chiefs of Staff have taken favorable action on the Bolte report, but some time must elapse before the responses of the services can be evaluated.[24]

The developments related in this chapter illustrate not only the position in which the joint colleges find themselves, but the broader problem of armed services unification. Here is a situation in which the value system is not adequately supported by institutional arrangements. The Joint Chiefs, in fact the services themselves, make many pronouncements about the importance of joint education. But the administrative structure is oriented more toward the separate services than toward joint undertakings. Although significant recommendations have been made from time to time by such responsible groups as the Service Academy Board and the Baxter board, only the services themselves can enforce them. The failure of the services to agree to any sort of administrative machinery, whether it be an Academic Council or Board for the academies, a director of military education, an assistant secretary of defense, a Joint Education Committee, or a civilian Advisory Board, results directly from their insistence upon retaining their freedom of action. The boards that have made the recommendations, being *ad hoc* bodies, have gone out of existence upon making their reports and have had no means of checking up on compliance.

This present situation is most serious with respect to the National War College. It violates the original concept of the college as the highest institution of officer education—a concept that we believe was and still is valid. The present trend to equate the college with other War Colleges places emphasis upon quantity rather than upon quality; it minimizes the unique character of the college and the special contributions that it alone can make

[23] *Report by the National War College Ad Hoc Committee to the Joint Chiefs of Staff*, dated 30 June 1956.

[24] Also the responsibilities of the Bronze team with respect to joint education were transferred to another team of the Joint Staff.

to the preparation of officers for responsibilities involving participation in the formulation of national policies, and to the allevia-
tion of interservice rivalry. Continuation of the *status quo* involves risk to the college. Up to the present its prestige has been
high. But the effect of the recent personnel policies of the services
upon selection of students and faculty might well initiate deterioration, which in turn would stimulate a further diminution of
support by the services and the Department of State.

Presuming that fully adequate support is available to the National War College, what changes should be made? These should
include return to the original concept of the college as the highest
educational institution of the armed forces. Emphasis should be
placed upon quality rather than upon quantity. In assigning officers to the college the services should select only highly qualified
individuals who are likely to move on to the highest responsibilities in their respective services. We would favor decreasing the
size of the college to accomplish this purpose and believe that it
would bring other benefits as well. At the present time personnel
agencies oppose the suggestion that only officers with promise of
promotion to general or flag rank be assigned to the National War
College. They argue that this practice would create a service
morale problem among those officers who were not selected for
the college. These officers might conclude, it is said, that failure
to attend the college would diminish chances of promotion. We
believe that this factor is exaggerated. Particularly if the college
is reduced in size as we recommend, it would be recognized that
by no means all potential general and flag officers will attend, and
that there are many other ways of achieving distinction and promotion. We also would favor assignment of some brigadier generals and rear admirals as students to the college. This is done by
the British at the Imperial Defence College and also by the Ca-
nadians and others abroad.[25]

If these policies were to be followed, personnel agencies would
find it easier to avoid dipping into the pool of marginal officers to
fill their quotas, and would find it easier to assign graduates to
highly responsible positions. There would be less reason to rely

[25] We note that the Bolte committee observed that smaller enrollment at the
National War College would bring an improvement in instruction but for other
reasons it recommended that the present size be retained.

on branch and other intraservice quotas. It would be possible to eliminate the practice that prevents an Army or Naval officer from attending both a service and the National War College.

Finally, these policies would induce the National War College to raise its sights and to think not in terms of preparing future brigadier generals and rear admirals, but future three and four star officers. With a smaller number of officers, there would be room for a modest increase in the number of civilians and a modest contingent of foreign personnel, both of which would add an important leavening influence and contribute much to the educational experience of the military students. A smaller student body might also lead to a more informal, less highly organized, and better-tailored program to meet the needs of each individual officer. There would be no rigid schedules, no formal lecture programs, no standard curriculum; these would be reserved for the service War Colleges. These policies might also lead to a different kind of faculty, more intimately concerned with instruction and research.

What we are suggesting is that if the National War College is to be restored to the apex of higher military education it must be different and distinctive. The service War Colleges are now doing what the National War College set out to do in 1946. The time has come for it to raise it sights. This might be accomplished by making it a smaller institution devoted to studies of the highest quality.

The basic problem of the Industrial College is similar to that of the National War College, though complicated by lower prestige, and solution lies along the same lines. Selection criteria should be stiffened, and more combat arms, line, and rated officers should be assigned, not only to raise the standing of the institution but to increase the number of graduates among future commanders. This also would cultivate a greater understanding of the logistics dimension throughout the services.

It is unlikely that these conditions will be fulfilled by the services if the present arrangements for administrative support of the joint colleges are retained. The principal problem appears to be to induce the Joint Chiefs to take more seriously their responsibility for supervision of the colleges. The Joint Chiefs presently do not do this; they follow rather than lead the services with respect to military education. They established the committee to review the National War College only when hard pressed to do so by the chairman, Admiral Radford. Adequate supervision requires the formulation of policies supporting the mission of the colleges and defining the criteria for the selection of students and faculty. It includes use of the veto if need be when these policies are abused by the services.

As a minimum, approval of the recommendations of the Baxter survey board is both necessary and practicable. These provided for the creation for the Joint Chiefs of a Joint Education Committee and a civilian Advisory Board. In addition to the commandants of the joint colleges, as recommended by the survey board, the committee also might include the chiefs of personnel of the three services. It should meet at regular intervals to review the problems of the colleges and their relationship to service education. It should assure that high standards are maintained in the selection of students and faculty. The committee should consult with the Advisory Board, which also should review the accomplishments of both joint and service education and report independently to the Joint Chiefs.

This matter is intimately associated with the larger question of the effectiveness of the Joint Chiefs of Staff in the years to come. If the Chiefs represent no more than an alliance of convenience, then little if any improvement in the status of joint military education can be expected. But if, on the other hand, a real federal union emerges, then joint military education will prosper. Developments in other areas of military activity where interservice cooperation has been inadequate suggest that if the Joint Chiefs do not provide adequate support, then the Department of Defense might step into the picture. This would have its disadvantages. We already have noted that the department, particularly its Office of Manpower and Personnel, has not shown much interest in officer education so far. This development also would tend to separate the joint schools further from the services and from their needs and requirements. Moreover it would antagonize many in the services who are already critical of what they believe to be undue "civilianization" of the military. And lastly, until civilian secretaries and assistant secretaries develop the habit of remaining in office for longer periods, we doubt that they would be adequately qualified to provide the support that joint education needs. If supervision by the Department of Defense were to succeed, it would require the continued attention of an official with fairly long tenure, experienced and knowledgeable in the ways of the Pentagon.[26]

It has been suggested by some that support of the National War College be lodged with the National Security Council. The council is the highest organ of the government for the formulation of advice to the President on all matters relating to national security. Functionally its field of responsibility is the same as that for which the National War College presumably prepares its graduates. The subjects with which the council and its staff are concerned are those which are examined at the college. Also the various executive agencies of the government represented either on the council itself or on its planning staff are also represented at the college. Thus the council would appear to be a logical supporting agency.

Such an arrangement is of course possible. Already the Central Intelligence Agency, a complex operational organization, is under the direction of the National Security Council. But to place the National War College under the council would change its basic character. It would no longer be a military institution but a government-wide one. While a very strong case can be made for the need for such a school, we do not believe that its creation should involve the absorption of the National War College. The need for a joint military institution, under military command and enrolling principally military personnel, would remain. In the first place preparation for high level military assignments requires more attention to military affairs than this civilian-sponsored institution would likely give. Moreover there would be risk that the military services would have less interest in an institution that would be outside of their organization, placing their support on a less secure basis. Ideally we would favor a strengthened National War College under strong Joint Chiefs of Staff leadership *and* a small, high level civilian school closely associated with the Na-

---

[26] We have in mind an individual of the experience and stature of W. J. McNeil, assistant secretary of defense (comptroller).

tional Security Council to which a few outstandingly well-qualified military officers would be assigned.[27] Even if this civilian school were to be established, the Department of State should still assign representatives to the National War College, for reasons suggested above.

The Industrial College also should benefit from stronger administrative support. The proposed Joint Education Committee and Advisory Board would have responsibilities for its success as well as that of the National War College. Because of its preoccupation with preparation for joint operational responsibilities, supervision of the Armed Forces Staff College should remain with the Joint Chiefs, but experienced officer personnel should be assured for both faculty and student assignment. In the case of the Industrial College, transfer of supervisory authority to the Department of Defense might be necessary for the same reasons as obtain for the National War College, but it would offer the same disadvantages as well. Another possibility for the Industrial College, similar to placing the National War College under the National Security Council, would be to place responsibility in the Office of Defense Mobilization, which also is part of the Executive Office of the President. But this would place the Industrial College even further from the main stream of military affairs.

There remains the issue of the relationship of the National War College and Industrial College. The survey board recommended no change in the present separate identities of the two institutions, and the decision to proceed with a new building for the Industrial College constituted endorsement of the *status quo* by the services. Yet the issue is likely to be raised again from time to time.

A valid case may be made for a merger. From an intellectual standpoint the formulation of national policies is a seamless web, in which strategic and economic considerations are inseparable. On this basis it is unrealistic to separate these two main areas and to assign one to the National War College, the other to the Indus-

[27] Such a high level school has been proposed by numerous individuals, most notably by John J. McCloy; see his *Challenge to American Policy*, Cambridge, Mass., 1953. See also Harold D. Laswell, *National Security and Individual Freedom*, New York, 1950, pp. 100–101, and Society for Personnel Administration, *Proposal for a Federal Administrative Staff College*, General Series, Pamphlet No. 5, Washington, 1953. The Brookings Institution, a private organization, has made plans for a prototype school. In this connection see Robert D. Calkins, "Executive Training," *Personnel Administration*, November 1955, pp. 5–12.

trial College. In the second place there is a possibility that a merged institution would be sufficiently different from the service War Colleges to avoid the present problem of duplication.[28] It might then also be different not only with respect to the curriculum but also in terms of the rank and career prospects of the students. And lastly the merger, by bypassing it, would solve the problem of the Industrial College's prestige.

On the other hand there are substantial arguments against a merger. Intellectually it would be an extremely difficult problem to compose a workable course combining elements of both programs. We fear also that the net result might provide inadequate preparation in the logistic aspects of strategic planning. But the principal argument against the merger is that it would result

---

[28] The outline of a curriculum for a merged NWC-ICAF might look something like this:

Part One

1. *Historical Introduction.* Soviet theory and practice. Role of underdeveloped and uncommitted areas. Policies of selected allies. Internal pressures on their leaders.
2. *Nature of International Politics.*
3. *Instruments of National Security Policy.* Diplomacy, alliances, force, economic foreign policy, psychological, etc.
4. *The Revolution in Weaponry.*

Part Two

5. *Strategic Doctrines and Roles and Missions.* What they currently are. How they have changed in past. Present tension points and possible future developments.
6. *War Planning: Inputs.*
   a. *Strategic Intelligence.* How knowledge and assumptions regarding intentions and capabilities affect decisions as to types of forces needed, and as to state of readiness. Case studies showing past errors.
   b. *Trends in Weaponry.* What gadgets are worth developing? At what stage? With what effects on other plans and needs? Case studies.
   c. *Resource Limitations.* When are plans utopian? Case studies.
   d. *Budget Ceilings.* Including effect on plans of last minute changes in budgets. Stretch-outs. Case studies.
   e. *Public and Legislative Support.* How much insurance is the nation ready to buy? Case studies.
7. *War Planning: Outputs.* Joint plans. Force level decisions. Allocation of resources and dollars.

Part Three

8. *Special Problems.*
   a. *Nuclear Attack on U.S.* Continental defense. Civil defense. Industrial mobilization capabilities after attack.
   b. *Coalition Planning.* Effect of different national objectives. Problem of allocating missions and weapons. Different concepts of strategy. Different concepts of support. Case studies.

in a larger enrollment than at either of the present colleges, and this would mean a lowered standard of performance. Since the decision has been made to construct a new building for an Industrial College of the present size or even larger, we would favor continued separation of the two institutions. But there should be some integration of the two courses of instruction. Students at the National War College should be exposed to some of the curriculum of the Industrial College. Students at both schools, for example, might work together in the study of the international scene, and in the determination of force level requirements. This would be facilitated if both schools were reduced in size.

This chapter concludes on a note of uncertainty. After ten years the momentum toward joint military education generated at the conclusion of world war ii has been expended and there has been serious retrogression. There are difficult intellectual and organizational problems at all levels, from the academies and ROTC programs to the service War Colleges and the joint colleges. These problems are intimately intertwined with the larger issues arising from the relationship of the three services to each other. Their ultimate resolution will be determined by alterations in the roles and missions and organizational structure of the separate parts of the military establishment. But measures to strengthen joint military education should not wait upon these developments.

CHAPTER TWENTY-TWO

EDUCATION FOR POLICY ROLES: SOME

FINAL OBSERVATIONS

How well does professional military education prepare career officers for policy level positions in the government? We have directed attention to this question throughout; here we add a few final observations, conclusions, and recommendations.

In chapter two we discussed certain qualifications for officers assigned to policy positions and suggested that these might serve as criteria for the evaluation of military education. In addition to military competence, which is a prime requisite for all assignments, certain general executive qualifications and certain more specialized military executive qualifications were listed. The former included the ability to grasp large, complicated situations, the ability to adapt creatively to changing circumstances, and freedom from parochialism. The latter included versatility, job motivation, and creative service under civilian leadership.

The record of accomplishments of professional military education has been described and commended in preceding chapters. It is a record of which the armed forces justly may be proud; it is far better than many civilian educators and laymen realize. The services recognize the need to prepare officers for the newer demands that have been placed upon them. This awareness has led to both specialized training programs and broader general educational opportunities. We have been most interested in the latter.

Whether or not such educational developments actually contribute to more effective performances cannot be easily demonstrated. There has been insufficient time for the full effect of many of them to be felt. Moreover a precise answer to this question would require construction and administration of a battery of tests designed to measure exact "before" and "after" levels of knowledge, skill, adaptability, attitudes, and so forth of graduates and nongraduates of military schools. The tests also should distinguish between the influence of educational experience and the influence of other relevant experiences. Except for the questionnaire that we administered to a limited number of graduates of the senior joint and service colleges and other officers in selected offices in the Pentagon, we have not attempted any analysis of this sort. The observations that follow are based upon our own subjective judgment.

We conclude that military education does make a very substantial contribution to the preparation of officers for policy roles. Within a matter of a few years it is likely that officers assigned to these positions will have had significantly *more* formal educational preparation than comparable civilian officials. This preparation does enhance an officer's ability to grasp large, complicated situations and to adapt creatively to changing circumstances. The range of subjects presented in military schools helps him to see the relevance of his task to the larger context in which he operates. It helps him to see broader technical, organizational, and social relationships, and to appreciate the dynamic quality of decision making in an era of revolutionary change. In many cases the educational experience helps to diminish a narrow parochialism and to increase versatility. Because the schools make it possible for an officer to understand the purpose of policy positions, they diminish the likelihood that he will be poorly motivated toward them. They facilitate creative military service under civilian leadership in a democratic society.

At the same time military education can and should be better. In preceding chapters we have called attention to limitations upon its effectiveness. If in the pages that follow we appear to be unduly critical, we would declare again that we wish to emphasize the areas, already well known to many responsible officers, in which efforts for improvement might be concentrated. We would repeat that many of the shortcomings identified here are by no means limited to military institutions; unfortunately they are characteristic of many civilian institutions as well. Actually military schools seek help and guidance to a unique degree. We have encountered more genuine humility in this respect than is found at civilian institutions.

Perhaps the most serious limitation upon military education is a tendency toward conformity. The executive, whether he be a military executive or the director of any large undertaking, cannot afford to be unduly limited by dogma, orthodox practice, or prevailing policy. Yet the urge to conform is naturally strong in the military profession. Higher level military schools should serve as built-in devices to counteract this urge, but they find this hard because they are so closely related to the policy-making centers of their own services and of the government generally. It is not easy for the head to challenge the heart. It is not enough simply to announce or decree that school solutions are out of order or that complete freedom of expression prevails. There must be forceful and continuous challenge of basic assumptions. Is it realistic to assume that the cold war will continue in its present form? Have we correctly appraised the intentions of other nations? Does it make sense to stockpile material in an era of nuclear warfare? Does the present organization of the armed forces make sense for the future? We conclude that if the schools are to serve as built-in devices to counter conformity, they in turn need some kind of devil's advocate in residence who can challenge prevailing doctrine forcefully but intelligently. This might be one of the functions of advanced study and research.

A second limitation relates to the issue of parochialism. Many features of military education are designed to prohibit the development of narrow, biased, or parochial attitudes and behavior. Courses of instruction increasingly have been broadened to enlarge the horizons of officers. Arrangements are provided for instruction in the organization and operations of the other services, of civilian agencies, and of foreign governments. The other services are represented among the faculties and students of almost every single-service military school. Foreign officers are often welcomed as students, and American officers are assigned to foreign military schools and occasionally to civilian schools abroad. Much is done to lift the officer above his own speciality and his own service. Yet most military schools remain service-oriented, and in this respect the intangibles—the traditions, slogans, and unwritten customs—are of more significance than the formal programs. In an era in which technological advances rapidly outmode prevailing organizational relationships, military education must promote the most intimate interservice associations. Yet there remains a wide gap between the ideals of joint education expressed by General Eisenhower and other wartime leaders and present accomplishments. A separate Air Force Academy has been established and even the modest suggestions of the Service Academy Board for interacademy cooperation have been set aside. While officers are sent to the schools of other services, the quotas are relatively small. The senior joint institutions, the National War College and the Industrial College, are rivaled in prestige by the service War Colleges. Clearly these trends should be reversed.

The last chapter suggested measures that might be taken to strengthen the National War College and Industrial College. In addition the three service War Colleges might assume more of the characteristics of joint institutions. While present command and organizational relationships could remain the same, we would favor equal representation of the three services among faculty and students. Likewise it is important that the Armed Forces Staff College be maintained and strengthened. Our observations suggest that the joint character of this institution is one of its most important features and that its students, because they attend at an earlier age than at the War Colleges, are more favorably impressed by this.

At the international level, present cooperative arrangements should be extended. The practice of accepting foreign officers in the Command and Staff Schools and at the Armed Forces Staff College should be extended upward to the senior joint and service colleges. The British and Canadian air officers at the Air War College are the only foreign officers in the senior institutions. This is a mistake. The advantage to American officers of contact with foreign officers far outweighs the inconvenience arising from present laws and regulations that necessitate exclusion of foreign officers from certain classified lectures and source materials. Our defense policies have become increasingly dependent upon successful cooperation with our allies. The senior military schools are a natural setting for American officers and their foreign associates to study and to work together in committees on problems of close mutual interest. In this manner they can learn to appreciate each other's characteristic motivations, attitudes, customs, and interests.

One other aspect of the issue of parochialism deserves reemphasis. In chapter seventeen we suggested that the preoccupation of the senior joint and service colleges with the Soviet threat narrowed their view of the rest of the world. There is need for greater understanding of the factors motivating the peoples of Asia, the Middle East, and Africa. As an officer at one of these colleges observed to us: "We are wrong to call these the 'uncommitted nations.' It merely means that they are not committed to *our* way of looking at the world."

A third limitation relates to the principle of civilian supremacy. Americans can be proud of and reassured by the devotion to this principle displayed at the academies and all higher military schools. It is drilled into every officer. But, as suggested in chapter two, more is required than mere acceptance of the principle of subordination to civilian authority. Officers have a positive or affirmative duty to contribute their best judgments to the decisions in which they participate. We identified this as an important element of creative service and noted that it raised difficult problems of application. Military schools, particularly the senior colleges, might devote more attention to these problems, including relationships of officers to appointed civilians, to elected officials, and to the public. There is need for deeper understanding of the ideals underlying American democratic society, and more candid discussion of tension points and areas of controversy. Such discussion is needed to balance the thorough consideration of organizational and institutional relationships.

Other limitations upon the effectiveness of higher military education stem from the tendency of many responsible officers to associate education with training, a function with which they are more intimately acquainted and toward which they are often more sympathetic. While there is no fixed line between training and education, there certainly is a vast difference between training thousands of troops in military maneuvers or producing a highly skilled bomber crew, and cultivating those habits of mind that make an officer an effective representative of his service in high level policy negotiations. The failure to appreciate fully these differences is reflected in such features of military education as excessively rigid and standardized curricula, preoccupation with form and technique rather than with content and purpose, and ceaseless tinkering with the organization of the program.

The schools would profit from a less tense approach to officer education. They might take a lesson from operating officials in their own services. Some officers have a curiously ambiguous attitude toward officer education, particularly at the advanced levels. They are for it. Yet they insist that it is the man who counts, not his formal schooling. In screening a candidate for a vacancy they want to know what kind of fellow he is and what practical experience he has had. This attitude is stronger in the Navy than in the other two services, but it can be found everywhere. There is certainly something to it so long as it is not pushed to the extreme conclusion that all advanced schools should be abolished. Few officers, even those who are skeptical of the effect of advanced schooling on an officer's performance, would be willing to go that far.

Yet if one concedes that there is something to the argument, one should conclude that the process of advanced education ought to be approached in a more relaxed manner. This means simply that one should not get too doctrinaire over particular curricular designs or methods of instruction. It would be irrational to be dogmatic about these matters if one realized that it is something of a gamble whether the mature student will get anything significant out of school attendance or not. Yet despite (or perhaps because of!) some inner misgivings about the value of education, the military usually take a very inflexible attitude toward it.

One unfortunate carry-over from training to education is the principle that the inclusion of a subject or area of study in a curriculum should be determined on the basis of "need to know" rather than of "nice to know." There are reasons for this rule with respect to a highly specialized training mission, but in the realm of higher education it is dangerous. As one observer pointed out to us, "need to know" is likely to mean narrowly vocational and immediately useful; "nice to know" is likely to mean broadly professional and ultimately useful. High level command and policy-making responsibilities are not those for which a neatly packaged bundle of requirements can be determined and assembled. They call for the broadest sort of intellectual and personal qualities.

507

Some of the best kinds of preparation for such responsibilities are likely to be excluded by a rigid application of the "need to know" formula.

The official regulation for the Army's civilian institution program is an example of this danger. This regulation declares: "Training will be limited to the extent necessary to qualify the individual to meet anticipated Army requirements in accordance with job descriptions. Training will not be given for the primary purpose of raising the educational level of the individual." While such a rule might be needed to justify before Congress the assignment of officers to graduate study, it is not in the best interests of the Army, for it places the emphasis upon the immediate rather than the long run value of the program. The interests of the Army are best served when the intellectual level of the individual officer is raised. This should be an aim of all education at all stages of an officer's career.[1]

The "need to know" formula is also reflected in the subject content of the curricula. Naturally and properly there is heavy emphasis upon matters of immediate military consequence. But in the selection of nonmilitary subjects an attempt is made to stick to so-called "practical" matters. This explains the heavy emphasis upon oral and written communication, conference techniques, community relations, and so forth. Here the purpose is not to stimulate the officer's understanding of human relations but to equip him as an effective negotiator or spokesman for his service. If such ability is used on behalf of inappropriate policies, its presence is a curse rather than a blessing. This is the fundamental reason why emphasis should be placed on quality of thought rather than on technique. In the selection of material from the social sciences, military schools characteristically lean heavily upon the descriptive portions of economics and political science. They generally avoid sociology and anthropology, and limit their use of psychology largely to its application to study of military leadership. Likewise they generally avoid historical perspective and theoretical or abstract principles. Some military schools have been oversold on "geopolitics." In general there is too much of an arithmetical, power calculus, or "stockpiling" approach to inter-

---

[1] On this same line see Colonel John D. Byrne, "New Vistas in Education," *Army*, February 1956, p. 44.

national economic and political issues. The consequence is that military education is weakest in cultivation of the creative, imaginative, analytical mind.

Another direct consequence of a training approach to officer education is the tendency to stress quantity rather than quality. For reasons that have been explained in previous chapters, personnel agencies like to put as many officers through the schools as possible, including the advanced schools. They look upon military education as mass distribution of information rather than as an individual inquiry for knowledge and understanding. Here they reflect a development in American public education generally. Traditionally our society accepted the principle that an individual was selected for a particular job according to his special qualifications. We now seem to be shifting to the concept that any individual can be prepared for a given job by exposure to an appropriate formal educational experience. Instead of selecting the round pegs for the round holes, the square pegs are sent to school.

Lastly, the training approach to officer education shows insufficient understanding and respect for a truly intellectual enterprise. In spite of their notable achievements, American military schools have not furnished intellectual leadership in the investigation of military subjects. As we pointed out earlier, they are not pushing out the frontiers of knowledge in their professional field; they are not making notable contributions to advanced study and research.[2] The principal analysts and writers on military affairs today are civilians. The War Colleges rely on these civilians to lecture to their students on various subjects of military strategy. Where are the successors to Luce, Mahan, and Upton?

Our concluding observation concerns the importance of undergraduate education both at the academies and at civilian institutions. The experience that a young man receives at this stage can have a decisive impact on his future habits of mind, his attitudes, and his intellectual curiosity. It can also determine whether he acquires a genuine interest in continued self-education. We have not spoken much about self-education in this book because we have set ourselves the task of analyzing schools. But we would be the first to concede that a major function of any school is to push

[2] See the editorial comment by Rear Admiral J. D. Hayes in *Military Affairs,* Spring 1955, p. 64.

that particular button within each man that makes him ready as
well as able to continue his education under his own steam. This
is a goal to which the service academies must give greater attention
in the future. We are not certain that it can be attained without
a further liberalization of program and method and without some
reduction in the total work load carried by the student. More
technical studies will have to be postponed until after graduation.
This is the trend in engineering and other professions.[3] The men
now graduating from the academies will lead our armed forces
in the 1980's. Clearly they will require the broadest and deepest
kind of understanding in order to grapple successfully with the
uncertainties and imponderables of the future.[4]

There are enough unresolved problems of professional military education to warrant attention from the highest authority of
the United States. In the normal course of events they are not
likely to receive such attention because more dramatic and immediately urgent issues constantly dominate appointment calen-
dars and committee agenda in the upper reaches of our government. In order to secure action of the kind we believe necessary
we recommend the appointment by the President of a special
commission on the education of American military officers. In
1956 President Eisenhower established a committee on education
beyond the high school in civilian institutions. The problems of
higher education in military institutions are of comparable importance. In a thermonuclear age the survival of our society requires that officers of our armed forces be as well prepared for
their duties as the intellectual and material resources of the country will permit.

The primary task of such a commission, as we conceive it, would
not be to conduct a lengthy inquiry into curricular details and
teaching methods. The strengths and weaknesses of military education are recognized by many responsible officers; they have been
discussed by many review boards and supervisory agencies. The
primary task of such a commission would be to break through
the obstacles to change by dramatizing the importance of the

[3] American Society for Engineering Education, *General Education in Engineering*,
Urbana, 1956.

[4] See the commencement address of Secretary of the Army Wilbur Brucker at the
Military Academy, June 5, 1956.

major issues, by providing an over-all rather than a partial approach to those issues, and, above all, by assuring that necessary reforms are given proper consideration by the responsible authorities of our government. The first task might well be to review the reasons why earlier efforts to improve military education have so often failed for lack of support from the services themselves.

The principal matter of concern to the commission should be joint military education. It is clear that interservice rivalries continue to plague strategic planning and the formulation of the highest national policies. Military education alone cannot eliminate these rivalries but it can and should help to confine them within tolerable limits. The commission should consider the possibility of introducing more common courses, joint training, and extracurricular cooperation at the service academy level. The establishment of a separate Air Force Academy should not preclude reexamination of the question whether a system of three separate academies, each intimately associated with a single service, is the best that can be devised to prepare the future officers of the nation's armed forces. It should reexamine the desirability of three separate ROTC programs. It might also address itself to the desirability of providing a joint educational experience for which an officer would be eligible after a shorter period of commissioned service. The Armed Forces Staff College might be reconstituted for this purpose. At the highest level the commission should formulate proposals to introduce a joint perspective into the Army, Naval, and Air War Colleges, and to make their student bodies fully representative of all three military services. It should formulate proposals designed to insure that each service will give full support to the joint study of war resources at the Industrial College of the Armed Forces. It should formulate proposals to insure that each service will regard the National War College rather than its own institution as the apex of the pyramid of higher military education.

The commission should review present statutes and policies governing appointments to the service academies in the light of the competition these institutions now face from leading universities with ample scholarship funds to dangle before superior students. It should consider the feasibility of abolishing or deferring for future study parts of the academic program that interfere unduly with the general education of midshipmen or cadets. At this same level it should examine the problem of recruiting more career officers from the nation's colleges and universities. The armed forces should have a fair share of the graduates of these institutions in their career ranks. They are not now getting that share. In the light of recent experience, is the ROTC program the most effective device to attract college students to a career as an officer in the armed forces? Do curricular changes within civilian colleges suggest that a change in the basic structure of the ROTC programs is required?

At the senior level the commission should establish the highest standards for the selection of commandants, faculties, and students. More important, it should formulate proposals designed to insure that these standards are respected by the services. It should also define the responsibility of the senior colleges to advance the frontiers of thought by study and publication.

Lastly, the commission should devise arrangements to centralize further the responsibility for military educational policy. These arrangements should permit continuing review of both joint and service schools in the light of the demands of a changing world and the increasing responsibilities of career officers.

APPENDIX

A NOTE ON OFFICERS IN POLICY ROLES

This appendix supplements the brief historical sketch in chapter one of the growth of military responsibilities. It uses three devices to suggest the extent to which officers are engaged in policy positions today and the nature of the duties they assume thereby. The first device is a statement of the actual functions of several military agencies in a single selected field: international security affairs.[1] The second is an analysis of the deployment of senior officers at a given point of time. The third is a selection of personnel code designations and job descriptions illustrating positions in our modern armed services that bear only an indirect relation to the operation of forces in the field.

1

At the highest level in the military establishment, international security affairs are the responsibility of an assistant secretary of defense. In recent years his staff has included about 45 senior officers drawn from all three services. This office helps the secretary of defense formulate views on United Nations affairs, National Security Council actions, North Atlantic Treaty affairs, defense aid, intergovernmental conferences, and similar politico-military matters. It arranges for Department of Defense representation on governmental and intergovernmental organizations, including those concerned with regulation of armaments, hemispheric defense, and military aid. After the representatives have been selected, it gives

[1] Similar statements could, of course, be prepared of the functions of military agencies in other fields such as research and development, finance, logistics, or legislative liaison and public relations. See Timothy W. Stanley, *American Defense and National Security*, Washington, 1956.

them policy guidance and staff support. It furnishes a representative to the planning board of the National Security Council. It develops policy for Defense officials concerned with occupied areas. It coordinates Defense views on foreign economic policy, intergovernmental economic mobilization plans, and economic defense matters. The assistant secretary in charge of the office has always been a civilian, but military men have served as deputy director, assistant for National Security Council affairs, director of the military aid and the foreign military affairs offices, and chiefs of the geographical divisions of the latter.

The Joint Chiefs of Staff, as the principal military advisers to the President, the National Security Council, and the secretary of defense, are also heavily involved in international security affairs. In recent years they have addressed themselves to such matters as: the kind of military organization that should be established under NATO; the crossing of the 38th parallel in Korea; the selection of Latin American states to receive military aid and the amount of such aid; the rearmament of Western Germany; the wisdom of seeking air bases in the Mediterranean, of blockading Communist China, of suggesting revisions of the Italo-Yugoslav border, and of relieving the French of part of their burden in Indo-China. Much of the preliminary work that supports their recommendations is done by interservice subcommittees backed up by the more than 200 members of the Joint Staff who are employed full time on joint work.

These organizations have large counterpart units within the operations offices of each of the three services. The Air Force, for example, has a Directorate of Plans containing about 100 senior officers. One of its divisions develops the Air Force position on interservice and international military plans, including those for continental defense. Another provides Air Force support for the National Security Council, the Joint Chiefs of Staff, and other interdepartmental, combined, or international agencies dealing with international security affairs; it supplies guidance to Air Force representatives; and it reviews the military implications of political proposals or decisions by other agencies. The latter division also formulates Air Force policy on base and other rights in foreign countries; provides support for negotiations for such rights; takes part in international conferences; keeps in touch with the State Department; and studies the reports of other agencies to ascertain foreign developments of interest to the Air Force.

The Army assigns similar duties to the Operations and Plans Divisions in the Office of its Deputy Chief of Staff for Operations. The Plans Division, for example, with about 57 senior officers, works with the State Department in an effort to make certain that foreign political problems will be considered when military policy is made, and vice versa. It also coordinates Army help in the drafting of treaties and other international agreements with long range military implications. The Navy vests comparable functions in a deputy chief of Naval operations for plans and policy. Four of his divisions, containing nearly 100 officers, are responsible respectively for: strategic plans, including interservice and international plans and psychological warfare; international security affairs, including those related to the United Nations, the National Security Council, and the Joint Chiefs of Staff; foreign military assistance; and Pan American affairs and Naval missions to foreign countries. The headquarters of all three services contain additional units that supervise their respective mutual defense aid programs.

2

In 1953 the Army had about 500 general officers.[2] Roughly one third of these were assigned to continental divisions, corps, armies, or anti-aircraft commands, or to tactical units or commands overseas. Of the remaining two thirds:

9 were in civilian agencies.

8 were in the Office of the Secretary of Defense.

14 were with joint agencies in the United States, e.g. the Joint Chiefs of Staff, the Weapon Systems Evaluation Group, the Armed Forces Special Weapons Project, and the National Security Agency.

---

[2] This year has been selected because relatively complete information is available. The figures are based upon detailed justifications presented to Congress by each service in connection with a study of the number of authorized general and flag officers. See House of Representatives, 83rd Congress, 1st Session, Committee on Armed Services, *Hearings*, March 5 to August 3, 1953.

40 were overseas in agencies with major international responsibilities, e.g. in NATO organizations or joint missions to foreign countries.

5 were in the Office of the Secretary of the Army.

55 were in General Staff agencies concerned with personnel, intelligence, logistics, and operations, or in such special staff units as those concerned with law, finance, psychological warfare, military history, and reserve and ROTC affairs.

10 were in administrative services.

16 were in medical, dental, or hospital activities.

23 were in schools and training centers, including joint colleges and technical service schools.

11 were assigned to Army-wide or technical service activities relating to research, development, and testing.

29 were in depots, arsenals, engineering districts, and ports of embarkation.

26 were in technical service activities other than those in the preceding four categories.

79 were engaged in essentially administrative work in overseas headquarters and area commands, and in overseas technical service or communication zone organizations.

The figures for the Navy and the Air Force were comparable. Three out of four admirals were assigned to administrative work in the Navy Department; in continental districts, shipyards, schools, or bases; in overseas districts and stations; or in billets external to the Navy. Three out of five Air Force generals were assigned to administrative duty in the headquarters of the Air Force, in the Matériel or Research and Development Commands, in the Military Air Transport Service, in the Air University, or in agencies external to the Air Force. In all three services these general or flag officers were backed up by much larger numbers of less senior personnel.[3]

It is striking to note that a majority of our very highest ranking officers were assigned to duties requiring them to deal with the economic, scientific, or political aspects of military functions, and that only a minority were assigned to operating units in the field.

[3] For example, for every Army general in such activities there were 6 colonels, 10 lieutenant colonels, and 10 majors. The figures for the other services are comparable.

Undoubtedly, many of the former positions did not bring generals or admirals into policy issues of national importance. But many of them did. This was particularly likely when the position to which an officer was assigned was outside his parent service. In this connection it is interesting to note that about 200 generals or admirals of all services are usually on assignment to interservice or international agencies or to other departments of the government; they constitute roughly 17 percent of all officers of that grade. The number of colonels or Naval captains with comparable duties is about 1,400; they constitute roughly 11 percent of all officers of that grade. An additional 6,000 or more officers of lower grade assist them in their work.

A few other points must be made in connection with all the foregoing figures. One is that the services, in peacetime, rarely have enough troop units, air units, or ships to accommodate all the senior officers they are authorized to have. The surplus of available officers constitutes a kind of reserve or cadre that must be maintained to organize and direct the additional forces that would be created in an emergency. In the absence of an emergency, a relatively large number of officers are therefore assigned to administrative or overhead positions. To the extent that this occurs, figures on the total number of officers in such positions, if taken as firm military requirements, may be exaggerated. On the other hand this argument cannot so easily be applied to those officers who are assigned to duty outside their own service. These assignments are not initiated by personnel offices anxious to dispose of surplus colonels or generals. They usually constitute forced drafts on the services by influential external agents who stipulate in detail the qualifications they desire. Finally, it must be appreciated that all officers, whether assigned to their own service or to outside agencies, have limited tours of duty; and that many of them, especially senior line officers, move on to totally new functions at the expiration of their tours of duty. Thus a Naval captain may spend two or three years in the Office of Foreign Military Affairs or in the Office of the Comptroller of the Navy, and then be replaced by another captain who has just completed a tour as commanding officer of a destroyer squadron. Because of this practice, the number of officers assigned to political, economic, or scientific functions over a decade is far greater than the number assigned at any given moment.

3

In recognition of the magnitude and stability of the demand for officers in policy positions, each service has incorporated appropriate code designations and job descriptions in its classification manuals. A few examples will suffice. In 1953 the Air Force added to its specialty codes the category of *international politico-military affairs officer*. A few dozen senior officers bear this title. The classification manual describes their duties in the following way: "Plans, formulates, coordinates, and implements Air Force aspects of international politico-military policies, advises and briefs commanders and Government officials on international problems affecting the Air Force; and represents the Air Force in international and interdepartmental conferences and negotiations." [4]

The Navy utilizes the category of *international affairs officer*. His duties are described in similar language: "Advises and assists in planning and implementation of policy with respect to naval aspects of international affairs; provides background information and studies in international developments relating to the Navy; serves as Navy representative in foreign surveys and projects; furnishes policy guidance for naval advisory groups abroad; arranges diplomatic clearances for visits of United States naval ships and aircraft to foreign countries; maintains liaison with other branches of the armed services and with civil agencies of government concerned with international affairs." [5]

The Army, because of its particularly great responsibility in the field, has a highly detailed description of a *civil affairs / military government officer*: "Advises commander on matters pertaining to administration of civil affairs / military government operations. Directs and coordinates one or more civil functions, such as enforcement of law and order, political administration, establishment of courts and administration of law, public finance, civilian defense, public health, and sanitation, public welfare, disposition of refugees and displaced persons, education administration, civil administration, custody and administration of property, currency and banking, commerce and trade, price control and rationing,

[4] Department of the Air Force, *Officers' Classification Manual*, AFM 36–1, January 1, 1952 (as revised).

[5] *Manual of Navy Officer Billet Classifications*, Navpers 15839, revised 7 June 1954.

food production and distribution, manufacturing, transportation, communications, and restoration of monuments and archives." [6] There is not much left!

A further study of officers' classification systems confirms the view that combat operations constitute only a fraction of the task of our armed forces. The Air Force divides all its jobs into 21 major occupational fields, only one of which is entitled combat and operations. The Navy divides all jobs into 10 fields. One deals with naval operations, another with aviation; four deal with engineering; the remaining four deal with medical, personnel, supply and fiscal, and sciences and services. The naval operations field includes a number of positions in the area of international security affairs. Examples are: civil affairs officer, military government officer, attaché, head of mission, and international affairs officer. The sciences and services field includes such designations as anthropologist, economic officer (military government), and mathematical sciences research administrator. Examples of code designations in the supply and fiscal field are: comptroller, price analyst, contract negotiation officer, and foreign requirements procurement officer. The growing importance of research and development is attested by categories added to the Navy's manual between 1953 and 1954. Examples are: national science research administrator, staff gunnery officer (guided missiles), staff special weapons officer, ship's engineer officer (nuclear).

A few Army code designations, selected at random, illustrate the almost bewildering range of military functions at the present time:

Highway traffic engineer	Yardmaster
Clinical psychologist	Labor relations officer
Machine records officer	Civil defense officer
Tissue pathologist	Real estate officer
Forestry officer	Radio broadcast officer
Postal officer	Laundry and fumigation officer

Obviously, very few officers in these positions have much to do with matters of high national policy. But each stands at the base of a pyramid that reaches up to heights on which other military officers, by conference, staff study, and directive, help dispose of pressing national business.

[6] Department of the Army, *Commissioned and Warrant Officer Personnel Military Occupational Specialties,* SR 605–105–5, March 1954.